Word across the Water

THE UNITED STATES IN THE WORLD
Edited by Benjamin A. Coates, Emily Conroy-Krutz, Paul A. Kramer, and Judy Tzu-Chun Wu
Founding Series Editors: Mark Philip Bradley and Paul A. Kramer

A list of titles in this series is available at cornellpress.cornell.edu

Word across the Water

American Protestant Missionaries, Pacific Worlds, and the Making of Imperial Histories

Tom Smith

Cornell University Press
Ithaca and London

Copyright © 2024 by Cornell University

All rights reserved. Except for brief quotations in a review, this book, or parts thereof, must not be reproduced in any form without permission in writing from the publisher. For information, address Cornell University Press, Sage House, 512 East State Street, Ithaca, New York 14850. Visit our website at cornellpress.cornell.edu.

First published 2024 by Cornell University Press

Library of Congress Cataloging-in-Publication Data

Names: Smith, Tom, 1990– author.
Title: Word across the water : American Protestant missionaries, Pacific worlds, and the making of imperial histories / Tom Smith.
Description: Ithaca, [New York] : Cornell University Press, 2024. | Series: The United States in the world | Includes bibliographical references and index.
Identifiers: LCCN 2024000033 (print) | LCCN 2024000034 (ebook) | ISBN 9781501777417 (hardcover) | ISBN 9781501777448 (paperback) | ISBN 9781501777424 (epub) | ISBN 9781501777431 (pdf)
Subjects: LCSH: Imperialism—History—19th century. | Imperialism—History—20th century. | Protestantism—UnitedStates—Influence—History—19thcentury. | Protestantism—United States—Influence—History—20th century. | United States—History—19th century—Historiography. | United States—History—20th century—Historiography. | Hawaii—History—19th century—Historiography. | Hawaii—History—20th century—Historiography. | Philippines—History—19th century—Historiography. | Philippines—History—20th century—Historiography.
Classification: LCC E713 .S645 2024 (print) | LCC E713 (ebook) | DDC 996.9/00072—dc23/eng/20240220
LC record available at https://lccn.loc.gov/2024000033
LC ebook record available at https://lccn.loc.gov/2024000034

Contents

Acknowledgments vii

Introduction: History, Religion, and the American Imagination of the Pacific 1

PART I. Hawai'i 25

1. "Venerated Fathers": "Missionaries," Mission History, and Native Hawaiian Sovereignty 31

2. "From the Beginning of the World": The Contested Terrain of History in Hawai'i 64

3. "A Past That Is Often Noble": Memory, "Unwritten Literature," and the Consolidation of an American Hawai'i 98

PART II. The Philippines 133

4. "A Sudden Turn of History": Providence, Crisis, and US Empire in the Philippines 137

5. "A Dark and Troubled Past": Missionaries and Historicism in the Philippines 168

6. "A Chosen People": Filipino Nationalism, Protestant Missionaries, and the Long Philippine Past 204

Conclusion: The Purposes and Ambivalences of Missionary
Knowledge Production   234

Notes   241
Bibliography   283
Index   311

Acknowledgments

This book was completed during my time as the Keasbey Research Fellow in American Studies at Selwyn College, University of Cambridge. I would like to thank the master and fellows of the college for their support and friendship throughout the process. Selwyn is a very special community and I am extremely grateful for the opportunities it has given me. Before I took up my post at Selwyn, this book was enabled by the financial support of the Arts and Humanities Research Council (grant reference AH/L503897/1); Trinity Hall, Cambridge, and its Nightingale studentships; and the Cambridge History Faculty and its Prince Consort and Sara Norton funds. I am thankful to staff at the Andersen Library, the Bancroft Library, the Burke Library, Cambridge University Library, the Hamilton Library, Hawaii State Archives, the Hawaiian Historical Society, the Hawaiian Mission Houses Museum, the Houghton Library, the Huntington Library, the Library of Congress, the National Archives and Records Administration, the Presbyterian Historical Society, Yale Divinity School, and Yale University Library. Some of the material on Hawai'i, most substantially that in chapter 3, has appeared before in "History, 'Unwritten Literature,' and U.S. Colonialism in Hawai'i, 1898–1915," *Diplomatic History* 43, no. 5 (2019): 813–39. Many thanks to Oxford University Press and the Society for Historians of American Foreign Relations for permission to republish this material.

At Cornell University Press, I am thankful to the editors of the United States in the World series for their belief in the book, especially Emily Conroy-Krutz, who has been extraordinarily generous both with the time she invested in helping me refine the manuscript and with her encouragement throughout the process. The anonymous peer reviewers gave me much to ponder and challenged me to expand the book's horizons while reassuring me that I was onto something. Sarah Grossman has guided this first-time book author through the process with patience and kindness.

I am grateful for the generosity and insight of Andrew Preston, my mentor at the University of Cambridge. His knowledge and enthusiasm have buoyed me throughout the project, his wisdom in matters both intellectual and practical has been priceless, and our meetings have always been productive and encouraging. Gary Gerstle and Axel Schäfer have also been greatly supportive, and their suggestions have been instrumental in helping me improve the work and push it in new directions. Sujit Sivasundaram and his graduate reading group and David Maxwell were also extremely helpful at various stages, asking challenging and thoughtful questions that enabled me to think beyond the frame of US history.

The Cambridge US history community has been a constant source of support, insight, and friendship. Among the friends who have been alongside me on the journey are Rob Bates, Nico Bell-Romero, Jethro Calacday, Lewis Defrates, Ruth Lawlor, Jeanine Quené, Jeffrey Rosario, Emily Snyder, and Evelyn Strope. Seth Archer's arrival at the faculty early in my PhD was serendipitous; his advice on all things Hawaiian was invaluable, as was his boundless generosity and attentive friendship. His successor as Mellon Research Fellow, Emma Teitelman, also closely read parts of the work and offered hugely useful commentary. Both the Cambridge American History Seminar and the graduate workshop are stimulating intellectual forums that I feel lucky to have been a part of and even more fortunate to have presented my work to.

Research fellowships at the Huntington Library and the Library of Congress were made unforgettable by the people I encountered, not least my fellow AHRC International Placement Scheme scholars with whom I was able to explore all that Los Angeles and Washington, DC, had to offer. At the Huntington, Juan Gomez was a wonderful landlord and friend. At the Library of Congress, the Kluge Center staff (not least the inimitable Travis Hensley) fostered an energizing environment, while my next-carrel neighbor, Samira Mehta, became a friend for life. My trip to Hawai'i was also formative for the project, and I am grateful to a number of local scholars who gave up their time to point me in the right direction, especially Ron Williams, who bought me a birthday beer, reassured me that what I was doing was valuable, and gave me some very useful leads. Many others helped orient a lone British traveler in the

United States both socially and intellectually over the course of a year's archival research—from those with whom I lived to friends passing through to those who sat down for a coffee with me at archives or conferences. Space prevents me from listing them all, but they are remembered fondly and with gratitude. Elsewhere, it was a pleasure to join with other scholars of US religion and empire in Mainz, Germany, in 2018 to share new research in the field. Dan Geary and Gene Zubovich, who were both in attendance, have subsequently offered valuable commentary on parts of the book.

Friends old and new have been sources of laughter and comfort across the span of this project. Mattin Biglari, Lottie Field, Phil Howell, Tim Heimlich, and Allison Neal deserve special mention. My parents, Wendy and Steve, have championed me at every turn and in a multitude of ways. Although I cannot do the feeling justice here, I am unreservedly thankful. The most extraordinary journey that I have been on over these past few years, however, is with Carys Brown. Meeting her was the best imaginable by-product of embarking on a PhD, and I am overflowing with gratitude every day for her love, support, wisdom, and generosity, not to mention her astute reading of many different parts of the book. Although Reuben has been less well placed to offer constructive feedback, watching him grow and learn about the world has been a source of joy that has helped carry this project over the finish line. I am now excited to see what comes next.

Introduction

History, Religion, and the American Imagination of the Pacific

On September 7, 1907, aboard a vessel returning him to the Philippines following a six-month furlough in the United States, the Presbyterian missionary George William Wright penned a letter to Bethlehem Presbyterian Church in Chicago, where he had previously been pastor.[1] Wright wrote of his profound sense of dislocation when traveling on the ocean. Although the vast breadth of water on which he sailed tantalized him with the possibility of comprehending "a thousand other worlds," it ultimately isolated him. The only world that existed for Wright as he wrote was the ship, "a little frame of wood and iron . . . tossed upon a great infinity." The United States had "faded into dream," and it was difficult to "conceive that there can be lands ahead." Wright expressed his sense of dislocation temporally as well as spatially. Cut adrift by the ocean's vastness and existing in a world that was so compacted, he began to doubt "if there was a past or . . . a future."[2]

Wright's experience of the water as a discombobulating expanse contrasted sharply with the way a fellow Midwesterner, the politician Albert J. Beveridge, had characterized the Pacific Ocean to a meeting of Indiana Republicans nine years earlier, in September 1898. Engaging with a national debate about what should be done with the Philippines, which the United States had wrested from Spain's control during the Spanish-American War but had not yet formally annexed, Beveridge passionately outlined the case for US seizure of the islands, insisting that "distance and oceans are no longer arguments. . . . The ocean does not separate us from the land of our duty and desire. . . . Steam joins us; electricity joins us. . . . Hawaii and the Philippines not contiguous!

Our navy will make them contiguous.... American speed, American guns, American heart and brain and nerve will keep them contiguous forever."[3] Beveridge envisioned the expansion of the United States into the Pacific as continuous in method and spirit with its expansion across continental North America. Hawai'i and the Philippines could be seized as "contiguous" territories and the Pacific would cohere under American auspices, connecting the United States to the riches of Asia, particularly to China.[4] Although other territories closer to US shores—Cuba and Puerto Rico—were also central to the Spanish-American War and subsequent debates, there was particular rhetorical power in the idea of the United States expanding farther west and into the vast Pacific, transforming it into what contemporary journalists called an "American lake."[5]

Moreover, although Wright was the Protestant evangelist, it was Beveridge who explicitly tied his vision of the ocean to a confidence in God's ability to shape history. His speech associated the idea of a contiguous Pacific with an unfolding providential drama in which the United States was playing a starring role: "It is a glorious history our God has bestowed upon His chosen people; ... a history divinely logical, in the process of whose tremendous reasoning we find ourselves to-day." To go against the expansionist convictions of President William McKinley, Beveridge argued, who had acted "under the guidance of Divine Providence," would be to "reverse the wheels" of that history.[6] The historian Hubert Howe Bancroft similarly linked the idea of a "new Pacific" under US dominance to the fulfillment of the historic destiny of the United States: "It is not so much a question of the will of the people as of the destiny of the people whether or not the United States, in the westward march of progress, will step forth into the sea, and, placing foot upon islands at convenient distances apart, cross to the shore of Asia.... Nowhere is history so rapidly being made as in and around the Pacific ocean."[7] Both Beveridge and Bancroft conceptualized expansion into the Pacific as the irresistible conclusion of a history driven by a higher power—a natural extension of the manifest destiny that had supposedly carried the United States across the American continent.[8]

One might expect George William Wright to have been a fervent believer in the notion that God was steering history toward the US conquest of the ocean. After all, his Philippine mission work was facilitated by the stretching of the tentacles of US colonialism out to the ocean's furthest reaches. Before the islands were annexed, a process that was completed in December 1898, Protestant missionaries had been barred from the archipelago during more than three centuries of Spanish Catholic rule. Yet when

Wright was on the ocean, he did not experience the same seamless contiguity that Beveridge believed Americans would impose. From the perspective of the North American continent, Beveridge may have looked at the Pacific on a map and seen the future of the United States unfolding inexorably westward. On the vast ocean, however, Wright found only the immediate present and felt disconnected from his homeland and from either past or future. By writing about his travels, Wright was producing knowledge about the world for Chicagoans living in a city whose late nineteenth-century boosters had styled it as the epicenter of a US empire sweeping westward.[9] Indeed, missionaries were key sources of foreign intelligence for Americans more generally across the nineteenth and twentieth centuries through their letters to mission boards and home churches, their published works, and their lectures when they were back in the United States.[10] Yet as Wright conveyed his perspectives, he evinced not imperial confidence but uncertainty about the ability of the United States to fulfill a historic destiny to collapse oceanic space. He evoked disjuncture and the subservience of human polities to the enormity of the ocean.

By interrogating American Protestant missionaries' historical thinking from different points in the Pacific, this book argues that the relationship between religion, history, and empire was less straightforward than imperialist ideologues liked to suggest. It pays attention on a granular level to the ways missionaries, as self-styled interpreters of history, negotiated their own status between the imperial and the local through historical narratives and philosophies of history. By generating historical knowledge, missionaries sought to justify and stoke interest in their cause among audiences in the United States, locating US imperial interventions and their own evangelistic projects in divinely ordained historical trajectories. For these missionaries working in the shadow of their nation's empire, however, religiously inflected historical narratives were not simply a mode of affirming the destiny of the United States to project its power across the vast Pacific Ocean. Rather, these narratives were a way of coming to terms with the heterogeneity of the Pacific and the refusal of its different island locales to conform to the grandiose spatial-temporal categories imagined from the United States. In showing this, the book encourages scholars of empire and religion alike to acknowledge both the pernicious nature of imperial claims over oceanic space underpinned by religious and historical arguments and the fragility of those claims on the ground.

Historians of US empire have drawn our attention to the importance of context, contingency, and conflict across imperial settings in various ways.[11]

This book affirms that attention to locality, difference, and actors with a specific religious purpose is crucial in revealing that the US presence in the world was often defined by uncertainty, improvisation, and competing priorities.[12] However, the book additionally underscores that such attention allows us to contest hegemonic ideas about history and geography that continue to resonate. This is a particularly important argument to make in the context of the Pacific Ocean—a vast expanse of water whose inhabitants' ways of thinking about time and space have often been smothered by metanarratives developed from large continents at the ocean's edge. The two island groups studied in this book—Hawaiʻi and the Philippines—were each drawn into an American imaginary of an empire sweeping westward toward Asia that was imbued with providential purpose, an imaginary that served the needs of those who sought to promote the projection of US power. In both archipelagoes, however, Americans had to contend with ideas that already existed about the connections between history, sovereignty, and spirituality that were rooted in specific places and were resistant to American categorization. Charting the interactions of missionaries with these alternative modes of historical thinking allows us to move past hegemonic spatial-temporal categories and to view places in the US Pacific empire on their own terms.

The Heterogeneous Pacific

Albert Beveridge's claim that US power would collapse the Pacific is emblematic of a pernicious idea that is recurrent in descriptions of the ocean—one that renders oceanic space as connective only insofar as it serves the needs of large continental powers at its rim, reduces islands to stepping-stones between the United States and Asia, and naturalizes imperial domination of a vast expanse.[13] Privileging the idea of an "American Pacific" risks characterizing the ocean in such ways.[14] Indeed, this labeling might be viewed as one of many attempts of foreigners to make sense of the Pacific's vastness and render it legible and controllable through categorization and representation.[15] Outsiders have drawn lines on maps to designate the Pacific's peoples as either Polynesian, Melanesian, or Micronesian.[16] They have sometimes represented the ocean as an Edenic escape for sailors and tourists.[17] At other times, they have regarded it (especially its islands) as a site for scientific exploration, discovery, and innovation, as the laboratory of James Cook, Charles Darwin, and others.[18] In the twentieth century, in addition to becoming a key site where Bronisław Malinowski, Franz Boas, and Margaret Mead developed cultural anthropology, it was increasingly viewed through the lens of international competition and warfare as a site of naval bases and nuclear testing.[19] In more recent times, Pacific islanders have been recognized as among the first victims of human-induced climate change as rising sea levels threaten their lives and homes.[20] In each case, the emphasis has been on the Pacific as acted on by outsiders, potentially obscuring the fact that it has long been a diverse and contested space—a site of multidirectional mobility and interconnection for its inhabitants with its own intellectual traditions and an expanse traversed by numerous empires and Christian missions.[21] It is a "multilocal" space of many "seas" or "worlds," covering a third of the world's surface area, and is incomprehensible through broad-brushstroke categorizations or through the kinds of historical grand narratives applied to the Mediterranean or Atlantic.[22]

For late nineteenth-century Americans, the notion of a contiguous American Pacific carried weight. The nation's western "frontier" had been declared closed in 1890, and the construction of the United States as a bicoastal power with naval influence in the Pacific made strategic sense. This point was forcefully made by the historian, naval strategist, and devout Episcopalian Alfred Thayer Mahan.[23] The ocean also offered the possibilities of overcoming the deep economic crisis that hit in 1893 through trade and overcoming the national crisis of masculinity that greeted the post–Civil War generation who no longer had an ideational frontier through warfare.[24] Frederick Jackson Turner's frontier thesis provided the intellectual foundations of a belief that in order to protect the nation's vitality and democracy, the manifest destiny of the United States had to be extended by continuing to move outward from the West Coast into the ocean.[25] More critically, understanding these visions of the ocean as an extended West and highlighting continuity between continental expansion and overseas empire illuminates long histories of US colonial violence moving across land and water.[26]

A teleological vision of westward movement nonetheless obscures the fact that Americans' interest in the Pacific dated back to long before they could have considered the ocean to be contiguous to them. From the late eighteenth century and across the nineteenth, in fact, Americans had been in the Pacific in various guises. Traders had extracted a variety of products to trade with China; missionaries had sought converts; writers, notably Herman Melville, had conveyed romantic visions of the ocean to audiences in the United States; Charles Wilkes, sponsored by the US government, had become perhaps the most famous of a number of American explorers in the Pacific; and "blackbirders" had seized labor.²⁷ The Adams-Onís Treaty of 1819, the Treaty of Wanghia in 1844, the Oregon Treaty in 1846, California statehood in 1850, the opening of Japan by Commodore Perry in 1854, the Guano Act of 1856, and William Seward's purchase of Alaska in 1867 had all served to bring concrete realities to Americans' ideas about their prominent role in the Pacific. The late nineteenth century did not represent a completely new departure nor the fulfillment of inexorable westward progress, as connections not based on contiguity had long linked the United States and the Pacific.

The year 1898, however, focused Americans' minds on two particular archipelagoes—Hawai'i and the Philippines—that were now apparently being made "contiguous," having both been formally claimed as territories of the United States within months of one another. This book focuses on Americans' presence in and ways of thinking about these two island groups across the late nineteenth and early twentieth centuries. Sitting respectively around 2,400 and 7,000 miles away from the continental United States, Hawai'i and the Philippines represented two vastly different Pacific worlds that were always bound to refuse straightforward absorption into a teleological narrative of US Pacific dominance moving westward. The former is situated in a centuries-old milieu of interisland migration and cultural contact, sustained by remarkable long-distance voyages undertaken in canoes. The latter is a diverse group of around 7,000 islands with historical ties to both Pacific and Indian Ocean worlds, shaped also by its experience of nearly four centuries of Spanish colonialism prior to the arrival of the United States.

Yet, as Beveridge's idea that these two archipelagoes were being made "contiguous" to the United States suggested, the experience of US colonialism bound them together both rhetorically and materially. The scholar Vernadette Vicuña Gonzalez notes that their fates became "linked" and "interdependent" as "the first and most sustained military occupations in Asia and the Pacific," as "the linchpins of American domination in the region," and as "pivotal American tropics" that have been feminized and styled as tourist paradises to be protected by "masculinized modes of security." From the start of the US occupation of the Philippines in 1898, troops fueled their bodies and ships in Hawai'i on their way to "pacify" Filipino resistance. In turn, as time went on, Filipinos migrated to Hawai'i in significant numbers to find work on plantations in a pattern of mobility that followed the contours of US empire.²⁸ The scholar of American religion Kathryn Gin Lum also points out the ways Hawai'i and the Philippines were connected by the tendency of colonial officials and imperialist ideologues to designate the peoples of these archipelagoes as "heathens" with atavistic instincts.

In significant ways, this perception shaped discussions about the terms on which they both might be "included" in the US empire and linked debates about the possibility of assimilating overseas populations to debates about Indigenous peoples on the North American continent.[29]

Despite being two places with very different historical relationships to the idea of the Pacific, Hawai'i and the Philippines were shoehorned into a particular US vision of the ocean in ways that served the purpose of imperialists while undermining the sovereignty of islanders. From a continental rather than an oceanic or island perspective, it becomes easy for these ideas about the natural unity or homogeneity of the Pacific to go without interrogation and thus to unwittingly replicate the idea of the ocean as a space whose history American actors had unbridled power to reorient. In recent years, some scholars—particularly those with interests in the Pacific—have started to draw critical attention to the "tyranny of the continent" in US history.[30] Over the past 150 years or so, beginning with the Guano Act of 1856, the United States has claimed a multitude of island territories as its own and the right to unfettered economic and military action in the waters around them. Taken together in terms of area, these claims actually make the United States a "majority-ocean nation."[31] Islands themselves, however, have often been rendered in scholarly and popular perceptions as isolated tropical idylls that are interchangeable and easily passed through or passed over rather than as culturally or intellectually meaningful entities in their own right.[32]

These scholars have instead called for an "archipelagic American studies" that might encourage us to think critically about the ways the United States has become "an archipelagic and oceanic nation-state" in whose history oceans and islands—in other words, the "borderwaters" of the United States—have been "crucial spaces, participants, nodes, and networks."[33] They draw attention to the way the US "rhetorical archipelago" overlaps and interacts with alternative "rhetorical archipelagoes" that are more meaningful to islanders. Although none of these archipelagoes are fixed or natural, they have been constructed around different ideas about history, connection, the ownership of certain symbols, and where political and spiritual power resides.[34] One particularly influential paradigm that has centered islanders' vision of the Pacific is that of the Fijian anthropologist of Tongan descent, Epeli Hau'ofa, who envisions the ocean not as a space that renders islands weak, isolated, and subject to foreign domination, but as profoundly connecting island peoples and confounding imperialist designs.[35]

The scholar Lanny Thompson has argued that too often a failure to think across the US "imperial archipelago" among American historians has given rise to a generalized idea of US power acting on isolated island groups, missing both the deliberate ways they were rhetorically connected by US imperialists and the diverse modes of rule and representation that emerged from the process of colonization.[36] This book takes up the call to pay more critical attention to the "rhetorical archipelago" of the American Pacific that was established in the late nineteenth and early twentieth centuries, turning attention to how its foundational assumptions might be deconstructed in order to see islands as spaces of meaningful cultural and intellectual production rather than as ciphers in an American grand narrative of the ocean. It shows how, through a granular reading of what white Americans on the ground in different places wrote and said, scholars of US empire and religion can find cracks in the superficially confident and cohesive ideas about history, geography, and Christianity that were used to legitimize oceanic colonialism.

A comparative analysis of the different pathways American missionaries' historical thinking took in Hawaiʻi and the Philippines reveals that the category of the Pacific as formulated by Americans and the historical narratives they deployed to help create it were fragile constructions. By studying these two archipelagoes alongside one another, we see more clearly the attempts Americans made to pull disparate places into a narrative of sweeping US power, Christianization, and civilization. We also see the ways imperial histories formulated from different oceanic places diverged from one another as they were challenged and reshaped by engagements with specific island peoples, environments, and pasts. If we view the production of historical narratives not simply as a tool for establishing authority but as an act of constant adjustment to local particularities and disappointed expectations, we can dismantle the logic of colonization that held that "objective" historical thinking and religious certainty were hallmarks of American superiority that legitimated control over swathes of oceanic space. We can also in the process demonstrate the potency of the island and oceanic intellectual traditions that white Americans denigrated.

Many of the most effective critical perspectives challenging US-centric representations of the Pacific have come from Native Hawaiian scholars. Prevailing American perceptions of Hawaiʻi's history, they argue, have too long been rooted in English-language sources written by advocates of the islands' annexation to the United States that naturalized the idea of Hawaiʻi as a American place and lent legitimacy to colonialism.[37] Even in the decades before 1898, US boosters had sought to rhetorically connect the islands to California as a site for white settlement and tourism, and such assertions of a natural linkage only intensified in the aftermath of annexation.[38] As a result, wrote Native Hawaiian scholar and activist Haunani-Kay Trask a century after annexation, Americans came "to believe that Hawai'i is as American as hot dogs and CNN."[39] Trask questioned whether written history could ever truly represent Native Hawaiians who understood their past through orally transmitted genealogies.[40] However, a rich vein of nineteenth-century Hawaiian-language newspapers and petitions shows exactly how Indigenous people felt about their colonization.[41] These Indigenous voices confound the notion that Native Hawaiians consented to colonization and suggest strategies of resistance that might be revived.[42] They also defy the insinuation that Hawai'i was a "fait accompli" after 1898—that annexation brought an end to Native Hawaiian history and transformed the islands unequivocally into a site for American business and tourism, Asian migration at the behest of foreign planters, and ultimately US statehood in 1959.[43]

Rather, Indigenous voices situate Native Hawaiians in a connected oceanic world, seeking opportunities to travel and to engage with outsiders, "sincerely but strategically" incorporating Christianity, and imagining themselves relative to Black and Indigenous peoples in the United States.[44] Hawai'i's mō'ī (monarchs) and other ali'i (chiefs) of the nineteenth century were not puppets of US influence but fought to preserve Hawaiian independence in a changing Pacific marked by competition between empires. They forged diplomatic networks, asserted their independent authority, and adapted their political and legal systems, even if the ultimate outcome was the erosion of their sovereignty.[45] Hearing these Indigenous voices and considering both sides of the encounter between the United States and Hawai'i more carefully opens up new perspectives on indigeneity, settler colonialism, and race, key themes in US history.[46] Most radically, the historian Gary Okihiro thinks about how Hawai'i "stirs and animates" the United States, viewing the former as the "mainland" and the latter as the "periphery."[47]

Therefore, Native Hawaiians engage Americans, critiquing egregious settler colonial practices that most Americans continue to be ignorant or unconcerned about, even in the wake of an official apology from the US Congress in 1993.[48] They stress that the overthrow of the monarchy and annexation were blatant colonial actions, following on from the incursion of disease, Christianity, and foreign legal frameworks across the nineteenth century.[49] Throughout this story of colonialism, Native Hawaiians were by no means passive.[50] They reoriented and defended their traditional understandings, asserting their sovereignty both as Indigenous people and as a modern nation.[51]

From the Philippines, we perceive another island world that cuts across colonial "seascapes of desire." Culture, kinship, and patterns of mobility historically connected the Malay peoples of the Philippines not only to Pacific peoples as far east as Rapanui but also to Southeast Asia, southern China, and Indian Ocean islands as distant as Madagascar.[52] Thus, to straightforwardly accept that the Philippines is a "Pacific" place might in itself be privileging a colonial construction. The archipelago's orientation toward a Pacific world was to a degree an invention of the Spanish empire from the sixteenth century, which made the islands a nodal point in a "Spanish lake" that connected Asia to South America by way of the Manila galleon trade. This serves as a reminder that Americans were neither the first nor the last imperial power to devise their own idiosyncratic version of a connected Pacific.[53] Spain's conquest of the islands remained far from complete, however, and a vast array of cultures, languages, and world views endured outside the colonial purview, contesting and limiting Spanish rule and continuing to suggest other forms of orientation than that across the Pacific.[54] For example, although Spanish colonization led to the dominance of Catholicism, that religion continued to exist alongside the animism prevalent among hill peoples who were unreached by Spanish rule and Islam, a religion that dominated in the southern islands. The peoples who did fall under Spanish jurisdiction appropriated aspects of colonial culture, particularly Catholicism, to make sense of their changing world and evolving patterns of colonial governance and to generate strategies of resistance.[55] Filipino nationalism emerged in the second half of the nineteenth century, precipitating a revolutionary movement against Spanish rule in 1896. Particularly influential in providing the underpinnings of this revolution were the *ilustrados*, a group of Filipino intellectuals who had been educated in Europe and were plugged into transnational networks including pan-Asianist anticolonial movements.[56] They used literature, historical writing, and the press to enable Filipinos to imagine themselves as a people with a history and culture outside the confines of colonial rule, as deserving of rights as colonial subjects, and ultimately as an independent nation.[57]

Yet having accepted the military help of the United States in throwing off Spanish rule, Filipinos found themselves subject to another empire and rhetorically situated in another colonial vision of the Pacific. The US colonization of the Philippines says a lot about the conceits of US power in the late nineteenth century. It exemplified an impulse to project an image of an exceptionally benevolent and tutelary empire to the world while also providing the United States with the westernmost node of its grand strategic vision to create a "highway" across the Pacific that placed it "at the gates of Asia."[58] These American fantasies about the Philippines belied the reality.[59] As the Philippine population resisted Americans' "benevolence," the most sophisticated US attempt to construct an overseas colonial state became fraught with astonishing violence and racism that was particularly visible during the Philippine-American War (1899–1902). Moreover, the United States did not transcend a global context of interimperial competition and exchange but instead partook in it. "National-exceptionalist" ideas about US empire shared a complex relationship with "racial-exceptionalist" ideas of Anglo-Saxon superiority, while the precedents the Spaniards set in the Philippines provided important templates for American imperial administrators' production of social categories.[60]

Histories of Hawai'i and the Philippines draw out the richness and diversity of the Pacific worlds that Americans sought to dominate in the late nineteenth century and show how the peoples of both island groups deployed their own ideas about geography and history that spoke back to and looked beyond American representations. *Word across the Water* focuses on white missionaries instead of claiming to speak for Native Hawaiians or the people of the Philippines; there are rich traditions of writing and activism in both contexts that speak for themselves. This study listens to that scholarship and develops a critical lens through which to examine the ideas about history that missionaries generated, noticing the contingencies and encounters that underpinned them. By doing this, the book aims not only to open up new lines of dialogue between US historians and Pacific or Indigenous scholars but also to further empower an island-centered critique of historical and present-day US colonialism in the region.[61] If closer attention to missionary sources reveals that the historical and religious ideas used to legitimize US colonialism were neither as certain nor as insulated from Indigenous perspectives as they first appeared to be, their claims to distinction and to authority might be eroded in ways that have previously been overlooked.

Protestant Mission and US Empire

The period 1880 to 1930 marked the apogee of the American foreign missionary enterprise. Across these five decades, tens of thousands of Americans—many of them college-educated recruits of the hugely successful Student Volunteer Movement—found their way to distant lands, communicating their achievements and needs to an audience of millions of American Christians they relied on for financial and moral support.[62] It was a time when the broad evangelical coalition of the nineteenth century became increasingly fractured as Christians responded in varying ways to modern intellectual currents and a changing nation.⁶³ Nonetheless, most still shared an activist spirit and what the historian Grant Wacker calls a "historical hopefulness," epitomized by the Student Volunteer Movement and its watchword—"the evangelization of the world in this generation."⁶⁴ Evangelicals disagreed about how and when the end of time would come and about what weight should be given to education or medical work in foreign missions as opposed to pure evangelism. Nonetheless, for most of the years from 1880 to 1930, they all remained confident in their cultural superiority and in the idea that God had a plan for the world's redemption that Christians needed to be attentive to.⁶⁵ This fragile conviviality began to collapse in response to the seismic shaking of confidence engendered by World War I. Modernist Christians more fully embraced a liberal and ecumenical vision, seeing good in modern science and non-Christian religions, while fundamentalists laid claim to an uncompromising, urgent, apocalyptic faith.⁶⁶

The period of greatest confidence and unanimity in the American foreign missions movement mapped onto the period when the United States was bursting onto the world stage as both a major industrial power and an imperial hegemon. In particular, the Spanish-American War, which the United States embarked on in May 1898 as an ostensible response to Spanish repression of Cubans and the alleged sinking of the U.S.S. *Maine* by Spain off the coast of Havana, triggered a wave of overseas territorial seizure. Over eighteen months, the United States took Guam, the Philippines, and Puerto Rico as spoils of the war and annexed Hawaiʻi, Samoa, and Wake Island. None of this happened without dissent from within the United States. An anti-imperialist coalition railed against the un-Americanness of overseas empire, many perhaps fearing most of all the implications of allowing non-white others into the American family.⁶⁷ Indeed, enthusiasm quickly waned for a high-maintenance and frequently violent project, and by the 1930s it seemed that the whole enterprise had been a brief mistake that Americans would rather forget, giving rise to the historian Samuel Flagg Bemis's exceptionalist fantasy that US empire was a "great aberration."⁶⁸

Both hopes and fears were wrapped up in the rapid postbellum rise of the United States that motivated American Protestants to spread the gospel abroad. In one framing, their nation's growing confidence and assertiveness translated into a conviction that global spiritual leadership was the nation's destiny.⁶⁹ From a different angle, the missionary enterprise might be read as a desperate attempt to reinscribe Protestant spirituality and morality in the face of the upheavals brought about by industrialization—immigration, materialism, anomie, and overseas empire.⁷⁰ Either way, the results were that the number of US missionary societies had swelled from sixteen in the 1860s to ninety by 1900, and the United States surpassed Britain as the world's leading exporter of Protestant evangelists by 1910, supplying nearly half of the globe's missionaries by 1925.⁷¹

While American mission and empire were rising together to global dominance in the late nineteenth and early twentieth centuries, the question of Protestant missionaries' complicity in imperialism is more vexed.⁷² Certainly white missionaries' confidence in Western "civilization" and in the truth of their religion led them to express a set of racist assumptions about non-Christian others across the globe.⁷³ In this sense, missionaries from the United States and Europe alike were archetypal cultural imperialists, denigrating foreign cultures, disseminating a "liberal-developmentalist" ideology alongside the gospel, and effecting a "colonization of consciousness."⁷⁴ Missionaries were also often crucial informants and intermediaries for a US foreign policy establishment, encouraging their nation to wield its power to moral and evangelistic ends and ultimately exercising an "extraordinary" influence over US overseas expansion on either side of 1900.⁷⁵

At the same time, however, missionaries were more inclined than most Europeans and Americans abroad to look beyond national and imperial frameworks, enthused by opportunities for transnational and ecumenical collaboration.⁷⁶ They often emerged as the conscience of imperial projects, critiquing administrations, engaging dialogically with proselytes, and developing cultural sensitivities that led them to question racist and colonialist assumptions.⁷⁷ In the long run, perhaps the biggest legacy of their endeavors was a transnational and decolonial movement centered not on imperial metropoles but on the Global South.⁷⁸ Converts "translated" Protestantism in ways that dovetailed with existing cosmologies and underpinned movements for social change.⁷⁹ In response to this complexity, historians have developed a variety of descriptions that acknowledge the imperial outlook of American missionaries but also assert their distance from other expressions of empire: they offered a "moral alternative to imperialism" or a "spiritual imperialism"; built a "Christian moral empire," spinning "webs of humanitarianism" that were "analogous to empire"; or practiced an "imperialism of ideas and . . . human rights."⁸⁰

Despite this nuance, US colonization of the Philippines in 1898 furnishes an example of US Protestant missionaries operating self-consciously under the banner of US empire. Missionaries embraced a national mood that found a basis for a unified sense of moral purpose in the notion that the decisive US victory in the Spanish-American War was providential and that its resultant new empire was for the good of humanity.[81] A number of American mission boards enthusiastically responded to the God-given opportunity to evangelize the Philippines and to work among its unusual constellation of Catholic, Muslim, and animist populations.[82] Missionaries often acknowledged their reliance on the colonial administration and colonial administrators in turn frequently praised the influence of missionaries.[83] In this sense, the Philippines provides a concrete example of an experiment undertaken jointly and confidently by a burgeoning, bombastic US imperial power and a foreign missionary enterprise at its heady apex, beginning a new venture in the Pacific Ocean hand in hand.

At the same point in history, however, over 5,000 miles away from the Philippines in the Hawaiian Islands the inheritors of another missionary enterprise resided and served as a living reminder that American engagements in the Pacific had a long and multifaceted history. The missionaries of the American Board of Commissioners for Foreign Missions had first arrived in Hawai'i in 1820. They were emblematic of the fact that long before an age of US industrial might and numerical dominance in the mission field, missionaries had thought beyond national boundaries and had thought about the ability of racial others to acculturate to Anglo-American Protestant life.[84] For Hawaiian scholars, these missionaries "introduced a religious imperialism that was as devastating a scourge as any venereal pox," promulgating a "rhetoric of revulsion" that laid the groundwork for US colonialism.[85] For the student volunteers of the late nineteenth century, however, the mission to Hawai'i served as a touchstone. Its history provided evidence that a Christian nation could be created of a "heathen" people if sufficient faith and resources were deployed in response to God's call. Still, for the missionary community remaining in the islands by the 1890s, the story continued to unfold. Having gained political and economic influence in the islands while also starting families, missionaries and their descendants had formed the core of a white settler society that in 1893 conspired to overthrow the Indigenous monarchy. They saw opportunities in "formal" US empire to protect both economic interests and a spiritual legacy and lobbied the US government for annexation. Though initially unsuccessful, they took advantage of the clamor surrounding the Spanish-American War to achieve their goal in July 1898.

The historian of religion Laurie Maffly-Kipp has called on fellow scholars to pay closer attention to the Pacific as a site not of westward movement and "discovery" by Americans but as an ocean whose space has been sacralized and perceived as a site of religious encounter and experience by many different groups of people thinking from different locations and moving in different directions.[86] This book shows how even for American missionaries who ostensibly shared in a national and religious project, the Pacific was generative of diverse ideas about how history was unfolding and about where spiritual power was centered. As missionaries and their descendants thought about history from Hawai'i and the Philippines, they did so not only from two different geographical locations in the ocean but also from the perspective of different generations of mission work and different relationships to the concept of US empire. In Hawai'i, US empire was founded on a settler mission that consisted of northeastern Congregationalists and Presbyterians. The mission began in the early nineteenth century and was deemed complete by the mid-nineteenth century. It was represented in the late nineteenth century by second- and third-generation "missionaries" who were utterly convinced of their inherited moral and racial superiority yet were more familiar in many ways with their Pacific island setting than with American politics and culture. In the Philippines, meanwhile, a new mission emerged from a confident foreign missionary movement that still had its center of gravity in the Northeast but took on a far more national cast. The Philippine mission viewed US empire as running before it, opening a crucial front in a Protestant world struggle with Catholicism and Islam.

Religion served no monolithic function across time and space. For the missionary community in Hawai'i, religious associations and institutions mattered greatly, connecting second- and third-generation "missionaries" to a history of spiritual endeavor in the islands and becoming central to a broader struggle over sovereignty in the late nineteenth century.[87] For missionaries to the Philippines, the question was about how they could assert a break from a religious past in the islands that they perceived to be too bound up with a formalistic institution—the Catholic Church—and encourage a deeper spiritual life among Filipinos. While US policymakers may have invoked religion when outlining their grand imperial designs, missionaries firmly believed that God was at work in the minutiae of Philippine life and that he might facilitate profound spiritual transformation. Thus, although religion certainly played a critical role in defining US global activity, it functioned at numerous interrelated but different levels—as an institutional presence, as a language deployed for political ends, and as a sincere set of beliefs.

This study reiterates that missionaries mattered because through their communications with US Christian audiences they sought to make significant contributions to American knowledge about the world and imbued US global endeavors with religious and moral purpose.[88] Yet it also emphasizes the ways the perspectives missionaries developed from different Pacific sites reconfigured their relationship to their homeland and its imperial culture and left them uncertain about their ability to persuade Christians and politicians in the United States to meet their needs. They were certainly aware of the importance of their nation's power and politics for their work, and they persistently mobilized arguments about US empire and its historical purpose in order to raise expectations for their work and secure backing for it. However, when they were on the ground in Hawai'i and the Philippines, they also realized the benefits of articulating visions of history that resonated at an island level. In this way, they established themselves as authorities attuned to local particularities and positioned themselves as actors who existed between the imperial and the local.

Without a doubt, missionaries constructed a sense of themselves as figures with feet in imperial and local worlds in a bid to cope both with their distance from the metropole and with their uncertain relationship to local people, places, and traditions. After all, as Albert Memmi argued several decades ago, this kind of liminality was central to the colonial experience and tended to provoke a series of psychological and rhetorical defense mechanisms on the part of white interlopers.[89] Yet this book goes further to suggest that these personal anxieties and coping mechanisms could actually be reflective of broader fissures in hegemonic conceptualizations of space and time in the Pacific and of the failure of US empire to marshal the ocean's multitudinous geographies and histories. Missionaries paid particularly close attention to the relationship between religion, history, and empire and were therefore acutely aware of and anxious about the fragility of the categories devised in the United States. An analysis of their intellectual production helps us see how in negotiating their own position they exposed the hubris and limits of American imperial visions of the ocean, often unwittingly.

Missionaries and Historical Consciousness

Historical narratives and particular ways of understanding historical change have been key weapons in the imperial arsenal.[90] By the late nineteenth century, new conceptions of history were emerging in the United States that helped white Americans situate themselves relative to other peoples. As history and social science professionalized, Americans increasingly imbibed historicism, the idea that history was characterized by continuous change and perpetual cause and effect and was not simply the working out of higher laws.

In part because of a continued belief that God was the driving force behind history, Americans were late to integrate such a concept, which for European thinkers emerged from the Enlightenment.⁹¹ Nonetheless, as it came into vogue, US imperialists appropriated a particular understanding of historicism to help them conceptualize their role. If history was marked by gradual progress, human populations could be placed on a developmental timeline culminating in modernity, and the job of Americans—particularly white Anglo-Saxon Protestant Americans—was to catalyze others' passage out of the past.⁹²

Yet Americans were emerging from the nineteenth century during which they had been more likely to think of history as moving in cycles, or as echoing the past, than they were to think about progress.⁹³ Some white Americans, for example, especially in New England, obsessed over genealogy and used the Puritan past as their point of reference, venerating the foundational role of their ancestors at the expense of Indigenous histories and inheriting from those ancestors a view of white supremacy over Native Americans.⁹⁴ Late nineteenth-century American Protestants were also heirs to a long tradition of thinking about Providence as an active guiding force in history and about the United States as a chosen nation in a divine historical plan.⁹⁵ Although historicism was supposedly secularizing Americans' ideas about how history moved, there was no wholesale revolution. The late nineteenth century was, after all, still an age when future president Woodrow Wilson's career as a historian was dependent on his ability to satisfy prospective university employers that he "believed that the hand of Providence was in all history."⁹⁶ As Albert Beveridge's pronouncements show, an ongoing reading of US history as the fulfilment of Protestant history and of the nation's supposedly sudden turn to overseas empire in the late nineteenth century as divinely ordained sat alongside "imperial historicism."⁹⁷

As they sought to discern God's plan for the evangelization of the world, missionaries saw themselves as among their era's deepest readers of and thinkers about history: "Missionaries are the interpreters of History," declared one Presbyterian woman who attended a missionary convention in Columbus, Ohio in 1905.⁹⁸ Prominent mission leader Robert E. Speer's two-volume book *Missions and Modern History* (1904) is one particularly good example of ongoing missionary attempts to read evangelistic significance into major world events of the nineteenth century.⁹⁹ In the process of their engagements with history, missionaries embodied the whole gamut of American historical consciousness. Of course, they found room for God's hand in their ideas about history and about empire's purpose. However, they were also educated to engage with the latest intellectual trends, invoking historicism and sharing a dialogic relationship with nascent American historical and social scientific disciplines. Some missionaries claimed the authority of these disciplines, sought their readership, and used their arguments as models to describe how the work of mission and empire would unfold. The missionary enterprise also contributed to the development of social scientific research. Missionaries established museums and exhibitions, for example the exhibit the ecumenical Bureau of Missions in New York set up in the aftermath of a major conference on foreign missions in 1900. Here, cultural artifacts gathered in the mission field were displayed, constituting significant repositories of data for social scientists including Franz Boas.[100] Furthermore, in their writings, missionaries had long offered influential assessments of what was history and what was not to US audiences. They evaluated the different cultural modes of engaging with the past they encountered in the mission field and asserted that true history was something that only "civilized" and Christian peoples truly possessed.[101]

However, missionaries' juxtaposition of secular and providential ideas about history did not always foster confidence that the United States was playing a transformative and divinely ordained role in the Pacific Ocean.[102] Their peculiar and ongoing attentiveness to the way history moved in different mission fields shared an uncertain relationship with US imperial confidence and with conventions and disciplines in the United States. In Hawaiʻi, the missionary community fell back on local religious histories and genealogies to find meaning when faced with an American public who seemed indifferent to their needs. In the Philippines, missionaries sought purpose in the history of the islands themselves, plagued by their perception that US empire seemed to be responding inadequately to a historic opportunity God had presented to transform the archipelago's religion. Their ideas about history came to reflect fragmentation, disappointment, warnings, crisis, stasis, and lack of control as much as imperial triumphalism, optimism, order, and progress. They oscillated between imagining themselves as agents in an unfolding history and as being subject to forces beyond human agency. In the process, they revealed the instability of both providential and imperial historicist understandings of American presence in the Pacific and indeed the tensions between these two conceptualizations.

Missionaries' kaleidoscopic and sometimes anxious articulations of history also stemmed from the fact that the peoples colonized by the United States with whom missionaries engaged also deployed history. At stake for the people of Hawaiʻi and the Philippines was their political and spiritual autonomy, and their engagements with history in various forms anchored them in conceptions of political and spiritual power that resisted Americans' assumptions. History was etched into the landscapes, oral traditions, and cultural practices of the Pacific locales Americans encountered. It was also employed in writing by Indigenous peoples who were developing nationalist intellectual traditions. Native Hawaiian genealogies were both written down and performed in the late nineteenth century, asserting the insufficiency of white Americans' claims to Hawai'i by demonstrating the longevity of Native Hawaiians' relationship to the land.[103] In the Philippines, meanwhile, the potency of the Spanish Catholic past remained evident in the built environment, and Filipinos claimed capacity for spiritual and political independence by narrating the past outside the framework of Spanish and US colonialism.[104]

Missionaries did not fully grasp the dynamism of these modes of historical narration but understood that they had to respond to them. Articulating their own versions of history was in part an attempt to assert authority over the narratives of the colonized in ways that were consistent with white Americans' broader efforts to silence others. On the North American continent, white Americans had created a national narrative by effacing, denigrating, and appropriating Indigenous histories.[105] In the late nineteenth and early twentieth centuries, they rehashed Civil War history to emphasize white brotherhood and nationhood, obscuring African Americans' experience.[106] Missionaries tried to use history to similar ends in the Pacific, obscuring rich and dynamic Indigenous intellectual cultures, deflecting attention from colonial violence, and helping underpin US imperial projects. The imagination of the Pacific as an American space was predicated on subsuming island histories into a broader narrative of Providence and progress. Yet historical narratives people in the ocean told disrupted these imperial geographies and shaped the priorities and arguments of missionaries—self-declared "interpreters of history"—in meaningful ways. To understand this is to understand the contingent and fragile nature of American spatial and historical renderings of oceanic space and to reconceptualize the relationship between Christian-inflected views of history and US imperial thought.

The emergent historical discourse analyzed in this book was most often generated by white men who asserted a formidable combination of firsthand experience and white American scientific analysis. The book also thinks often about the roles missionary women played in reading, writing, and interpreting history. Women's presence was significant in both the Hawaiian and Philippine mission fields. The mission to Hawai'i was founded in large part on exchanges between missionary wives and chiefly Indigenous women who became crucial to Christianity's success in the islands, although these strong traditions of women's leadership gave way to more patriarchal norms as European and US influence increased across the nineteenth century.[107] By 1890, two out of every three American missionaries were women, and accordingly one of the first missionary societies with formal representation in the Philippines was the Woman's Foreign Missionary Society of the Methodist Episcopal Church. Its workers viewed themselves as "pioneer Americanas" who were running ahead of Methodist men into the new mission field.[108] The Woman's Foreign Missionary Society was representative of a mass movement with a transnational outlook that sprang up in the late nineteenth century. The mission field presented educated women with opportunities to become teachers, doctors, and social workers, drawing on the financial and moral support of hundreds of thousands of middle-class women back in the United States.[109]

While it was men who most often claimed the platform to talk authoritatively about history, the book shows at various points how women claimed a voice in a patriarchal landscape, upholding certain gendered expectations of women's role in "domesticating" colonialism to carve out a space for themselves and at the same time displaying their knowledge of and interest in history.[110] In Hawai'i, after the United States annexed the islands, female descendants of earlier missionaries emerged as key figures in the presentation of historical narrative through performances and through a new associational culture that promoted the view of Hawai'i's prior mission history as harmonious and apolitical. They thus became crucial agents in the obfuscation of previous politicized contests over Hawaiian history in which missionary men had taken the lead. Missionary women—Laura Fish Judd in Hawai'i and Alice Byram Condit in the Philippines—also used the form of the memoir to articulate their versions of history, although in Judd's case we see what happened when women's writings were mediated and edited by a man's hand. Finally, the book considers evidence from women's missionary society periodicals in which missionary women and their supporters encouraged one another to learn together about the histories of the places American evangelists were working. While we might have to look harder for this evidence of missionary women discoursing on history, we can certainly find it by scratching the surface of their "domestic" self-presentation and by understanding this self-presentation as closely tied to the needs of empire.

Kathryn Gin Lum has recently explored the ideas about religion that underpinned the foundation of history as a discipline. Specifically, she emphasizes the contrast white Protestant Americans asserted between themselves as "progressive history makers" operating under the "blessings of Providence" and the "heathen world," which they characterized as "a lethargic realm of unchanging pitiables" without any true sense of history. She also exposes the fallacy of this dichotomy, evident in the relatively unchanging view of the heathen that white Protestants clung to from one generation to the next, and considers how white Protestants veiled their anxieties about the actual "blurriness of categories" through "constant invocation and reinvocation" of their binary world view.[111] Developing this critique, *Word across the Water* takes a granular look at the process by which the idea of Americans as providentially ordained history makers in the Pacific became insufficient for missionaries. In the course of missionaries' attempts to assert authority in their engagements with local traditions of historical narration, the boundaries they sought to erect between the producers of knowledge and the objects of study, between those who truly had history and those who did not, proved more porous than they would have liked their readers to believe. They had to grapple with competing Indigenous and colonial legacies, with the perceived inertia of the US government, and with the lack of history they and their religion had in the island groups they worked in. Hopeful visions of a divinely ordained Pacific transformation gave way to a more fragmentary vision of the ocean and of history itself as missionaries sought a hearing. Diversity, uncertainty, and competition between multiple voices were evident throughout the historical narratives of American missionaries, which became unstable and malleable tools for establishing authority in the ocean from different points in it.

Sources and Structure

The principal sources analyzed across the book are missionary writings that include missionaries' various outlooks on history. These include letters to mission boards, periodicals, sermons, personal papers, pamphlets, and books containing both formal historical inquiries and memoirs. In many cases, these sources were produced for the purpose of encouraging moral and financial support from the United States, an exercise that required the correct balance between optimism and urgency. Because of this purpose, some scholars have critiqued missionary sources as too sanitized, exaggerated, and glossy to be of much use, seeing them as distilling coherence "out of the often chaotic, episodic stream of missionary experience."[112] However, by looking closely at these sources, by exploring their internal contradictions and conflicts and the rhetorical tools used to create a veneer of authority, we can notice about the missionary archive what the historian Ann Laura Stoler noticed about the Dutch colonial archive—its "granular rather than seamless texture" and the shifting and competing uncertainties, anxieties, and definitions of "common sense" that informed it.[113] In particular, reading the missionary archive in the context of Hawaiian and Philippine histories and traditions of historical narration illuminates the structures in which missionaries were producing historical knowledge and suggests how these alternative traditions established the "common sense" that defined missionary thought.

The book consists of three chapters on Hawaiʻi followed by three on the Philippines. This structure reflects the book's intention to emphasize difference over similarity—to "critically juxtapos[e]" as much as to compare, to borrow the words of Vernadette Vicuña Gonzalez from her work on Hawaiʻi and the Philippines.[114] Chapter 1 shows how in the decades before 1898, descendants of missionaries in Hawaiʻi and their allies formed an associational culture to attach themselves to a successful historical project to Christianize the islands, underscoring their claims to be rightful sovereigns. In pursuing their political goals, they sought with mixed success to change the perception of American audiences that Hawaiʻi's mission history was complete, arguing that there was more work to be done to secure a Christian future for the islands. Chapter 2 argues that the missionary community's need to justify its religious and political agenda prior to 1898 with reference to history was particularly acute, given Native Hawaiians' deployment of historical narration as a claim to sovereignty. Descendants of missionaries responded to a potent Native Hawaiian culture of historical narration that employed genealogy in performance and print to assert the connection of the islands' Indigenous people to the land long before the arrival of settlers from the United States. As a result of this encounter, memory, kinship, genealogy, and performance all became vital to fashioning a white settler identity in Hawaiʻi. Chapter 3 shows how the descendants of missionaries established their authority as chief interpreters of the Hawaiian past after the United States seized the islands. It focuses on the genre of the missionary memoir, which was used to sell the idea of Hawaiʻi as a space that was both exotic and thoroughly Americanized to US audiences. It then turns to the social scientific studies of Nathaniel Emerson, the son of two missionaries, who aestheticized Native Hawaiian modes of historical narration in his work. In both cases, descendants of missionaries claimed authority by deploying supposedly objective forms of writing that were recognizable to Americans, but woven into these were local and personal histories that reflected the subjectivity and emotional responses to Hawai'i of these descendants of missionaries.

Chapter 4 shifts to the Philippines, analyzing how missionaries' experience on the ground disappointed their expectations that US empire, ordained by Providence, would facilitate a radical break with the islands' Spanish Catholic history. They instead began to worry that the United States was exacerbating a historic crisis in its lukewarm commitment to Protestant evangelism, failing to respond adequately to a God-given opportunity to take a significant step in the evangelization of the world. Chapter 5 considers the alternative philosophies of history missionaries turned to in order to escape these anxieties. Ideas about racial development furnished by the social sciences assured them that Filipino society needed to pass through many stages before it would become a full-fledged Christian civilization. The power of the Spanish Catholic past, which was particularly evident in the built environment, encouraged missionaries to recognize that Philippine history could not simply be obliterated by US empire but required engagement and negotiation. Finally, chapter 6 builds on the previous two by arguing that missionaries' belief in Providence, their turn to social science, and their obsession with the Spanish colonial past all obscured the ways Filipinos sought to narrate history outside the confines of colonial perceptions. However, by the mid-1920s, in a remarkable turn prompted by World War I and the US commitment to decolonization, missionary texts began to echo Filipino nationalist ideas about history. They argued that Philippine spirituality did indeed have a long history that proved the inherent ability of the people of the Philippines to lead the evangelization of the world. In the process, missionaries completed their turn away from centering an American imperial project in their world view but also hijacked a Filipino nationalist language and historiography, bending it to Protestant purposes without acknowledging the intellectual agency of Filipinos. Taken together, the six chapters demonstrate how the historical arguments missionaries made undercut any sweeping conceptualization of the historic purpose of the United States in the Pacific. They prompt us to appreciate the heterogeneous nature of US presence overseas and to consider both the construction of hegemonic spatial-temporal categories and their fragility on the ground.

PART I

Hawai'i

The United States completed its annexation of the Hawaiian Islands in July 1898, just months before it annexed the Philippine Islands. The timing was undoubtedly dictated by the strategic imperatives of the Spanish-American War. Although imperialists' rhetoric surrounding the Philippines focused on the unexpected and novel nature of Americans' engagement with that archipelago, however, the annexation of Hawai'i seemed instead to be the completion of a historical process—one that was more akin to the creation of earlier settler territories on the North American continent than to the new colonial project in the Philippines.[1] Indeed, whereas significant numbers of Americans were not present in the Philippines until after the US victory in the Spanish-American War, in Hawai'i there was already a contingent of white settlers of American heritage. They had long been entangled with the islands without being dependent on or protected by formal US empire, operating instead in what was for them a more uncertain world that was defined by Indigenous sovereignty, interimperial competition, and an influx of laborers from China, Japan, and the Portuguese empire.[2] Accordingly, in July 1898, one of their main organs, the Honolulu-based Protestant newspaper *The Friend*, celebrated "annexation at last," reporting that the drawing of Hawai'i "into Columbia's fold, and under shelter of the Star Spangled Banner" represented "the successful ending of [a] long struggle."[3]

As these settlers saw it, annexation to the United States was essential to the fulfillment of a political project that had gathered momentum over the preceding decade. This was a project designed to wrest power away from an

Indigenous monarchy that had presided over an independent kingdom for more than a century and then to gain the security and tariff-free trade that would come with making Hawai'i a US territory. To these ends, in 1887, a group of white lawyers and businessmen formed the Hawaiian League and imposed upon the Native Hawaiian king, Kalākaua (r. 1874–91), the infamous Bayonet Constitution that stripped the Indigenous monarchy of its executive powers. Six years later, in January 1893, enraged by the plans of Kalākaua's successor, Queen Lili'uokalani (r. 1891–93), to return some power to Native Hawaiians by promulgating a new constitution, these same men established a Committee of Safety. Backed by US troops stationed in Honolulu harbor, they elicited the queen's abdication. Although the desired annexation to the United States did not happen immediately, the provisional government that filled the political vacuum declared the Republic of Hawai'i in July 1894, which endured until US president William McKinley finally intervened to take the islands four years later not by treaty but by a congressional joint resolution. The Organic Act of 1900 subsequently affirmed that Hawai'i was to be an incorporated territory of the United States. Its people thus became US citizens.

For the white settlers who drove these political changes, annexation was the culmination of an even deeper history. A significant core of the supporters of the overthrow and annexation were the children and grandchildren of American Protestant missionaries who had first begun to arrive in Hawai'i in 1820. Born in the islands, these figures frequently recited the history of their ancestors' efforts to Christianize Hawai'i's Indigenous population and in so doing sought to make a moral case for their political actions. They styled annexation as the only way of protecting the civilizational gains missionaries had made earlier in the century by taking power away from an Indigenous monarchy that supposedly could not be trusted to uphold the moral and religious standards that Americans had established. They turned to the idea that Native Hawaiians were at their core still "heathen," invoking a word long used by Calvinists and settler colonialists alike to supply the rationale for both evangelistic and acquisitive endeavors.[4] Hawai'i's nineteenth-century population certainly consisted of more than missionaries and Native Hawaiians; traders, sailors, diplomats, adventurers, and laborers all contributed to what the anthropologist Sally Engle Merry calls a "deeply fractured" cultural field.[5] Nonetheless, for the descendants of missionaries, the history of the relationship between their community and Hawai'i's Indigenous leadership loomed particularly large, and it was this narrative that demanded completion.

What was at stake for Hawai'i's Indigenous population was their sovereignty. Throughout the nineteenth century, Native Hawaiians had endured rapid depopulation as a result of diseases outsiders brought to the islands. They had witnessed the breakdown of a system of communal land tenure in favor of private ownership. They had grappled with the encroachment of numerous foreigners who sought political, economic, or religious influence in the archipelago or some combination of the three.[6] Yet going into the 1890s, Hawai'i still had an Indigenous monarchy that, for many Native Hawaiians, represented the continuation of a venerable lineage of *ali'i* (chiefs) that dated back many centuries before the arrival of American missionaries and even to the beginning of the world itself. Because the overthrow and annexation threatened to sever this chain of sovereignty, tens of thousands of Native Hawaiians mobilized to sign anti-annexation petitions.[7] Hawai'i's final queen Lili'uokalani traveled to Washington to present her case to US audiences in an attempt to counter the concurrent efforts of white settlers such as Lorrin Thurston, the grandson of two of the first missionaries to Hawai'i, to present the annexationist cause.[8]

While *The Friend*'s idea that Hawai'i was coming "into Columbia's fold, and under shelter of the Star Spangled Banner" gave voice to an imperialist vision of the United States stretching its flag out across the Pacific and gathering islands into it, a more granular analysis of the missionary community's intellectual production reveals less certainty about this sweeping conception of oceanic space. The first half of this book considers how the arguments descendants of missionaries made, particularly the historical narratives they developed, did not foreground the imperial archipelago of a US Pacific but were instead centered on the islands. Descendants of missionaries often lamented continental Americans' ignorance of Hawai'i's history and used their own engagements with island history to establish themselves as authorities who were able to mediate between American and local sensibilities. Of course, these claims were in large part a colonizer's defense mechanism that sought to palliate a sense of distance from the United States and to establish a sense of local belonging by marshaling and overriding Indigenous understandings. At the same time, however, we can read into them very real contestations over Hawai'i's significance and future in which local understandings could undercut imperial metanarratives. The idea developing in the continental United States of Hawai'i as a node in a broader American Pacific often coexisted uncomfortably with claims that a particular history of religious endeavor and cultural encounter in Hawai'i required protection. On the ground, descendants of missionaries competed with Indigenous actors over ownership of

Hawaiian history and tradition, again in ways that centered religion, sovereignty, and place at the island level. Although the seizure of Hawai'i and the Philippines prompted Americans from their continental perspective to deploy religious and historical arguments about the connectedness of the Pacific that minimized island agency, American settlers on the ground grappled with histories that emphasized Hawaiian distinctiveness.

The following three chapters also demonstrate the malleability of historical narratives as they became linked to the politics of annexation in Hawai'i, evolving in response to the changing needs of the missionary community. Chapters 1 and 2 both consider the period before annexation. Chapter 1 shows how arguments for annexation from among the missionary community became contingent on overturning an idea prevalent in the United States that Hawai'i had become a Christian nation earlier in the nineteenth century through the efforts of Protestant missionaries. They instead made the case that mission history was incomplete and that evangelistic work in the islands needed salvaging through renewed missionary efforts and, indeed, through annexation, undermining Native Hawaiians and their leadership in the process. Chapter 2 then sets the missionary community's pre-annexation uses of history in the context of a vibrant Native Hawaiian culture of historical narration that burgeoned in the last decades of the nineteenth century in direct opposition to the erosion of Indigenous sovereignty. This culture played a part in prompting descendants of missionaries to see claiming a place not only in US religious history but also in Hawaiian history on the basis of their birth and ancestry as necessary to their political project. Chapter 3 turns to the post-annexation period, exploring how the demands of creating an Americanized Hawai'i that would be attractive to settlers, businesspeople, and tourists required a further restyling of Hawai'i's nineteenth-century history. A vision of a harmonious historical project that white missionaries and Native Hawaiians had both partaken in to uplift the nation and create a space that was simultaneously civilized and exotic was prevalent from this point forward.

These three chapters complicate ideas about what it meant to be an American settler in the islands in the late nineteenth and early twentieth centuries. The descendants of missionaries certainly felt a pull toward their ancestors' homeland and campaigned for annexation, using ideas about the mission past to naturalize Hawai'i's place in the US order. They also often sought to establish their authority as narrators of history by drawing on American principles and on the conventions of historical and social scientific disciplines in the United States. However, they simultaneously used history in ways that betrayed the fact that they were removed from the United States by a generation or two and from the new imperialist project in the Philippines. They often justified themselves with recourse to Hawaiian rather than US history, seeking to overturn what they believed to be American misrepresentations of Hawai'i and its religious past. Also, despite their claims to scientific authority, they frequently appeared to value their intimate knowledge of the islands' people, traditions, and environment over any dispassionate analysis. In this sense, they distanced themselves from other white Americans. Although Hawai'i was drawn into the United States as part of a broader US strategy for the Pacific, this diasporic community had its own agendas and historical sensibilities that did not always align neatly with those of their ancestral home.

Chapter 1

"Venerated Fathers"

"Missionaries," Mission History, and Native Hawaiian Sovereignty

On June 9, 1895, Sereno Bishop spoke at Central Union Church in Honolulu to commemorate the seventy-fifth anniversary of American Protestant missionaries' arrival in Hawai'i. He recounted how when the first missionaries of the American Board of Commissioners for Foreign Missions (ABCFM) arrived in 1820, they discovered that the old Hawaiian religious system had already been destroyed. Seizing their opportunity, these missionaries, working with noble Native Hawaiian chiefs, had effected a thorough and rapid transformation of political, social, and religious life.[1] The apparently astonishing success of the mission that Bishop alluded to had been widely trumpeted in the United States, not least by the ABCFM, which by the 1850s was declaring that its religious work in the islands was complete. Adulation and fame endured. By the 1880s, one of the leaders of a new wave of American foreign missionary activity across the globe was holding up the Hawaiian mission as an exemplar, noting that to a Christian audience in the United States, the details of its history were "too familiar to need repetition."[2]

Sereno Bishop was born in 1827 to Artemas and Elizabeth Bishop, who had arrived in Hawai'i in 1823, part of the second company of American missionaries to the islands. Having spent his early years in the archipelago, Bishop was sent away for an education in the United States in 1839, graduating from Amherst College in 1846 and Auburn Theological Seminary in 1851, and subsequently received ordination into the Presbyterian Church. He returned to Hawai'i with his new wife Cornelia in 1853, taking up the position of seaman's chaplain at Lāhainā on the island of Maui. He then became principal of an industrial school in Lahainaluna in 1866. After he retired in 1877, he worked as a land surveyor. Speaking at Central Union Church in 1895, at the age of sixty-eight, Bishop positioned himself as an authoritative narrator of the early days of mission work in the islands, adding personal reminiscences to the familiar narrative of success. He had witnessed the "constant enthusiasm" and "millennial vision" of the early missionaries, the "squalid poverty" of ordinary Native Hawaiians, the imposing stature of Christianized chiefs, and the "strange, supernatural power" of missionary-led revivals. He recalled how when he returned to Hawai'i in January 1853 after his education abroad, he had been struck by the complete overhaul of Hawaiian politics led by missionaries since his departure, marking a transition from what he characterized as feudalism to private ownership, democracy, codified law, and constitutional monarchy.[3] Bishop was not the only one in the church that day who felt they had a personal share in Hawai'i's missionary past. He addressed an audience that included a number of fellow descendants of missionaries—"the lineal and spiritual progeny of the missionary fathers"—and challenged them to prove themselves worthy heirs by "building up . . . God's kingdom of righteousness and salvation."[4]

Bishop spoke at a time of political turmoil between the overthrow of the Native Hawaiian monarchy in 1893 and the annexation of the islands to the United States in 1898. He was a vocal supporter of the overthrow and of annexation, backing fellow descendants of missionaries active in the Hawaiian League who had conspired to depose the monarchy. As a result of these shared political convictions, Native Hawaiians and some in the United States accused descendants of missionaries of corrupting a religious enterprise for profit and power. Indeed, the label "missionary" was pejoratively employed in the late nineteenth century to identify white annexationists. Against this backdrop, Bishop's invocation of the mission past took on particular significance. In the face of criticism, descendants of missionaries sought the appearance of continuity with a successful American religious enterprise. While few took up formal mission work, they formed an associational culture, dominated by white male voices, that emphasized the idea that they were perpetuating a spiritual project in the islands. They were involved in the continued direction of churches through the Hawaiian Evangelical Association, formed in 1853 to take up the work of the ABCFM, and the Hawaiian Mission Children's Society. Through correspondence with the ABCFM in Boston, they sought to convince a US Christian audience both that they were inheritors of the missionary torch and that further political and religious intervention from the United States was needed to protect the successes of previous generations. This chapter emphasizes that these descendants' invocation of the ancestral past went beyond incidental assertions of moral superiority, as previous studies have seemed to suggest.[5] Rather, an expression of a specific and continuous religious purpose lay right at the heart of the associations and political arguments that descendants of missionaries constructed.

The chapter also introduces a theme that runs through the next three chapters: the ways descendants of missionaries were discursively cast as liminal to the United States, partly by their detractors but also as a part of their self-presentation. Even in an age of imperial bombast and of the apparent projection of US power across oceanic space, some of their fellow Americans regarded those on the frontline of US colonialism in Hawai'i with suspicion. In response, descendants of missionaries styled themselves first and foremost as local experts with a deep investment in island politics, religion, culture, and history. They recast their perceived liminality as a virtue to stave off the fear that what their detractors said was true—that they belonged in neither Hawaiian nor American worlds. The idea of the descendants of missionaries as liminal figures does not suggest that they stood apart from the general thrust of US colonialism. Indeed, the colonizer's perception of themselves as liminal was central in shaping their relationships to "home" and to the colony across colonial contexts.[6] By appreciating this core dynamic and the particular ways the missionary community in Hawai'i engaged with it, we might understand Hawai'i not as conforming neatly to a hegemonic vision of oceanic space and history developed from the United States but as a space in which white Americans were constantly negotiating their status as imperial or local through the production of historical narrative. We will see in the first half of this book that descendants of missionaries sought to rewrite American perceptions of Hawai'i's religious history, were drawn into contests over genealogy, and marshaled Indigenous renderings of the past for their own purposes, both personal and imperial.

In this chapter, an analysis of how descendants of missionaries engaged with the religious past in Hawai'i reveals their self-presentation as actors who above all were concerned with their local situation and who sought American assistance to help them perpetuate a "missionary" agenda in the islands. Unlike in the Philippines, the American presence in Hawai'i was multigenerational by 1898 and was already deeply rooted in a particular Pacific world. Therefore, although descendants of missionaries recognized the political, economic, and spiritual benefits of closer ties to the United States, they persistently asserted their unique understanding of and connection to Hawaiian history, making the case that they were better equipped to lead in spiritual and temporal affairs than either Native Hawaiians or American outsiders. In this sense, their perception of imperial authority was not that it was projected from the United States outward but that it was negotiated in Hawaiʻi by actors who placed the islands rather than their ancestral homeland front and center. Although from a US perspective, the 1898 moment seemed to draw Hawaiʻi into an "American lake," the spatial-temporal category of the US Pacific was punctured by instances in which local religious history seemed to be of primary concern to those on the ground.

Hawaiʻi's Mission History in the United States

On October 27, 1852, Rufus Anderson, the influential foreign secretary of the ABCFM, wrote to the board's missionaries in Hawaiʻi that "the time has come . . . to recognize the Sandwich Islands as having been *virtually Christianized*." Laboring among a "Christian community, and no longer upon a heathen people" was wasteful, so the task now was to "prepare the way for the gospel to stand alone."[7] In making this case, Anderson built on British missionary leader Henry Venn's idea that it was the responsibility of missions not to "civilize" but to rapidly build up Indigenous churches.[8] He also pragmatically responded to the pressures the ABCFM experienced after the financial panic of 1837 and as a result of attacks on the board by abolitionists in the Hawaiian mission, who accused the ABCFM of temporizing over the question of slavery.[9] Anderson continued to push for the swift transfer of work to Native Hawaiian pastors in the following decades, visiting Hawaiʻi in 1863 to make his case in person.

Meanwhile, publications in the United States reflected on a job well done by missionaries.[10] Anderson authored two histories of the successful effort to Christianize Hawaiʻi.[11] After his successor, N. G. Clark, visited the islands in 1870 to mark the fiftieth anniversary of the first missionary landing, the effusive words of Clark's subsequent report to the ABCFM's annual meeting were disseminated to American Christian audiences through the board's flagship periodical, the *Missionary Herald*: "The first missionary company . . . found a people sunk in ignorance. . . . I found a Christian nation. . . . Where in all the course of human history have results so grand, so beneficent, been achieved in so short a period?"[12] Similarly positive assessments of mission work in Hawaiʻi reached broader US audiences in the popular travel writings of Richard Henry Dana Jr.[13] Even Mark Twain, better known for his biting critiques of missionary hypocrisy, offered his readers and lecture audiences an impression of the remarkable changes he perceived that missionaries in Hawai'i had wrought.[14]

Before the mission was declared complete, the writings of ABCFM missionaries Hiram Bingham and Sheldon Dibble that were published in the United States constituted key parts of a canonical historical literature on Hawai'i's successful evangelization and the divinely ordained chain of events that led to it.[15] The story began with Captain Cook's "discovery" of the islands and his death at the hands of Native Hawaiians, an act that exemplified the archipelago's apparent pre-Christian degradation. The next key event was the Native Hawaiian orphan 'Ōpūkaha'ia traveling as a cabin boy aboard a ship bound for the United States and finding his way to New Haven in 1809. There, he converted to Christianity, attended the short-lived Foreign Mission School at Cornwall, Connecticut, and begged to return to his homeland accompanied by missionaries. 'Ōpūkaha'ia died before he was able to make the return trip. By the time an ABCFM mission reached the islands in 1820, the first Native Hawaiian monarch, Kamehameha (r. 1795–1819), who had completed the unification of the archipelago in 1809, had also passed away. Then, in an episode deemed providential, two of Kamehameha's wives, Keōpūolani and Ka'ahumanu, as regents to Kamehameha's son Liholiho (Kamehameha II, r. 1819–24), overthrew the *'ai kapu*, the sacred system that regulated Hawaiian life and had been deemed prohibitive and superstitious by foreign observers. Soon after that, missionaries arrived, gained influence with Indigenous elites, and oversaw the transformation of the islands, culminating in a great revival from 1837 to 1839 and the promulgation in 1840 by Kauikeaouli (Kamehameha III, r. 1825–54) of a written constitution. Under Kauikeaouli and his successor, Alexander Liholiho (Kamehameha IV, r. 1855–63), the Hawaiian government went on to promote temperance and to reform education and land tenure.

Stories of Hawai'i's Christianization were disseminated across the United States in newspapers, pamphlets, and religious periodicals from the early decades of the nineteenth century, as missionaries' need to drum up financial support entered a reciprocal relationship with the demands of US audiences for tales of the benighted heathen and their improvement. In the words of the Native Hawaiian scholar Noelani Arista, "Hawaiian history, politics, genealogies, and social relations" were "available for fabrications.... History was a thing that could be crafted and honed as an instrument of the mission."[16] The shadow of the missionaries' narrative was so long that only relatively recently have historians reframed it from a Native Hawaiian perspective. 'Ōpūkaha'ia, for example, was not "an awkward, dull-looking heathen boy," as nineteenth-century American narratives suggested, helpless but for the intervention of kindly New Englanders, but rather a religious expert who traveled in order to master outsiders' religious traditions.[17] Moreover, Native Hawaiian leaders were not mere puppets of missionaries. Indigenous governance was viable for decades after contact, and Native Hawaiian leaders were making careful political and spiritual calculations when they overthrew the ʻai kapu, converted to Christianity, forged a written constitution, and shifted to a system of private land ownership. They were active innovators, seeking education and alternative religious, legal, political, and economic systems to preserve Hawaiian independence in a world of competing empires.[18] Of particular importance were the staunchly Christian kahu (royal attendants), including John Papa ʻĪʻī, who worked closely with missionaries across several decades and monarchical reigns.[19] While these figures never gave up aspects of Native Hawaiian epistemology, as ʻĪʻī's historical writing makes clear, they were instrumental in imbuing Hawaiian politics with a Christian sense of morality even when their monarchs succumbed to alcoholism, as was the case with Kauikeaouli.[20]

However, advocates of American mission work in the late nineteenth century obfuscated any nuanced sense of Indigenous agency. By the 1880s, a new age of Protestant mission was beginning. Meetings at Northfield, Massachusetts, led by the renowned revivalist Dwight L. Moody gave rise to the Student Volunteer Movement and its watchword, "the evangelization of the world in this generation." As this new era of activism began, the Hawaiian case was used to show that divine favor rested on the missionary enterprise. In his influential 1886 work *The Crisis of Missions*, the "elder statesman" of the student movement, Arthur T. Pierson, wrote of the mission to Hawaiʻi as an enterprise that "humanly speaking" was hopeless.[21] However, Providence had wrought a remarkable transformation before the first missionaries arrived, as the Hawaiian monarchy ended the notorious ʻai kapu and burned their wooden idols.[22] From this point, in a story "familiar" to Christians in the United States, "within fifty years an entire people . . . took their place in the great brotherhood of Christian nations."[23]

Pierson sought to convince Protestant readers that missions had reached a crisis point: individuals and churches could either take advantage of the many opportunities God presented to rapidly evangelize the world or remain apathetic and risk losing such opportunities forever.[24] In the case of Hawaiʻi, however, the work was complete and had receded into history, its memory galvanizing a new, more ambitious project. Congregationalist minister Austin Phelps's introduction to another widely read and now infamous book on the notion of crisis written by a supporter of foreign mission work—Josiah Strong's *Our Country* (1885)—further reinforced the notion that Hawaiʻi's Christian story had been rendered entirely historical by pointing to the death of the islands' Indigenous people: "Seldom has a nation been converted to Christ, only to die."[25] The Native Hawaiian population had indeed declined precipitously between the late eighteenth and late nineteenth centuries, from several hundred thousand to around 40,000 in the wake of contact with foreigners and their diseases—venereal disease, tuberculosis, measles, smallpox, typhoid fever, and leprosy, among others.[26] Even so, Phelps's formulation was indicative of a common settler-colonial desire to naturalize and preempt Indigenous disappearance as symptomatic of racial weakness rather than of violent colonial incursion.[27] Tales of historical missionary glory and contemporary ideas about the inevitable death of "weaker" races in the face of "civilization" worked together to reinforce the impression among US audiences that the tale of Hawaiʻi's evangelization was finished.

Yet in Hawaiʻi in the late nineteenth century, as they operated at a distance from the United States and its new age of mission, the children and grandchildren of ABCFM missionaries were convinced that the missionary story in the islands was ongoing, embodied by them. Through a rich associational culture, they countered accusations that they had abandoned their forebears' spiritual goals in pursuit of political power, by reminding themselves and others that there was mission work still to be done. In the process, they rooted themselves in a particular story of intergenerational American presence in one Pacific archipelago, claiming a place in the history of Hawaiʻi that was not dependent on any broader narrative of US empire sweeping westward across oceanic space.

Defining the "Missionary"

Although the missionaries who arrived in Hawaiʻi in 1820 did not have political and economic agendas, having children in the islands transformed their priorities. Seeking security for their offspring and finding their evangelistic work increasingly squeezed by Rufus Anderson, some of the original missionaries took advantage of their close relationship with the Hawaiian monarchy to become royal advisors, landowners, lawyers, and businessmen.[28] In so doing, they forged paths that their children and grandchildren followed. In particular, many of these descendants developed interests in the islands' burgeoning sugar industry, represented not least by the companies Castle &

Cooke (founded by two missionaries) and Alexander & Baldwin (founded by two sons of missionaries), two of Hawaiʻi's notorious Big Five corporations by the early twentieth century. Moreover, through their childhood interactions with the Hawaiian landscape, their peer culture, and their ambivalent relationship to the United States, descendants of missionaries developed a "bicultural identity" marked both by certainty that they belonged in Hawaiʻi and a sense of supremacy based on their white American Protestant heritage.[29] A combination of their economic interests with their confidence that Hawaiʻi was their inheritance inspired them to overthrow the Hawaiian monarchy in 1893, colluding with the US minister to Hawaiʻi, John L. Stevens, and troops aboard the U.S.S. *Boston*, all of whom acted without any explicit instructions from Washington.[30] These descendants of missionaries subsequently lobbied for annexation to the United States.

Sanford Dole, the first and only president of the Republic of Hawaiʻi and the first governor of Hawaiʻi as a US territory, was the son of missionary Daniel Dole and his wife Emily, who came to the islands in 1841. The Dole family's influence in Hawaiʻi increased with the arrival in 1899 of Sanford's cousin once removed, James Dole, later Hawaiʻi's most prominent industrialist. Lorrin Thurston was the grandson of Asa and Lucy Thurston, members of the first missionary company in the islands. He was the lawyer and businessman who authored the Bayonet Constitution of 1887, led the Committee of Safety that overthrew the monarchy, and represented the cause of annexation in Washington thereafter.[31] Even those among the descendants of missionaries who were not directly involved in the Hawaiian League were said to be "practically unanimous" in their support for these political actions.[32]

By the late nineteenth century, the term "missionary" had taken on heavily political connotations in Hawaiʻi, employed pejoratively by critics of the overthrow and annexation. "The missionaries as a sect are an abomination to us the Hawaiians," wrote "Young Hawaiian" in a letter to the pro-monarchy newspaper *Hawaii Holomua* in January 1894. "They deprived us of our liberation and rights and self-government" and "robbed us of our country by the misuse of the Boston marines in obedience to the command of Stevens."[33] Samuel K. Pua, the Native Hawaiian representative for Honolulu's Fifth Ward in the Hawaiian House of Representatives, expressed his hope in the aftermath of the overthrow that "the President [of the United States] will not notice the attempt of these missionaries to humbug him, but will ... banish the dark cloud which hangs over our heads and deliver us from the hands of these people."[34]

James H. Blount, a recently retired Democratic representative from Georgia and former chair of the House Committee on Foreign Relations, noted such uses of the word "missionary" when President Grover Cleveland sent him to Hawai'i in 1893 to investigate Stevens's involvement in the overthrow. Blount observed that "the revered missionary had disappeared. In his stead there came . . . his son, ambitious to acquire wealth and to continue the political control reverently conceded to his pious ancestor. Hence, in satire, the native designated him a 'missionary.'"[35] Blount (and consequently Cleveland) supported the claim of Lili'uokalani, the deposed Hawaiian queen, that Hawai'i's lawful government had been illegally overthrown, and the president refused to pass an annexation treaty to the US Senate. It is worth properly contextualizing Blount's conclusions. He was a southern Democrat, a former Confederate, and a white supremacist who was undoubtedly suspicious about the idea of adding racial others to the US body politic through annexation. Blount did amplify Native Hawaiian voices to a certain extent, and his government's approach evinced a desire to cautiously and thoroughly scrutinize the claims of white settlers in Hawai'i, also to a certain extent. Yet Blount, like many anti-imperialists of the late nineteenth century, approached the question from a standpoint of racism, paternalism, and southern antipathy to the idea of Yankee invasion and occupation rather than being motivated by any belief in equality.[36] Nonetheless, his findings corroborated concerns expressed by Rufus Anderson and some late nineteenth-century travel writers that the descendants of missionaries were failing to match the piety of their forebears.[37]

Even some descendants of missionaries broke ranks and echoed these critiques. Charles Thomas Gulick, for example, was the nephew of the missionary Peter Gulick. His impoverished father had sent him to live with his uncle in Hawai'i at the age of ten, where he attended school with a number of his cousins in the 1850s and 1860s.[38] The Gulicks were one of the few Hawaiian missionary families to initiate a missionary dynasty. Peter's son Luther embarked on a mission to Micronesian island groups from Hawai'i. Luther's sister Julia taught and evangelized in Japan, while his brothers Orramel, John, William, and Thomas performed ABCFM work in Japan, China, and Spain.[39] Most famously, Sidney Gulick, Luther's son, became an influential missionary to Japan in the early twentieth century.[40] Charles, however, remained in Hawai'i, where he became a prominent politician, and by the 1890s he stood in support of Lili'uokalani, against the political ambitions of other descendants of missionaries. Writing in early 1894, citing the role Lorrin Thurston,

Sanford Dole, and members of the Judd, Castle, and Alexander missionary families played in the overthrow, Gulick found evidence of enough "traits and peculiarities" to make any "careful observer . . . revise many of his notions, respecting the Hawaiian Missionaries and their descendants. . . . The term 'Missionary' hardly deserves notice at this stage of Hawaiian history."[41]

Liliʻuokalani argued that the missionary community's hunger for power had a longer history. Writing to a US audience after her overthrow, she undermined the received wisdom in the United States that the early missionaries had encouraged and defended the authority of noble Native Hawaiian leaders. She suggested that the original missionaries had initiated "a project of many years" to seize power.[42] She still reserved particular ire for the descendants of missionaries, referring to the "unchristian . . . Missionaries" who sought "power and control," abusing her from the pulpit.[43]

Since the 1820s, many nonmissionary white businessmen, too, had been engaged in a struggle against the missionary community's perceived moral absolutism, political influence, and, increasingly, economic dominance.[44] Although several such men aligned themselves with the missionary community's political and economic interests in the late nineteenth century, ongoing tensions remained evident in an 1881 pamphlet by John C. Allardyce, a small businessman in Lahaina. Allardyce wrote for an American audience, seeking to shatter myths that might entice others to follow him in emigrating to the archipelago in search of opportunities. Central to his disillusionment was the domination of island society by a "missionary 'ring,'" of whom his sarcastic criticism was relentless. "These worthy folk long since formed an internal alliance . . . against all outside influence," Allardyce began. Like Liliʻuokalani, he drew little separation between descendants of missionaries and first-generation missionaries. Through their historical influence over the monarchy, they had imposed "restrictive legislative ordinance and selfish, illiberal regulations" and "succeeded in civilizing and moralizing the Hawaiian native race off the face of their country." He accused these "money-making, land-grabbing Pharisees" of hypocrisy, noting the contrast between their oppressive laws and their "self-satisfied" services at Honolulu's Fort Street Church and frequent scandals reported in the local press, even implying that the original missionaries had fathered children with Native Hawaiian women. It was only a matter of time, he added, before the "patient Hawaiians" rose up against their "oppressors."[45]

The *Missionary Herald*, as the ABCFM's main organ in the United States, had long defended its missionaries from rumors resentful businessmen circulated and the American press amplified, and it continued to do so in the final decade of the nineteenth century.[46] It leaped to the defense of missionaries after the *New York Herald* published a story in April 1894 that drew on a letter that supposedly originated with a Honolulu correspondent. The article suggested that Hiram Bingham, one of the first missionaries in Hawai'i, had colluded in 1826 with the US navy to extort goods from the Hawaiian people that were subsequently sold in China. The *Missionary Herald* described these claims as "preposterous," motivated by "bitter hatred": "A proper climax to such fiction would be that these enterprising but avaricious missionaries . . . kept straight on to the moon where they obtained cheese in such quantity that they afterward made themselves rich by selling it to the Patagonians."[47] Descendants of missionaries also refuted such narratives. Hiram Bingham II, the son of the accused missionary and himself a missionary to the South Pacific, wrote to Honolulu's *Pacific Commercial Advertiser* in June 1894 to chastise the newspaper for engaging with the *New York Herald*'s claims. He wrote that even though the *Advertiser* had dismissed the allegations, voicing them anew was irresponsible: "*You* will know that it is indeed preposterous; but perhaps *some* of your readers may not."[48]

Amid such suspicion about the true nature of missionary ambition, most descendants of missionaries rallied around the "missionary" label. Sereno Bishop, for example, responded in an 1890 edition of *The Friend*, Hawai'i's monthly Protestant periodical that he edited, to the charge by the Hawaiian royalist Robert Wilcox that "Missionaries" had "captured the government." Bishop turned the criticism on its head by noting that "they mean by a missionary a man who pays his quarterly account," implying that "missionaries" had earned their supremacy.[49] Another son of missionaries, William DeWitt Alexander, stated that the epithet was "a title of honor," while Frank Damon suggested that it was a marker of character inherited from the first-generation missionaries: he claimed that his father, Samuel C. Damon, had been not just a missionary by profession but also a "missionary" in the same sense as his descendants, as an upstanding white settler.[50]

Although descendants of missionaries embraced "missionary" as a social and political label, they also continued to cluster around a religious institution: Fort Street Church in Honolulu, which relocated in the city and became Central Union Church in 1887. As Allardyce's pamphlet suggested, the congregation at Central Union was perceived from the outside as exclusive, elitist, and racist, having inherited the rigid moralism of Calvinist missionaries and a disdain for Native Hawaiians and foreign outsiders alike. Descendants of missionaries had grown up in a bubble, protected from the supposed evils of Native Hawaiian culture through practices that Rufus

Anderson had warned were setting them up in "hot houses."[51] As children, some had been kept in homes with high-walled gardens, and after 1840 all had been educated at the Punahou School, which opened exclusively for them after their parents decided that sending young children back to the United States for their education was unsustainable.[52] Through such institutions as Central Union, descendants of missionaries maintained these social bubbles as they grew older.

The church was just one expression of a multifaceted associational culture that rooted the "missionary" community in a history of religious endeavor and thus challenged accusations of worldliness. The centerpiece was the Hawaiian Mission Children's Society (HMCS), founded in 1852 as a "Social Missionary Society" to raise financial support for missionary son Luther Gulick's evangelistic work in Micronesia. At its inception, it had a pool of 282 missionary children and sixteen grandchildren to draw on.[53] By 1895, it boasted over 900 living members and maintained a correspondence network that included many who no longer lived in the islands.[54] This was a small group in the context of a Hawaiian population of nearly 110,000, as an 1896 census estimated, but the community's self-presentation through the HMCS imbued it with special historical and religious significance.[55] Even though most descendants of missionaries did not pursue the same course as Gulick and enter formal mission work, the HMCS sought to "cultivate the missionary spirit" among them.[56] Annual presidential addresses frequently reminded them of the history they were a part of and the spiritual duties incumbent on them to continue religious work, if not by becoming missionaries then by extending moral and financial support for ongoing evangelistic projects in Hawai'i and beyond. HMCS members combined celebratory reflection with admonishments and challenges, worrying that not enough was being done to keep up the work of their forebears. "Why do not the descendants of the missionaries to these Islands, engage in foreign missionary work, as their parents did?" asked missionary son William O. Smith at the society's 1882 meeting. "We may challenge ourselves on this subject, or we may await the challenge of others."[57] Sanford Dole explored similar themes in his 1888 address: "It is our privilege to claim their story and their work as our inheritance, and it is for us to take up and prosecute this heritage of work in their spirit of consecration."[58]

The Hawaiian Evangelical Association (HEA), which was tasked with continuing the ABCFM's work as a largely self-supporting home mission after 1853, acted as another concrete institutional expression of the late nineteenth-century missionary community's commitment to upholding a spiritual legacy. The purpose of the ABCFM in drawing the mission to a close and handing its legacy over to the HEA was to facilitate the indigenization of the Hawaiian church. At its grassroots, the HEA was an overwhelmingly Indigenous organization—the ʻAhahui ʻEuanelio o Hawaiʻi (Evangelical Association of Hawaiʻi), as Native Hawaiians referred to it—whose business was conducted in the Hawaiian language.[59] At the top of the association, however, it was a different story. Descendants of missionaries became well represented on the HEA's board. As the last of the missionary "fathers" passed away in the 1880s and 1890s, their sons stepped into their shoes. Although sons of missionaries were only five of the twenty-seven-man board for 1879–80, by the time of Hawaiʻi's annexation they were fourteen of thirty-two.[60] The board's officers continued to be white settlers, sons of missionaries in particular. One of them, Albert Francis Judd, was president from 1883 until his death in 1900. Hiram Bingham II, Anderson O. Forbes, and Oliver P. Emerson each served as corresponding secretary for a number of years, and another descendant, William W. Hall, was a long-serving treasurer. Sereno Bishop was also a perennial board member. Beyond this, a large portion of support for the HEA came from economically successful descendants of missionaries.[61] Accordingly, donations were subject to vacillations in their success, a fact that was particularly noted in the period following the McKinley Tariff Act of 1890, which stripped Hawaiian sugar planters of the privileged position they had enjoyed as sugar exporters to the United States under an 1875 reciprocity treaty.[62]

While women were prominent on the membership rolls of Central Union, the HMCS, and the HEA, those who led and spoke for the descendants of missionaries were usually men. Indeed, descendants of missionaries effaced the crucial role of mothers in raising a settler mission in Hawaiʻi and women's agency in mission history more generally in their persistent, exclusive references to missionary "fathers" as those to be celebrated and emulated. This veneration of missionary masculinity was particularly apparent in the way Albert Judd framed the memoirs of his late mother, Laura, when preparing them for publication in the United States in 1880. Although he clearly believed these memoirs to be of interest to an American public already fascinated by the Hawaiian mission, he stated in his introductory note that they did not constitute history. Judd thus rendered missionary wives' accounts ephemeral, in direct contrast to the supposedly more robust histories written by the famous male missionaries Bingham and Dibble, who warranted the title "historians" in Judd's eyes. Judd also suggested that despite his mother's authorship, it was his father's story that readers would uncover: "This work is occupied so largely with describing his agency in building the ship of State of this little kingdom, that it may be regarded more as a tribute to his memory, than as an attempt at history-writing."[63]

In making these claims, Judd was to some extent drawing on words his mother had written in 1861, eleven years before her death. She denied any claims to "literary merit," apologized for any appearance of "egotism," and stated that she had "not pretended to write a history of the Hawaiian kingdom."[64] What Albert ignored, however, was the wide-ranging nature of his mother's writing, which interspersed accounts of her personal experience with details of key events in Hawaiian political history, reflections on Indigenous practices, and stories involving an array of important figures in the islands that included missionaries, Native Hawaiian leaders, diplomats, sailors, and explorers.[65] Laura Judd even laid claim to the same kind of objectivity as Bingham in her statement that she had "endeavored to obtrude personal feelings and affairs as little as possible."[66] We might think of Laura Judd as engaging in an act of dissembling, carving out a space in a supposedly masculine enterprise and finding a standpoint from which to write history by denying that it was actually history in which she was interested. In this sense, she adopted the same tactic as many other women engaged in missionary and colonial enterprises in the late nineteenth century. On the one hand, they affirmed that their role in these enterprises was a "domestic" one that was qualitatively different from that of history-making men. On the other, under the cover of "domesticity," they contributed significantly to imperial meaning making in ways that served both their personal ambition and the imperial project.[67] Another example from the Hawaiian context is the letters of the young Congregationalist schoolteacher Carrie Prudence Winter, who arrived in Honolulu from Connecticut in 1890. While she did not author a history of the islands as such, her letters back home to her fiancé included an array of reflections on the Native Hawaiian monarchy, missionaries, the health of Hawai'i's Indigenous people, and the political turmoil of the 1890s. The letters thus became a way that Winter could demonstrate her colonial expertise and contribute to colonial perceptions of Hawai'i's history and culture without breaking from the "domestic" frame of the love letter.[68]

More broadly, the reality that Albert Judd's framing of his mother's writing obscured was that contrary to contemporary New England conventions, missionary wives had significant agency in the conversion of Native Hawaiians in the early decades of the nineteenth century. Because it was Native Hawaiian chiefly women who wielded the most significant religious influence in the islands, missionaries achieved success only by promoting their wives to intermediary roles.[69] Given this, Judd's suggestion that the women of the mission were secondary characters even in their own writing speaks of a retrospective effort to place masculinity at the forefront of Hawaiian mission history in the late nineteenth century, a time when, as Gail Bederman has shown, "Americans were obsessed with the connection between manhood and racial dominance" against the backdrop of Jim Crow, Chinese exclusion, and imperial warfare.[70]

At the same time, Native Hawaiian chiefly women featured heavily in histories of the mission. Three in particular were prominent: Keōpūolani and Kaʻahumanu, the wives of Kamehameha who were instrumental in breaking the ʻai kapu after his death, and Kapiʻolani, who gave the most famous public display of Christianity in Hawaiʻi, defying the goddess Pele in 1824 by walking into Kīlauea, the volcanic crater on Hawaiʻi island where Pele resided. The centering of women was evident in Hiram Bingham's history: he clearly framed the breaking of the ʻai kapu as Kaʻahumanu's effort, supported by a number of other chiefly women, to overthrow the restrictions on them.[71] Rufus Anderson authored a pamphlet about Kapiʻolani, "the heroine of Hawaii," in 1866, describing her life as emblematic of "the genial and beautiful Christianity introduced by American missionaries."[72] Into the 1880s, the *Missionary Herald* kept Kapiʻolani and Keōpūolani's stories alive for a new generation of Christian youth.[73] The prevalence of Native Hawaiian women in these narratives that were popularized in the United States, and the comparative erasure of Indigenous men, has led one recent historian to wonder how far it gave rise to the problematic colonial perception that the story of US empire was one of white masculinity acting on a feminized nation.[74]

Whatever the reason for missionaries' ongoing celebration of Native Hawaiian women's historical Christian leadership, the reality was that in the nineteenth century, patriarchal norms triumphed in Hawaiʻi. In the shift to a constitutional, elected government after 1840, women began to lose their status. Over time, they were denied the right to vote and the right to govern as Hawaiian leaders increasingly recognized women's political subordination as intrinsic to modern nationhood.[75] By the time the constitution of the Republic of Hawaiʻi was drawn up in 1894, Sereno Bishop dismissed out of hand the Hawaiian expressions of a transnational "boom for woman's suffrage" because of the "numerical preponderance of women of degraded character" in the islands. Delegates to the constitutional convention agreed, striking down a proposal for woman suffrage by 22 votes to 8.[76] Bishop also cast aspersions on Hawaiʻi's final monarch in terms that were both racist and misogynistic, denigrating Liliʻuokalani for her association with "the very impure living women of her own kindred," for whom "chastity was not at all a virtue."[77] If there had indeed been a time when women had been seen as the vanguard of Hawaiian Christianity, it had clearly passed away by the 1890s as far as the missionary community was concerned. This fact was reflected in the dominance of male voices in their associational culture.

While direct descendants of missionaries were at the core of "missionary" culture, their associations were not entirely closed to outsiders. Although the constitution of the HMCS stated that while any direct descendants of missionaries could become a member for an annual fee of $1 or a onetime fee of $10, it also stated that any person who was not a direct descendant was allowed to join for the same price "by the consent of four-fifths of the members present at any regular meeting," modified to two-thirds in 1865.[78] This suggests how those from outside the missionary "family" might be adopted. Sereno Bishop's speech at Central Union in 1895, discussed at the start of this chapter, also implied this possibility, conditional on acceptance of a spiritual mantle. Bishop stated that "the true children and heirs of those venerated fathers" were not just the "lineal descendants" but included all those "who make those men your fathers by . . . applying yourselves to fulfil the work which they began."[79] As a result, the "missionaries" that critics referred to in the late nineteenth century included some of the businessmen and lawyers, mostly Americans, who had established themselves in the islands, a handful of surviving first-generation missionaries, and a small number of new religious workers who arrived after the mission was declared complete.

The businessmen Joseph B. Atherton, Peter C. Jones, and Henry Waterhouse, for example, all gained adoptee status and spent significant amounts of time as officers in the HMCS, the HEA, Central Union Church, and the Honolulu Young Men's Christian Association (YMCA). The latter was another local religious association, this one exclusively male, that was founded in 1869 and was heavily populated by descendants of missionaries.[80] Atherton, Jones, and Waterhouse were all also associated with the Hawaiian League, the organization that was instrumental in overthrowing the monarchy. Charles McEwen Hyde was another successful adoptee. In 1877, the ABCFM sent Hyde to oversee the North Pacific Missionary Institute, a training school for prospective Native Hawaiian pastors in Honolulu. Called from his role as a Congregationalist minister in Haverhill, Massachusetts, he became the first new ABCFM missionary to Hawai'i since Rufus Anderson had declared evangelistic efforts complete. At first, Hyde expressed ambivalence about the political machinations of descendants of missionaries and their "absorption" in secular pursuits: "'Missionary' is a term of reproach in Honolulu" because "so many of our good people have done things utterly inconsistent with their professed beliefs."[81] With such admonitions, Hyde inherited the role of missionary parents, who had often worried about the spiritual condition of their children and feared that they did not intend to continue religious work.[82] However, Hyde increasingly ingratiated himself, fully participating in the missionary community's associational culture, for example by serving as president of the HMCS for 1879–80 and 1884–85.[83] He stayed in Hawai'i until his death in 1899. By the beginning of the 1890s, he seemed to have revised his initial assessment: "The reality so far exceeds anything thought possible when the work was begun, that all the criticism you may hear about failure and hypocrisy and greed of missionaries and their children will melt away as smoke."[84] When Native Hawaiian pastors attempted to remove missionary son Oliver Emerson from the HEA board in 1894 in protest of his anti-monarchical stance, Hyde opposed them, stressing "the importance of historical continuity.... The present Hawaiian Evangelical Association ... is the successor of the American Mission."[85]

Through the HMCS, the HEA, Central Union Church, and the YMCA, descendants of missionaries and their allies presented themselves as guardians and perpetuators of a historical legacy. They were far from being a numerically dominant element in late nineteenth-century Hawaiian society, yet through an associational culture that constantly reinforced their sense of centrality and significance to local history, they assuaged anxieties and shielded themselves from detractors. Facing criticism of their worldliness from Native Hawaiians and fellow Americans, they used these associations to conspicuously reiterate the Hawaiian mission's spiritual goals and achievements and to develop the idea that descent from the mission marked a continuation of this religious ideal, not its corruption. They set their hegemonic white settler identity on these foundations. The next section shows that in asserting their ownership of Hawaiian religious history, descendants of missionaries also sought to recalibrate Americans' perceptions of it, impelling American Christian audiences to recognize that Hawai'i's Christianization could not be regarded as complete after all. When they argued that the mission's legacy was under siege in an ever-changing island world and in need of protection, "missionaries" insisted that they were being truer than other Americans to their parents' evaluation of the mission. When American Christians responded to these pleas, however, the intellectual distance between descendants of missionaries in Hawai'i and the late nineteenth-century missionary enterprise in the United States became all the more apparent. New impetus from outside the missionary community threatened the traditions that the descendants of missionaries saw themselves to have inherited.

Recalibrating Mission History

In the early 1880s, the missionary community was still contributing to Americans' celebration of a successful and complete mission. Albert Francis Judd's introduction to his mother's memoirs, for example, reminded Americans of "the only instance of a nation lifted from the darkness of heathenism to the light of Christian civilization without the destruction of the native Government."[86] The publication of missionary Titus Coan's memoirs by a New York press in 1882 further amplified tales of "the wonderful changes wrought in Hawaii during a life time."[87] As the 1880s went on, however, and particularly as Native Hawaiian Christians began to contest the HEA board's authority after it supported the Bayonet Constitution of 1887, "missionaries" increasingly stressed to American mission backers that the perception of the mission's completeness was not wholly correct.[88] When ABCFM foreign secretary N. G. Clark visited Hawaiʻi for the fiftieth anniversary of the mission in 1870, he had argued that "the past at least is secure," that the legacy of mission work in Hawaiʻi was safe no matter what the future held.[89] However, in the last two decades of the nineteenth century, some members of the missionary community vehemently argued that this was not the case and appealed to the ABCFM for new evangelists to shore up the work of the previous generation. One adopted "missionary," W. B. Oleson, a Maine native who had travelled to Hawaiʻi in 1878 to become principal of the Hilo Boarding School and in 1887 became the founding principal of the Kamehameha School for Boys, stated that "the results of the past" were "in real jeopardy."[90] While "the great Christian public, conversant with the historical facts of the evangelization of the Hawaiian race, would naturally expect a development of religious life in keeping with the phenomenal emergence from heathenism," subsequent "extraordinary conditions" had stunted this development.[91]

In the eyes of the descendants of missionaries and those who associated with them, an explosion of commercial activity and the resultant influx of white businessmen and non-Christian immigrants from China and Japan in particular had overwhelmed the still-nascent church.[92] Even "the momentum of the early work" had not brought "this people safely through the trying ordeal of . . . the large influx of ungodly men."[93] At the same time, the perceived decline was described as rooted in the essential nature of Native Hawaiians. They were fickle and easily led, "missionaries" argued, and their Christianity had only been superficial.[94] In celebrating the Hawaiian mission, Bishop wrote, churches in the United States had failed to appreciate "the inherent weakness and necessities of 'Nature people.'"[95] In response to the dual curses of supposed Native Hawaiian racial inferiority and new corrupting influences, it was the responsibility of good Christian Americans to forget what they thought they knew about Hawaiian history and to act to save the good work the first-generation missionaries had only managed to begin.

There was a fine line between suggesting that mission work remained incomplete and suggesting that the mission itself had been misguided. This tension surfaced particularly in the work of Samuel Chapman Armstrong. Armstrong, son of the missionaries Richard and Clarissa Armstrong, who arrived in Hawai'i in 1832, was best known for his role as a Union Civil War general and for establishing the Hampton Institute for the industrial training of African Americans and Native Americans in Virginia. At Hampton, Armstrong taught Booker T. Washington, directly inspiring his influential philosophy of racial uplift through the creation of a Black manual laboring class that was made manifest at the Tuskegee Institute in Alabama. Armstrong's work also flowed across the Pacific, inspiring the efforts of US colonialists to bring industrial education to the Philippines.[96] Armstrong was thus the child of the Hawaiian mission who made the most significant impact in the United States, and his ideas about industrial education and Hawaiian mission history were closely connected. Armstrong retained a keen interest in the land of his birth, epitomized by his 1884 article "Lessons from the Hawaiian Islands" in which he argued that with hindsight, it was possible to see that the ABCFM had "fatally" neglected to train Native Hawaiians in mechanical arts and agriculture. Armstrong argued that this failure "to train and harden the soft Hawaiian hand," or in other words to build up Indigenous "manliness," had led to the religious indifference, moral turpitude, and physical decline of "a soft and pliant race."[97] Only a few missionary-run institutions provided notable exceptions. One example was the Hilo Boarding School for Native Hawaiian boys, which missionaries David and Sarah Lyman had founded on Hawai'i island in 1836. The combination of Armstrong's convictions about the shortcomings of the ABCFM's approach and the exceptional example set at Hilo inspired him to take a different tack with African Americans and Native Americans.[98] Armstrong did not brand the original missionaries as failures and praised the rapid social transformation they had effected. However, for some in the missionary community, he had strayed beyond the bounds of acceptable critique. Charles Hyde lambasted Armstrong for his "materialistic views" and his disrespect for "higher spiritual realities," and other descendants of missionaries echoed such a perspective.[99]

In seeking to recalibrate US audiences' perception of the completeness of Hawaiian religious history, other descendants of missionaries were more careful to emphasize that their arguments did not constitute a critique of the original missionaries. Instead, they insisted that these arguments were an inheritance from the previous generation, who had been critical of the ABCFM's original decision to declare the mission finished. Indeed, the few first-generation missionaries who remained in the field in the 1880s and 1890s argued that mission work remained incomplete and feared that perceptions of a wholly successful mission history were injurious. In one letter to the ABCFM, Elias Bond stated that he was "fully aware that the world has been assured that the Board here has 'wound up its Missionary work' & left the Islands 'Christianized.'" However, he continued, the number of "faithful & efficient" Native Hawaiian pastors could now "be counted upon the fingers of one hand."[100] Another first-generation survivor, Lorenzo Lyons, offered to help the ABCFM correct such misapprehensions in 1885 by assisting them in writing a new history of the mission emphasizing that "Drunkenness, Popery, Mormonism, Atheism, Paganism, Ungodliness are the Devil's agents for destroying the good work that missionaries have done."[101] Accordingly, an HMCS letter to ABCFM donors in 1887 stressed that requests for the renewal of work in the islands by descendants of missionaries were not the whimsical desires of a new generation but represented a continuation of their forebears' historical concerns.[102] This sentiment was echoed in an essay by Jared and Juliette Smith, children of an early missionary, in the same year: "This step [of ending the mission] was taken with many questionings on the part of the missionaries, and the result has justified many of their fears." The Smiths ultimately accused Boston of abandonment: "The people have been sadly neglected by their older Christian brothers, who should have redoubled their care and aid in this crisis of their history."[103]

"Missionaries" underpinned their claims about the need to reevaluate Hawaiian mission history with the argument that as Americans embarked on a new and more ambitious phase of foreign mission work epitomized by the Student Volunteer Movement, it would not look good if older enterprises were allowed to fall. The HMCS had already expressed this sentiment to the ABCFM in a letter by the time W. B. Oleson articulated it in his 1889 presidential address to the HMCS.[104] Oleson acknowledged that the fact "published world-wide by missionary organizations that the Hawaiian Islands have become Christianized . . . has been dwelt upon as a motive to the speedy culmination of missionary effort in other lands." If visitors were to see that "the glowing descriptions of the former days" were not a truthful reflection of the actual state of Hawai'i, there would be ramifications for "every mission enterprise in the world."[105] This attempt to connect the fate of the Hawaiian mission to that of a new age of global missions revealed that those in Hawai'i had a sense of being left behind. In one plea to the ABCFM, Hiram Bingham II's wife Clara asked, "where are all 'the student volunteers'?"[106] Arthur Pierson and his student evangelists may have rhetorically exploited the Hawaiian mission's exemplary success in response to an apparent crisis in the broader world mission field, but they seemed to care little for its actual fate.

When the ABCFM responded to the wishes of descendants of missionaries, however, different tensions surfaced. In 1887, the HMCS requested that the ABCFM recommence foreign mission work in Hawai'i by sending out at least five new missionaries.[107] The board accepted the society's assessment of the situation and soon plans were in place to send workers, with the board bearing all expenses.[108] The ABCFM sent out the Ohio-born and Oberlin-educated pastor William D. Westervelt in 1889, but he quickly became frustrated. On entering the field, he encountered a five-man, all-white Committee on Hawaiian Evangelization set up jointly by the HEA and HMCS, three of whom were direct descendants of missionaries. The establishment of this separate body cut Native Hawaiians, who still had some representation on the HEA board, out of the decisions on new mission work.[109] Westervelt initially acknowledged the "unique" nature of this local committee and the need to remain open minded.[110] Just a few months later, however, he reported to the ABCFM that he was having "to meet continually the strong feeling" of the local committee "that the labor of the missionaries should be local. . . . The suggestion is continually made [that] the Board does not understand the situation."[111] By the end of the year, Westervelt was warning the ABCFM of "a large opportunity for trouble" in continued dealings with "arbitrary" local agents.[112] His subsequent criticisms only became more damning: "The Missionary Party while in power may have forgotten the interests of the natives."[113]

"Missionaries" moved to counter Westervelt's arguments. In their perception of the situation, Westervelt understood himself to be accountable only to Boston and refused contact with the HEA and the HMCS. While HEA board members registered their dissatisfaction with the ABCFM, Nathaniel Emerson, the son of missionaries who chaired the Committee on Hawaiian Evangelization, outlined his grievances directly to Westervelt in an April 1891 letter.[114] He first argued that "men working in these Islands" would be "hampered . . . if obliged to defer" to those "6000 miles away." He then accused Westervelt of being out of step with "the traditions of the Haw[aiia]n mission," questioning why, after seventy years of success, those laboring for Christianity in Hawai'i should countenance new ways of working directed from afar.[115] Emerson valued the experiential knowledge of descendants of missionaries over the ABCFM's expertise and authority and sought to cling to the very autonomy that the missionary community had criticized the ABCFM for extending to them. Although the missionary community acknowledged that the board's financial clout and high profile were useful, Emerson's ideas of wise missionary policy were derived entirely from the "traditions" of his parents' generation.[116]

As the only other direct ABCFM appointee in Hawai'i, Charles Hyde expressed some initial misgivings about the new mission. He presciently asked whether the ABCFM could manage the "giant enterprise" of resuming "a work which was 25 years ago declared completed," especially given the potential difficulties of acting "jointly and wisely and unanimously" with the HMCS and the HEA.[117] After Westervelt arrived, Hyde took the missionary community's side, echoing Emerson by arguing that Hyde had failed to appreciate that the work was one of "re-habilitating and re-invigorating the institutions" established by the missionary "fathers."[118] What was needed was a worker who would learn the Hawaiian language and "mingle" with the people "as the old missionaries did."[119] Westervelt left the islands after just two years, advising the ABCFM that the Hawaiian mission was not worth their resources given "the far more important openings among the vast populations of other lands."[120] He claimed that Native Hawaiians had great affection for the early missionaries, exemplified when a woman tearfully approached him after he had preached at Hilo, exclaiming that "this day is like the days of the Fathers."[121] However, he clearly did not feel that the descendants represented meaningful continuity.

After Westervelt's departure, relations between the ABCFM and the descendants of missionaries cooled. The Committee on Hawaiian Evangelization dissolved in early 1892 and there was a distinct scaling back of ambition. An HEA report in March 1892 stated that there was no need for a regular

Hawaiian mission after all and that one or two associates to train up Native pastors in the North Pacific Missionary Institute would suffice.[122] John Leadingham was sent to do this work in 1894. He had an easier time than Westervelt, no doubt partly because he viewed "missionary descendants and those who sympathize with them" as "the people who feel a responsibility for the moral and religious welfare of the country" and urged that the ABCFM "keep the work here in line with its past history."[123] In another twist, Westervelt returned to Hawai'i in 1899 and settled there until his death forty years later, becoming an authority on Hawaiian history and folklore. His comfort on his return was facilitated by a new mutual acceptance between himself and the missionary community that was symbolized by his marriage to a daughter of missionaries, Caroline Dickinson Castle. The other new workers who received enthusiastic "missionary" backing in the 1880s and 1890s were Oliver Emerson, who arrived from the United States in 1888, and Orramel Gulick, who relocated from Japan in 1894 after the missionary community lobbied the ABCFM for his services, principally to work among the islands' growing Japanese migrant population.[124] Tellingly, Emerson and Gulick were both sons of earlier missionaries.

Indeed, the Westervelt episode reinforced a conviction that what was really needed were "Hawaiian born men to help us, who knew the native language & the people & who were yet white at heart."[125] The logic descendants of missionaries applied in their requests to Boston for new workers in the late 1880s had been completely inverted in just a few years. Whereas before, a perceived crisis in Hawai'i's Christian history necessitated an influx from abroad, now that same crisis meant that external influences should be excluded: "White men who do not know Hawaiian & who cannot come into touch with the natives cannot do the work of these ten or fifteen years so big with fate."[126] History weighed heavy on evangelistic efforts: they could only be driven forward with reference to ancestral successes, embodied by the new generation of "missionaries." The only other category of Christian who might have adequately fulfilled the need for evangelists who were "Hawaiian born . . . yet white at heart" were Native Hawaiian converts who accepted the molding hand of the descendants of missionaries.[127] The HEA, hoping that John Henry Wise would be such a figure, sent him to Oberlin College in 1890. To their disappointment, however, he returned to Hawai'i not only as a talented preacher and a star football player but also as a supporter of Lili'uokalani.[128] While descendants of missionaries and their allies repeatedly stated their need for new men and methods, in actuality they were reluctant to relinquish control of the work they saw themselves to have inherited, and they stifled innovation. Their resistance betrayed an intellectual distance from the United States and its contemporary missionary movement.

Nonetheless, the missionary community's efforts to perpetuate a particular, delicate historical conception of the Hawaiian mission also served another purpose that dovetailed neatly with the actions of the settler-colonial opponents of Native Hawaiian monarchy in the late 1880s and 1890s. As shown throughout the chapter so far, a focus on "missionary" as a purely political label obscures the missionary community's expressions of religious purpose. Nonetheless, the spiritual claims of descendants of missionaries that they had inherited and were protecting their forebears' Christian work constituted a political argument. "Missionary" efforts to recalibrate Americans' sense of Hawaiian history developed a logic whereby further US intervention in both church and government was of profound spiritual importance.

Mission History, the Overthrow, and Annexation

In early 1895, remarks about the Hawaiian mission made at a prayer meeting of Brooklyn's Plymouth Church, where the prominent liberal Congregationalist theologian Lyman Abbott was pastor, found their way into the *New York Evening Post* under the heading "A Missionary Disgrace." Lawyer Thomas G. Shearman, a church trustee, had spoken of "a weaker race" being "practically enslaved" by "Congregationalists and sons of Congregational missionaries." Native Hawaiians had been deprived of their land, subjected to laws that limited their freedom of speech, and overrun by foreign workers. Not only that, but their trust in missionaries had been repaid by a volte-face in which descendants of missionaries had suddenly turned away from their parents' boasts about the education, behavior, and religiosity of Native Hawaiians to deride them as filthy, ignorant, idolatrous, and not to be trusted with self-rule. If this were true, suggested Shearman, then "the result of sixty years' unbroken missionary government" in Hawai'i had been that the population was "as debased, licentious, and brutal as they were when the missionaries began their labors." The proposal to annex Hawai'i, with its "Congregational heathen, Christian idolaters," further illuminated the paradoxes in the missionary community's representation of the situation.[129]

"Missionaries" defended their community's historical record against this attack from inside their traditional denominational constituency. Sereno Bishop, missionary "mother" Mary Rice, and missionary son Titus Munson

Coan all issued rebuttals in American newspapers, while another missionary son, William W. Hall, assured the ABCFM that Shearman's words had "caused much indignation here among all classes who are acquainted with the true facts."[130] Yet Shearman's remarks perceived the generational shift in the narration of the Hawaiian mission's history, from boasts of Native Hawaiian religiosity by the original missionaries to derision of Native Hawaiian heathenism by those missionaries' descendants. Speaking as white settlers petitioned for US annexation, Shearman implied that this generational shift was closely related to the missionary community's political ambition to see Hawai'i become a part of the United States. Indeed, some of those descendants of missionaries most active in the HEA and HMCS were among the most vocal supporters of overthrow and annexation—W. D. Alexander, Sereno Bishop, Albert Judd, and William O. Smith in particular. Even Charles Hyde, despite his wariness of the political and economic ambitions of the descendants of missionaries, increasingly commented on political affairs, condemned the Hawaiian monarchy in strong terms, and noted that the political opinions of those like Bishop and Judd, "born at the islands," outweighed those of any "Tom, Dick and Harry" who opposed them.[131]

The issue of annexationists' connection to Hawaiian mission history entered the American political sphere in debates about whether the overthrow of the Hawaiian monarchy was legitimate. In Congress in February 1894, a year after the overthrow, Elijah Adams Morse, a Republican representative from Massachusetts, defended the involvement of descendants of missionaries in terms of this connection. He recalled "the efforts that resulted in reclaiming these islands from barbarism, cannibalism, and heathenism of the most revolting and degrading form." Then, with reference to the instigators of the overthrow, he expressed his disappointment that President Cleveland appeared "hostile and unfriendly to these men and women, many of whom are descended from the missionaries and are bone of our bone and flesh of our flesh."[132] Morse's attitude indicates that those who sympathized with the overthrow and the annexationist cause in the United States did so in part because they recognized white settlers' historical connection to a successful missionary project.

Yet that perception presented a potential problem for the political ambitions of descendants of missionaries. The notion that the missionary enterprise in the islands was merely historical—successful and complete—simultaneously allowed Americans to believe that Hawai'i was a Christian nation and that the Native Hawaiian leaders the descendants of missionaries sought to supplant were Christian actors. Cleveland's commissioner, James Blount, made a special point of Native Hawaiians' religiosity when he condemned the overthrow, observing that Native Hawaiians were affiliated with both Protestantism and Catholicism and that idolatry had "long since disappeared."[133] The missionary community more broadly feared the sympathy for Native Hawaiians emanating from the press in the United States. Charles Hyde had noted in the mid-1880s that the ABCFM in Boston would "see in the papers only admiration of the Hawaiian people and their King. You will hear much talk about the missionary gang, and how they have robbed the Kanakas and live a life of selfish ease."[134] A decade later, Sereno Bishop frequently used his regular column in the *Washington Evening Star* to defend the missionary community from attacks, citing the *San Francisco Call*, the *San Francisco Chronicle*, the *New York Evening Post*, the *New York World*, and *Harper's Bazaar* as examples of publications that had discredited the government of the Republic of Hawai'i as inept and cruel, extolled Lili'uokalani, and opposed annexation.[135] "So many Americans," he wrote in 1896, "think there was a crooked work in our Revolution."[136] In fact, one historian has found that in a number of debates between US collegiate debating teams in the 1890s on the question of Hawaiian annexation, the side presenting the case against annexation and for Hawaiian independence consistently won.[137]

Against this backdrop, the argument the missionary community had made to the ABCFM when appealing for fresh impetus to evangelistic work in Hawai'i—that mission history among Native Hawaiians remained incomplete—became a political weapon. On December 17, 1893, eleven months after the overthrow and just two weeks after Cleveland had used his State of the Union address to reaffirm the illegality of the coup, missionary son and ordained minister Oliver Emerson, who was visiting from Hawai'i, addressed the Metropolitan Presbyterian Church in Washington, DC.[138] In his sermon, given just a few blocks away from the US halls of power and reprinted the following day in the *Washington Evening Star*, Emerson pronounced to the congregation that "there is a chapter in the history of Hawaiian Christianity which the churches of this land know little about." The revisionist history Emerson outlined pushed back against the narrative of a completed mission that he clearly believed had prevailed in the United States and explicitly made the case that the overthrow of the monarchy was necessary to fulfill the mission's early promise. Hawaiian Christianity under "the Kalakauan dynasty" had been "in the presence of most depressing and harmful, corrupt, idolatrous influences" of a "heathen court." These had now been taken away by "the kind providence of God," liberating the churches to thrive once again.[139]

Emerson outlined the familiar deeds of the early missionaries in education, translation, conversion, and "civilization" that had given rise to a "really Christian nation" prior to Rufus Anderson's visit to encourage an end to the mission in 1863. After that, the "heathen" influences within the monarchy had soon awakened. Starting with Lot Kapuāiwa (Kamehameha V, r. 1863–72), Emerson explained how chiefs had sponsored sorcery, the worship of fetishes, healing practices, traffic in rum and opium, and "pagan" ceremonies, drawing Native Hawaiians away from their churches and insidiously corrupting the churches themselves. He was careful to state that these accusations applied as much to Liliʻuokalani as to her predecessors Lot and Kalākaua, aware of a particular sympathy for the deposed queen in the United States. Thus, the overthrow was not simply a coup by oligarchic settlers but a brave bid, resonant with biblical history, to rescue the fruits of missionary labors: "They are building up that outpost of civilization and holding it, as [Jerusalem] was held and built of old, with the spade in one hand and the sword in the other." Those who had undertaken this Christian act now required the protection of US annexation, and Emerson hoped that Americans would not instead "look on, as did Edom in that day, only with a purpose to stop it."[140] Emerson's sermon demonstrates that it was important to descendants of missionaries that they be seen not just as the scions of mission history but as authoritative interpreters of it who were writing a new chapter through their political actions.

Frequent letters to the ABCFM from the missionary community that tied political arguments to spiritual necessity might be read in the same vein, not least because the board had significant capacity, through the *Missionary Herald*, to shape American Christian opinion. As early as 1886, Charles Hyde wrote to the ABCFM about Hawaiian affairs, stressing that his letter was "to be read and destroyed" given the potential sensitivities surrounding a Christian minister involving himself in politics. In this letter, Hyde asserted that "the King is the great obstacle to our Christian work" and that this argument came not from the standpoint of the "color line" but from one of "social purity and fundamental righteousness."[141] That monarchical failings were associated with a heathen tendency that had not been properly rooted out, despite perceptions of a successful mission, was a particular recurring theme of letters to the ABCFM during Kalākaua's reign. Jared and Juliette Smith argued that Kalākaua's opposition to the "missionary party" was characterized as much by "a revival of heathenish dances" as by political corruption.[142] Sereno Bishop similarly tied "the prevailing sins of sensuality" and the "labors of the King . . . to detach the people from all 'missionary' influence" to Kalākaua's bid to secure "absolute political subserviency."[143] Bishop was particularly inclined to read the political struggle of descendants of missionaries in "prophetic" terms and ultimately styled the overthrow as divine deliverance from "the dreadful incubus of a heathenizing monarchy."[144]

"Missionaries" also directly linked their perception that Kalākaua was politically corrupt to the supposed corruption of church governance in Hawai'i, which they argued was proceeding unchecked in the absence of the revered previous generation of missionaries. Perturbed by a suggestion that Kalākaua sought to supplement the declining salaries of Indigenous pastors in order to draw them away from the HEA and instead intertwine church and state, the missionary community repeatedly claimed that Kalākaua sought to subvert the HEA, establish himself as head of a Hawaiian church, and influence Native Hawaiian pastors to revive traditional spiritual practices.[145] The claims the missionary community made, however, only ever appeared to represent a fear of something taking place outside their purview. They remarked on Native Hawaiian "duplicity and guile," on idolatrous practices that had "hood-winked" outsiders and were "apparent only to the initiated," and on the "dark mystery" of Hawaiian "diabolism and pollution."[146] As keen as Hyde in particular was to emphasize to the ABCFM small-scale cases of doctrinal misunderstanding, financial mismanagement, syncretic practice, sexual immorality, and resistance to HEA control, no Kalākaua-led conspiracy to subvert the churches and turn them into heathen temples ever came to pass.[147] Hyde even admitted that Native Hawaiian ministers had been unresponsive to what he perceived to be Kalākaua's attempts to foment schism, and in 1892, he stated that he believed that a rising generation of church members was "outspoken against the old heathenism."[148]

Individual accusations of apostasy prior to the overthrow were associated directly with political opposition to the missionary community rather than with un-Christian practice. Hyde branded a set of Native Hawaiian deacons "lunatics" when they voted to seek independence from the HEA in 1890 in response to the HEA board's condemnation of royalists.[149] Moreover, when Hyde wrote to the ABCFM in 1892 about the lamentable condition of Hawaiian churches, the only specific example he offered was of a Native pastor at Kohala on Hawai'i island who put himself forward as a parliamentary candidate for a royalist faction.[150] In short, while missionaries wrote in general and hyperbolic terms to the ABCFM about a grand conspiracy drawing together alleged heathenism in the churches and political opposition, they presented little concrete evidence connecting the two.

After the overthrow, too, as settlers lobbied for annexation and some Native Hawaiian Christians continued to express their opposition to the missionary community's dominance in political and spiritual affairs, Oliver Emerson wrote to the ABCFM to suggest that Native Hawaiians stood against the missionary community because that community upheld true Christianity. He then drew a remarkable historical parallel between the conflict between descendants of missionaries and Hawaiian royalists and the conflict between "the royalist & the puritan" during the British Civil Wars. In doing so, he suggested that the spirit of royalism always ran counter to good Christianity. He equated good Christianity with Puritanism, which in his account characterized the religion of both the Roundheads and of Emerson's own ancestors; it was good Christians who had fomented revolution against the English monarchy in the seventeenth century and pioneered the Hawaiian mission in the nineteenth century.[151] Through an allegory that was resonant with Americans, Emerson used history to justify the missionary community's political work as primarily spiritual.

There is evidence that "missionaries" successfully convinced the ABCFM of the connection between religious and political goals and that the board in turn sought to persuade American Christian audiences of this link. The *Missionary Herald* of March 1893 pronounced that "facts . . . seem fully to justify the action taken in displacing the Queen." Those who had participated in the overthrow were "the best men at the Islands," many of whom were "sons of American missionaries, born on Hawai'i" who sought "social, moral, and religious prosperity."[152] Native Hawaiians, however, often expressed their opposition to the overthrow in sincere Christian terms. Membership of HEA churches declined by more than 70 percent from 1863 to 1887, but many were converting to Catholicism, Anglicanism, or Mormonism rather than repudiating Christianity altogether.[153] Those who stayed in the HEA asserted that devotion to Protestantism and devotion to Indigenous sovereignty were not diametrically opposed and battled to define the politics and theology of their churches against those of the white HEA hierarchy. In the aftermath of the overthrow, early morning church bells rang to call congregants to meetings of prayer and fasting for the queen across the islands. Letter writers in the Hawaiian-language press claimed that God was on their side—the side of "true Christianity."[154] Congregations engaged in protracted and conspicuous struggles to wrest control of their churches from pastors who supported the HEA board and the overthrow.[155]

In their appeals to President Cleveland, Lili'uokalani's supporters noted the cynicism with which they believed descendants of missionaries had intertwined religion and politics as they conveyed their message through the press in the United States. They reproached US newspapers "for their unchivalrous and untruthful abuse of our Queen who, only a year ago, was in the acknowledged lead of the Christian work in Hawaii and the gracious patron of the sycophantic church society that now maligns her."[156] Lili'uokalani herself, in her English-language book *Hawaii's Story by Hawaii's Queen*, defended her religiosity and her people's, contrasting the sense of threat that missionaries conveyed in writing about Native Hawaiians with their peaceable Christian disposition. No people, she said, had "a tenderer Christian conscience" or "a greater reverence and love for their Christian teachers." After all, "where else in the world's history is it written that a savage people . . . have made equal progress in civilization and Christianity in the same space of time?"[157] Lili'uokalani and her supporters understood that the way to appeal to US audiences was to restate the trusted narrative that Hawai'i was governed by a Christian monarchy, enabled by early missionaries, and to imply that suggestions to the contrary were belated attempts to rewrite this history. Thomas Shearman's characterization of the historical narratives peddled by descendants of missionaries as contemptuous and politicized shows that some Christians in the United States agreed with this assessment.

Although at least for the first year of Lili'uokalani's rule, the missionary community had expressed hope that she would prove to be compliant, their view of Kalākaua was more unequivocally negative.[158] However, not all Christians shared this straightforwardly negative view. Upon Kalākaua's death in 1891, the Anglican bishop of Honolulu, Alfred Willis, whose church the king had been a confirmed member of, acknowledged that the late monarch had not been "wholly emancipated from the influence of the religion of his fathers" and had been tempted by "modern scepticism" but praised him for his "true faith."[159] While this was hardly an unqualified endorsement, it made the repeated attacks of descendants of missionaries appear extreme and politicized. Americans in the islands and those in the United States when Kalākaua visited during his 1881 world tour had also often been impressed by the king's dignity, intelligence, and courtesy, countering the missionary community's presentation of him as corrupt and comical.[160] Indigenous agents thus constantly unsettled the assertion of "missionaries" that they had declined into heathenism, an assertion that was made to justify divesting them of sovereignty.

The claims of descendants of missionaries that they were the inheritors of the mission past, which they carefully curated to show that Americans had misapprehended the situation and that there was still work to be done, facilitated a broader discourse in which claims to political supremacy and fears for the spiritual legacy of a heroic missionary generation were closely linked.

Claims of the inadequacy of Native Hawaiian pastors mapped onto claims of the inadequacy of Native-led government. Appeals to the ABCFM for mission reinforcement mapped onto appeals to the United States for annexation. Insistence that mission work could be done only by those who understood the Hawaiian people and subscribed to the traditions of the mission mapped onto insistence that there was insufficient comprehension of the situation in Washington. The work of delegitimizing Native Hawaiians as Christians and delegitimizing them as political actors was done in tandem.[161]

A deeper understanding of ongoing "missionary" efforts in the sphere of religion complicates a simpler narrative that explains how a Christian mission evolved into a nakedly political project. The question naturally arises as to whether descendants of missionaries were sincere in their claims to be perpetuating Christian work in Hawai'i, given the apparent cynicism with which they bent religion to political and economic ends. The fact is that whatever "missionaries" believed, religion and politics were inseparable throughout Hawai'i's history in the nineteenth century. Descendants of missionaries not only gleaned their ideas about how Hawaiian governance and race relations should look from their reading of a historical religious project but also went to great lengths to institutionalize and extend that project for a new generation. While it was true, as Ronald Williams writes, that "the Hawaiian 'mission' circa 1893 was not the result of a teleological seventy-year presence," the appearance of continuity was vital to descendants of missionaries, both in their own organizations and in their appeals to the United States, in ways that transcend any straightforward assessments of their sincerity.[162]

What tied the religion and politics of the missionary community together in particular was an interest in overturning the perception of Hawaiian mission history that was prevalent in the United States. However, there is no doubt that there was some ambivalence. In order to make the case that Hawai'i was special and deserving of Americans' attention but also that Hawai'i's Christianization was incomplete and Native Hawaiians were unfit to govern their nation or their churches, descendants of missionaries oscillated between celebrating the achievements of their ancestors and reflecting on the incompleteness of their work. Significantly, they also appealed for new external impetus while still clinging to "traditional" methods and asserting that their understanding of mission history was superior to that of outsiders, reflecting how they saw US power as a means of achieving local ends instead of wanting to be completely absorbed and changed by it.

How much of this filtered back into popular and political opinion in the United States in any decisive way is questionable. Despite the confidence Sereno Bishop projected that the Republic of Hawai'i would "have much to say about the conditions" under which it would be taken by the United States, Hawaiian annexation was completed on US terms.[163] It happened because it suited the long-held strategic designs of a cabal of late nineteenth-century US expansionists that included James Blaine, John L. Stevens, Alfred Thayer Mahan, Benjamin Harrison, and Theodore Roosevelt, and the timing was dictated in large part by the Spanish-American War of 1898 at a time when fears that European or Japanese designs might undercut the vision of the United States for the Pacific took on greater urgency.[164] In other words, it was an expedient and strategic maneuver and little space was left for arguments about a mission that began for the sake of a foreign people, even as Bishop continued to insist on the benefits of empire for "feeble but amiable" Native Hawaiians who had for decades been reliant on Americans' care.[165] In fact, those arguments only served to highlight the racial otherness of Hawai'i, which imperialists knew they had to avoid mentioning if they were going to allay white Americans' fears about seizing colonies.[166]

Descendants of missionaries had to learn to speak a strategic language when they made arguments for annexation. In the 1850s, when the missionary community was looking for new mission fields that were reachable from Hawai'i, its members had oriented themselves southward toward Micronesia. By the end of the century, however, they had pragmatically invested in a vision of Hawai'i as a strategic midpoint between the United States and Asia that was beneficial for US commerce and security and would inevitably fall into the sphere of another colonial power without American protection. In particular, they played on Americans' fears by inventing the idea that Japanese sugar plantation workers in the islands were the vanguard of a Japanese empire that was no friend of white American civilization.[167] Sereno Bishop's frequent letters to the *Washington Evening Star*, to be further examined in chapter 2, frequently used such language, and he was supposedly the first to speak of Hawai'i as "the crossroads of the Pacific."[168] A tension emerged between the attempts of descendants of missionaries to center Hawai'i and its mission history, on the one hand, and their need to style the islands as useful to the United States in a broader Pacific, on the other.

The idea that there was still mission work to be done often seemed to fall on deaf ears among Christians in the United States. This is evident in a book published in 1898, against the backdrop of annexation, by Fleming H. Revell, a leading New York evangelical press. The writer was Belle M. Brain, an artist, educator, and author of books on Christian mission and temperance. The title of her book boasted of "transformation" and argued that American missionaries had given a "Christian nation" to the world. The work was aimed at young people who might not have been familiar with the stories of the successful Hawaiian mission. Brain did not link the need for annexation to a need to save an evangelistic work, as descendants of missionaries had. She viewed annexation as the product of a successful and complete mission history, arguing that it came about "not by purchase, nor by conquest, but by the vote of the Hawaiian people, who offered [the islands] to us as a gift."[169] Only the story of "how a race of degraded savages became an intelligent, God-fearing Christian nation" explained this.[170] This conceptualization was as egregious as the missionary community's formulation, given the tens of thousands of Native Hawaiians who petitioned against annexation, but it indicated that the historical revisionism of the "missionaries" had failed to fully take root.[171]

These disjunctions between the religious and historical arguments descendants of missionaries in Hawai'i made and the reasons for annexation articulated in the United States indicate the intellectual distance from metropolitan imperial discourse of "missionaries" in Hawai'i. Chapter 2 will scrutinize the distance between US imperialists and "missionaries" further by showing that even if there were ways that descendants of missionaries saw their historical narration as meaningfully connecting them to the traditions and culture of their ancestral homeland, there were slippages in their discourse that indicate a sense of alienation from the United States and the profoundly local nature of their concerns. In particular, "missionaries" needed to assert themselves on a contested terrain of history in Hawai'i, where competing religious groups fought to establish legitimacy for themselves using history and Native Hawaiians made sovereignty claims through genealogical traditions that, like "missionary" narratives, integrated notions of spiritual and political inheritance. While descendants of missionaries denigrated Indigenous narratives, they recognized that their own claims to sovereignty needed to be founded on a vision of history that asserted their place in both American and Hawaiian stories. In the process, the dichotomy the missionary community had long tried to assert between written histories, on the one hand, and genealogy, oral tradition, and performance, on the other, frequently broke down. Local contingencies significantly shaped the histories and forms of historical narrative US colonialism attached itself to in ways that pulled against concurrent attempts to impose a particular US-centric vision of space and history across the wider Pacific.

Chapter 2

"From the Beginning of the World"

The Contested Terrain of History in Hawai'i

In the late 1880s, as the missionary community deployed evidence of a supposed resurgence of "heathenism" among Native Hawaiians to underscore the need for white leadership in political and religious affairs, James Bicknell published the pamphlet *Hoomanamana—Idolatry*. Bicknell was the son of a British missionary to Tahiti but had married into the ABCFM missionary family in Hawai'i as the husband of Ellen Bond. Ellen was the daughter of Ellen and Elias Bond, who had arrived in 1841 as part of the ninth ABCFM company to the islands. Bicknell did not subscribe to some of the mission's orthodoxies and was deemed a "religious crank" by Charles Hyde for his belief in direct communication with the Holy Spirit and faith healing.[1] Nonetheless, he was active in the Hawaiian Evangelical Association (HEA) and won praise from descendants of missionaries for his studies of Native Hawaiian "paganism" during King Kalākaua's reign, which he undertook in order to prove its pernicious effect on the churches, better understand its content, and suggest how a "purer" spiritual practice might combat it.[2]

Hoomanamana covered a range of issues relating to Native Hawaiian religious practices but contained a particularly striking passage on Kalākaua's Hale Nauā society. At a time of ongoing depopulation and of the increasing influence of white settlers within the Hawaiian government, Kalākaua founded the Hale Nauā in 1886 as an association of chiefly men and women seeking the reinvigoration of the Native Hawaiian people and their culture.[3] It continued the work of a previous society, the Board of Genealogy, that had been founded in 1880 but closed down under "missionary" pressure. It had undertaken genealogical research and cultural preservation work, seeking to imbue Kalākaua with a legitimacy and an authority derived from the sacred ancestral past.[4] Genealogy undergirded Native Hawaiian cosmology and conceptions of time, proving the high ancestry of *aliʻi* (chiefs) and anchoring *makaʻāinana* (commoners) in a shared ancestral past. The preamble of the Hale Nauā's constitution, which was translated into English and published in San Francisco, declared that "the foundation of the Hale Naua is from the beginning of the world" and that Kalākaua had revived the society in the 825th generation, or 24,750 years, after the first woman and 40,000,000,000,024,750 years from "the commencement of the world."[5] Native Hawaiians deemed this assertion of Indigenous genealogical longevity, encompassing not only humans but also natural phenomena as ancestors, to be an important tool in the face of colonial incursion. The findings of the Board of Genealogy and the Hale Nauā were both published and publicly performed as *hula* dances. In the words of the historian Noenoe K. Silva, "the revitalization of these ancient ways armored people against the pernicious effects of the constant denigration of Kanaka [Native Hawaiian] culture by the U.S. missionaries and their descendants and allowed them to know themselves as a strong people with a proud history."[6]

Part of a broader Native Hawaiian cultural revival encouraged by Kalākaua, the Hale Nauā also promoted traditional Hawaiian dress and crafts, sponsored Hawaiian exhibits at world's fairs, and propagated Indigenous astrological knowledge. It also incorporated elements of modern science, art, and literature.[7] As far as the members of the missionary community were concerned, however, its true purpose was shrouded in secrecy, and they strongly suspected that it was a front for perpetuating religious and healing practices they had used their influence in the Hawaiian government to criminalize.[8] Their attempts to write about the Hale Nauā snatched at fragments derived from rumor and hearsay. They struggled even to find a precise English translation for the phrase "Hale Nauā," although Nathaniel Emerson suggested that it might have been a genealogical challenge, meaning "whose house?" or "what is your ancestry?"[9] One historian suggests that it thus "became a symbolic *tabula rasa* on which the sons of missionaries and business leaders could project their most fearsome nightmares of a return to the 'unholy terror' of 'heathen idolatry.'"[10] Given this, we might assume that Bicknell's account in *Hoomanamana* reflects something of his community's peculiar understanding of and fears about the society.

Bicknell saw the Hale Nauā as one of the key means by which Kalākaua was "striving to bring the system of fetich worship into a concise form of which he shall be the acknowledged head." He focused on one particular practice of the society. Allegedly, Kalākaua kept a copy of *Ka Moʻolelo Hawaiʻi*, a book of Hawaiian history and tradition, in a small room in his residence, ʻIolani Palace. This book was composed around 1838 by David Malo, a prominent early Native Hawaiian convert to Christianity, at the behest of his ABCFM missionary teacher Sheldon Dibble. Bicknell alleged that the book lay on a table in the center of the room and that Kalākaua read it in ritualized ceremonies: "A circuit of the table is made seven times, after which the book is opened with a show of reverence, and then the credulous owner of the sanctum holds converse, in imagination, with the gods and demi-gods."[11]

To a contemporary "missionary" observer—in other words, to those who were not necessarily professional missionaries but nonetheless saw themselves to have inherited the mantle of missionary work in Hawaiʻi—the scene described would have been uncanny. The missionary community had broader fears about the ways they believed the Hale Nauā was incorporating Christian ritual and setting the Christian God among a pantheon of other gods, but the materiality of the ceremony Bicknell described revealed particular concerns about the subversion of mission-inspired modes of narrating Hawaiian history.[12] The supposed object of worship was Malo's book, which originated in a mission-led project to record previously unwritten Hawaiian lore, partly in order to ossify and repudiate its content. Kalākaua's supposed fetishization of Malo's book was a potent and unsettling symbol of the apparent corruption of Hawaiian rulership and Indigenous Christianity and the missionary community's inability to control historical interpretation any longer.

Whatever truth lay in this story, Bicknell's particular attention to the alleged practice of revering an Indigenous history book is indicative of a "missionary" obsession with the question of who could appropriately lay claim to Hawaiian history. As chapter 1 showed, the missionary community persistently dwelt upon local history and its religious purpose as they sought to establish settler-colonial sovereignty in the islands. This chapter argues that engagements with history by the descendants of missionaries prior to the annexation of the islands in 1898 were also shaped by a need to come to terms with a contested terrain of history in Hawaiʻi. Multiple voices within the islands sought to establish legitimacy and meaning by situating themselves within local religious pasts, just as the descendants of missionaries did. Challenges came from other groups besides Native Hawaiians. Competing religious sects that included Mormons, Anglicans, and Catholics all questioned the ABCFM-centric version of the Hawaiian past and engaged the missionary community in battles over historical primacy. Without a doubt, however, "missionaries" were most exercised by a vibrant culture of Native Hawaiian historical narration. Because this culture was inseparable from both Native Hawaiians' cosmology and from their claims to present-day sovereignty, it was profoundly threatening to descendants of missionaries on both spiritual and temporal fronts. Despite Bicknell's clear attempt to denigrate the Hale Naua's practice as secretive and archaic, Indigenous traditions of historical narration were constantly evolving in the late nineteenth century. They used print, incorporated scientific discoveries, and sought recognition as both thoroughly authentic and thoroughly modern modes of understanding the world.

The chapter shows that by reading "missionary" sources in light of Indigenous traditions and Hawaiian scholarship, we can understand why descendants of missionaries found history to be such an important tool and why they selected particular forms of historical narration. In the missionary imagination, having a proper written history was one of the things that separated the West from the rest. According to missionaries and their descendants, Native Hawaiians' lack of a written history confirmed their status as heathens whose supposedly childlike and unsubstantiated oral traditions were insufficient to bear the weight of either true history or true religion.[13] Thus, the missionary community had long sought to differentiate their traditions of narrating the past from those of Indigenous peoples, setting supposedly objective written histories apart from genealogy, oral tradition, and performance. In this way, they claimed a place within US history and American traditions of historical narration. In actuality, however, this dichotomy frequently broke down. This was because American cultures of narrating and commemorating history furnished the missionary community with plenty of genealogical and performative tools of their own for amplifying their assertions of their connection to ancestral pasts while suppressing the narratives of Indigenous and nonwhite peoples. It was also because although they treated narrations of the past in the Indigenous voice with suspicion and ridicule, descendants of missionaries simultaneously chose particular forms of historical narration that responded to Native Hawaiian traditions and underscored their own attachment to Hawai'i. As descendants of missionaries sought to mobilize their sense of liminality as a strength rather than a liability, they attached themselves to histories and traditions of historical narration that did not emphasize grand providential narratives of US empire sweeping westward across oceanic space but instead engaged with ways of claiming authority through history rooted in a particular Pacific place. Although they did this to bolster their own credentials as white American claimants to Hawaiian sovereignty, at the same time they revealed their physical and intellectual distance from the United States and the discrepancies between visions of the Pacific from the United States and from island locations.

Hawaiian scholars have made important interventions that have shown that the way the history of the islands is told matters. They stress the nuances of the Hawaiian language, the richness and dynamism of oral tradition, and the centrality of genealogical connection to land and ancestors as key components of Native Hawaiian understandings of history.[14] It is also worth considering the uncertain and contingent processes by which dominant American interpretations of Hawaiian history were created, suppressing particular voices and forms of knowledge about the past while simultaneously reflecting the world around them and claiming connection to it. By drawing on Indigenous scholarship to better understand the context in which "missionaries" made their historical claims and by paying closer attention to the form these claims took, we can see that Native Hawaiian resistance was evident throughout "missionary" discourse. Indigenous historical traditions not only interrupted missionary visions of progress, as Noenoe K. Silva argues.[15] They also established the conditions under which descendants of missionaries might claim sovereignty and led them to turn to the past in search of legitimacy and identity.

History as Contested Terrain

The Board of Genealogy and the Hale Nauā exemplify the importance for late nineteenth-century Native Hawaiians of linking religion, sovereignty, and history and of refusing to sacrifice their traditional ways of understanding the past. Both of these societies incorporated modern science. For example, the Board of Genealogy used data from ocean soundings to theorize about migration patterns and the Hale Nauā styled itself as a "Temple of Science" in the English version of its constitution.[16] However, these groups used scientific methods only to corroborate Indigenous understandings of the past, which stretched back through generations of ancestors to divine beginnings. Researchers operating under the auspices of these chiefly societies principally collected *mele*—traditional songs that narrated the genealogies of Native Hawaiians—and used them to validate the genealogical claims of chiefs.[17] When it came to the past, wrote the Board of Genealogy, there was "no other guide than that furnished by ancient folklore."[18] These groups refuted the historiographies of outsiders when they did not concur with traditional narratives. The Hale Nauā, for example, dismissed "the reverend historian"—the early missionary Hiram Bingham—as "irreverently ignorant" in his narration of history designed to justify the "taming, civilizing and christianizing" of Native Hawaiians.[19]

Publications by the final Native Hawaiian monarchs underscored the centrality of Indigenous historical knowledge when making sovereignty claims. Kalākaua published the *Kumulipo* (1889), or account of creation, in Hawaiian, which included over 1,000 lines detailing genealogical descent that linked him to the genesis of the islands. Lili'uokalani subsequently translated it into English in 1897. She followed this with her widely circulated English-language history, *Hawaii's Story by Hawaii's Queen* (1898), which emphasized genealogical connections while also presenting her narrative of the recent past of US colonialism. There was a fine line, however, between Hawaiian monarchs' publication of narratives in support of Native Hawaiian sovereignty claims and outsiders' potential appropriation and fetishization of Hawaiian tradition to serve colonial ends. Another volume of Hawaiian "myths and legends" in English that Kalākaua had compiled appeared in the United States in 1888. However, the former US minister to Hawai'i, R. M. Daggett, introduced it as a collection of the "fables and folk-lore of a strange people" and assured readers that the islands would soon "pass into the political . . . system of the great American Republic."[20]

The idea of genealogies linking chiefs to the divine beginnings and ancestral past of the islands and the notion that longevity of lineage was the most effective claim to sovereignty underpinned Native Hawaiian conceptions of time.[21] It also tied Native Hawaiians to a broader, interconnected Pacific island world of shared origins and cultural motifs that took on renewed significance for Kalākaua as he sought transoceanic alliances to help reinvigorate the dwindling Indigenous population and provide a bulwark against colonialism.[22] Genealogies are not straightforwardly chronological; they are, in J. Kēhaulani Kauanui's words, "a uniquely Indigenous way of knowing and understanding lineage."[23] Prior to the publication of some of them in the second half of the nineteenth century, they were transmitted orally, taking the form of epic poems that specialist genealogists composed, memorized, and recited.[24] They were dynamic and heavily politicized, "contingent rather than absolute," according to Kauanui, and part of the genealogist's role was to make a convincing case for a particular chief through skillful composition and recitation.[25] In this way, a claimant might "[attach] himself to the chiefly genealogies, even though his father may have been of no great rank."[26]

When Kalākaua's predecessor, Lunalilo (r. 1873–74), died without naming an heir, it was up to the Hawaiian legislature to elect a new monarch under the terms of the 1864 constitution. Still, genealogical claims were of the utmost importance in establishing legitimacy, and Kalākaua battled his rival Emma, formerly queen as the wife of Alexander Liholiho (Kamehameha IV), to prove the superiority of their respective lineages through newspapers and broadsides. Emma, for example, announced in one broadside that she was "a chiefess of the highest blood" who was "the nearest living connection of Kamehameha I, the conquer[o]r of these Islands," of whom she claimed her great-grandfather was a brother.[27] Although Kalākaua won the election, he was not directly of the Kamehameha line, and thus his legitimacy was challenged throughout his reign. Accordingly, he sought to demonstrate the validity of his claim in his *Kumulipo* by emphasizing particularly resonant motifs in Hawaiian tradition, for example the story of Maui who struggled for power having been born into a chiefly family following an alliance with outsiders.[28] Indeed, after Kalākaua's election, one Native Hawaiian member of the legislature was keen to note that "the present King came to the throne by his hereditary claims to the position" and "not exclusively 'by *virtue*' of the votes of the Representatives."[29] Kalākaua continued to defend his legitimacy in these terms. At Kalākaua's coronation, for example, which was held nine years after he became monarch, an account of Kamehameha's life was read that established a link between the current king and the first Hawaiian monarch.[30] Kalākaua's sister Lili'uokalani also defended her lineage against attacks in both the Native Hawaiian and the "missionary" press. She showed that while her family was not directly descended from Kamehameha, it was certainly chiefly in its own right and was intimately connected with the Kamehameha line through a long history of devotion and alliance.[31]

The genealogical assertions of Hawaiian elites underpinned Native Hawaiians' collective identity. According to the historian Lilikalā Kame'eleihiwa, "even though the great genealogies are of the *Ali'i Nui* [high chiefs] and not of the commoners, these *Ali'i Nui* are the collective ancestors, and their *mo'olelo* [histories] . . . are the histories of all Hawaiians."[32] Through the Hale Nauā, for example, Kalākaua sought not only to assert his own heritage but also "to further the humble and careful way of life as nurtured by our ancestors from the beginning of time."[33] In this way, Native Hawaiians as a community were able to establish their connection to the islands and their presence in the archipelago long before the missionaries arrived. Indeed, descendants of missionaries were barred from the Hale Nauā because of their lack of genealogical claim, further heightening white suspicion of the society.[34] For the scholar Judy Rohrer, Native Hawaiian assertions were "less about possession than . . . about relation; less about to whom the islands belong and more about who belongs to the islands," and they "interrupt[ed] the teleological march of settler time" by upsetting "the narrative of discovery and disappearance."[35]

Native Hawaiians were not the only group in Hawai'i that upheld their political and religious status against the missionary community through the use of history and claims to historical longevity. Mormons, for example, who originally initiated work in the islands in 1850, when they sent a group of ten missionaries to find white converts, became increasingly fascinated with Native Hawaiians after engaging with their traditions and seeing in them an affirmation of Mormon cosmology.[36] Early Mormon missionary Henry W. Bigler, for example, noted in his diary the resemblances between Native Hawaiian narratives and Mormon stories of creation and subsequent deluge, which led him to believe that "the Hawaiian race was once a favored people of the Lord and must have had the law of Moses and observed its teachings but through transgression they fell into darkness, error and superstition."[37] The impact of Mormonism on Native Hawaiians was equivocal. On the one hand, it gave them a channel through which to claim connection to the land and to perpetuate Indigenous practices, especially at the Mormon colonies founded at Lāna'i and Lā'ie. On the other hand, the Mormon church was founded upon the racial hierarchies of white Americans.[38] However, the assertion of a historical connection between Native Hawaiians and Mormon cosmology and Mormonism's consequent reification of Indigenous narratives facilitated the relative success of the Mormon faith as an alternative to "missionary" Christianity by the late nineteenth century. The Mormon mission claimed nearly 3,000 members within its first three years, winning converts among the chiefly classes, including their most influential proselyte, Jonathan Nāpela.[39] By the 1870s, it declared over 4,000 converts, making it a significant challenger to the Christianity of HEA churches, whose membership had declined to 5,787 by 1887.[40] The claim that Native Hawaiians somehow inhered within Mormon visions of history seemed to provide an adequate substitute for the ABCFM enterprise's claims to longevity, which Mormons worriedly acknowledged.[41] Mormonism thus presented a religious threat to the late nineteenth-century missionary community and, briefly, a political one, in the shape of Kalākaua's controversial advisor Walter Murray Gibson, who first arrived as a Mormon missionary in 1861.[42]

Descendants of missionaries also found their historical advantage challenged by the Anglican Church in Hawai'i. The first Anglican mission to the islands led by Bishop Thomas N. Staley was sent from Britain in 1862 at the behest of the reigning monarchs Alexander Liholiho and Emma. They saw in Anglicanism an ecclesiastical form better suited to monarchical rule and to the intertwinement of church and state. Relations with US missionaries were rancorous from the start. The ABCFM lodged a protest with the Archbishop of Canterbury against Staley's arrival, and within three years the bishop had engaged in a vitriolic pamphlet war involving both the board in Boston and missionary son W. D. Alexander.[43] Anglicans in Hawai'i deliberately and repeatedly emphasized the superiority of their heritage over that of American Congregationalists. One pamphlet stated that Native Hawaiians and their rulers had begged for religious teachers from England for decades before the arrival of the ABCFM mission—since the late eighteenth century, when British explorers James Cook and George Vancouver had visited the islands—and had only "reluctantly admitted" Americans.[44] Moreover, the main Anglican organ in Hawai'i, the *Anglican Church Chronicle*, juxtaposed the historical steadfastness of the Anglican Church with "the degenerate sons of heroic ancestors" who were "dependent upon the religion, which they discard, for any privilege they enjoy"—a clear reference to ABCFM "missionaries."[45] By way of implicit contrast with these flighty descendants of missionaries, the *Chronicle* stated that although the English church was not only the denomination that had stripped away the errors of Roman Catholicism during the English Reformation, it was the one that for centuries before that had carried the true light of the gospel in opposition to Rome.[46] As the Anglican Church faltered in Hawai'i after an initial period of success, Bishop Alfred Willis redoubled efforts to draw in Kalākaua toward the end of his reign using similar historical arguments and successfully won over the king.[47] Interreligious competition in the islands was thus once again framed by historical argument and by dueling claims to longevity and stability.

A third main group of religious competitors to the Protestant missionary community also had cause to claim a longevity of presence in Hawai'i superior to that of the ABCFM mission. French Roman Catholics had baptized two influential Native Hawaiian chiefs—Boki and Kalanimoku—in August 1819 when visiting the islands aboard *L'Uranie*, two months before the first company of ABCFM missionaries even left Boston. Even W. D. Alexander, the man whom his fellow descendants of missionaries deemed the leading authority on Hawaiian history, acknowledged this episode in his history of Hawai'i that was published in 1891.[48] Yet Catholic missionaries had not used this success as a springboard to further work among Native Hawaiians, and by the time a group of Catholic priests did try to settle in the islands in July 1827, Protestantism was the preeminent religious influence among the chiefs. The monarchy expelled Catholic missionaries in December 1831 after the unceasing work of the Protestant queen regent, Kaʻahumanu, to ensure that competing religious forces were kept out of the islands. It took the intervention of a French gunboat in 1839 to finally secure equal rights of access for Catholic missionaries.[49]

As Americans in the late nineteenth century looked back on the resistance to Catholicism of earlier Native Hawaiian leaders, it was clear that particular ideas had taken hold, ideas that had filtered down through missionary sources in the intervening decades. The early missionary Hiram Bingham had argued in his book that a desire to avoid "civil divisions" motivated Kaʻahumanu to reject Catholicism.[50] The more enduring interpretation, however, was articulated by Sheldon Dibble: Protestant Indigenous chiefs had turned away Catholics because they brought a form of worship that too closely resembled the kind of ritualism that Native Hawaiians had just given up with the overthrow of the ʻai kapu.[51] Although Protestant missionaries had urged compassion and tolerance, Bingham argued, Native Hawaiians had proved incorrigible in their rejection and suppression of Catholicism.[52] An 1884 article by Samuel Chapman Armstrong and an 1898 book by Belle M. Brain both articulated these prevalent notions for a US audience in the late nineteenth century.[53] In drawing straightforward analogies between Catholicism and the traditional practices of Native Hawaiians, Protestants were to an extent caricaturing both, but Native Hawaiians recognized some resonance. In fact, Samuel M. Kamakau, a prominent historian and a convert to Catholicism, gave this as a reason why he switched his allegiance from Protestantism.[54] Accordingly, "missionaries" in the islands continued to highlight evidence that true Christian Native Hawaiians saw Catholicism as a retrograde step toward materialism and superstition. *The Friend*, for example, reported in early 1891 that when a new Protestant church at Waialua on Oʻahu was initially built with a cross on the steeple, "the Hawaiians disliked it so much, as indicative of Papistical formalism, that the cross was replaced by a finial of less distinctive conspicuousness."[55]

A new struggle over Hawaiian history was brewing between Protestants and Catholics in the late nineteenth century, related to the legacy of the Belgian priest Father Damien. Damien's story threatened to undercut Protestants' historical triumphalism about their hegemonic role in the "transformation" of the islands just as Catholics were redoubling their efforts to convert Native

Hawaiians.[56] Heralded as a hero and martyr by the Catholic Church (and ultimately canonized in 2009), Damien spent most of the 1870s and 1880s among Hawaiian lepers on the island of Molokai. He contracted the disease and died in 1889. Disagreements over the details of Damien's story commenced a war of words immediately after his death that attracted attention beyond the islands. It began when Charles Hyde wrote a private letter to the Australian pastor H. B. Gage in mid-1889 decrying Damien's character and habits and expressing frustration that the world did not know the truth about him.[57] The letter found its way into a number of publications, and in early 1890 it drew a reply from the Scottish writer and friend of Kalākaua, Robert Louis Stevenson, who at that point was in Sydney, Australia. In an open letter, Stevenson launched a scathing attack on Hyde and the missionary establishment in Hawai'i. Drawing on knowledge gained on a visit to the islands in 1889, he contrasted the grand Honolulu abodes of the missionary community with Damien's asceticism, accused Hyde of jealousy and guilt over his church's inertia on the problem of leprosy, and said that while Damien may have been simple and coarse, he displayed "intrusive and decisive heroism."[58] The New York lawyer and church trustee Thomas G. Shearman, whose criticisms of Hawai'i's missionary community in 1895 were published in several US newspapers, further lambasted Hyde's treatment of Damien, and the prominent Catholic author Charles Warren Stoddard published a hagiographic account of Damien for Americans in 1901.[59] The vitriolic nature of Hyde's response to Damien's veneration manifested frustration that an alternative version of Hawaiian history was gaining currency in which Catholics could figure as patriarchs and heroes at a time when some descendants of missionaries still declared the pope to be "the Man of Sin, the Wicked one, the Antichrist, the False Prophet."[60] The transmission of Damien's story threatened to create the perception that the islands had been uplifted by a multifaith endeavor, and Hyde had to set the record straight.

The fact that "missionaries" came into conflict with Europeans and even fellow Americans over Hawaiian history and its religious significance indicates that the missionary community had always operated within a "deeply fractured" cultural field.[61] In addition to its historical struggles with Mormonism, Catholicism, and Anglicanism, the missionary enterprise in Hawai'i had from its beginnings been confronted with licentious merchants from both Britain and New England, sugar planters from Europe and China, and adventurers from around the world. Foreshadowing the efforts of the "missionaries" to raise the US flag in Hawai'i without the formal sanction of their government, rogue Russian, British, and French actors had even attempted to claim sovereignty over the islands on various occasions in the first half of the nineteenth century, prompting Britain, France, and the United States to formally recognize the archipelago's independence in the 1840s.[62] Cooperation with British missionaries and their Tahitian converts was also decisive in the ABCFM mission's early success.[63] In asserting a special connection between American Protestantism and Hawai'i, "missionaries" were effacing much of this complexity and alternative understandings of Hawaiian history. The complexity continued into the late nineteenth century. By the start of the 1890s, the Catholic and Mormon churches had more than 18,000 members between them, while HEA numbers had declined to under 3,000.[64]

Competing claims to historical legitimacy by Native Hawaiians and various religious groups in Hawai'i prior to annexation, all of which served the purpose of bolstering claims to political and religious authority, provide context for the "missionary" culture of historical narration described in chapter 1. The members of the missionary community were not reflecting on the religious past in a vacuum, nor did they take for granted the hegemony of their narrative; they were responding to the surrounding conditions. As the rest of this chapter will show, their reactions to Native Hawaiian retellings of history demonstrated a particularly acute concern. On the one hand, the eagerness of descendants of missionaries to denigrate and suppress these retellings spoke of a vibrant culture that troubled and threatened them. On the other, evidence that descendants of missionaries mirrored some of the forms of Native Hawaiian history telling shows that Indigenous culture was to an extent shaping how history could be effectively employed and how legitimacy could be claimed.

"Missionary" Denigration of Indigenous Understandings

Nathaniel Emerson, the son of two missionaries, condemned Kalākaua's coronation ceremony in 1883 and its attempt to establish historical legitimacy for the king as "a costly pageant" in which "the pomp and circumstance of barbaric pearl and gold were married to the voluptuous obscenities of the Hawaiian hula."[65] The king's fiftieth birthday celebration in November 1886 elicited similar responses that denounced it as an extravagant public display of heathen practice. The historian and missionary son W. D. Alexander—"a gentleman whose accuracy and fidelity no one ever ventures to call in question," in Sereno Bishop's words—watched events unfold.[66] In recounting what he witnessed, Alexander homed in on two particular elements of the proceedings. First, he described a "so-called historical procession" that wended its way through the streets to ʻIolani Palace, "consisting chiefly of canoes and boats carried on drays, containing natives in ancient costume, personating warriors and fishermen, mermaids draped with sea moss, hula dancers, etc." The "notorious Hale Naua" also made an appearance, marching around the palace, "over which the yellow flag of their order was flying." Second, five days later, the jubilee closed with a series of "historical tableaux" at Honolulu's opera house, "concluding with a hulahula dance."[67]

Alexander recognized that Kalākaua's pageantry was a highly conspicuous display of Hawaiian history as told by Native Hawaiians. Like the Board of Genealogy and the Hale Naua, it represented an attempt by Kalākaua to revive traditional Native Hawaiian modes of genealogical narration, this time through performance, as an expression of resistance to US colonialism. Central to both the historical procession and the tableaux in Alexander's description was the *hula* dance, an art form inherently connected to genealogy. The scholar Adria L. Imada underscores the "connection between historiography, politics, and hula." The dance was "a form of embodied and kinesthetic historical knowledge" able to accommodate "flexibility, change, and innovation as its practitioners and political patrons shifted."[68] Although the missionary community seethed over the return to heathenism that Kalākaua's encouragement of *hula* performance apparently symbolized, Indigenous newspapers were more preoccupied with the implications of the content of the revived *hula* for Kalākaua's genealogical contest with Queen Emma. The "obscenities" descendants of missionaries identified in the *hula* represented the sexual vigor that had allowed for the perpetuation of the Hawaiian land and people dating back to the birth of the islands—an invocation that was particularly resonant against the backdrop of an Indigenous population crisis.[69] The dance had been banned earlier in the century by chiefly converts working with Alexander's missionary ancestors, and Kalākaua's revival was a pointed act of defiance against the missionary community.[70] To undermine the potency of this conspicuous Native Hawaiian history telling, Alexander called both its morality and its accuracy into question. He pointed out that the displays "gave offense" to most of those watching in Honolulu of the 1880s, thus rendering them unacceptable in a Hawaiian society in which the majority were "civilized" and Christianized. Moreover, the title of Alexander's pamphlet in which he described the celebrations, *Kalakaua's Reign: A Sketch of Hawaiian History* (1894), laid claim to historical truth, set against the "so-called historical" content of Kalākaua's procession.[71]

Taking a different approach to Alexander, the pamphlet *Gynberg Ballads* (1887) employed satire in response to Kalākaua's birthday celebrations. Alatau Tamchiboulac Atkinson, the apparent author of this pamphlet, was not a descendant of missionaries—he was the son of British explorers in the Russian empire—but following his arrival in Hawai'i in 1869, he became an adopted "missionary," allying with descendants of missionaries in opposition to Kalākaua and ultimately in advocacy of annexation, which he expressed through his editorship of the *Hawaiian Star*.[72] William R. Castle and Sanford Dole, both sons of missionaries, supported his work, bringing legal proceedings against the Hawaiian collector of customs on his behalf when 1,100 copies of *Gynberg Ballads*, which had been published in San Francisco, were seized at port.[73] The pamphlet took its title from a derogatory name for Kalākaua derived from his alleged proclivity for spirits and included a poem entitled "A Stranger Asks Bliff about the Historical Procession." In this rhyme, a silent "stranger" shows interest in determining from "Bliff," presumably a Native Hawaiian man, exactly what the historical procession during Kalākaua's birthday celebrations had been about. But "Bliff" is ignorant of its meaning and is not interested in talking about anything other than the amount of alcohol he has consumed: "What! that don't interest you—you say, nor yet what we imbibed? / Historical Procession, then, is what you want described. / Well, honestly, I'm up a tree, I really can't pretend / To say where history came in, unless right at the end."[74] The Indigenous historical voice was thus dismissed as a cover for licentiousness and Native Hawaiians were portrayed as being dispassionate about the historical content on display during the festivities—they recognized, insofar as they thought about it at all, that it did not measure up as history.

Taken together, the responses of Alexander and Atkinson to Kalākaua's birthday celebrations stripped Native Hawaiian historical narration of claims to accuracy, morality, or dignity. This was a tactic descendants of missionaries also frequently employed in relation to the Hale Naua: Alexander referred to the society as a "travesty of Masonry, mingled with pagan rites" that provoked "general disgust"; Bishop said it "embrace[d] the very worst elements of organized sorcery, of idolatry, and of heathen impurity"; and Hyde wrote of "a grand secret society . . . designed to entangle and embrace the whole Hawaiian people" in "pagan practices."[75] The missionary community branded it the "Ball of Twine" Society, an epithet Lorrin Thurston originally devised in response to the alleged playing of a game involving a ball of twine that was used to select sexual partners.[76] Confronted with

Indigenous traditions of historical narration that they did not fully comprehend, descendants of missionaries perceived them as a threat to both their morals and their sovereignty, responding with ridicule and condemnation. Ultimately, after the overthrow, a "missionary" government suppressed the very medium of these traditions—the Hawaiian language—by establishing English as the sole language of school instruction in 1896.[77] Descendants of missionaries deployed their self-proclaimed, inherited moral and spiritual superiority to make clear that Indigenous history telling had no place or meaning in contemporary society or politics.

Seeking Connection to American Epistemologies

A claim to white Americanness was implied in the denigration of Native Hawaiian historical accounts descendants of missionaries engaged in, by way of asserting a stark dichotomy between white American and Indigenous ways of knowing the past. This was important to these descendants of missionaries, given that their opponents in both the United States and Hawai'i focused on their liminal relationship to the United States. Detractors made the argument that "missionaries" were not fully of the United States and that they had diverged from US political traditions in their treatment of Native Hawaiian rule. Indeed, the report of President Cleveland's commissioner, James Blount, expressed a belief that, having been born and raised in the islands, the children and grandchildren of missionaries had fallen out of step with US history. This undermined the petition they made as Americans to have Hawai'i annexed to the United States. Blount referred to "natives of foreign parentage, some of whom were the descendants of missionary ancestors," and to "native-born subjects of foreign origin."[78] In choosing this language, Blount refused to associate the descendants of missionaries with the United States, placing them instead as being simultaneously "native" to Hawai'i and of generic "foreign" stock. He also evoked the fact that various changes to the definition of citizenship in both Hawai'i and the United States over the course of the nineteenth century had left the legal status of the descendants of missionaries highly ambiguous.[79] Sent to examine whether "historical precedents, and the general course of the United States" had been followed when the US flag was raised on Hawaiian soil, Blount concluded that they had not been. Similar grievances in the United States, he argued, would have been resolved through democratic processes.[80] Blount's framing did not escape Sereno Bishop's attention: "We were outcasts in his view—men without a country."[81]

Although Cleveland did not completely efface the American origins of the children and grandchildren of missionaries, as Blount did, he suggested that the overthrow of the Hawaiian monarchy was an act that was not aligned with US history. He stated that the United States was in danger of having "set up a temporary government on foreign soil for the purpose of acquiring . . . territory" and that "we are not without precedent in showing how scrupulously we avoided such accusations in former days," using the example of Andrew Jackson's refusal to immediately annex Texas after colonists had secured independence from Mexico. Not only that, but the provisional government had assumed a form that was antithetical to US political traditions—"a mere executive council or oligarchy"—and thus "due regard for our national character" dictated that the United States should "endeavor to repair" the wrongs done.[82] Cleveland's supporters in Congress agreed. John W. Daniel, the former Confederate major and senator for Virginia, pointedly underscored the majority "alien" makeup of the Committee of Safety by labeling the six members who were descendants of missionaries as Hawaiians. They stood alongside an Englishman and a German, outnumbering the five members Daniel identified as actual Americans.[83] J. F. Stallings, a Democratic representative from Alabama, spoke in the House of his desire to back the president in "following the precedents laid down by Washington, Jefferson, Jackson," declaring counterresolutions to be "un-American."[84] These critiques by Democrats should certainly be read at least in part against the backdrop of sectional antagonisms and racist anxieties over the possibility of annexing Hawai'i, and they of course drew on a selective reading of US history that was in reality founded on government-assisted settler colonialism.

Similar charges that the descendants of missionaries were un-American were made elsewhere. The Republican senator for South Dakota, Richard F. Pettigrew, a purveyor of racist arguments against expansion, broke ranks with his party on the issue after visiting Hawai'i in 1897, denouncing the political actions of settlers whom he said wanted "simply to lute [sic] the treasury of the United States."[85] Julius A. Palmer, a Boston journalist who became Lili'uokalani's personal assistant in the United States, accused "missionaries" of having "imported one of the most Un-american of organizations" to Hawai'i.[86]

Anxieties about the possibility that Americans might perceive the expanse of water between Hawai'i and the United States as a cultural chasm were evident in "missionary" writing. Satire was one response, as when descendants of missionaries produced for their own amusement a parody letter purportedly from President Cleveland to Congress in which he asserted that Hawai'i's provisional government had sent a "kahooner"—a *kahuna*, or priest—to kill him using the supposed Native Hawaiian practice of "praying to death." In laughing at the exaggerated notion that white settlers might deploy a practitioner of Native Hawaiian ritual to kill the US president, the descendants of missionaries revealed a more salient and subtle fear that lawmakers in the United States perceived them as having somehow "gone native."[87]

Sereno Bishop's regular letters to the *Washington Evening Star* tried more directly to reorient the perceptions about the missionary community emanating from the United States. After agreeing terms with an agent of the Associated Press in a Honolulu hotel in early 1894, Bishop wrote 102 columns over the next thirteen years that were distributed via the *Evening Star* and other East Coast newspapers.[88] These were an attritional campaign to put white settlers' arguments for annexation before the American public. The letters denigrated both white and Indigenous opponents of annexation and warned of grave consequences if the United States missed its opportunity. Throughout these letters, Bishop was clearly concerned that it was all too easy for Americans to believe that a settler community across the ocean would be out of step with the political traditions and societal needs of the United States. A significant number of US newspapers had long appeared willing to further this impression, as did pro-monarchy Hawaiian publications, one of which undermined Bishop personally by claiming that the US flag "is not, nor ever will be the flag of S. E. Bishop."[89]

Clearly, Bishop saw his letters in part as a way of asserting Hawai'i's place in the story of the United States and its suitability to be an incorporated territory rather than a colony. He often did this by demonstrating that settlers in Hawai'i were well attuned to white Americans' repressive and racist instincts on the continent.[90] Against the charge that annexationists were overriding the Indigenous majority by restricting suffrage, Bishop likened their situation to that of "southern states where an ignorant negro majority exists"—a resonant argument during a decade when the US Supreme Court continued to validate the prerogative of white southerners to chip away at African Americans' rights as citizens.[91] Against the charge that Hawaiian planters needed a continued influx of "Asiatic" labor and thus would undercut the US exclusion of Chinese migrants, Bishop repeatedly responded that the American element of the islands' population recognized the need to end East Asian migration and foresaw a future of white settlement and labor in

Hawaiʻi.[92] Against the charge that Hawaiʻi's population was too mixed race to become a territory of the United States, Bishop emphasized the Americanness of Hawaiʻi's institutions. The fact that they were rooted in a missionary heritage, he claimed, made Hawaiʻi a more suitable candidate for annexation than some other territories that were now full-fledged members of the union had initially been.[93] "All Americans now find themselves at home," he wrote. Even newcomers "forget they are out of America" and "habitually speak of 'this country' when they mean America." Hawaiʻi was "already an American commonwealth, except in the name."[94] Setting aside any insecurities about the fact that the pro-annexation contingent of white Americans made up as little as 2 percent of the population of the islands, propped up only by threat of force, Bishop attached himself to the language of manifest destiny to rhetorically naturalize Hawaiʻi's place in US history.[95] In this sense, Bishop partook in a common enterprise across settler colonial contexts—seeking inclusion within a metropolitan identity by deploying racial arguments in order to lay claim to support, counter "humanitarian" detractors, and justify colonial violence in all its forms.[96]

Meanwhile, in their associations, political institutions, local newspapers, and correspondence, descendants of missionaries rehearsed a number of other arguments to demonstrate that they were not out of step with the US past. To a degree, these claims were successful. For example, US senator George Frisbee Hoar, who later was famous for his opposition to the seizure of the Philippines, appeared to publicly accept the argument that Hawaiʻi could be annexed as it was already an American place.[97] When Sanford Dole spoke at the Honolulu Social Science Association in 1887, he said that Hawaiian annexation would be consistent with the principles of the Monroe Doctrine because European colonizers would otherwise collect the islands.[98] Elsewhere, Dole claimed that the longevity of American civilization in Hawaiʻi was superior to substantial parts of the continental United States thanks to its mission heritage. When gold was being discovered in California, Hawaiʻi already had "a constitution and good laws, a legislature and a Supreme and subordinate courts. . . . Schools were found in all parts of the country, churches were numerous and well attended."[99] W. D. Alexander argued that "missionary" action was consistent with American precedent in an 1894 letter that tried out three different historical frames. First, he likened the vilification of settlers in Hawaiʻi to the initial vilification of the Texas colonists, second, he asserted that "renegade white royalists" corresponded to the "'carpet-baggers' and 'scalawags' of the South," and third, he reminded his correspondent that, much as pro-annexationist settlers represented a numerical minority within Hawai'i, "the American Revolution was commenced and carried through by a minority of the colonists."[100] The missionary community was, after all, overthrowing a monarchy just as those revolutionaries had, argued one pro-"missionary" newspaper, and Cleveland might be considered "somewhat in the dictator line" for obstructing "popular sentiment."[101] Lorrin Thurston argued to the Hawaiian legislature in 1898 that history showed "Congress and the Executive annexing territory under every conceivable method" and that "every such annexation has been upheld by . . . the supreme court."[102] Most conspicuously of all, the declaration of the Hawaiian Republic on July 4, 1894, was a pointed counterclaim to the idea that the new government was out of step with US political traditions.

The mode in which history was told was just as important as the content of historical argument for attaching "missionaries" to American historical epistemologies and establishing the supremacy of their narratives. The missionary community had long denigrated the forms in which Native Hawaiians understood and narrated history, building on a Euro-American conviction that those who did not write could not have a history. This view was evident as early as the interactions of Christopher Columbus's crew with the Taíno in the late fifteenth century.[103] The early missionary Hiram Bingham had denied orality and memory as appropriate media for history, railing against "stupid, unlettered" Native Hawaiians for their inability to offer "a trustworthy history of their country . . . even for a single generation."[104] Even as Native Hawaiians embraced the written word en masse over the subsequent decades, W. D. Alexander continued to embody the idea that the versions of Hawaiian history written by white outsiders were unimpeachable. His *Brief History of the Hawaiian People* (1891), which was written at the behest of Hawai'i's Board of Education and was used as a school textbook, claimed the sole authority to impart Hawaiian history to schoolchildren. In his role as commissioner of public instruction, Alexander was also instrumental in banning the Hawaiian language in schools in 1896, thus further distancing a new generation of Native Hawaiians from their traditional narratives.[105] In drawing the line anew between apparently scientific or objective history and the poetic forms associated with savagery, Alexander participated in a process that characterized the beginnings of history as a professional discipline in the late nineteenth-century United States.[106]

Indeed, as claims to objective historical inquiry and scientific investigation became increasingly important to US thinkers, they became central to the missionary community's associational culture. The Honolulu Social Science Association and the Hawaiian Historical Society (HHS) complemented the HEA, the Hawaiian Mission Children's Society, the Honolulu YMCA, and Central Union Church as key venues where "missionaries" gathered. Both provided echo chambers in which an identity based on authoritative knowledge of the Hawaiian past was continually reaffirmed, countering conspicuous Native Hawaiian retellings of history that constituted claims to sovereignty. The Honolulu Social Science Association, which was founded in 1882, two years after the Board of Genealogy, provided a forum for the missionary community to share and discuss the Hawaiian past through the lens of social science. It remained independent of Native Hawaiians and received high-profile scholarly guests from the United States.[107] The HHS, which was founded in 1892, was another exclusive space for interpreting history from a "missionary" perspective; it was established right at the time when the missionary community stepped up its claims to sovereignty. It was the second incarnation of a Hawaiian Historical Society. The first had been formed in 1841 by Samuel M. Kamakau, a Native Hawaiian historian and a vehement critic of the "post-missionary progress" narrative of Hawaiian history.[108] The makeup of the new society was quite different. Missionary sons W. D. Alexander, G. P. Castle, William R. Castle, Sanford Dole, Joseph Emerson, and Nathaniel Emerson were all prominent members during its early years.

Vice-president Joseph Emerson went out of his way to eschew any political or religious purpose for the HHS at its first annual meeting on December 5, 1892, a little over a month before the monarchy was overthrown.[109] Emerson was protesting too much. Especially in the context of the febrile political atmosphere, it is impossible not to identify a political and racist argument in the work of the HHS: that Native Hawaiians were a dying race incapable of adequately accounting for or preserving their own history and therefore that "missionary" intervention was needed. The society's reports show how the settler community claimed the authority to collect, speak, and publish on an extraordinary range of topics under the rubric of history: the development of the Hawaiian monarchy and its laws, Hawaiian legends obtained from Indigenous informants, objects of sacred significance to Native Hawaiians, and the precontact past of the islands. "It is the desire of this Society," said Joseph Emerson, "to gather up the threads of our history which may otherwise be permanently lost, in order that hereafter they may be woven by the future historian, into a lasting and symmetrical whole."[110] This was because, added Alexander, the HHS's long-standing corresponding secretary, "the few who still possess some knowledge of the ancient folk-lore of Hawaii are fast passing away."[111]

The HHS consolidated its authority in a transnational context. It situated Hawai'i within its historical place in Polynesia by forging links with other white ethnologists across the Pacific, notably S. Percy Smith of New Zealand, who founded the Polynesian Society.[112] It also claimed a place within professionalizing historical and scientific disciplines in the United States by sending its publications to US institutions that included the Smithsonian, the New York Public Library, the Field Museum, Harvard and Yale Universities, and various state historical societies.[113] In the content of their research and in the networks they built, HHS members made the case that history was a scientific endeavor in which the task of preserving culture and discerning truth fell largely to white men. One woman of Indigenous descent, Emma Nakuina—the daughter of an American sugar planter and a female *ali'i* who became a judge, a women's suffrage campaigner, and a writer on Hawaiian folklore—briefly served as a vice-president of the society and had a paper read at one meeting, albeit by a missionary son.[114] The role of HHS librarian was nearly always filled by a white woman. Other than that, the proceedings of the society were overwhelmingly dominated by white male voices.

There were other ways, too, in which "missionaries" generated knowledge about Hawai'i's origins and precontact history that claimed objectivity and connected them to professionalizing scientific disciplines in Europe and North America. W. D. Alexander, Sereno Bishop, and John T. Gulick contributed theories about the migratory past of the Hawaiian people, about the geological origins of the archipelago, and about evolution as seen through specimens collected in the islands.[115] Bishop's geological studies were published in US journals and he corresponded with the prominent scientist Alexander Winchell, whose arguments about the inferiority of nonwhite races dovetailed neatly with Bishop's own views.[116] Gulick exchanged letters with such famous counterparts as George John Romanes, Charles Darwin, Alfred R. Wallace, Louis Agassiz, and Alpheus Hyatt.[117] Sanford Dole refined his Social Darwinist justifications for white rule in Hawai'i through extensive correspondence with the American social scientist John W. Burgess.[118]

In their scientific commitments and networks, descendants of missionaries in many ways built on the interests of their forebears. Missionary mothers and fathers were educated New Englanders who keenly observed and collected natural phenomena, sought evidence of God in nature, and were instrumental in sparking the curiosity of their offspring.[119] The early missionaries' desire to collect and categorize also extended to Indigenous heritage. From early on in their work, they gathered emblems of Native Hawaiian culture in order to assert control over their meaning, in particular to emphasize their diminishing relevance as Christianity and civilization took hold. Their descendants helped to institutionalize and professionalize this practice: Samuel M. Damon, William O. Smith, Charles M. Cooke, and Charles Hyde were trustees of the Bishop Museum, which American businessman Charles Reed Bishop (no relation to Sereno) founded in 1889 to gather and display artifacts from across Polynesia, using a bequest left by Bishop's chiefly wife Pauahi.[120] Early missionary collections came full circle in the 1890s: missionaries had first sent them to the ABCFM in Boston for display in the United States, and now the Bishop Museum requested their return to exhibit them in Honolulu.[121] Despite these continuities with their parents' impulses, however, when it came to drawing conclusions about the past based on science in a Darwinian age, descendants of missionaries often perceived themselves to be embracing something that their forebears had held at arm's length because of their biblicism. Gulick's pursuit of evolutionary science put him at odds with his father, even though he took pains to explain to other members of the scientific community how evolutionary theory affirmed biblical revelation for him.[122] Sereno Bishop noted that he had learned nothing of his geological expertise in childhood, when he had been taught that "the globe had been created in six ordinary days, and there was no mystery about it. . . . Six thousand years was the limit of past earthly chronology."[123]

It would be wrong to suggest that science was totally at odds with Native Hawaiian historical narratives. As we have seen, the Board of Genealogy and the Hale Nauā engaged with scientific methodologies insofar as they did not encroach upon genealogical understandings. Nonetheless, science certainly furnished evidence about the distant past that to the "missionary" mind undercut traditional cosmogonical accounts and established white settler authority in the language of the evolving epistemologies of Americans. Nineteenth-century science was an ideological tool with multifaceted significance as a weapon in a settler-colonial cultural arsenal. The volcanological studies prolifically undertaken by the missionary community in Hawai'i and fed back to the United States, for example, were not only protoscientific but were also a refutation of a competing Indigenous cosmology in which Pele, the goddess who resided in the volcano, was central.[124] In other words, for descendants of missionaries, science partially replaced Christian dogma as a mode of asserting cultural superiority.[125]

Moreover, engagements with scientific theories about geological time and migration helped nineteenth-century Europeans and Americans sense their connection to specific locations. The historian Thomas Allen argues that emergent scientific understandings of deep time helped Americans overcome a sense of cultural inferiority by finding historical roots for the United States that were independent of the shared traditions that characterized European nationhood.[126] Social scientific theories about the racial origins of Polynesians, like those Alexander engaged with in his *Brief History*, repeatedly styled Polynesians as primitive prior iterations of white civilization in ways that allowed white settlers to think of whiteness as somehow indigenous to Polynesia.[127] By studying geology, volcanology, or ethnology in Hawai'i, descendants of missionaries were developing their own felt connection to Hawaiian history while simultaneously linking themselves to American cultures of historical understanding.

However, the dichotomies between written history and oral tradition, or between objective science and unreliable collective memory, were not as stark as descendants of missionaries or Americans more generally might have liked to believe. For a start, throughout the second half of the nineteenth century, Native Hawaiians enthusiastically embraced technologies of writing and print that missionaries had introduced. They pressed their own claims to sovereignty, previously enshrined in oral tradition, through a vibrant print culture, of which Kālakaua and Lili'uokalani's published genealogies were just one element. In newspapers in particular, beginning with *Ka Hoku o ka Pakipika* ("The Star of the Pacific," established in 1861), Native Hawaiians preserved and perpetuated their historical narratives, asserted their indigeneity, and defended their sovereignty against the claims of descendants of missionaries who sought to dominate and control the Hawaiian press.[128] Indigenous scholars have shown that through newspapers, Native Hawaiians replicated some of the dynamic, dialogic forms of oral tradition. These publications provided a format in which interpretations could be printed and then contested in an ever-evolving discourse.[129]

Lili'uokalani's *Hawaii's Story by Hawaii's Queen*, which was published in the immediate aftermath of annexation, was in the words of the scholar Lydia Kualapai not "a backward look into a kingdom's monarchical history but a timely and constructive strategy for a newly restored Hawaiian nation."[130] Facing the challenge of producing a narrative in written English that would outline the wrongs of US colonialism to an audience in the United States but would also be true to her Native Hawaiian outlook, the queen found a solution in the form of the memoir. That form allowed Lili'uokalani to make personal, genealogical claims intelligible to Native Hawaiians, beginning with a traditional cosmogony and moving through a lineage of venerated ancestors to the present. At the same time, building on a more general Native Hawaiian interest in how the Western tradition of life writing could be adopted as a political act in the late nineteenth century, she offered her interpretation of more recent events and asserted the steadfastness of the contemporary monarchy, thus undermining the "missionary" narrative in a manner that was intelligible to Americans.[131] Although the fact that the narrative was written rather than oral indicated Liliʻuokalani's adaptability to the international political stage on which she made her claims, she was able to assert a cultural gap through her use of untranslatable Hawaiian words and ambiguous motifs, inscribing *kaona*, the notion of hidden meaning that was central to Indigenous oral tradition, into a text written in English.[132] Even when Native Hawaiian historical interpretations were written rather than performed, however, descendants of missionaries found ways to denigrate them. Sereno Bishop questioned whether Liliʻuokalani had authored *Hawaii's Story by Hawaii's Queen* at all, suggesting that it had been "carefully edited by some very competent person," at the same time proclaiming it to be "utterly and deliberately false."[133] Significantly, the title of his *Washington Evening Star* letter about the book was "No Value as History." Like Hiram Bingham before him, Bishop used the insinuation that Native Hawaiians could not properly write history to bolster an argument that Indigenous lifeways and sovereignty had no place in a modern world.[134]

Although Native Hawaiians subverted Bingham's dichotomy between written and oral histories by writing down their historical claims derived from oral tradition, US culture also blurred the distinction that Bingham tried to make, suggesting to the missionary community that genealogy, memory, and performance were potent forms of historical narrative for white Americans seeking to suppress the voices of racial others. However much history writing in the late nineteenth-century United States professionalized, embracing historicism and objectivity as ideals, American historical consciousness was founded on a great diversity of ways of thinking about time and about forms of historical narration.[135] Genealogical sensibilities, an obsession with historical beginnings, and the idea that spiritual legitimacy flowed down the generations from more pious ancestors were all familiar to the New England Puritan context that the majority of the original Hawaiian missionaries emerged from.[136] In the North American context, these historical framings proved critical for overriding Native American connections to the land and establishing roots for the United States as a nation.[137] They represented a broader trend Kathryn Gin Lum has identified across the long nineteenth century whereby recognizing "other people's competing claims to historical significance and longevity," Europeans and Americans turned to "doing just what they derided childlike 'heathens' and geriatric 'pagans' for: relying on myth and glorifying ancestors." Against this backdrop, claims to historical authenticity were rhetorical assertions that diverted attention from the fuzzy lines between supposedly trustworthy written history and its alternatives.[138]

Orality, too, was more important to the missionary community's sense of history and identity than Bingham's straightforward association of truth with writing suggested. Sermons and catechisms had always been at the heart of missionary practice in Hawai'i.[139] Members of the missionary community were also dependent on Indigenous oral tradition in their attempts to reconstruct precontact history. Bingham had been confronted with this problem in his written history of the islands, in which within the space of a few pages he paradoxically dismissed oral tradition as offering nothing of use to the historian and then outlined the migratory past of the Hawaiian people with reference to "traditionary history."[140] Around forty years later, Bingham's successor as the supposed authority on Hawaiian history, W. D. Alexander, also acknowledged his reliance on tradition when considering the origins of the Hawaiian people and their migratory voyages across the ocean.[141]

Moreover, although Alexander derided Kalākaua's historical displays, at the turn of the twentieth century, public performance of historical narrative was taking on heightened significance in US culture, deployed to affirm particular ideas about local and national identity and memory in the aftermath of the Civil War. In Decoration Day parades and speeches, white Americans performed a reconciliatory collective history at the expense of Black civil rights.[142] New Englanders joined in this craze for public memorialization by reaffirming their Puritan heritage through jubilees, dances, and historical tableaux, for example at the Old Days and Ways festival in Plymouth, Massachusetts, in 1896.[143] "Missionaries" engaged with this burgeoning culture from afar, extending their own associational culture to celebrations of US history. A branch of the Sons of the American Revolution was founded in Hawai'i in 1895 that attached itself to the US organization founded six years earlier. Alexander hoped it would "connect us with the United States" and "help to show the intensity of American feeling here."[144] A branch of the Grand Army of the Republic drew together veterans of the Union Army in the islands, which several descendants of missionaries fought in during the Civil War.[145] This epitomized how even though "missionaries" took many of their ideas about the disfranchisement of nonwhite populations from the South, they equated their struggle for freedom with that of the North.¹⁴⁶ Decoration Day became something of an institution in Hawai'i, with descendants of missionaries serving as orators to evince their "ardent American patriotism."¹⁴⁷

However, in addition to connecting descendants of missionaries to cultures of historical pageantry and collective memory in the United States, genealogy and performance became useful to them as they sought to assert themselves on the contested terrain of history in Hawai'i. Although the foregoing section of this chapter has principally focused on how "missionaries" sought connection to white Americans' histories and epistemologies, the next section considers how descendants of missionaries inadvertently cut across their assertions of Americanness by betraying a parallel and sometimes contradictory need to establish legitimacy as Hawaiians. Responding to Indigenous genealogies and performances, "missionaries" invoked their ancestral connection to the Hawaiian religious past at communal gatherings and built up extensive kinship networks that imitated Native Hawaiian genealogical recitation and allowed descendants of missionaries to psychologically overcome the comparative paucity of their claim to the land and justify their claims to sovereignty on both American and Hawaiian terms. They did not straightforwardly appropriate Native Hawaiian epistemologies or cultures; as we have seen, traditions in the United States provided them with plenty of models for genealogical invocation and historical performance, and in any case they failed to grasp the nuance or dynamism of Indigenous genealogies. Nonetheless, some of the specifics of their modes of historical narration bore the hallmarks of a cultural encounter with local traditions and a willingness to deploy a sense of liminality and cultural and intellectual distance from the United States that descendants of missionaries elsewhere fought so hard to deny.

Claiming Hawaiian Identity

The bid for sovereignty in Hawai'i on the part of descendants of missionaries was largely based on their claim that they had redefined Hawaiian identity, replacing an outmoded indigeneity with a self-proclaimed morally responsible and physically vital white Hawaiian.¹⁴⁸ However, Indigenous genealogical performances and print cultures served as a constant implicit reminder of the insufficiency of "missionary" claims in a world where genealogical recitation was the basis for proving Hawaiianness.¹⁴⁹ As much as political opponents of descendants of missionaries denied "missionaries" an American identity, they also declared them, in Julius Palmer's words, to be "posing as Hawaiians," not as having established government on behalf of the Hawaiian people.[150] Descendants of missionaries were thus rhetorically left in a liminal place between American and Hawaiian identity: "Fair-minded people," argued President Cleveland, "will hardly claim that the Hawaiian Government was overthrown by the people of the islands."[151] James Blount distinguished "natives of foreign parentage" from the "native race," to whom a "deep wrong" had been done.[152] Lili'uokalani's supporters also assailed the claims of "missionaries," asserting that they did not "represent the Hawaiian nation," adding for good measure that they were also "in direct violation" of "principles for which Americans have repeatedly shed their blood, viz, the government of the people, by the people, and for the people."[153]

In the land of their birth, these criticisms stung descendants of missionaries badly, as clearly shown in one of Sereno Bishop's *Washington Evening Star* letters in June 1894. "We belong here," Bishop asserted, "fully as much as do the aboriginal population." He argued that many of the descendants of missionaries had been born in the islands and, in the case of third-generation "missionaries," including Lorrin Thurston, their parents had been too. Bishop deployed the well-worn settler-colonial argument that settlers and Indigenous peoples were just immigrants of different vintages: "We fail to understand why the aboriginal population have any superior right to ourselves in the country. Their ancestors came here from the Friendly Islands, in the neighborhood of Samoa, about twelve hundred years ago." Of course, this was a logic that contemporary US nativists seemed less willing to apply in their own context.[154] Overall, Bishop complicated his insistence on the Americanness of Hawai'i and its settler community with his expression to US audiences of hurt and confusion that he was not taken seriously as a Hawaiian: "Our white people have settled here. We have made Hawaii our home, with these aboriginal Polynesians."[155]

A consequent desire to prove the missionary community's Hawaiian credentials by claiming not just intellectual authority over the Indigenous past but a visceral connection to it explains the appearance of some passages in Bishop's letters that would perhaps have struck his US audiences as jarring, given that they emerged from the supposedly all-American, Protestant white community that Bishop was simultaneously desperate for Americans to recognize. Consider his lengthy description of a birthday celebration held for Sanford Dole in April 1895, which involved about seventy-five descendants of missionaries arriving at the president's house, "each armed in native fashion with a hookupu, or tribute." Trooping into Dole's residence carrying an array of local produce, flowers, "native fans and fancy mats," the company exchanged Hawaiian salutations—"'Alohamei' (great love), 'Maikaioe' (you are looking well), 'Elemakule no oe' (you are getting to be an old fellow)." Lorrin Thurston meanwhile led mimicry of "the pathetic native accent of deep adulation" and "wailing emotion, . . . praising the 'Alii' (chief)," in "a travesty of scenes frequently witnessed when a native chief was among his people."[156] On the one hand, this performance sits squarely in recognizable traditions of ironic cultural appropriation designed to underscore white supremacy—donning blackface or playing Indian, for example.[157] As the cultural historian Eric Lott argued about blackface minstrelsy, such performances always evinced "envy as well as repulsion, sympathetic identification as well as fear."[158] On the other hand, however, the choices of these descendants of missionaries also said something to US audiences about the extent to which this community was au fait with hallmarks of the Hawaiian past that were entirely alien to US culture and were willing to adopt its symbols as a sign of their own authority. Gone was the severe condemnation evident in their ancestors' response to Indigenous traditions and indeed the moral outrage with which descendants of missionaries greeted Kalākaua and Lili'uokalani. Instead, Bishop playfully elevated Dole to the status of *ali'i* and claimed to have a "strong sympathetic feeling for the fine old native customs."[159]

Bishop also appeared keen to show audiences in the United States that the overthrow of the Hawaiian monarchy was justifiable not only according to the principles of good American government but also from a Native Hawaiian genealogical perspective. Bishop was not wrong that some Native Hawaiians disputed Kalākaua's genealogical claims, but he mobilized the idea of genealogical contestation to make simplified assertions about the connection between missionaries, race, and monarchical legitimacy. In reviling the final two Hawaiian monarchs, who were not direct descendants of Kamehameha, he repeatedly presented "missionaries" as guardians of the true Hawaiian chiefly line. In the most striking example, from a letter published in June 1897, Bishop responded to the *Harper's Bazaar* columnist Harriet Prescott Spofford's sympathetic portrait of Lili'uokalani with a lengthy meditation on the insufficiency of her claims to royal blood. Kalākaua and Lili'uokalani, Bishop stated, were the children of Keohokālole, "a chiefess of the third grade" who could perhaps "trace descent from royalty somewhere from six to ten generations back." It was rumored that the two monarchs were the illegitimate products of Keohokālole's relationship with "a Jamaica quadroon," a shoemaker named John Blossom, a fact "which betrays itself in [Lili'uokalani's] wavy hair." The only living Native Hawaiian with a remotely legitimate claim to the throne, Bishop continued, was Jonah Kūhiō Kalanianaʻole, or Prince Cupid, who was later a delegate to the US Congress. Confusingly, Bishop indicated that Jonah and Cupid were two separate people, perhaps undermining his claims to familiarity with the royal lineage.[160] Bishop's digressions were striking, combining racist fears of Native Hawaiians' potential proximity to Blackness that were also evident in other derogatory representations of Kalākaua and Liliʻuokalani with a desire to demonstrate that the political actions of descendants of missionaries could be viewed as a restoration of propriety on Hawaiian as well as American terms.[161] Other descendants of missionaries followed a similar line of argument. Orramel Gulick argued to the ABCFM that it was "due to the missionaries from America, and their sons, that the Hawaiian chiefs held power till all the legitimate representatives of ancient Hawaiian royalty had passed away."[162] Nathaniel Emerson concurred that "Kalakaua had no place in the affections of his native countrymen as an alii or hereditary chief."[163] Although they misunderstood the dynamism of genealogy, descendants of missionaries clearly felt the need to justify their politics through what they recognized of the Hawaiian world view.

Also, descendants of missionaries conspicuously performed their own ancestral pasts in the late nineteenth century with the specific aim of demonstrating their innate and personal connection to Hawaiian history. The cultures of Native Hawaiian historical narration perhaps demonstrated to them that connections to Hawaiʻi were to be asserted not through written histories but through genealogical invocation, collective memory, and performance. Bishop's speech in Central Union Church in 1895 to commemorate the seventy-fifth anniversary of the first missionary landing provides a particularly good example. He recounted his childhood memories of the early missionaries, of Native Hawaiian chiefs, and of sweeping spiritual revivals and political reforms. He also sought validation by Indigenous memory, co-opting the reminiscences of a recently deceased Native Hawaiian convert to Christianity, Daniel Puhi, "who might have watched the brig Thaddeus [the ship on which the first missionaries arrived] as she lay to off the north point of Hawaii." Puhi "remembered what this new generation of Hawaiians often strive to deny, the squalid poverty of their ancestors, . . . their nakedness, indolence and stupid ignorance."[164] By performing his own memories, seemingly corroborated by those of a venerated Native, Bishop offered a direct counterpoint to the Hawaiian monarchy's public displays of history and proved that descendants of missionaries also did not need documents and books to construct and display their vision of the Hawaiian past. It was being kept alive in the present through recitation by those who claimed living links to it.

Bishop's speech was not an isolated example. Eight years before the seventy-fifth anniversary celebrations, for example, in April 1887, a gathering at Kawaiaha'o Seminary in Honolulu was part of a three-day extravaganza commemorating the fiftieth anniversary of the landing of mission reinforcements in 1837. Bishop offered his personal reminiscences before Lowell Smith and James William Smith, missionaries who had arrived in 1833 and 1842 respectively, spoke of their experiences and Lydia Bingham Coan and one of John and Ursula Emerson's sons recalled their parents' pioneering work.[165] The community found frequent excuses to gather and commemorate the early days of mission work through oral testimony and historical oration led by descendants of missionaries. Examples include the centennial of Hiram Bingham's birth in 1889; the fiftieth anniversary of Oahu College in 1891, originally Punahou School for the children of missionaries; and the rededication of Kawaiaha'o Church after refurbishment in 1895.[166] The broader associational culture of descendants of missionaries provided additional spaces for the affirmation of a shared heritage through oral testimony that blurred the lines between history and memory. The HHS, for example, relied on its members "to bring forth the stores of their experience" in order to generate discussion. The paper missionary son Rufus Lyman read at the society's 1894 annual meeting recounting his experiences of Kamehameha V's court during his time as a royal advisor is one example of the performance of "missionary" memory being institutionalized and labeled as history.[167]

This foregrounding of performative historical testimony suggests that a missionary community that wanted to lay claims to leadership in Hawai'i attempted to fashion a public identity based not only on their sense of racial superiority but also on a historical connection to the islands. There are even clearer examples of the efforts of descendants of missionaries to establish historical identities for themselves not simply as "missionaries" but as Hawaiians. At a so-called Great Reform Meeting prior to the imposition of the Bayonet Constitution on Kalākaua in 1887, missionary grandson Lorrin Thurston, a lawyer and key player in the annexation of the islands, announced himself in such terms: "I am here to speak as a Hawaiian. My ancestors came here in the reign of Kamehameha I. I was born and brought up here, and I mean to die here."[168] Thurston established his legitimacy not only in terms of his genealogy but also by linking that genealogy explicitly to the Hawaiian chiefly past: the only name he mentioned was that of Kamehameha, not any of his missionary ancestors. This was an attempt, admittedly crude, to imitate the forms of Native Hawaiian genealogical invocation, whereby "through verbal introduction, people attempt to see how close they can get to others, dead or living," in this case specifically to the most elevated of chiefly names.[169] Bishop established an imagined yet visceral connection between his ancestors and Kamehameha in one of his letters to the *Washington Evening Star*, noting that the first member of the mission to die in 1828 was buried "among the rugged lava rocks of Kailua but a few rods from the ruined walls of a house where died the old conqueror, Kamehameha."[170] Moreover, Bishop signed those letters under the pseudonym "Kamehameha," embarrassed to lend the name of a Christian minister to vitriolic political content but clearly believing that appropriation of the Native voice and in particular of the name of Hawai'i's first monarch might lend him authority, even to a US audience.[171]

With all this in mind, a remark Charles Hyde made in December 1886 when he took the minutes for a meeting of the Honolulu Social Science Association is telling. Following a paper on "Heredity" in which the question was raised about how far the children of missionaries inherited the characteristics of their ancestors, "family trees and pedigrees were still further discussed until it seemed there was some danger of the Association resolving itself into a Board of Genealogy had not the novelties of the host's cuisine diverted attention from Hawaiian antiquities."[172] Although this was clearly intended as a sarcastic comment, by tying a discussion of the heritage of descendants of missionaries to Native Hawaiian genealogical invocations and to "Hawaiian antiquities," Hyde suggested a recognition of the historical landscape the missionary community operated on and the desire of descendants of missionaries to conceive of themselves as both inheritors of the missionary project and claimants to a Hawaiian past.

Particular understandings of kinship came with these claims to Hawaiian identity. As chapter 1 showed, the creation of a missionary "family" in Hawai'i was less about direct lineage by blood and more about expansive definitions of inclusion based on shared acceptance of the parenthood of the first missionaries and a recognition of one another as cousins. Indeed, the Hawaiian Mission Children's Society was sometimes referred to as "the Cousins Society," because the missionary fathers had referred to each other as brothers.[173] These conceptions of kinship bore striking similarities to Native Hawaiians' competing claims to inheritance made through genealogical assertion. Just as "genealogy is a form of world enlargement" for Native Hawaiians, allowing for fluid definitions of connectivity that potentially encompasses all Pacific peoples, descendants of missionaries sought to expand their worlds through certain ideas of kinship.[174] They built up a community that might together claim inheritance of a morally superior version of Hawaiian identity, rooted in the mission past, against the potent collective claims of Indigenous people. In so doing, they accepted a definition of relation that, according to the anthropologist Jocelyn Linnekin, characterizes Native Hawaiian designations: "One can be called a relative whether or not there is a known genealogical tie, if one meets the behavioral expectations for a relative."[175] Descendants of missionaries were familiar with how Native Hawaiians established such kinship networks: several of them had been adopted by Hawaiian chiefs when they were young as *aliʻi* used the customary practice of *hānai* to cement a bond with the missionary community.[176] Although they had clearly rejected the reciprocal relationship this adoption entailed, descendants of missionaries continued to understand the importance of kinship in Hawaiʻi. This is not to suggest that the missionary community was respectful of Indigenous kinship practices. Indeed, missionary-inspired laws had been responsible for tying Native Hawaiians to white normative ideas about marriage, gender, and the family across the nineteenth century.[177] Having denigrated Indigenous practices, however, missionaries and their descendants were then free to cherry-pick the language that was most useful to them in their bid to supplant Native Hawaiians as the most legitimate claimants to the islands. Noenoe K. Silva suggests that Americans dismissed Indigenous genealogical claims to sovereignty because "rule by virtue of illustrious ancestors is anathema to the American discourse of democracy."[178] The missionary community, however, *were* keen to both expand their definitions of family beyond the biological and invoke their ancestral past as a source of legitimacy. Perhaps, after all, one historian provocatively suggests, they "were no less clannish than the Hawaiian *aliʻi*."[179]

The desperate attempts of descendants of missionaries to find historical roots in Hawaiʻi were emblematic of a tension that bled through Sereno Bishop's letters to the *Washington Evening Star*. Despite his strident assertions of Hawaiʻi's Americanism, Bishop's foremost concern was for the Hawaiian life that "missionaries" had established. Over the course of his correspondence, Bishop painted a picture of a Pacific where imperial powers came and went. Although he consistently appealed to US strategic interests against the British and Japanese empires, he also repeatedly combated American indecision about Hawaiian annexation with the threat that white settlers in the islands could just as easily turn to Britain as to the United States.[180] Hawaiʻi was the exceptional nucleus around which the vast Pacific revolved: "Hawaii, although minute in territory, occupies, as sole center, an enormous tract of ocean; and it has had the honor of contributing to history an unusual number of peculiar incidents."[181] Bishop was a US annexationist, but one who often seemed to see himself as Hawaiian first and foremost, betraying a world view that decentered the United States and remained comfortable with the Hawaiian past even as he appealed for an Americanized future. Although it might have been the case that newcomers to the islands perceived nothing but an American space, he argued, "we old settlers are more sensible of a difference."[182] Therefore, while imperialist narratives produced in the United States at this time represented Hawai'i and the Philippines as being brought smoothly into a US-centric vision of Pacific space and history, descendants of missionaries demonstrated that particular local ideas about history, kinship, and legitimacy could prove more salient to those on the ground. Narratives of Pacific dominance were of little use to white Americans born in Hawai'i who were trying to overcome anxieties about their perceived liminality and to instead leverage that sense of liminality as a basis for sovereignty. To understand this is to understand the importance of island spaces and their cultures within imperial and religious enterprises that often spoke in more grandiose terms about their historical purpose across continents and oceans.

The descendants of missionaries did not fully appreciate the richness and dynamism of Indigenous historical narration and genealogical traditions, and by no means did they altogether abandon written histories as carriers of truth and authority in narrating past events both distant and recent. Nonetheless, there are suggestions of the creativity of cultural encounter flowing in multiple directions as descendants of missionaries and Native Hawaiians responded to each other's attempts to mobilize history as a claim to religious and political sovereignty. Against this backdrop, Native Hawaiians deployed their genealogies using the written word and descendants of missionaries became peculiarly interested in memory, performance, and ancestry in ways that suggested that the Hawaiian setting was drawing out particular forms of historical narration. Although none of these ways of narrating history would have been entirely alien to Americans, there was a clear impulse on the part of the missionary community members, who had considered Hawai'i their home for two or three generations, to use ideas about the past and about kinship to establish themselves as sovereign on the basis that they were Hawaiians rather than just white Americans. "Missionaries" selected forms of historical narration that they felt most effectively allowed them to claim this identity and in so doing retained a sense of Hawai'i as an exceptional space and of themselves as an exceptional people, even as they successfully encouraged the arrival of US empire. In the process, they showcased a sense of liminality that certainly caused them anxiety but that they also at times emphasized in order to present themselves as ideal colonial rulers, not in a general sense but within the particular Pacific context of Hawai'i.

The next chapter shows how the missionary community once again reframed the religious past once they had achieved their political goal of annexation in 1898, this time in order to consolidate US authority in Hawai'i while encouraging tourism, business, and settlement. Here, "missionaries" styled themselves as brokers between a harmonious Hawaiian past and a frictionless Americanized future, publishing their memories and appropriating traditional Hawaiian narratives under the rubric of social science to style the islands as a place that white Americans had tamed but that was still exotic. As they portrayed this particular version of the mission past and Hawaiian history, their narratives betrayed an ambivalence about the transformation of the island world over which they had asserted sovereignty. Even in the aftermath of annexation and of the creation of a broader US Pacific empire, they manifested a sense of intellectual distance from the United States.

Chapter 3

"A Past That Is Often Noble"

Memory, "Unwritten Literature," and the Consolidation of an American Hawai'i

In February 1911, a debate erupted in Honolulu's *Pacific Commercial Advertiser*—traditionally the newspaper of the "missionary" establishment—over the propriety of *hula* performances that were to be staged at the Mid-Pacific Kirmess, a fund-raiser for the Pālama Settlement in Honolulu. Individuals closely connected with the Hawaiian Evangelical Association (HEA) had founded the Pālama Settlement in 1906 on the model of a Progressive Era settlement house. The project grew out of philanthropic work undertaken by the congregants of Pālama Chapel in an area of Honolulu that was largely populated by poor Chinese migrants and was blighted by disease, fire, and crowded tenement housing.[1] Predictably, given their responses to the *hula* performances King Kālakaua had sponsored prior to annexation, some descendants of missionaries expressed indignation at the idea that the dance might be employed in support of this "missionary" endeavor. Orramel Gulick fired the opening salvo, arguing that "hula is a word that can scarcely be spoken in good society."[2] A couple of days later, William De-Witt Alexander weighed in, agreeing that *hula* dances were "in the minds of most Hawaiians so closely associated with demoralizing accessories" that it was best "to leave them severely alone."[3]

In between the appearance of these two "missionary" opinions, Native Hawaiians wrote back. The Hawaiian Booth Committee, which was arranging the *hula* performances for the Kirmess, derided Gulick's "utter ignorance of the subject" and his interpretation, which derived from "intolerance and bigotry." The *hula*, argued the committee, was a tradition dating back "far beyond the knowledge of even a man so supposedly versed in Hawaiian history as is Mr. Gulick." Properly performed, it dealt "with events in the history of the Hawaiian people that occurred long before Mr. Gulick's ancestors ever came to the Hawaiian Islands" and was "a dignified dance that tells in words and gestures the story of certain historical events of old Hawaii."[4] Abraham K. Palekaluhi, an elderly Native Hawaiian born in 1830 to the high chiefess Liliha, added that the *hula* reenacted the "beauties of creation." He expressed his shock at Gulick's ignorance of Hawaiian language and culture and affirmed the consonance of the dance with Indigenous professions of Christianity: "We still adhere to the Ten Commandments, taught to our kings and queens by the good missionary fathers and mothers."[5]

Thus far, the battle fought in the *Advertiser* over the *hula* in the aftermath of annexation demonstrates continuity with contests over Native Hawaiian traditions of historical narration in the pre-annexation period, with Native Hawaiians asserting their gravity in the face of "missionary" denigration. However, the newspaper debates also suggested that some new dimensions were emerging. For a start, there were indications that Indigenous people were finding it increasingly difficult to uphold the integrity of their traditions of historical narration after annexation. The Hawaiian Booth Committee wrote that Gulick was saying "things that he would not have dared to say a few years ago." In other words, white settlers seemed to be increasingly free to lay claim to Hawaiian history and to denigrate Indigenous forms of narration without significant challenge. The Republic of Hawai'i's banning of the Hawaiian language in schools in 1896 no doubt had something to do with this sense that Indigenous people were increasingly unable to defend their traditional modes of understanding the past. Palekaluhi added that lamentably, there was an increasing amount of truth to what Gulick said about the *hula*'s immorality, thanks to its perversion in response to the demands of white visitors. Some Native Hawaiians were said to be making money out of performances that appealed to the "immoral lust" of tourists, suggesting in a different way that Indigenous people were increasingly unable to protect their traditions of historical narration from corruption by colonialism.[6]

At the same time, responses to the controversy in the *Advertiser* by descendants of missionaries other than Gulick and Alexander suggested that a new reaction to the *hula* was developing among some "missionaries" in a post-annexation age. William R. Castle Jr., a grandson of missionaries whose father had for a time represented the annexationist cause in Washington, argued that the *hula* was "interesting and free from harm—especially if looked at in an artistic and historical sense." Castle pointed readers to a recent book published by Nathaniel Emerson, the son of two missionaries, that he believed presented evidence to support this opinion.[7]

This chapter argues that in the post-annexation moment, descendants of missionaries took advantage of Native Hawaiians' increasing sense of alienation from their traditional modes of historical narration to invent a new historiographical turn that simultaneously underlined the exoticism and Americanness of the islands. Although the perspectives on the *hula* that Castle and Emerson articulated diverged from Gulick's and Alexander's obvious denigration of Hawaiian tradition, they were pernicious in a different way: they appropriated Indigenous customs under the guise of preserving a dying way of life, divorced these customs from their historiographical and political potency, and aestheticized Native Hawaiians and their culture in a way that presented the islands as a safe space for American settlement, business, and tourism. To entice white Americans after annexation and to smooth the path for Hawai'i to be fully incorporated into the United States, descendants of missionaries set aside the uncertainties about Hawai'i's Christianization they had expressed prior to 1898. They instead returned to the popular idea that Hawai'i had profoundly transformed since the arrival of missionaries, who had lifted the archipelago out of its alleged barbarism by working with friendly and welcoming locals. They also invoked Native Hawaiians and their traditional culture, sterilized and robbed of actual agency, to obscure the contested nature of Hawai'i's colonization and to offer a sense of continued otherness. This was clear in their public commemorations of mission history, their memoirs, and their social scientific studies of Indigenous traditions, including the *hula*. Under US rule, Hawai'i thus existed at the nexus between tradition and transformation, summoning and reinventing the past as much as it emphasized a new future. The missionary community that facilitated colonialism in Hawai'i did not "obliterate the past," as missionary son Samuel M. Damon had claimed that it wished to when it was overthrowing the monarchy, but continued to dwell upon the local and the historical.[8]

On the one hand, these post-annexation developments were emblematic of broader processes taking place across the parts of the Pacific under US rule as colonial authorities sought to style the islands under their control as American tropics ripe for both tourism and domination. In doing so, they drew on romanticized versions of history that emphasized the consent of local peoples. In the words of the scholar Vernadette Vicuña Gonzalez, "even as the fates of Hawai'i, Guam, and the Philippines were officially decided, . . . these colonial fictions continued to do the work of claiming these territories."[9] On the other hand, to create an image of an Americanized Hawai'i, descendants of missionaries once again mobilized a sense of their own liminality to style themselves as having deep-rooted expertise in a particular Pacific place that they had gleaned from multigenerational experience rather than just objective study of a new US possession. This sense of liminality was a double-edged sword. It could be a source of anxiety—as is particularly clear in this chapter's analysis of Nathaniel Emerson's studies of the *hula*—that led descendants of missionaries to suggest that they were not fully comfortable in either American or Indigenous intellectual traditions. Yet it was also central to their attempts to construct a colonial identity as people with an ability to mediate between US audiences and Hawaiian history. They drew on tropes of the strenuous imperial life and asserted their authority as white American scientists to render Hawai'i recognizable and appeal to fellow white Americans while also playing up the idiosyncratic nature of their knowledge and experience. To them, the most effective way of securing the future Hawai'i they wanted was not to assert the islands' place in a homogenized US Pacific but rather to lean into their own precarious positionality and point out what was particular about Hawai'i, its community of settlers, and its Indigenous people. Hawai'i was not a fait accompli after 1898. Through historical narrative, descendants of missionaries were still wrangling with the Indigenous and religious past and making claims for their own specialness in the context of a new US Pacific empire.[10]

Annexation and the Completion of Mission History

After the United States annexed Hawai'i in 1898, the missionary community's prior insistence that mission history in the archipelago remained incomplete gave way to a more positive outlook. Whereas evidence of Indigenous Christianity had to some extent been inconvenient for descendants of missionaries who wanted to underscore Native Hawaiian depravity and unfitness for self-government, annexation made Native Hawaiian Christians useful again. They could now become emblems of a harmonious and civilized multicultural community that was fit to be incorporated in the United States. As early as 1899, Sereno Bishop noted in his correspondence with a former resident of the islands that Hawai'i was "striding fast away from its past, into a great future."[11] In 1901, Oliver Emerson declared his confidence to the ABCFM that despite everything that had been said before, Native Hawaiian pastors were "doing a good work, such as white men would find it hard & perhaps impossible to do."[12] In 1906, Nathaniel Emerson reflected in *The*

Friend on the "tidal-wave of paganism" that had swept the islands in the late nineteenth century, but noted that such stories of a resurgent heathenism in Hawai'i's recent past seemed like "imaginative words" to readers in the post-annexation period, given the islands' rapid escape from this troubled history in the intervening years.[13]

This apparently clean break with the recent past also allowed Hawaiian history to be celebrated anew and without reservation in multiple public forums. In 1900, O. H. Gulick attended a major ecumenical conference on missions in Edinburgh and gave a speech outlining the remarkable historical changes in Hawai'i, celebrating its Christian influence across the Pacific.[14] Bishop authored a series of articles for the *Missionary Herald* in 1904 and 1905 that reiterated the "special providences in the Christianization of Hawaii," returning to a straightforward narrative of how Hawai'i had become a Christian nation.[15] The shifting landscape was also evident in new expressions of connection to Hawaiian history, notably in the 1903 establishment of the Daughters of Hawai'i, founded by seven daughters of early missionaries. Unlike the Hawaiian Mission Children's Society (HMCS) at its formation, the Daughters expressed little missionary impulse, instead declaring themselves guardians of "Hawaii's rich tradition" as embodied in its history, poetry, land, buildings, and relics. The founders declared their intention "to perpetuate the memory and spirit of old Hawai'i and of historic facts, and to preserve the nomenclature and correct pronunciation of the Hawaiian language."[16] Their existence indicated that Hawaiian history telling was entering a maternalistic realm of "deep sentiments" that claimed to "cherish" a fading culture, a departure from the narratives of the self-consciously masculine "missionary" spaces like the HEA, the HMCS, and the Hawaiian Historical Society (HHS) that often weaponized history to undermine Native Hawaiian claims to sovereignty.[17] Here we see a prime example of white women's particular forms of engagement with historical narration and its relationship to the colonial project. The Daughters of Hawai'i gained a platform for themselves to authoritatively discuss history by eschewing any academic or missionary purpose and instead presented themselves as sentimental guardians of the past of a land that they claimed to love. Yet in making these claims, they also played an important and pernicious role in the ongoing process of colonizing Hawai'i: they domesticated the practice of narrating Hawaiian history in a way that suggested it was no longer politicized or contested and could be treated as a curiosity. This was an act that attempted to silence Native Hawaiians who linked the narration of history so closely to their claims of sovereignty.

In another step of great symbolic significance, in 1907, the HMCS changed its constitution to become a "memorial society." Any sense that it was an active religious organization was left behind.[18] The reason given was that the HMCS's work as a benevolent society was rendered irrelevant by the existence of the HEA. However, those two organizations had overlapped in their advocacy of mission work for over half a century, suggesting that other factors explained the shift, in particular a feeling that after 1898 the legacy of the mission was secure and the work of the early missionaries could safely recede into memory. One of the reframed society's key activities was the establishment of a museum in the Honolulu houses built by the first ABCFM missionaries, which opened in 1923 and exists to this day.

Relations between the HEA and the ABCFM also shifted. In 1903, the ABCFM completely cut off the limited aid that it had offered over the previous decades. Hiram Bingham II, Oliver Emerson, and Orramel Gulick all argued that support from Boston was needed more than ever in the years after annexation, partly in response to an increasing shortfall in donations from the islands' missionary community. Gulick wrote that "the spirit of some of our men of wealth who have been generous givers for years past . . . seems now to have entered into an eclipse."[19] This shortfall in donations from the local community was indicative of the reason the remaining relationship between the ABCFM and the HEA was breaking down. It was sustained in the late nineteenth century by a feeling among the missionary community that Americans needed to atone for their abandonment of the missionary parents' project. Annexation had served as US atonement, so there was little to bind the two organizations any longer. Local enthusiasm failed, and although the ABCFM continued to offer positive assessments of the descendants of missionaries in the *Missionary Herald*, it no longer wished to support a community that had questionable evangelical credentials over whom further doubts were being raised, for example by Gulick's complaints in 1900 that some sons of missionaries proposed to buy up old mission property for nonreligious purposes.[20]

The fact that the handwringing of descendants of missionaries over the state of Hawaiian Christianity and governance in the late nineteenth century gave way to an unequivocal celebration of the mission past in the early decades of the twentieth century was nowhere more evident than in the events marking the centenary of the ABCFM mission, which lasted for over a week in April 1920. The multiple committees involved in planning the centennial were conspicuously populated by direct descendants of missionaries, including but not limited to members of the Castle, Damon, Dole, Emerson, Judd, and Thurston families, and thus the historical interpretation presented throughout the jubilee had "missionary" fingerprints all over it. The vision of the past was a harmonious one in which the ABCFM, other Christian groups, Native Hawaiians, and Asian immigrants had worked together to build up an "American" Hawai'i. Now, declared the centennial program, "the continuation of the work of our forefathers" rested not solely in the hands of the descendants of missionaries but in those of "the citizens of Hawaii, regardless of color, creed and parentage."[21]

Walter Frear, the son of a missionary, wrote in a commemorative volume that "the history of Hawaii is a great history in miniature" that over the course of a single century had exhibited "the problems and their solutions that have made up in large part the histories of great nations of centuries' growth." He reclaimed a familiar history in which whites and Native Hawaiians worked together to forge a "Christian nation . . . without violent shock" and "the two races soon found themselves akin in spirit and aim."[22] The "differences of the later monarchial years" were simply "by-gones"—the overthrow and annexation had removed barriers to both Christianity and pro-US sentiment, facilitating what the centennial volume referred to elsewhere as a "renaissance" in Hawaiian Christianity.[23] The Hawaiian antiquarian Thomas G. Thrum reinforced the idea of a successful interracial project of Christianization in an essay on the "native leaders of Hawaii" and "their contribution to . . . Christian civilization."[24] The Anglican bishop of Honolulu, Henry B. Restarick, wrote that although he deemed the Hawaiian mission to be ongoing, this was only in the sense that "it has gone out into the Islands of the Pacific" and "other far distant lands," not in the sense that Native Hawaiians required further evangelization.[25]

Restarick's celebration of the ABCFM's work also indicates that once the politicized antagonisms of the nineteenth century were put to bed by annexation and the political and social supremacy of the missionary community was assured, a sense of white Christian affinity across denominations developed that had been conspicuously absent in the pre-annexation era. Representatives from the Catholic and Anglican Churches and the Methodist Episcopal Church, which had commenced a small work in Hawai'i in the 1890s, contributed to the commemorative volume for the centennial, suggesting a shared history of Christian endeavor rather than separate and competing histories.[26] To further underscore this rapprochement, Restarick elsewhere described descendants of missionaries as "not decayed stock, but the backbone of the islands." He wrote his own sweeping history of Hawai'i in 1924 that told "the story of English and American churchmen."[27] In the late 1900s, Reginald Yzendoorn, the Dutch Catholic historian of Hawai'i, became an active member of the HHS, bringing tales of a Catholic past in the islands to a space that had previously been dominated by the voices of descendants of Protestant missionaries.[28]

The public performance of history was particularly conspicuous during the centennial. Although W. D. Alexander had derided Native Hawaiian performance of "so-called history" during Kalākaua's jubilees of the 1880s, at the centennial, descendants of missionaries fully embraced the connection between history and creative performance to consolidate their grip on narration of the past in a Hawai'i under US rule. Native Hawaiian ancestors, Indigenous dress, and "bizarre customs" of the kind that Alexander had loathed when they appeared in Kalākaua's processions were now appropriated and marshaled to lend vibrancy and a sense of collaboration in retelling the mission past, and Indigenous people were said to have acted as consultants. Given the vitriol the missionary community had directed at the alleged extravagance and wastefulness of Kalākaua's historical processions and tableaux, there was irony in their boasts about the "wealth of detail and elaborateness not limited by expense" in "picturing the old-time life of the native islanders and the missionaries," using the best "musicians, authors, playwrights, and historians" for the task.[29] It seemed that the missionary community saw historical performance as worth spending money on when it was oriented toward acceptable interpretations. A commission appointed by the governor of Hawai'i that consisted of missionary grandsons Alfred Castle, Clarence Cooke, and Lorrin Thurston lent the proceedings the imprimatur of the state, much as Kalākaua's jubilees had been state events.[30]

Historical performance at the centennial took many forms. Sermons were held on the "heritage of the past." A play written by missionary granddaughter Ethel Moseley Damon dramatized the story of the first Native Hawaiian convert, 'Ōpūkaha'ia, while another performed by "Oriental students" from Honolulu's Mid-Pacific Institute entitled *A Thousand Years Ago* recognized the East Asian historical cultures that immigrants had brought to the islands. On the centennial's Civic and Industrial Day, local businesses and associations sponsored parade floats that depicted historical scenes, including the arrival of the first missionary ship, Ka'ahumanu's acceptance of Christianity, and Kapi'olani's defiance of Pele. The appearance of the *lū'au* (traditional feast) and performances of Native Hawaiian chants on the program suggested that mission history and traditional Indigenous culture could sit comfortably side by side.[31]

The pièce de résistance was a grand historical pageant titled *One Hundred Years of Christian Civilization in Hawaii* that was performed on April 13 in the shadow of a giant cross erected in the dramatic environs of the Mānoa Valley on the fringes of Honolulu. The organizers boasted that it was "the biggest thing of the kind ever shown in the Islands," involving thousands of Indigenous and missionary-descendant men, women, and children. In eight tableaux vivants and a "mammoth" final procession, the participants rendered "the drama of their race's progress from the era of idol-worshipping to the present time of highly-ordered Christian living and civilization." The chiefs of "old Hawaii," with their costumes of "gorgeous coloring" and their "bizarre customs," burst forth "with their hordes of retainers and warriors, to hold court with all the splendor and pomp of bygone days."[32] White women were prominent in the planning of this event. As was the case with the Daughters of Hawai'i, this suggests that there was a new and important role for the missionary community's women in the post-annexation era. The pageant was an example of how they gained platforms for their creative talents by reinforcing the idea that the Hawaiian past was harmonious and could be domesticated. Ethel Moseley Damon was the pageant's chair and the author of its text, and Jane Lathrop Winne, great-granddaughter of the early missionaries Asa and Lucy Thurston, was responsible for the music. Despite the heavy presence of Native Hawaiian performers, there was no doubt that at heart this was a white settler enterprise. In the program, Damon expressed her debt of gratitude to "the historians"—not Native Hawaiians but Sheldon Dibble, W. D. Alexander, and other white authorities who had put pen to paper—and to the "sound learning and phenomenal memories" of Sanford Dole and Joseph Emerson. Winne asserted the pageant's place in a Western cultural canon by bookending proceedings with the music of Beethoven and Haydn, and the program situated the tableaux in the tradition of "ancient Greek drama."[33]

Pageantry certainly had a place in early twentieth-century US culture, not least among missionary women who dressed in ethnic costumes to teach audiences in the United States about foreign lands and to allow them to imagine a cosmopolitan global Protestant community.[34] Although the centennial pageant in Hawai'i was similarly authored by white, middle-class, Protestant women, it celebrated the local over the global. Anyone watching would have recognized that it was an attempt to co-opt Native Hawaiian cultural forms. Instead of "stage left" and "stage right," Damon self-consciously described in the program how she had used the Hawaiian orienting words *makai* (toward the sea) and *makua* (toward the mountains). The carefully choreographed movements of the performers and the poetic narration, which a chorus of 700 local schoolchildren chanted, clearly evoked the *hula*. Indeed, the cover of the pageant's program (figure 3.1), designed by Jessie Shaw Fisher, great-granddaughter of the first missionaries of the Bishop family, even depicted a *mele* singer performing as the chiefly and missionary ghosts of the past whose tales he sang rose behind him. Among the ghostly figures was the child of a missionary, thus placing descendants of missionaries at the center of a pivotal moment in Hawaiian historical narrative and further underscoring the intergenerational nature of the missionary project. Just as the Hawaiian Booth Committee for the Mid-Pacific Kirmess had asserted the dignity and gravity of the *hula*, the pageant's promoters declared the "simplicity and reverence" of their enterprise, a "lofty and dignified panorama of local history."[35]

Drawing Indigenous people and their cultures of historical narration into celebration of the mission's successes presented an apparently uncontested narration of Hawai'i's past through the lens of missionary-community values. This narrative rhetorically stripped Native Hawaiian culture of the political and spiritual power it had manifested in the pre-annexation period. It treated it as a benign curiosity and further nullified it by the assertion that it was dying out. A pamphlet that advertised the centennial claimed that although Indigenous customs could "be reproduced today," within a few years, they "[could] never be retold because the men and women familiar with them will have gone."[36]

Indeed, descendants of missionaries now styled themselves as the last defenders of Hawaiian heritage in a world that the United States was transforming. Writing in 1918, Orramel Hinckley Gulick and Ann Eliza Clark Gulick, husband and wife who were both children of missionaries, said that young Native Hawaiians under the tutelage of American schoolteachers "care very little and know still less" of "the famous names of Kamehameha, Kaahumanu, and Kapiolani."[37] Descendants of missionaries filled this vacuum with romanticized, exoticized, and decontextualized visions of Hawaiian history. In the process, they obscured the fact that it was the actions of their own community that had helped ensure exactly what the Gulicks purportedly lamented—the separation of Native Hawaiians from their history—by banning the teaching of the Hawaiian language and overriding oral tradition with school history textbooks. Sereno Bishop had been rather more candid about this fact prior to annexation when he offered a rebuttal to unnamed critics of the missionary community: "We have been bitterly accused of stealing [Native Hawaiians'] government. . . . They might with more truth charge us with robbing them of their language, which we are

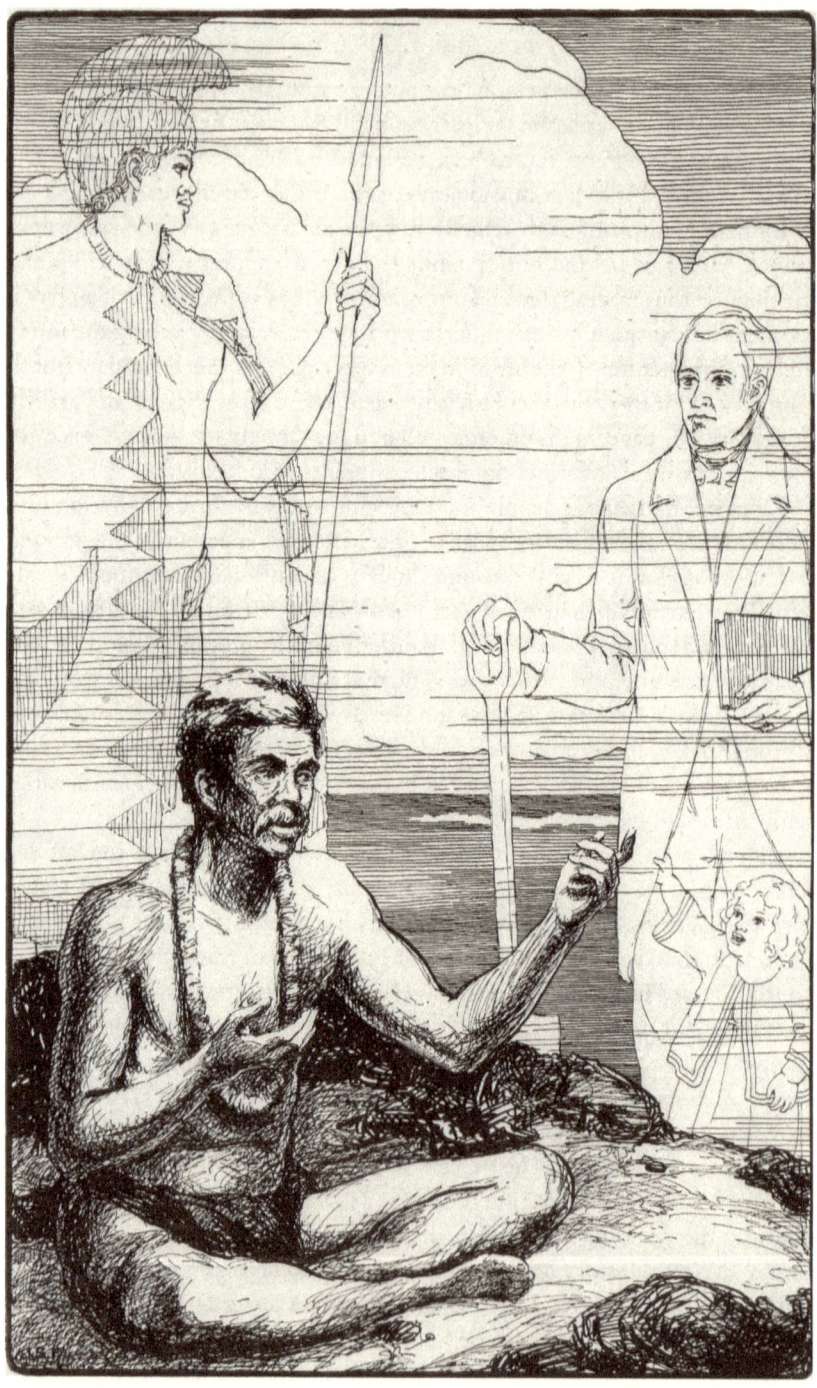

Figure 3.1. Image designed by Jessie Shaw Fisher to introduce the "historical pageant" *One Hundred Years of Christian Civilization in Hawaii*. *Source*: Hawaiian Mission Centennial, *Official Program for the Events of Centennial Week* (Honolulu: Centennial Committees, 1920), 15. Courtesy of The Burke Library at Union Theological Seminary, Columbia University Libraries.

really and rapidly doing."³⁸ Just as education proved a key tool for distancing Indigenous North Americans from their culture and assimilating them in the US body politic from the late nineteenth century onward, English-language education was a way of bringing young Native Hawaiians into an American conception of modernity.³⁹ Those who had most derided Indigenous culture swept in to lament its demise and claim ownership of it.

After annexation, the notions of Hawaiian history as harmonious and of Indigenous people and culture as present but thoroughly compliant were central to the image descendants of missionaries wanted to convey to US audiences of contemporary Hawai'i as a space for tourism, business, and settlement. This image took root in a series of memoirs published by Henry Lyman, William R. Castle Jr., Sereno Bishop, Orramel and Ann Gulick, and Oliver Emerson in the first three decades of the twentieth century. Like the centennial celebrations, these narratives remembered mission work as a complete enterprise that had rooted out all but the most agreeable elements of Native Hawaiian culture. In an overview chapter on nineteenth-century history, Castle presented a narrative of Christian progress, ending in annexation, in which even Kalākaua and Lili'uokalani received rehabilitative treatments.⁴⁰ Emerson, quoting another observer, wrote that "out of the turmoil and confusion of Hawaii's middle period has come the fascinating and helpful Hawaii of today. . . . The religious spirit has risen up . . . in a way worthy of the missionary pioneers."⁴¹ The Gulicks included a retrospective chapter that celebrated the transformative work of missionary "pilgrims" and ended their book with a lengthy section that asked the reader to visualize the scene they would have encountered in 1820 and the dramatic changes through the years.⁴² They retrospectively oriented themselves toward a celebration of "worthy, faithful" Native Hawaiian pastors and "illustrious pagan women," including in this frame not only the vaunted chiefesses of the early nineteenth century but also women of the late nineteenth century.⁴³ Such celebrations were reaffirmed in an introduction to the Gulicks' book by the long-serving ABCFM foreign secretary James L. Barton, who spoke of one of "the most romantic and even startling records in modern Christian history" and "a pagan people [who] have been transformed into a civilized Christian nation."⁴⁴

In these narratives descendants of missionaries wrote, laments for the physical and cultural death of the Hawaiian race in the face of white settlement ran up against memories of missionary childhoods that commonly featured imposing, noble, and brave islanders. As they sought to convince Americans that the islands were tame but also healthful, exotic, and strenuous, descendants of missionaries balanced a suggestion that Native Hawaiians were no longer a meaningful force in the islands with the perception that a vigorous and vibrant Indigenous culture could still be found. In the process, they asserted a very different role for Native Hawaiians than the one they had articulated prior to annexation. Despite the declarations that Hawai'i was striding away from its past into an Americanized future, memory and Indigenous histories became crucial to the creation of an American Hawai'i.

Memory, the Strenuous Life, and the Creation of an American Hawai'i

Although descendants of missionaries might not have recognized the subtleties of language and genealogical understanding Lili'uokalani employed in *Hawaii's Story by Hawaii's Queen*, several of them, like her, settled on the memoir form as the best way of setting out their vision of history. As it did for Lili'uokalani, the form of the memoir, rather than documentary history, offered descendants of missionaries the possibility of managing a cultural gap, in their case between their intimate knowledge of the islands they had grown up in and their status as Christian, "civilized" Americans who had apparently tamed Hawai'i and could impose further order on it through writing. The scholar Lydia Kualapai has noted that Lili'uokalani's text "preserves the ancestral link fundamental to Hawaiian identity and denounces the colonial attempt to appropriate and reconstitute 'Hawaiian' subjectivity."[45] The missionary memoirs that asserted their intimate knowledge of the islands constituted their counterclaim to that subjectivity. Moreover, laying aside documentary evidence and relying on memory allowed for a rewriting of history. What the historian Joy Schulz calls "the pleasant musings of aging memoirists" about a collaborative effort between "noble" Native Hawaiians and missionaries easily elided the denigrating comments about Indigenous people found in the discourse of descendants of missionaries prior to annexation.[46]

The children and grandchildren of missionaries used their recollections to meet the demand of tourists and new settlers for historical information about the islands, as Lorrin Thurston suggested in his introduction to Sereno Bishop's *Reminiscences of Old Hawaii* (1916), which was published seven years after Bishop's death. Bishop originally wrote this book, which collected snapshots of Hawaiian life in the mid-nineteenth century, in 1901 and 1902 for publication in *The Friend*. Introducing the collection, Thurston promised that the reader would encounter "lucid and almost photographic representations of the daily life and conditions existing in Hawaii." Although at that time, there was no comprehensive history of Hawai'i based on documentary evidence, Thurston suggested that "the best method of meeting the present public desire for information is to collect and publish the personal memoirs, reminiscences and writings of some of the older residents."[47] This privileging of memory over documentary history suggested that the Hawaiian past was best known not through written sources but through the memories of a man who was a direct conduit to the early days of mission work, even if some of those memories dated back to when he would have been a very young child. Indeed, Bishop himself had dismissed the possibility of compiling a history based on documents, eschewing the tradition of Hiram Bingham and W. D. Alexander in favor of recording his memories.[48]

Even when descendants of missionaries used a wider variety of sources, they privileged memory and personal experience. In *Hawaii: Past and Present* (1914), which missionary grandson William R. Castle Jr. wrote "to tell those who stay at home [in the United States] something about Hawaii" and "to help those who are going there," Castle emphasized that all information in the book had been "checked by my own personal knowledge" and that he had tried "to keep myself in mind so far as to tell things as I myself had seen them."[49] By referring to the United States as "at home," Castle asserted his affinity with his intended US audience and grounded his knowledge as being "American," but he also set that knowledge apart by tying it specifically to experience of Hawai'i. "There is no way to get any permanent impression of the charm of Hawaii except by a visit," he said. It was true that one could read history books and emerge with the sense that "thoroughly American ideals pervade all phases" of island life, but "the Hawaiian flavour" that "subtly impregnated" those ideals, emanating from "the misty hills, the whispering waters, the exquisite vegetation, the low voices of the people" could be grasped "only through the senses. Only this is full knowledge—and the sense of this no words can convey." By contrasting the value of written history with direct experience of the Hawaiian landscape, Castle not only promoted Hawaiian tourism but also established legitimacy for his own interpretation of Hawaiian affairs by showing that it derived from personal encounter. Castle moreover linked this to an Indigenous mode of knowing, arguing that Native Hawaiians had never traditionally felt the need to relate to the land through writing and that settlers and tourists too needed to embrace that way of understanding.[50] In other words, albeit in a romanticized and racialized fashion, Castle validated his observations in a manner resonant with the Indigenous perspective outlined by the Native Hawaiian scholar Haunani-Kay Trask, whereby historians must "put down their books" and "understand the land."⁵¹

The figure of a robust, vigorous Native Hawaiian also came to the fore as descendants of missionaries sought to hitch the missionary story in Hawai'i and ultimately the act of annexation to a broader imperialist mythology that was popular in the United States after 1898 that suggested that Americans' masculinity and nationhood were forged, in the words of Theodore Roosevelt, through "danger, . . . hardship, . . . [and] bitter toil" in dealings with Indigenous peoples and rugged "frontier" environments across the continent and overseas.⁵² Introducing Bishop's *Reminiscences*, Lorrin Thurston invoked Roosevelt, promising that the reader would gain from Bishop's recollections a sense of the "strenuous life" of the early missionaries.⁵³ Native Hawaiians themselves were emblematic of the strenuous world of the Hawaiian past; one detailed passage described Indigenous surfers as vigorous masters of nature.⁵⁴ Bishop admitted that "the great crowd of common people were miserably lean, and often very squalid," but he drew more attention to the upper class.⁵⁵ Corpulence was a sign of status in Hawai'i in the late eighteenth and early nineteenth centuries, and Bishop remembered Kuakini, the governor of Hawai'i island, as "an enormous man of great stature" who oversaw the building of a large church at Kailua using "immense timbers cut and dragged from the great interior forest."⁵⁶ Elsewhere, he described Keli'iahonui, a chief at Ewa on O'ahu, as "conspicuous for his stature and personal beauty" and the premier Kīna'u as "a tall and portly chiefess, weighing from 250 to 300 pounds."⁵⁷ The strenuous life in Hawai'i was not characterized by overt violence and thus diverged from the representations of frontiersmen and Native Americans that were popular in the early twentieth-century United States.⁵⁸ Nonetheless, Bishop emphasized that missionaries could physically hold their own and keep their Indigenous proselytes in check. They "enjoyed vigorous health, and labored hard" and were not intimidated by Native Hawaiian corpulence. Bishop recalled an instance when "Kuakini suffered a relapse into idol-worship, and . . . Father Thurston descended on the formidable old chief, and berated him with such severity that he submitted and repented."⁵⁹

As Thurston asserted Hawai'i's place in Roosevelt's strenuous imperial world, he pushed the image of depravity and dilapidation presented in one of Bishop's previous publications—the pamphlet *Why Are the Hawaiians Dying Out?*—into the background. The pamphlet was based on a speech Bishop gave to the Honolulu Social Science Association and was published in 1888, almost thirty years before his *Reminiscences*. It is uncertain how far Bishop was genuinely concerned for the reinvigoration of the Native Hawaiian population. His vocal support for supplanting the Hawaiian monarchy with US empire suggests that his goals were best served by the disappearance of Indigenous people. Whatever his intentions, Bishop used the issue of Hawaiian depopulation as a springboard for airing grievances about Indigenous sexual and religious practices. Drawing heavily on well-known settler-colonial tropes, he painted a sorry picture of an unchaste people who were ravaged by venereal disease and alcohol and were overreliant on superstition. Unless they assimilated to the model of the Christian family, their eradication was inevitable.[60] The contrast between Bishop's celebration of the Native Hawaiian body in his *Reminiscences* and his portrait in *Why Are the Hawaiians Dying Out?* suggests that different representations could be used for different purposes before and after annexation. Specifically, the idea of a vigorous and noble Indigenous people tamed by the endeavor of white men from the United States appealed to romantic ideas of pioneering across frontiers on the continent and overseas of the early twentieth century and invited further settlers and tourists to participate.

Ten years earlier, missionary son Henry Lyman had published a book entitled *Hawaiian Yesterdays* in which, amid his memories of the piety of the early missionaries and the strenuousness of missionary childhood, he too emphasized the physical strength of Native Hawaiians. Like Bishop, he remembered the dignity of "uncommonly tall and corpulent Hawaiian royals," but he also recalled the prowess of the *maka'āinana* (commoners), conjuring images of powerful Native Hawaiians carrying him and his mother on their shoulders across uplands and of Native Hawaiian boys performing death-defying feats while playing under a waterfall.[61] Orramel and Ann Gulick's volume not only reproduced the journals of the first missionaries to Hawai'i, likening them to the *Mayflower* pilgrims who sailed to the United States 200 years before, but also included stories based on Orramel's recollections.[62] These too documented the Christian fortitude and heroic physical feats of the *maka'āinana*, one of whom had saved the life of Orramel's younger brother Thomas when his canoe overturned. This suggests that in the Gulicks' memory, Native Hawaiians were associated with physical vigor, piety, friendship, and selflessness rather than the moral turpitude and pathetic frailty suggested in Bishop's pamphlet on Indigenous death.[63] Such descriptions were also evident deep into the 1920s in Oliver Emerson's *Pioneer Days in Hawaii* (1928). Emerson narrated a history in which "finely formed, statuesque Hawaiians with their tanned skin, straight black hair and friendly eyes" met "sturdy and devoted men and women . . . from New England" in an encounter described as a "romance."[64] From his childhood memories, Emerson told his readers of Indigenous "physical vigor and fearlessness," recounting feats of strength, agility, and skill, noting that Native Hawaiians were "sturdy, . . . lived abstemiously," had "keen . . . intelligence," and labored hard under "chiefish rule."[65]

As descendants of missionaries offered their recollections to US audiences, they tantalized with the possibility that although Hawai'i had been made comfortable for business, settlement, and tourism, the noble Native Hawaiian past that descendants of missionaries remembered had not passed away altogether. This was an important case to make because some travel writers asserted that "the average tourist anticipates entirely too much" of the exotic in Hawai'i and might find themselves disappointed by the degree to which "civilization" had reached the islands.[66] It moreover served as an implicit riposte to the continued suggestions of prominent figures in the United States that missionaries were in fact responsible for the decrepitude of Indigenous life and land, for example because they had forbidden Native Hawaiians to work on Sundays. Psychologist G. Stanley Hall made such an argument in the *Boston Journal* in October 1902.[67]

The idea that the past could still be found in the present was given a particularly interesting treatment in Castle's book. The ongoing power of Indigenous traditions of historical narration haunted his work even as he rhetorically dismissed them as bygone modes of knowing: "Early Hawaiian history is entirely legendary. There was no written language. . . . The history, therefore, can be traced only through ancient 'meles' or songs . . . which were handed down orally for many generations."[68] Even though he wrote off Hawaiian tradition as "entirely legendary," Castle immediately fell back on it as his only source for a *longue durée* history. The Gulicks similarly ran into problems when they tried to dismiss Indigenous oral traditions, arguing that "a people who have no written language can have no history in our sense of the word" and that "the recorded history of Hawaii can only begin with the work of the missionaries," but straightaway going on to say that "we may learn something of the life, customs, and history of the ancient Hawaiians from their legends, and chanted rehearsals or songs."[69] Like Bingham and Alexander before them, Castle and the Gulicks wished to distinguish between recorded history and Hawaiian tradition but could not overcome their reliance on Indigenous knowledge to do this effectively. This was one sense in which Native Hawaiian pasts and Indigenous modes of historical narration became crucial to the story that Castle sought to tell in the supposedly Americanized present.

Moreover, while Castle rhetorically bought into the notion of the dying race, at the same time, for aesthetic reasons he was keen to show the traveler in vivid detail that what he had seemingly written off as past could still be found. Having assured Americans that "most of the primitive Hawaiian life has disappeared for ever" and that Hawai'i was more "sophisticated" than it had been when his ancestors arrived, Castle immediately launched into a description laden with color and sound that suggested the conspicuous continuation of that "primitive" life. He noted that Native Hawaiians had "kept their simplicity of manner" and "many of the customs so deeply rooted in their nature," for example a "love of colour" that was "ineradicable." Fishermen still clung "to the picturesque but heavy dug-out canoe with its huge outrigger of lighter wood," and on the death of a chief "the ancient wailing makes nights and days tragically musical."[70] Castle made this juxtaposition again in a heavily exoticized description of Indigenous physicality. Having noted the "sad" disappearance of "beautiful" Native Hawaiians—"a people with a past that is often noble"—Castle immediately reverted to the present tense and assured the potential visitor that "physically admirable, tall, well-formed" Native Hawaiians "with high foreheads, good features, deep chests, slender limbs" were still there to be admired. "Nothing could be more physically beautiful," continued Castle, "than a Hawaiian fisherman, naked except for his loin cloth[,] . . . reminiscent of some Greek bronze or an athlete stripped for the games."[71] Surfing, dancing, music, and the *lū'au* all remained "to recall the ancient times," and some houses and settlements conveyed the tourist away from "civilisation" to the world of Indigenous "ancestors hundreds of years ago."[72]

Castle also sought to bring the past into the present in his description of Native Hawaiian history as etched into the landscape. This was particularly evident in his description of Kualoa Point on O'ahu, which "stirred" him to believe the Hawaiian legend that on one night each year, Kamehameha "marches with his ghostly army along the face of these hills and that all those who see the glimmer of the spears in the moonlight and who hear the trampling of the feet must surely die."[73] This was one of several moments in Castle's work when he tied particular locations to "ancient" battles and legends of "gods and demigods."[74] Although Castle noted that physical structures had fallen to ruin, including ancient *heiaus* (temples) and some of the old mission buildings, for him the past remained visible on the landscape through an act of imagination.[75] In this sense, he appropriated a Native Hawaiian understanding of how the past was inextricably linked to specific places in order to play into Americans' romantic vision of Hawai'i.[76]

The invocation of a vigorous Native Hawaiian past in the early twentieth century demonstrated a tension at the heart of the US colonial project between two divergent representations of Hawai'i. On the one hand, the annexation of the islands in 1898 broke with Hawai'i's Indigenous past, placing the archipelago as a strategic space between North America and Asia. Not only was it physically located in the middle of the Pacific but it was also a meeting point of different peoples: after 1898, Chinese, Japanese, and Portuguese laborers who had flooded into the islands to work for American businesses prior to annexation were increasingly joined by Koreans, as well as Filipinos, and Puerto Ricans who forged new patterns of mobility across the US empire.[77] Accordingly, descendants of missionaries suggested that they foresaw the problems of the twentieth century not as involving Native Hawaiians but as arising from the clustering of diverse races in an island space.[78] It has been easy for historians too to assume that Native Hawaiians simply faded from the story after 1898, reflecting a "dying race" hypothesis in the same way that Margaret Jacobs suggests scholars of the twentieth-century United States have when treating Native North Americans.[79]

On the other hand, the reflections of descendants of missionaries writing in the early twentieth century about the nineteenth century suggest that a romanticized old Hawai'i populated by courageous missionaries and larger-than-life Native Hawaiian characters retained real currency in their attempts to style the islands as a healthful, vigorous space where Americans could visit, live, and do business. Turning away from their ancestors' straightforward condemnation of Indigenous religious and cultural practice, descendants of missionaries complemented the work of the Hawaii Promotion Committee, founded in 1903, which restored *heiaus* and marketed surfing, co-opting the Indigenous past as a decontextualized aesthetic for tourists to consume.[80] The children and grandchildren of missionaries had been involved in enticing tourists and settlers at least since Henry Martyn Whitney, the son of two missionaries, wrote a guidebook in the 1870s that evidenced some similar tropes in small measure.[81] Bishop's letters to the *Washington Evening Star* had also tantalized with descriptions of surfing, volcanoes, elaborate *lū'au*, and a salubrious climate. These letters were precursors to his 1903 pamphlet for the Hawaii Promotion Committee, *Scenery in Hawaii*.[82] Lorrin Thurston had promoted volcano tourism at Chicago's Columbian Exposition in 1893.[83] After annexation, publications aimed at mainland US audiences were both more numerous and more effusive in their presentation of the strenuous, exotic, and authentic in the safe, cosmopolitan space of Hawai'i.

Despite their apparent attempts to will Native Hawaiians out of existence, white Americans needed their presence in history and culture to construct Hawai'i as a tamed yet exhilarating space belonging to the United States. Therefore, after annexation they turned away from attempting to persuade

US audiences of Native Hawaiians' dangerous inability to fully escape their heathen past and toward nostalgic narratives that created the impression that an exotic way of life could still be found in the islands. Although this was another form of silencing Native Hawaiians and objectifying them as noble savages, the romanticized appropriation of the past and of Indigenous stories undercuts notions that US Pacific ascendancy was founded on a cohesive vision of the ocean rooted in ideas about inexorable historical progress. In fact, the risk for descendants of missionaries in engaging with ideas about history with Hawaiian inflections, even when attempting to assert authority over them and override them, was the fragmentation of the white Christian self—a theme that emerges particularly strongly when looking at the appropriation of Hawaiian traditional narratives by one son of missionaries.

Nathaniel Emerson and the Classification of Hawaiian Tradition

Nathaniel Bright Emerson was born in 1839 in Waialua on the island of Oʻahu to John S. and Ursula Emerson, who had arrived in Hawaiʻi as missionaries in 1832. Educated first at Punahou, the school for the children of missionaries, Emerson continued his studies at Williams College in Massachusetts, where he was when the Civil War broke out. Serving in the Union Army, he sustained minor wounds at both Fredericksburg and Chancellorsville and saw action at Gettysburg. After he graduated from Williams, he trained as a medic at Harvard and in New York, where he worked as a doctor. He returned to Hawaiʻi in 1878 as general inspector of leper stations, then took up the presidency of the Hawaiian Board of Health in 1887.[84]

Emerson's greatest passion was for Indigenous tradition, stimulated by his parents' lack of concern about their children's contact with Native Hawaiians compared to most missionaries and their close relationships with experts in Indigenous lore, in particular the religious specialist Hewahewa. Emerson pursued his interest with vigor from the end of his tenure as president of the Board of Health in 1890 until his death in 1915. He worked as a private physician and then as a police surgeon, an occupation that brought him into contact with many potential Native Hawaiian informants. From 1898 to 1904, he served as president of the HHS.[85] He keenly collected folklore, asserting the need to commit fragments of oral tradition to paper before "civilization" transformed Indigenous culture beyond recognition or disease rendered Native Hawaiians extinct—a state of affairs with which, as a medical practitioner, Emerson was only too familiar.[86] Emerson published three major works on tradition, beginning with a translation of David Malo's *Ka Moʻolelo Hawaiʻi*, which was completed in 1898 and printed in 1903 under the title *Hawaiian Antiquities*.[87] Next came *Unwritten Literature of Hawaii: The Sacred Songs of the Hula* (1909), and then, shortly before his death, *Pele and Hiiaka: A Myth from Hawaii* (1915).

On the one hand, Emerson styled himself as an inheritor of his parents' faith and of their project to Christianize the islands. We have already encountered him advocating further mission work among Native Hawaiians as chair of the joint Committee on Hawaiian Evangelization of the HEA and the HMCS, defending the traditions of the ABCFM mission against newcomers from the United States, condemning the "voluptuous obscenities" of the *hula* performances at Kalākaua's coronation, and contributing to *The Friend*. He was also president of the HMCS for 1883–84 and 1891–92. In one letter to fellow missionary son Titus Munson Coan, Emerson stated that he had inherited the essence of his forebears' orthodoxies and had not found anything to replace "the God that I was taught to look up to, pray to, reverence and adore in my early days."[88]

On the other hand, Emerson's appreciation of Hawaiian tradition set him apart from his parents' generation. He noted this separation with reference to Sheldon Dibble, the missionary who first encouraged David Malo to gather and preserve Hawaiian traditional narratives while teaching him at Lahainaluna Seminary on Maui in the 1830s. In *Hawaiian Antiquities*, Emerson praised the broad-mindedness of Malo's teachers in encouraging him to record Indigenous traditions and suggested that the final work would have been better had Malo been supervised more closely. Elsewhere, however, Emerson branded Dibble "an enthusiast," claiming he had not truly valued folklore and only wished "to push the cause of American Missions."[89] He "utterly failed to penetrate the mystery" of "the Hawaiian mind and heart" due to his "false theology."[90] Emerson also expressed ambivalence about the transformations that his ancestors had brought about. Not only might the indiscriminate stripping away of any "primitive" knowledge of the divine "sink the . . . heathen" into "atheism," but Emerson also believed that in any case "it is a great wrong when a nation is at one stroke cut off from its past. . . . It is a mistake . . . not to hold on to the old lore of a people."[91] He reiterated this regret in introducing his translation of Malo, whose embrace of Christianity had caused him "to confound together . . . the harmless and depraved," to the "vain regret" of the contemporary student.[92] Emerson lamented that to Native Hawaiians in the

"American" present, the gods of the ancestors were "little more than vagrant ghosts" and felt that it was his duty to fill the vacuum left behind.[93]

Emerson's interest was particularly piqued by what he saw as the poetic expression of Native Hawaiians' relationship with the landscape in which Emerson grew up. In one essay draft, Emerson declared Hawaiian traditional narratives to be "saturated . . . with the salt air of the Great Ocean" and to be "thrilled by the changeful breath of its land-and-sea breezes, redolent of its perfumed mountains and rustling palms, tuneful with the warble and tinkle of its streams, ever reminiscent of the glory and awe of its volcanic mysteries."[94] Emerson wrote that it would "have been surprising indeed if such a people, under the influence of such an environment, had made no emotional utterance in response."[95] Emerson was fascinated by the Native Hawaiian conception of the ocean as a space of connectivity and by the ingenuity of Polynesians navigating the ocean by canoe using the stars. This had allowed them to hunt, migrate, and forge alliances across the "trackless prairie" of the Pacific over the centuries—a feat that some scholars doubted until well into the twentieth century.[96]

Emerson's appreciation of Indigenous tradition was connected to his contempt for modern life. On one occasion, he told W. C. Morrow, the San Francisco writer who helped Emerson revise his manuscripts, that "there is no city in this world I would accept as a gift, if the condition of my ownership was that I should live in it." Elsewhere, he linked "the growth of insanity" to the "lack of harmony between man and his environment" generated by modernity. Strikingly, he condemned prudish contemporary approaches to sex education, advocating instead the familiarity with the bodies of the opposite sex engendered in Native Hawaiians from a young age as a better way of fostering sexual morality.[97] Emerson stated that "only a few generations ago, we, in our ancestors, were as degraded as the savages of today," suggesting a stadial idea of societal and religious development that was at odds with the inherited tendency of the missionary community to dismiss Indigenous culture as idolatrous, heathen, or pagan. With this in mind, he asked whether it could truly be said that Anglo-Saxon nature was better than that of the Polynesian and spoke for the value of the knowledge of the "man on the sand-spit" to science and art.[98] After all, wrote Emerson, defending Native Hawaiian culture to his relatives, "God made the Hawaiian, and is therefore logically . . . responsible for them and their productions."[99] Most tellingly, Emerson confided to one correspondent that during his studies he had "been ready at times to exclaim with Wordsworth: 'Great God! I'd rather be a pagan.'"[100]

Nonetheless, though he was still wavering on the question as late as 1891, Emerson had become a fervent supporter of the overthrow of the Indigenous monarchy by 1893, making callous, racist statements about Native Hawaiians.[101] He argued that it was pointless to allow the Indigenous population a democratic voice on the question of annexation because "they are a short sighted set of children and will vote according to the instructions of the last plausible demagogue who addressed them."[102] Condemning Liliʻuokalani for exhibiting facets of the very paganism with which he elsewhere claimed great sympathy, he railed against "the disastrous failure of Hawaii's experiment at self government," argued that the building up of Hawaiʻi had been possible only because of the influence of the "white man," and concluded that the "ignorance of a child is no excuse for injustice, but it is good reason why the driving reins should be taken from its hand."[103]

Given these views, we might understand Emerson's writings on Indigenous tradition as intimately linked to the project of the descendants of missionaries to consolidate white settler rule. An analysis of how Emerson classified the material he gathered provides evidence. Although he privately acknowledged the difficulty of taxonomizing Native Hawaiian folklore because of the intertwining of mythological, traditional, and genealogical elements in each account, by the time his second book was published in 1909, Emerson had settled on the catchall term "unwritten literature."[104] Explaining this decision to Morrow, he wrote that while the "songs, poetical pieces, prayers and eulogies" he had collected and translated were not "worthy to be ranked in the same category with the volumes of the world's literature," they represented "the best attainment of the Hawaiian mind."[105] These attainments were made within the confines of a language that Emerson said lacked a "power of definition" and was unable to adequately express abstract ideas or cause and effect.[106] Although he appreciated that much meaning was conveyed in Indigenous oral tradition through nonverbal means, his ultimate assessment of the worth of the Hawaiian language and its narratives was based on their adaptability to "artistic form and literary unity," and here he found them deficient.[107] In *Unwritten Literature of Hawaii*, Emerson thus reduced what he referred to in his subtitle as "the sacred songs of the hula" to "unwritten literature"—the best poetry that the Native Hawaiian imagination, with all its limitations, could muster. In so doing, Emerson glossed over the profound historiographical (and therefore political) implications of the *hula* and the *mele* that accompanied it, which were evident in Kalākaua's performances before annexation and in the words of Native Hawaiians who wrote to the *Pacific Commercial Advertiser* that were quoted at the beginning of this chapter.

To some extent, Emerson acknowledged that history was bound up in the traditions he collected. Early in *Unwritten Literature*, he noted that the *hula* was a method by which "the race maintained vital connection with its mysterious past."[108] He asked in his conclusion whether the imagery in Hawaiian tradition might be derived from "vague memories of things which long ago passed from sight and knowledge."[109] In some of his earliest engagements with Hawaiian tradition, he had appreciated that "the principal data which we possess for fixing the dates of events" were "genealogies handed down from one keeper to another" that represented "a tolerable approach to the truth of history."[110] In *The Long Voyages of the Ancient Hawaiians* (1893), which he first read at a meeting of the HHS and subsequently published, Emerson read genealogical tales as evidence for twelfth- and thirteenth-century history, furnishing information about a world of Polynesian mobility that clearly enthralled him. In *Unwritten Literature*, however, any such treatment of tradition as historiography was buried under Emerson's concern with "what emotions stirred the heart of the old-time Hawaiian" and explanations of how "the poetry of ancient Hawaii evinces a deep and genuine love of nature, and a minute, affectionate, and untiring observation of her moods."[111] Although he briefly recognized that *hula* composition could be a matter of gravity undertaken by conclave in royal courts, "the great majority of songs," he wrote, were "the fruit of solitary inspiration, in which the bard poured out his heart like a song-bird."[112]

Emerson did not hide his cultural relativism in *Unwritten Literature*, and his concluding chapter was particularly saturated with it. Comparing contemporary Native Hawaiians with "our own race two or three centuries ago," he suggested that the former were no more superstitious, "absurd and illogical" in their cosmogony, inhumane in their theology, or unrestrained in their morals than the latter.[113] However, he saw virtue inscribed only in the *hula* of the distant past—ironically, the same form his missionary forebears had prohibited. He criticized Kalākaua's revival for its "riotous and passionate ebullitions," performed by those "to whom the real meaning of the old bards is ofttimes a sealed casket"; hence his condemnation of the *hula*'s "voluptuous obscenities" at the king's coronation.[114] It had always, stated Emerson, been "in times of royal debasement" that there was "the loudest poetic insistence on birth-rank" and "the most frenzied utterance of high-sounding titles."[115] Emerson thus presented himself as the guardian of the *hula*'s true meaning: it had no historiographical or political value as Kalākaua insisted, but its sacred and poetical dimensions could be salvaged.

For contrast, we might consider the work of Abraham Fornander. Fornander was born in Sweden but left his home country for the United States in the early 1830s. He left Massachusetts on a whaleship in 1841 and eventually settled in Hawai'i in 1844. He became a judge and a government minister who was known for his loyalty to the monarchy and married Alanakapu Kauapinao, a chiefly woman of illustrious descent. His three-volume *An Account of the Polynesian Race*, published in the 1870s and 1880s prior to his death in 1887, sought to draw out the historical value of Polynesian traditional accounts.[116] There were flaws in this approach also: Fornander's determination to absorb genealogy into history wrongly equated genealogy with chronology and overlooked the dynamism and politicization of genealogical narratives. *An Account of the Polynesian Race* might thus be read as just another way of claiming white settler authority over Indigenous traditions at the expense of Indigenous understandings.[117] But contrasting Emerson's emphasis with Fornander's recognition of the historical potential in traditional accounts reveals that some scholars of the late nineteenth century engaged seriously with tradition as history and that Emerson chose a different approach.

The relationship between the missionary community and Fornander was complex. Fornander was critical of missionaries, accusing them of ultimate responsibility for the slow death of Hawaiian culture and of preventing the free circulation of knowledge by controlling the press.[118] Yet the HHS, dominated by descendants of missionaries and their allies, celebrated Fornander's life at their annual meeting in 1907, Emerson and Charles Hyde expressed their admiration for his work, and W. D. Alexander cited him as a key source for his *Brief History*.[119] Fornander in turn cited Dibble and Alexander among his sources.[120] In other words, Fornander and a number of descendants of missionaries consciously existed in the same networks of knowledge production. In particular, they all saw themselves as engaged in a transoceanic work of salvage ethnology among a dying race. Echoing Fornander's claim in the late 1870s that "each year is fearfully diminishing the chances" of collecting Polynesian tales, the HHS continued after Hawai'i's annexation to stress the importance of "getting on record every scrap of folk lore that is obtainable before it is too late."[121] They sought dialogue with others doing the same work across the Pacific, looking to New Zealand's ethnologists in particular as furnishing an exemplary model of industrious preservation work that was deemed all the more urgent in "the rush and glare of the Twentieth

Century."[122] This was another sense in which descendants of missionaries were drawn into looking at the Pacific from the perspective of an interconnected island world rather than from the perspective of the United States.

Emerson certainly situated himself in this world of scholarship as a member of the Polynesian Society who collected artifacts and acknowledged ethnological work from across the Pacific. He exchanged ideas not only with Fornander but also with S. Percy Smith, the leading New Zealand ethnologist.[123] Emerson's stadial conceptualization of societal and religious development also chimed with the findings of early Christian humanist ethnographers and theorists of social evolution such as E. B. Tylor and James Frazer. For these men, in the words of the scholar Christine Weir, the non-European world appeared to be "a living museum of the history of present-day Western society."[124] However, whereas the ethnologists Emerson corresponded with viewed questions of history and chronology as the most interesting ones to arise from Polynesian tradition, Emerson saw these traditions through the lens of literature. He acknowledged this deviation from his contemporaries: "I would not claim that nobody has ever set foot in this territory, but . . . any diligent effort to explore it from a literary point of view, I doubt. . . . My friend Fornander['s] . . . point of view was almost purely historical."[125]

Emerson was perhaps not wrong to suggest that history was just one of many elements woven into Hawaiian tradition. However, his chosen emphasis was significant given the contested terrain of history in Hawai'i, where its narration in the Indigenous voice constituted a claim to sovereignty. As descendants of missionaries reinforced their political ambitions by cutting Native Hawaiians off from their language and traditions, Emerson rushed into the vacuum to insist on the primarily literary, rather than historical, nature of those traditions, branding them as vanishing curiosities and thus blunting any political force they may have had. During the time when Emerson was writing, Indigenous language, knowledge, and traditions of leadership retreated to particular places of refuge—small towns, isolated communities, and, indeed, Native Hawaiian-led churches.[126] These sites of survivance laid the foundations for Indigenous scholars and activists who pursued decolonial agendas later in the twentieth century to eschew quaint ideas about their traditions and to fully revive understandings of traditional narratives as powerful, practical, historiographical tools—a dynamic alternative to linear histories that connect Native Hawaiians to the land and to a broader island world.[127]

Thus, despite his apparently sympathetic approach and his understanding of himself as operating in a network of Polynesian ethnologists, Emerson simultaneously partook in efforts by missionaries and their descendants to nullify the Indigenous voice by suggesting that Native Hawaiian intellectual production could only be appreciated on the level of simple poetry. There were similarities in William R. Castle Jr.'s pronouncement on Hawaiian tradition: "Many of the printed legends are poetry in all but form. . . . There is material for many a solemn poem in the slow tragedy of the dying, lovable, Hawaiian people."[128] The roots of this perspective were to be found in earlier decades. Despite Hiram Bingham's general disdain for Native Hawaiian culture, he noted the "respectable specimens of poetic composition" among the Indigenous population.[129] The children of missionaries gathered fragments of Hawaiian tradition as curiosities during their years at Punahou School, and from the mid-nineteenth century, Native Hawaiian narratives and descriptions of spiritual practice appeared in the missionary press, which exhibited tradition but simultaneously condemned it and consigned it to the past.[130]

What is also striking is the extent to which descendants of missionaries relied on their own networks when constructing and disseminating their vision of Hawaiian tradition. Emerson on occasion enlisted his brother Joseph, who very much shared his interests, as a research assistant.[131] He also received intelligence from Albert Francis Judd Jr., employed Titus Munson Coan as an unofficial literary agent to deliver his *Unwritten Literature* manuscripts to New York publishing firms, and secured money for his efforts to publish *Unwritten Literature* from Samuel Alexander and Albert and George Wilcox. All of these men were the sons and grandsons of first-generation missionaries.[132] Although Emerson acknowledged the scientific community at large, his closest associates were his immediate peers.

Ultimately, in collecting traditional narratives Emerson drew attention to the successes of Protestant mission and settler colonialism in transforming Hawai'i. "When it found itself cut off and isolated from its old-time associates," he said in his notes on the *hula*, "forced to breathe the rarified air of new systems of thought and religion, it was unable to adapt itself to the new conditions and it rapidly went to decay."[133] Emerson seemed sincere in his cultural relativism and was genuinely conflicted about the transformations the missionary community had engendered. As a result, he helped perpetuate a dominant mode of talking about supposedly "heathen" cultures that saw them as representing primitive versions of white society from which an overly modernized culture could learn something.[134] Emerson's failure to engage with Hawaiian tradition on its own terms, however, demonstrates that he ultimately failed to escape his primary identity as "missionary" and colonizer. At the same time, Emerson's continuing need to deal with Hawaiian tradition even after annexation betrays the limits of transformation. There was still work to be done to turn Hawai'i into an American space after 1898, and in order to complete the transition, the Indigenous voice needed to be engaged and marshaled. That voice contained the continued potential of Native Hawaiian resistance that could undercut a US colonial project that depended on the idea that Native Hawaiians had consented to their colonization. As part of this process of marshaling the Indigenous voice, Emerson emphasized his own liminality and styled himself as the right person to correctly interpret and present elements of Hawaiian history to US audiences. Thus, the process of knowledge production was contingent on white actors' attempts to navigate their precarious position between the imperial and the local in particular Pacific places.

Between Two Worlds?

Collecting Indigenous traditions was often a project of knowledge gathering that underpinned colonial rule.[135] However, Emerson's case shows that there was also a process of self-fashioning inherent in the way he collected and presented what he deemed to be artifacts of the Hawaiian past. In her analysis of Emerson, Kathryn Gin Lum rightly situates him in a broader colonial project as one of many white Americans in the early twentieth century who became "nostalgic about the people whose lives, livelihoods, and lands they had been trampling for centuries" once these people had been "safely policed and domesticated."[136] Although this is undoubtedly true, there is more to be said about the particular anxieties that motivated Emerson and the contingencies that shaped his work. A focus on these helps us see that scientific approaches to preserving, classifying, and publishing Indigenous material, activities that were seen as bringing objective order to the chaos of tradition across continents and oceans, were heavily inflected with the personal and the local. This was not just because, as Gin Lum argues, Emerson worried that the Anglo world might be "becoming too brutal and destructive," thus failing to appreciate what it might learn from those at an earlier stage of human development.[137] It was also because Emerson claimed to have found in Native Hawaiian narratives an adequate language for responding to his environment and to his sense of being misunderstood.

Emerson's image of himself as liminal was in large part fictive. His loyalties had always fundamentally lain with his fellow white US colonizers. In many ways, he was the archetype of the "antimodernist" that historian T. J. Jackson Lears describes—a white Anglo-Saxon Protestant moral and intellectual leader who found individual solace from industrial modernity in supposedly simpler cultures but who did nothing to fundamentally challenge the drive toward capitalistic material progress.[138] However, a granular analysis of Emerson's knowledge production gives us a way to puncture his claims to objectivity about the Pacific and to recognize again that descendants of missionaries saw their engagements with history as a mode of negotiating their status as insiders or outsiders in a particular island group.

In presenting Hawaiian tradition as literature, Emerson not only suppressed the dynamism of Indigenous accounts and obscured their political potential, he also lived out his desire to respond creatively to his environment. He tried to do this through original writing, authoring short stories with themes of Native Hawaiian women, interracial relationships, the guardianship of disappearing Indigenous traditions, and the sense of alienation and loss his characters experienced when they left Hawai'i for New England.[139] However, in 1906, a literary agent in New York, though he was complimentary about Emerson's writing, informed him that his stories had "been declined by every periodical in New York City, as well as The Strand Magazine."[140] Finding his literary ambitions stymied, Emerson turned to the raw material of Hawaiian tradition, styling himself as mediator between these "unrefined" responses to the Hawaiian landscape and the written word. He admitted to Morrow in 1905 that he thought it a more "worthy" endeavor for him "to write one's heart into a faded Polynesian legend" than to write an original short story, adding that "I set the highest value on the 'short story' . . . though I do not seem to make any success of it."[141] In his self-proclaimed role as mediator, Emerson found his niche: he claimed unparalleled familiarity with the Hawaiian language, land, and people because of his upbringing and his knowledge of the true meaning of Hawaiian poetic expressions. These allowed him to navigate what he called the "jungle" of tradition so he could offer a translation that was "faithful but not servile," neither wholly Indigenous nor wholly foreign.[142] He recognized himself as one of the few who had been "granted the opportunity to acquaint themselves intimately with this isolated branch of the Polynesian race" and had induced them to share their "birthright." He wrote that few had thought it worthwhile "to study closely and sympathetically the intimate thoughts of the people and to report to the world the results and findings of their studies," presenting not "philosophic formulas and scientific propositions, but . . . the very language of their thoughts."[143]

Emerson's efforts to bring "literary unity" to Hawaiian tradition are most evident in his version of *Pele and Hiiaka*. The story of Pele and Hi'iaka, according to Emerson, "stands at the fountain-head of Hawaiian myth." It tells of the goddess Pele, who lived in the Kīlauea volcano on Hawai'i island. In a dream, Pele falls in love with Lohi'au, a human from Kaua'i, and sends her sister Hi'iaka on an epic quest to bring him to her. Stories about Pele were (and continue to be) of profound spiritual and genealogical significance. They are central to traditional religious practice and are indicative of the ancestry of Hawaiian land and people.[144] Variations in narratives had specific political and local meanings, in accordance with the dynamic nature of genealogical tradition. Rather than appreciating these differences, however, Emerson thought that "settling upon one authoritative version" was desirable. Hawai'i had been "denied a Homer capable of voicing its greatest epic in one song. . . . [It] has been handled by many poets and raconteurs, each from his own point of view." Synthesis would never be achieved through Native Hawaiian agency, argued Emerson, given that each Indigenous expert "was inclined to look upon every different . . . version" as "an infringement of his preserve," but in his sensitivity to both Indigenous tradition and Euro-American artistic form, Emerson could be the Homer that he perceived Native Hawaiians to need.[145] What followed was a synthetic account in which Emerson fused or omitted material in the interests of narrative cohesion.

In the process of producing his work, Emerson erased the names of his Native Hawaiian informants. When recording various fragments of tradition in his personal papers, Emerson frequently noted his sources, which sometimes consisted of written material by Native Hawaiians or outsiders but often were living native informants. Despite his promise to "ever preserve" the names of the "dear old men and women . . . who have shared with me . . . race-memories of far-off, sweet, pagan days," these informants largely disappeared from the final published works.[146] In *Unwritten Literature*, although Emerson thanked in general terms "native Hawaiians who have so far broken with the old superstitious tradition of concealment as to unearth so much of the unwritten literary wealth stored in Hawaiian memories," he mentioned no informants by name, using his extensive footnotes only to discuss the meanings of specific words and cite printed sources.[147] He also expressed doubts about how far his unnamed informants could be trusted, pointed to inconsistencies in their accounts, and took pride in his self-proclaimed ability to discern truth from the fragmentary information they provided.[148] Erasure was also evident in *Pele and Hiiaka*, where again Emerson offered general thanks to "the custodians of the material herein set forth" in his preface, but in the footnotes gave the full names only of authors of published works. Emerson sometimes referred to a living informant, but only as a "thoughtful Hawaiian" or with initials.[149] In fact, M. J. Kapihenui's version of the epic, printed in the Hawaiian-language newspaper *Ka Hoku o ka*

Pakipika in 1861, was the uncredited source for most of Emerson's book.[150] Once again, we see how descendants of missionaries relied on Indigenous forms of knowledge when constructing their narratives about the Hawaiian past but immediately claimed authority over the Native Hawaiian voice.

Despite basing his claim to authority on his supposed possession of both the Hawaiian sensitivity to the natural world and the white American propensity for order, there is evidence that Emerson was insecure in both these identities. He was uncertain about his position in relation to his Native Hawaiian informants, noting the "tendency on the part of the Hawaiian to put himself right with his interlocutor" by "coloring his statements to suit" or "assuming an apologetic attitude which leads him to an unconscious . . . suppressio veri."[151] Although Emerson was confident that annexation had opened new opportunities for a freer transfer of knowledge by breaking down old power structures, his ability to elicit information was often enabled not by intimacy with Native Hawaiians or understanding gained through immersion, as he would clearly have liked his readers to believe, but by payment of a fee. As Emerson told George Wilcox, "the mouth of the kahuna, the maestro, the ancient and venerable savage, will not open until the money has been placed in the palm."[152] Although he claimed a special connection to Hawai'i and its people by virtue of his birth in the islands, Emerson did not escape the problems any anthropologist faced of discerning truth or extracting information as an "inside outsider" or an "outside insider."[153]

Emerson, and indeed the New Zealand–born ethnologist and Bishop Museum curator Terence Barrow, who introduced a reprint of *Pele and Hiiaka* in 1978, presented the reluctance of Indigenous experts to part with their traditional knowledge as evidence of stubborn superstition and an inability to appreciate the need for preservation work in the face of imminent cultural death.[154] However, the dissemination of traditional accounts through the Hawaiian-language press in the late nineteenth century demonstrates that Native Hawaiians were concerned with cultural preservation and were using the written word to this end, producing a literature that Emerson used as source material.[155] It is altogether possible that Native Hawaiians simply used discernment about who could preserve knowledge and recognized that Emerson was not adequately equipped to carry out such work. There are grounds for doubting the sophistication of Emerson's Hawaiian linguistic and cultural expertise following his long stint in the United States as a young adult. His translation of Malo's work reflects his own presuppositions more than the original material, which was arranged according to traditional pedagogical forms that Emerson clearly did not understand. Malo's history centered the subtle concept of *pono*, referring to a state of social and cosmological harmony or balance, which Emerson translated in terms of a straightforward opposition between good and sin/evil.[156] Emerson's apparent distance from his Native Hawaiian interlocutors and his questionable grasp of the nuances of the Hawaiian language instill doubts about how effectively he could have mediated between Indigenous knowledge and an American readership.

At the same time, Emerson claimed to feel alienation from and even resentment for the United States. He had been profoundly affected by his time there, especially by the Civil War, which he commemorated as an active member of the Grand Army of the Republic, often speaking at gatherings of veterans in Hawai'i, and through correspondence with his regiment, the First Massachusetts Volunteers.[157] However, Emerson's short story, "The Prick of Honor," which he drafted in 1904 but never published, suggested a more difficult relationship with the land of his parents' birth. In the story, a sailor from New England returns home after a long time in Hawai'i and a love affair with a Native Hawaiian woman, only to find himself unable to converse with "pale" and "bloodless" women; confronted by Americans with crude, ignorant stereotypes of Hawai'i; and having to relearn "the A, B, C of his own race."[158] Emerson stated that his sense of inferiority in the face of American culture was the reason that he felt himself equipped to deal with only what he perceived to be Native Hawaiians' mediocre intellectual production: "When it should come to dealing with the more complex and more refined forces that surge in our own strenuous civilization, I fear lest I might find myself much out of my element."[159]

This sense of alienation was not uncommon among descendants of missionaries. When in the United States, groups of them would meet up to speak Hawaiian and would refer to each other sarcastically as "cannibals," a word that reflected their perception of difference from their supposed countrymen, whom they found overwhelmingly modern and morally coarse yet whom they also feared would perceive them as somehow backward.[160] In Samuel Chapman Armstrong's words, "a Hawaiian cannot become a thoroughly rooted American. . . . The roar of a distant surf is always sounding in our ears."[161] As was evident in the writings of Bishop and Lyman in particular, for descendants of missionaries, the islands were forever associated with childhoods of adventure and freedom amid great natural beauty, despite the fact that early years were often spent protected from the influence of Native Hawaiians due to the acute fears of missionary parents.[162] Recognizing that certain expectations had been thrust on him by his inheritance of a US culture from which he felt somewhat distant, Emerson found solace in a response to Hawai'i by Native Hawaiians—a people he deemed infantile—seeing something of his childhood self in it. This did not make him any less of a colonizer—in fact, Albert Memmi states that feelings of resentment and mediocrity in relation to the metropole were intrinsic to the colonial mentality—but it profoundly shaped the supposedly objective knowledge he produced about Hawai'i.[163]

Emerson was ultimately successful in establishing a reputation as a collector of Hawaiian folklore. *Unwritten Literature* was given the stamp of scientific authority when it was published as Bulletin 38 of the Smithsonian's Bureau of American Ethnology. Just as a number of his peers were connected to a scientific community in the United States, Emerson was no stranger to US social scientists. He presented papers at the International Folk-Lore Congress, part of Chicago's Columbian Exhibition, in 1893 and to the American Anthropological Association in 1905.[164] However, the scientific framing of *Unwritten Literature* was something of an afterthought. Emerson spent the earliest years of the twentieth century seeking to have the book published by major New York literary presses, desperately promoting it as being of interest to both scholars and the general reading public. He had no takers, even when he offered to bear the expense for the work in exchange for the international distribution power of these publishers.[165] The ultimate labelling of Emerson's work as science, which reflected a deepening impulse among Americans to categorize work as either science or literature, obscured how Emerson sought to transcend this disciplinary boundary from his liminal position in the Pacific.[166] His output was motivated more by an emotional response to the poetry he found in traditional accounts and by a visceral sense of connection to nature that he perceived Americans were alienated from because of modern life.

Although Emerson's adoption of the scientific voice ultimately proved to be his only route to publication, his latent romanticism made an impression on US audiences. One reviewer said that Emerson was "a scientist with the heart of a poet."[167] Another, writing in the *New York Daily Tribune*, expressed a newfound understanding that *hula* dances were not "exhibitions of savage license," as previous missionaries and travel writers had often suggested, but a "sacred grand opera" in which Native Hawaiians "could not help reiterating the love motive with a frequency that cold-blooded Anglo-Saxons would consider abandon." This interpretation, wrote the reviewer, was now "asserted on the authority of Uncle Sam himself," given its publication by the Smithsonian.[168] Such a statement lent a veneer of cohesion to the US colonial project, belying the idiosyncrasy of Emerson's conclusions among descendants of missionaries. As was clear at the beginning of this chapter, a number of Emerson's peers did not agree with him, instead upholding their forebears' denial that there was anything sacred or innocent in the *hula*. The enduring impact of Emerson's interpretation is evident in Terence Barrow's introduction to the 1978 reprint of *Pele and Hiiaka*, which uncritically echoed much of Emerson's language, emphasizing "the poetry of Hawaiian places" and the protagonists' "susceptibility to . . . emotions" that made possible "all the depth and conflict that are so essential to drama."[169]

Although Emerson did not attack the morality of the *hula* in the same way as some of his peers, in rendering it as a romantic and aesthetic production he largely obscured its links to the ways Native Hawaiians narrated their history and the connection between that history and Indigenous claims to sovereignty. He demarcated the kinds of material appropriate for consideration by historians, separating them from the kinds that were the preserve of ethnologists or folklorists. Ultimately claiming the authority of American social science to prop up his romantic notions, Emerson helped obfuscate contestation over US sovereignty, pave the way for the commodification of Hawaiian culture, and reaffirm that Hawai'i was an exceptional space in the Pacific that had been made safe for settlement, business, and tourism.[170] In the process, he also papered over his personal anxieties about the fact that he could not fully access either a Hawaiian or an American identity, instead constructing an image of himself as a liminal figure in a more positive sense with access to both American scientific and Native Hawaiian worlds. Acknowledging the contests and concerns that motivated Emerson's work in the early decades of the twentieth century causes us to see that despite the claims of descendants of missionaries to authority over Hawaiian history, the story of the US colonization of Hawai'i did not simply end with white settlers' political triumph and the folding of the islands into a broader US Pacific empire in 1898. In the early decades of the twentieth century, the idea of an American Hawai'i was still under construction by actors who saw themselves as liminal to the United States and who rehashed local histories and traditions as they searched for an anchor in an island world.

In the early twentieth century, hiding behind the veils of commemorative performance, memoir, or social science, a number of descendants of missionaries found outlets to express personal connections to Hawaiian history and roots in Hawai'i rather than the United States. At the same time, using these veils, they ostensibly presented an authoritative vision of a harmonious mission history that was punctuated by compliant islanders and their benign traditions. They encouraged Americans to view Hawai'i as both a tourist destination and a Protestant nation under white settler influence that was suitable for incorporation as a US territory, distinct from the unincorporated territories of the Philippines and Puerto Rico that the United States also seized in 1898. They quietly brushed aside their prior uses of the mission past that had questioned a prevailing narrative of harmony in order to encourage US intervention in Hawaiian institutions, in the process revealing malleability in their approaches to religion and history alike.

This chapter has shown how the discursive construction of Hawai'i as an American space continued after the 1898 moment, marked by ongoing negotiation at a local level between Indigenous knowledge traditions and white actors who placed the islands, rather than the United States, front and center in their world view. The personal and subjective nature of the histories of Hawai'i descendants of missionaries presented and the resolutely local nature of their concerns suggest that the notion of a wider US Pacific empire as an emergent spatial and historical category imagined from the United States meant little to those who were negotiating their status on the ground from Hawai'i. The diversity of perspectives and experiences that coexisted under this imperial banner is thrown into further relief by comparing the historical arguments generated by the missionary community in Hawai'i with those fostered by a US Protestant missionary enterprise that was only just beginning in 1898. Although the US seizure of Hawai'i represented the culmination of mission history for descendants of missionaries in those islands, its annexation of the Philippines over the course of just a few months marked the start of something new for missionaries from a range of denominations. Although both archipelagoes superficially shared a place in an American Pacific empire that was supposedly emblematic of the burgeoning global power and sweeping historic destiny of the United States, missionaries in the Philippines had to come to terms with a set of historical conditions that were quite different from those that animated descendants of missionaries in Hawai'i. Missionaries in the Philippines became equally drawn in by the local rather than by the spatial-temporal categories devised in the United States.

PART II

The Philippines

On the morning of May 1, 1898, Admiral George Dewey, on board the U.S.S. *Olympia*, led his squadron into Manila Bay on the west coast of the Philippine island of Luzon and routed a Spanish flotilla. This engagement in the furthest reaches of the Pacific from the United States might have seemed a somewhat odd beginning to the Spanish-American War, given that the conflict was ostensibly sparked by events closer to home in the Caribbean—by an intolerably abusive Spanish colonialism in Cuba and more immediately by the sinking of the U.S.S. *Maine* off the coast of Havana in mysterious circumstances. The truth, however, was that these excuses to strike at Spain presented the opportunity for leading foreign policy strategists in the Republican Party to press forward with long-held goals that were far more ambitious than saving Cubans or exacting vengeance. Taking the cue to remove an ailing transoceanic Spanish empire from the scene was a step toward controlling both the Caribbean and the north Pacific before ultimately connecting the two by way of the Panama Canal.[1] Within four months of Dewey's victory, Spain had surrendered, and through the Treaty of Paris in December 1898, the Philippines became a US territory alongside Puerto Rico and Guam, while Cuba became independent under close US supervision.

As we have seen, the missionary community in Hawaiʻi benefited from this chain of events and achieved their political goals. In July 1898, against the backdrop of the war, US lawmakers finally accepted the annexation of Hawaiʻi as a strategic necessity. But on the question of a broader US Pacific empire that seemed to draw Hawai'i and the Philippines together, the descendants of missionaries in Hawai'i were characteristically ambivalent. Sereno Bishop, despite being one of the most vocal advocates of the annexation of Hawai'i, wrote that the prospect of the United States taking the Philippines "disturbed and perplexed" him.[2] The leaders of the Hawaiian Republic initially considered remaining neutral in the war to stave off the risks of Spanish attack.[3] While they ultimately decided to roll out the red carpet for US troops stopping in Honolulu on their way to the Philippines, they emphasized the particularity of the local in doing so, mimicking the forms of a Native Hawaiian welcome by presenting troops with a *lei* as an act of *hookupu* (gift giving) and hosting a *lū'au*.[4] Because of this, troops and journalists passing through Hawai'i described it as a welcoming place. By perceiving and writing about Hawai'i in such a way, they overlooked ongoing contests over Hawaiian annexation but rhetorically softened the edges of US military presence in the Pacific.[5]

Nevertheless, even as both Hawai'i and the Philippines became US territories by the end of 1898, descendants of missionaries adopted rhetorical devices to underscore that, to paraphrase Bishop, Hawai'i was not just a Pacific colony equivalent to the Philippines.[6] Bishop, for example, morally elevated Hawai'i in the emerging "American lake" by arguing that it was the responsibility of those in the islands to exercise Christian influence over the colonial project from what Bishop called "this nearest American point."[7] The engagements of descendants of missionaries with history also reflected an ambivalence about the situation of Hawai'i in a US Pacific. On the one hand, the Hawaiian Historical Society produced historical knowledge and built intellectual networks that established linkages between Hawai'i and the other new possessions of the United States, seeking evidence of linguistic similarities and highlighting preexisting diplomatic connections.[8] On the other hand, W. D. Alexander still claimed Hawaiian primacy in oceanic history, maintaining that "no territory of the United States has had so varied and interesting a history or folk-lore as that of Hawaii."[9] If Hawai'i was a key node in a strategic American vision of the Pacific, "missionaries" on the ground continued to assert that it was also an exceptional place, rather than straightforwardly centering US power.

The second half of the book turns attention to a group that appeared far less ambivalent than the Hawaiian missionary community about the notion of US power radiating out across the Pacific and transforming it: US Protestant missionaries to the Philippines after 1898. Whereas the descendants of missionaries in Hawai'i were keen to fulfill the work that their ancestors had started in that archipelago, the missionaries to the Philippines were far more conscious of themselves as participating in a national imperial project. They were aware of their nation's growing power to shape world affairs and were part of an extraordinary wave of American foreign mission activity across the globe in the late nineteenth and early twentieth centuries, far surpassing that seen around the time the Hawaiian mission was established. Commensurately, in their letters, sermons, and publications for US audiences, missionaries heading to the Philippines frequently read the US seizure of territory across the ocean to be the unfolding of a divine historical plan. They were producers not only of historical narratives but also of whole philosophies of history that buttressed great expectations for the evangelistic potential of US empire in the Pacific.

However, missionaries' peculiar sense of expectation came with a heightened sensitivity to the prospect of failure. As chapter 4 suggests, if the US opportunity in the Philippines was indeed divinely ordained, then missionaries believed that the consequences of neglecting to adequately respond to that opportunity would be grave. Faced with prospective crisis, therefore, they punctuated their providential schemes with alternative conceptualizations of how history had unfolded in the islands. As chapter 5 shows, they derived comfort from ideas about racial development from the social sciences. They also recognized that the Spanish Catholic colonial past had not simply been obliterated but required engagement and negotiation. In the end, as chapter 6 demonstrates, they even reframed the history of the people of the Philippines as one of long preparation for spiritual leadership in Asia. As missionaries explored these different philosophies of history, they rarely acknowledged the paradoxes they were creating. They unreflexively invoked visions of history rooted in a genuine belief in divine agency alongside a discourse of an inherently "godless" linear historical time.[10] The audience for missionaries was usually back in the United States, and their writings were geared toward encouraging donations for their work and explaining how it related to the special US project in the Philippines. Accordingly, they rhetorically smoothed over ambivalence and contradiction, creating the appearance, in one historian's eyes, that "doubt and skepticism were alien" to them.[11]

Nonetheless, the granularity of the missionary archive shows that missionaries on the front lines of American religious efforts in the Philippines problematized grandiose religious and historical justifications for US empire in the Pacific. Taken together, the next three chapters show that even though missionaries to the Philippines consciously rode in the slipstream of US empire, they moved beyond a straightforward understanding of the United

States as God's tool for shaping Philippine, Pacific, and world histories. In fact, missionaries' complex and shifting ideas about history when faced with the concrete realities of conducting work in a Pacific archipelago ultimately reveal the fragmented nature of US imperial epistemology and doubts about the American imagination of the Pacific just as much as those of descendants of missionaries in Hawai'i.

Chapter 4

"A Sudden Turn of History"

Providence, Crisis, and US Empire in the Philippines

In the months following Admiral Dewey's victory, even before the Treaty of Paris cemented the position of the United States as a transoceanic colonial power, US imperialists began to style the arrival of their nation's empire in the Pacific as a critical moment in an unfolding providential history. As he outlined a colonial vision in which US power collapsed Pacific space and made Hawai'i and the Philippines "contiguous," senatorial candidate Albert Beveridge littered his September 1898 speech to Indiana Republicans with references to the idea that the United States had been driven to victory in the Spanish-American War and to an imperial destiny by the hand of God. Beveridge hinted that the need for a providential interpretation of the events that had unfolded over the preceding months was particularly acute given the ostensibly unexpected and sudden nature of those events. The presentation of an opportunity to build an empire must have been God's design, for it was an outcome only he could have foreseen when the war began. "We knew it not in the beginning," Beveridge said.[1]

After Philippine annexation, the need to imbue US foreign policy with moral purpose and godly design became even more pressing. The annexation had been opportunistic; events had escalated quickly from an initial hope that the United States could simply hold a strategic position in the port of Manila. It was also deeply divisive, mobilizing the same anxieties about the ingestion of racial others into the American body politic that had for so long forestalled Hawai'i's annexation.[2] Indeed, both the Philippines and Puerto Rico occasioned the need for a new legal category of "unincorporated" US territory to ensure that their affairs would remain as "insular" as possible.[3] The outbreak of the Philippine-American War in 1899, as Filipinos vigorously resisted the arrival of US colonialism, raised the stakes further still. Against this backdrop, in 1900, President McKinley famously justified the acquisition of the Philippines in a speech to a gathering of Methodist ministers, his co-religionists. He recalled his agony over the question of what to do with the islands after the US victory: "I am not ashamed to tell you, gentlemen, that I went down on my knees and prayed to Almighty God for light and guidance more than one night." One evening, like a bolt from the blue, a solution came to him: he had to take the islands and "uplift and civilize and Christianize them and by God's grace do the very best we could by them, as our fellow men for whom Christ also died."[4] By insinuating that God had "strangely guided" the United States to the Philippines, McKinley invoked a language of what the historian Nicholas Guyatt calls "historical providentialism," styling the nation as having been prepared by God to fulfill a divine historical purpose of spreading Christianity and civilization.[5]

Based on proclamations like those of McKinley and Beveridge, scholars have shown how ideas about the providential appointment of the United States were central to the framing of US imperialism in the late nineteenth century. Historical providentialism was given new life in the aftermath of the Civil War as Americans sought national healing and purpose. An interventionist "Christian nationalism" emerged from this search that underpinned the Spanish-American War and the turn to overseas empire.[6] Framing expansion as divinely ordained "destiny," as McKinley did in another famous proclamation, imbued the seizure of the Philippines with a sense of inevitability and soothed anxieties.[7] In addition, understandings of Protestant and US histories as one and the same—as a single, sweeping narrative of progress—provided an intellectual justification for the capitalist, racist, and developmentalist notions with which US policymakers approached the Philippines.[8]

This chapter focuses on how American Protestant missionaries to the Philippines responded to the idea that their nation's empire was divinely ordained. As might be expected, in many ways they bought into and amplified the notion that the United States was a providential tool and imbued it with particular spiritual significance. For them, the only way to explain why the United States had colonized the Philippines was to suggest that the archipelago must be a vital mission field that God had led the nation to. God had opened the door to a radical break with the islands' past and to a rapid spiritual transformation that had global ramifications. Missionaries joined US policymakers in deploying providential arguments to allay the anxieties engendered by the turn to US empire and to deflect attention away from the fact that US rule in the Philippines was above all propped up by astonishing violence.

This chapter argues that the idea of providential opportunity did more than simply increase missionaries' confidence in the US colonial project. Although they approved of the argument that Providence had guided the United States to break with historical precedent and take on an imperial role, they believed that Providence was also calling Americans to effect a further change in the Philippines: the overthrow of a stagnant Catholicism in favor of Protestantism. In this respect, missionaries often felt that their nation was falling short. They argued that even though the constraints of historical precedent had been thrown off in the US turn to overseas empire, imperial administrators remained too much in thrall to the Catholic past of the Philippines.

By considering the philosophy of history missionaries articulated, the chapter shows that the idea that Providence was operating in history could be a source of profound anxiety for some Americans instead of simply acting as a seal of approval for US empire. Missionaries' readings of providential history were not wholly teleological and optimistic; instead, they were cyclical and were infused with the notion of a crisis that threatened national ruin if the United States did not uphold its spiritual obligations. Providence may have used the United States to open the door to evangelism in the Philippines, but missionaries stressed that this door would not remain open indefinitely and characterized history itself as an agent that could overtake them and undercut evangelistic efforts if they were not prosecuted with sufficient urgency. When US imperial administrators appeared ambivalent about accepting the invitation of Providence to overthrow the Catholic past and facilitate Protestant triumph in the Philippines or indeed when politicians and voters appeared ready to give up their commitment to the Philippines altogether, missionaries feared that their nation would be found wanting in a moment of crisis. Their experiences in the Philippine archipelago when they crossed the Pacific led them to doubt whether the United States would become God's agent for transforming oceanic history after all.

American Protestant Missionaries in the Philippines

From early in the US occupation of the Philippines, men and women from the United States took advantage to commence evangelistic work in an archipelago that Protestant evangelists had previously been denied access to by Spanish Catholic authorities. YMCA workers entered just a week after Dewey's victory and other individuals also soon began evangelistic work on an unofficial basis, notably Arthur W. Prautch, a Methodist businessman and former missionary to India, and his wife, Eliza.[9] Another figure who commenced work during the early days of US occupation was Alice Byram Condict, a physician from New Jersey and a medical missionary who had previously spent twenty-five years in India. Arriving in the Philippines in 1899 on her own initiative, she supported herself as she distributed the gospel to thousands of Filipinos.[10]

Presbyterians commenced the first formal mission in the islands in April 1899 through James B. Rodgers, a New York native who transferred from work in Brazil.[11] Rodgers labored for thirty-six years in the islands. He became one of the strongest advocates of interdenominational cooperation between Protestant missions and published a historical retrospective on the Presbyterian mission in 1940.[12] He was soon joined by David S. Hibbard, who had been born in the Midwest and had trained at Princeton. Hibbard founded the Silliman Institute, an industrial school for boys, in Dumaguete on the island of Negros in 1901 and was its first president for nearly thirty years. Subsequent arrivals helped make the Presbyterian mission the largest in the islands; it had thirteen ordained ministers by 1903 and forty-four by 1912.[13]

Methodists also began formal missions in 1900. The first group to come was a four-woman delegation from the Woman's Foreign Missionary Society (WFMS) of the Methodist Episcopal Church to conduct educational work for the daughters of Filipino elites. The WFMS was one of the many women's missionary societies founded after the 1860s to provide institutional support to thousands of single women missionaries across the globe—a development that was unimaginable during the era of the ABCFM mission to Hawai'i. These societies promoted gender-separatist strategies for work among foreign women until most were absorbed into overarching denominational mission boards in the 1920s.[14] The WFMS workers in the Philippines included Julia Wisner, who had previously served for twelve years in Rangoon, and Cornelia Chillson Moots, who in 1903 authored a book about her experiences for the benefit of the 156,739 Methodist women she said subscribed to the WFMS at the time. Wisner, Moots, and their colleagues arrived in the Philippines in late February 1900 and managed to sustain a school for only eight months, although WFMS work in the islands was subsequently reignited by Winifred Spaulding, who in 1903 opened the Harris Memorial Training School in Manila for young Filipina women who wished to become deaconesses.¹⁵ By the mid-1920s, eighteen WFMS workers were in the field.¹⁶ Other denominational women's missionary societies followed suit, including that of the Presbyterian Church, which established the Ellinwood School for Girls in 1905 and the Mission Hospital School of Nursing in 1906.¹⁷ Women also still traveled to the field with missionary husbands, no longer having the subordinate status of those in the earlier Hawaiian mission field and instead being deemed missionaries in their own right, albeit often with childcare responsibilities that "prevent[ed] them from traveling around with their husbands."¹⁸ Methodist men commenced a mission alongside their wives in 1900. The most outspoken and influential of their number, Homer C. Stuntz, arrived in 1902.¹⁹ Hailing from New York City, Stuntz quickly styled himself as a key interpreter of the political and religious situation in the Philippines for US audiences through his articles for the Methodist journal the *Christian Advocate* and his monumental 1904 book *The Philippines and the Far East*.²⁰

From the start of the US occupation, Episcopalians had been represented in the archipelago by army chaplains. The denomination first sent formal missionaries in late 1901, followed by a man who became probably the most influential foreign Protestant in the islands, Charles Henry Brent.²¹ Born in Canada, Brent moved to the United States in 1886 to take up a ministerial position in Buffalo, New York, subsequently moving to Boston. Through the experience of working in some of Boston's poorest neighborhoods, he became committed to Social Gospel theology. After naturalizing as a US citizen, Brent accepted the invitation to become the first Episcopal bishop of Manila in December 1901, arriving in the islands the following August. He became well known not only for overseeing the establishment of hospitals, churches, schools, and societies in the Philippines but also for his tireless work opposing the opium trade and advocating ecumenical Christianity. He left the islands in 1917 to become chaplain general of the American Expeditionary Forces in France during World War I, returning to New York after the war.²² Brent's most vocal colleague was the straight-talking Texan evangelist Mercer Green Johnston. Never afraid to criticize insufficient advocacy for Protestantism on the part of the US government or even his fellow Episcopal missionaries, Johnston spent only five years in the islands from 1903 before his frustrations got the better of him.

The American Baptist Missionary Union, the Christian and Missionary Alliance, the United Brethren of Christ, the Disciples of Christ, and the ABCFM also all established small missions in 1901 and 1902, and the Seventh-day Adventists took up work later in the decade.²³ The Baptist missionary

Eric Lund traveled from Spain to begin a mission in the Philippines accompanied by Braulio Manikan, a Filipino who had converted to Protestantism in Spain, but it was Charles W. Briggs who became the leader of the Baptist mission.[24] Briggs was a difficult colleague. At first he was clearly scornful of the Philippine peoples he sought to evangelize, although his 1913 book *The Progressing Philippines* indicated something of a changing attitude.[25] The Woman's American Baptist Foreign Mission Society also sent a small number of workers, beginning with Anna Johnson in 1903.[26] The first ABCFM representative in 1902 was Robert F. Black, who labored with his wife in Davao on the island of Mindanao for six years before any more Congregationalists arrived. It was another seven years before the most recognizable member of the ABCFM mission, Frank Laubach, arrived in 1915. Laubach represented a new generation of American missionaries. He scolded his predecessors for missing important opportunities and saw greater value than they had in the Indigenous cultures he worked among.[27] He became particularly well known for his work from 1930 to promote literacy among the Muslims of Mindanao.[28] Another Congregationalist society, the Woman's Board of Missions, also partnered with the ABCFM to send women, including the New Mexico sisters Isabel, Florence, and Evelyn Fox, to the islands from the late 1910s.[29]

Many US missionaries in the Philippines, especially early on, were as much concerned with maintaining Christian worship and moral standards among their nation's troops in the tropics as they were with converting Filipinos. Cornelia Chillson Moots expressed her horror at the sight of "drooling, driving American men" spilling out of the saloons of Manila's main business street shortly after army payday.[30] In response to such scenes, the YMCA, Methodists, Presbyterians, and Episcopalians all retained strong presences in the city, working among both Filipinos and Americans.[31] All missions also developed work for either or both Catholic and non-Christian peoples in other parts of the Philippines. In a move that was heralded as unprecedented, seven of the US mission boards in the islands formed the Evangelical Union in April 1901, agreeing to divide the field such that work would not be duplicated and to parenthesize denominations when naming churches, foregrounding a united "Iglesia Evangélica."[32] The two largest denominations, the Methodists and Presbyterians, carved up the large northern island of Luzon between them, while the Presbyterians and Baptists agreed to share the central Visayas region, including the islands of Panay, Negros, and Cebu.[33] The ABCFM subsequently joined the Evangelical Union and labored principally in the southern island of Mindanao with both Catholics and non-

Christians.³⁴ Episcopalians, eschewing both the Evangelical Union and evangelism among Catholics, worked among the non-Christian mountain peoples of northern Luzon and later among Muslims in Mindanao and Sulu.³⁵

Both men and women who were missionaries in the Philippines had a sense that history was important, that knowledge of it was essential to interpreting God's designs and understanding the contexts they worked in. To that end, missionary men in the Philippines produced history for US audiences in published works that discoursed on the recent and distant past of the islands and on the prospects for mission work in the present. These included Arthur Judson Brown's *The New Era in the Philippines* (1903), Homer Stuntz's *The Philippines and the Far East* (1904), and Charles Briggs's *The Progressing Philippines* (1913). Later came Frank Laubach's *The People of the Philippines* (1925) and David Hibbard's *Making a Nation* (1926). Missionary men also outlined their philosophies of history and reflected on the ways history intertwined with their work through sermons, letters to mission boards, diaries, publications for Filipino students, and reports to ecumenical conferences.

Missionary women were perceived to be performing very specific roles in the Philippines. They joined women teachers and the wives of US officials in producing "colonial domesticity," styling themselves as emblems of American civilization against the backdrop of warfare and a military masculinity that for Moots developed "all that is domineering and tyrannical" and made it hard for soldiers "to live a Christian, a temperate, or even a moral life."³⁶ Moots, who had lost her adopted son early in the Philippine-American War, played an overtly maternal role with the soldiers. She cared for wounded troops at the Second Reserve Hospital in Manila, asking them: "You did not know you had a mother in the islands, did you?"³⁷ Other missionary women extended this maternalism to the archipelago's children, noting with horror an infant mortality rate of around 50 percent. They blamed this on the ignorance of Filipina mothers and resolved to instruct them in the basics of tender and hygienic childcare. This education was a key part of the role performed by the Methodists' Mary Johnston Hospital, established in Manila in 1906.³⁸ Another particular task of women missionaries was reaching Filipina women, who were believed by missionaries to be the key religious influence in Catholic households. They "modernized" these women by educating them about fashion, nursing, and domestic science and by training them to evangelize their peers. These goals were embodied by the training schools for Filipinas that Methodist, Presbyterian, and Congregationalist women founded. However, women missionaries struggled to elevate women's status in a predominantly masculinist missionary and imperial project that focused on raising a generation of young Filipino men as leaders and prevented Filipinas from voting or running for office until the late 1930s.[39]

Despite the separate and specific nature of their work, missionary women and their supporters were also engaged in producing and interpreting history. Alice Byram Condict's *Old Glory and the Gospel* (1902) was one of the first missionary-authored books to appear on the Philippines. It combined reflections on Philippine and world history with details derived from personal experience in the islands. Condict was fairly unapologetic about styling herself as an authority on the Philippines and on God's historical designs, although in a prefatory note she had the Methodist missionary bishop Frank W. Warne speak for her credentials as a medic and as someone who had "seen the inner home life of the Filipino people." This was a formulation that allowed Condict to discourse on history while affirming that she was speaking from her "domestic" role in the missionary enterprise.[40]

Moreover, the broader women's missionary movement fostered US Christian women's engagement with Philippine and Pacific histories. This fact was exemplified by Helen Barrett Montgomery's *Christus Redemptor* (1906), which appeared as the sixth volume in a series of seven books designed to educate Christian women about the world the US foreign missionary movement was expanding into.[41] This series, titled the United Study of Missions, was a mammoth effort to encourage women across denominations to embark on a course of learning and discussion in order to understand the ways God's hand had moved history in different parts of the world.[42] *Christus Redemptor* tackled the "Island World" of the Pacific, including the new US possessions of Hawai'i and the Philippines, in the belief that "the marvelous stories of the transformations of many of the Islands through efforts of heroic men and women must lead to greater enthusiasm and zeal and to an intensified faith in the ultimate triumph of the Cross."[43] Women's missionary magazines, just as much as men's, also consistently directed women to further reading in both the secular and Christian press, encouraging them to study and develop awareness of the histories, politics, geographies, and cultures that missionaries were encountering across the globe. Inspired by her studies, Mrs. J. H. Glotfelter of the Kansas Branch of the Woman's Board of Missions declared at her branch's annual meeting in May 1899 that "never, perhaps, has history making been so rapid as now."[44]

The following section considers how missionaries drew on their reading of history to generate lofty expectations for work in the Philippines, motivated by their apparent confidence that God had led US empire to a swift and unexpected imperial conquest because this empire was a crucial tool in a rapidly unfolding historical plan to convert the world. Although the subsequent analysis will show that this missionary conceptualization was infused with anxieties and contradictions, it is worth thinking first about how, in multiple forums and with remarkable persistence in the opening decades of the twentieth century, missionaries articulated a philosophy of history in which God directly caused seismic geopolitical shifts. In so doing, they negated questions about the propriety of US empire and their place in its slipstream.

Missionaries and the Providential Appointment of US Empire

The Philippines became a mission field that was overwhelmingly dominated by US missionary societies largely because US evangelists were excited by the opportunity to work under their own nation's flag in foreign climes. Julia Wisner, for example, was an experienced hand in the mission field but could not hide her excitement at involving herself in her own nation's imperial project: "One of the most thrilling moments of my life was when we dropped anchor in Manila Bay.... Not because it was my first touch with eastern life ... but because it was my first experience of this kind of life under the Stars and Stripes."[45] Missionaries and their supporters interpreted their nation's rapid and unforeseen acquisition of an island empire in terms of grand historical philosophies, as a divinely mandated and aided intervention in history. The speed with which Admiral Dewey had routed the Spaniards spoke of providential interposition, as Homer Stuntz reflected in his 1904 book: "So singularly complete and overwhelming was the victory that devout students" could not "refrain from believing that the God of nations helped mightily.... History furnishes no parallel."[46] In his report on a visit to the islands in 1901, Arthur Judson Brown, secretary of the Presbyterian Board of Foreign Missions, similarly concluded that "we obtained [the Philippines] in a clearly Providential way," as evidenced by the supposedly unlikely constellation of historical events that had directed the United States to the islands.[47]

Invocations of Providence served useful functions for supporters of US empire following the Spanish-American War. First, it soothed anxieties about the ostensibly new historical departure of the United States in turning to overseas empire. Brown acknowledged these anxieties, writing in his 1903 book that "no other Americans since Washington have had to grapple with more stupendous problems. Our history furnished no precedent to guide."[48] The seizure of the islands had given rise to "the most momentous question which our nation had faced since the Civil War," and "constructive statesmanship" was required as at no time since the Revolution if the United States was to avoid the "naked imperialism" that "furnished [the] motive for nearly all previous European occupation of the tropics."[49] Charles Brent, too, found "no exact counterpart in the past" and noted that the Philippine question was "the greatest problem this country had ever had to grapple" except the Civil War; "old traditions" had to be left behind.[50]

Yet American exceptionalism, suggested Stuntz, did not reside in an unmoving commitment to a set of historical precedents but in a unique sensitivity to the way Providence wanted to move history forward. In Stuntz's view, if "the President, Congress, Philippine officials, and missionaries submit themselves to Him who worketh all things," then the history that emerged would inevitably be "history creditable to Washington and Jefferson and Lincoln and McKinley."[51] In this sense, missionaries were on the same page as Albert Beveridge, who turned to Providence when speaking in the Senate in January 1900. He attempted to convince fellow senators that justification for imperialism was to be found by remaining attentive to where God was leading the United States. His argument transcended debates about historical precedent regarding the constitutionality of empire, the designs of the founding fathers, and the application of the Constitution to racial others.[52] The supposedly unprecedented nature of events and decisions was not the result of the United States having suddenly deviated from its historical values but a sign that God had laid radical new challenges at its doorstep that reemphasized its chosen status. As myths appeared to be under threat that trumpeted the nation's historical eschewal of imperialism, the idea that the swift call to empire was divinely ordained rhetorically reinscribed exceptionalism.

Second, the high-flown language of Providence in the aftermath of the Spanish-American War went some way toward deflecting attention from the reality of the situation on the ground in the Philippines. The "benevolent assimilation" of the islands McKinley committed to was in fact underpinned by astonishing violence, under the guise of disciplining a people deemed unfit for self-government and in need of paternal guidance. Beginning in February 1899, the Philippine-American War followed swiftly on the heels of the Spanish-American War, resulting in the deaths of 4,200 US soldiers and of anywhere between 200,000 and 1 million Filipinos over three and a half years.[53] As Filipinos who resisted US occupation turned to guerilla warfare as their best hope of success, the brutality heightened. The US Army, which racialized guerilla tactics as those of savages, came to see its enemy as fit for nothing better than torture and extermination. Seeing how the war might undercut its claims to exceptional benevolence, the United States unilaterally declared it to be over three times, desperately trying to draw a rhetorical line under the violence. On the second of these occasions, July 4, 1901, it deemed that enough had been done to initiate a transfer from military rule to an ambitious tutelary colonial project under a civilian government led by the Philippine Commission, an executive body that McKinley had appointed in 1899 to report on the state of affairs in the islands. Yet even after the war was declared at an end for the third and final time on July 4, 1902, "pacification" remained incomplete and US authorities continued to rely on force to quell periodic outbreaks of resistance across the islands. The devastation US troops wrought, especially with their policy of rounding up and confining supposedly threatening populations, continued apace, not least in the form of rampant disease epidemics.[54]

The resistance Americans faced had intellectual foundations in a rich tradition of anticolonial thought that Filipinos had developed during the final decades of Spanish rule in the archipelago. A reformed colonial education system after the 1860s had produced an educated urban class known as the *ilustrados* that emerged from Spanish-sponsored elites. Recognizing the ways they were exploited and denigrated by colonial rulers, especially the Catholic friar orders who dominated colonial policy, they traveled to Europe and became "Propagandists," engaging in intellectual exchanges and presenting themselves as worthy of assimilation into a Spanish body politic and representation in the Spanish Cortes Generales.[55] The Propagandist vision was exclusive; it developed a definition of the "Filipino" that left out animist hill peoples and Muslim polities the Spaniards had never been able to conquer and "civilize." Yet it was also one that provided the foundations upon which these Filipinos might begin to imagine themselves as a nation.[56]

By the early 1890s, disappointed by Spanish liberals' failure to do anything for them and disillusioned by the racism they encountered in the metropole, some Propagandists turned increasingly to a language of liberation. Concurrently, their intellectual ideas flowed into a Filipino or Tagalog revolutionary movement in the Philippines led by Andrés Bonifacio, who brought together rural and urban traditions of popular resistance in a secret society called the Katipunan after 1892. When the Spaniards discovered the Katipunan in 1896, Bonifacio's response was to hastily declare a large-scale revolt against friar rule. Quickly facing failure, he was displaced by a controversial new revolutionary leader, Emilio Aguinaldo, who briefly declared a new state—the Republic of Biak-na-Bato—in November 1897 and signed a truce with the Spaniards.[57] Aguinaldo, who initially saw the arrival of the

United States in the region in early 1898 as an opportunity to turn the tide against the Spaniards and secure liberation, welcomed US intervention and declared Philippine independence in the aftermath of Dewey's victory, establishing a new republic centered on Malolos, northwest of Manila, in early 1899. However, US military occupation and the Treaty of Paris disappointed revolutionary hopes that Spain's defeat would mean Philippine freedom of government, and the Philippine-American War soon commenced between Aguinaldo's forces and US troops.[58]

For Protestant missionaries entering the Philippines, the nuanced history of Filipino anticolonial struggle and the levels of violence required to undermine that struggle were of secondary concern to the conviction that the arrival of US empire in the Philippines was a significant act in an unfolding providential drama. In minimizing the role of violence in the Philippines, missionaries diverged from several members of the broader Protestant clergy in the United States who, despite their key role in stoking the Christian nationalism that underpinned the Spanish-American War, became increasingly horrified by the resistance and violence that accompanied the occupation of the Philippines.[59] American Christians elsewhere in the Pacific were openly critical too. Francis M. Price, an ABCFM missionary to Micronesia, acknowledged the need to evangelize the Philippines during the Ecumenical Conference on Foreign Missions in New York City in 1900 but did not see US empire's violence as particularly helpful to this mission, pointing to the historical successes of the ABCFM in the Pacific without "ammunition and guns and shedding blood." He proclaimed, "What we want to do is to send on missionaries to the Philippine Islands and to all parts of that Sea, not to subjugate them, nor to make them subjects of the American Government, but to bring the redemption that is in Christ Jesus."[60]

Missionaries in the Philippines participated in a process that was common among American civilians in the islands—a selective reading of events that avoided accountability for violence.[61] In missionaries' writings, colonial violence generally appeared only briefly and rarely as more than a temporary and necessary setback. Women's missionary magazines marshaled the voices of American and Filipina women to argue that the Philippine-American War was merely a by-product of a US colonialism that had staved off worse conflicts while introducing religious freedom, economic improvement, and education.[62] Homer Stuntz wrote about colonial violence perhaps more than any other missionary, defending the use of torture by US soldiers to audiences in the United States through the pages of the Methodist *Christian Advocate*. In his book, he described the bloodshed as the fault of "fierce personal ambitions in a few Filipino leaders."[63] Arthur Judson Brown claimed that "the blood-stained trenches around Manila" were "anguish to my heart" but expressed confidence that "the broad range of future years" would see "all the inhabitants of the Philippine Islands . . . come to look back with gratitude to the day when God gave victory to American arms."[64] The significance of colonial violence, in other words, paled against the prevailing narrative that US empire was a divinely ordained historic intervention.

Missionaries imbued the idea that God had directed the United States to the Philippines with peculiar spiritual significance. They persistently interpreted the sudden opening of the Philippines as a sign that the islands were to play a crucial part in the most important historical arc of all—the evangelization of the world. This idea was evident as mission boards commenced discussions about how best to take advantage of the opportunity. Arthur Judson Brown was a prominent voice in these discussions. Brown, who would become one of the best-known "missionary statesmen" of the twentieth century, worked with an illustrious array of public figures and advocated an ecumenical approach to mission work until his death in 1963 at the age of 106.[65] Brown's ecumenism was evident in his approach to the new US empire from 1898, when his Presbyterian board took the initiative in calling for an interdenominational missionary effort.[66] Less than two months after Dewey's victory, after convening a meeting of representatives from several Protestant mission boards, Brown spoke of "the political and military relations into which the United States has been so strangely forced" with its new possessions. In this formulation, his nation was a reluctant imperial power, compelled by external forces it did not fully comprehend. Brown did not believe it was the will of Americans that had led the United States to the Philippines. He believed that it was the unimpeachable will of God and argued that "the Christian people of America should immediately and prayerfully consider . . . entering the door" that the divine hand was opening.[67]

The missionaries who heeded Brown's call and went to work in the Philippines agreed that the sudden US seizure of the islands was God's intervention in history to facilitate Protestantism's rapid triumph in a field that could unlock the door to the conversion of Asia and the world. Hibbard wrote to the Presbyterian board's corresponding secretary in May 1899, very soon after his arrival in the islands, that he felt "sure that the Lord has opened here the greatest mission field of the century."[68] Charles Brent wrote to his colleagues just before his election as Episcopal bishop in late 1901 that the "pronounced and unequivocal" responsibility and the "unusual and immediate" opportunity granted to the United States called for a "conspicuously strong and venturesome" missionary effort.[69] Brent's US supporters shared his confidence that the rapidity with which events had moved was a sure sign that a particularly great Christian work was ahead. Henry Satterlee, the Episcopal bishop of Washington, DC, wrote to Brent shortly before the latter left for the Philippines that he would have "a truly Apostolic work to do," heralded by the fact that in the preceding five years in the archipelago it had been "the unexpected that has continuously happened, in a chain of events which I cannot but regard as Providential."[70]

This providential interpretation of events in the Philippines justified the provision of significant resources for missions to the islands. Mission work was a competitive enterprise, and missionaries in each field had to make a case for the continued channeling of financial and human resources toward their work rather than toward any other. Advocates for mission work in the Philippines mobilized their claim to specialness with some success on the basis that the islands were the site of the divinely ordained imperial intervention of the United States. The Episcopal mission board, for example, placed its work in the Philippines "on the same footing as the China Mission." Although the size of the field was not comparable, the "peculiar circumstances" surrounding US occupation suggested that Providence was at work. If Providence had indeed directed the United States to the islands, it could only be for an evangelistic purpose, and thus the Philippines demanded special treatment.[71] The fact that the Presbyterian board was still writing of its "favoritism as compared with older Missions" toward the Philippine enterprise in 1920 suggests that this perception did not pass away quickly.[72] Not all boards proved as receptive to this argument, though. Stuntz complained to his Methodist sponsors in 1905 that the "imperious openings" in the Philippines seemed to have "made no whit of difference in the treatment we received. Fields with no sort of promise such as this receive twice the sums allotted here."[73] The responses Brown received to his initial call to arms also revealed some of the pitfalls of a sudden providential intervention in history. One was that Christians in the United States might be found unprepared. The ABCFM, for example, recognized the "new responsibilities which have providentially come to the American churches in regard to the Philippine Islands" but nonetheless reckoned that the board could not suddenly take up work in a new field given its finite resources.[74]

Regardless of these nuances, during the first two decades of the US occupation, missionaries recalled the role of Providence in directing the United States to the archipelago with remarkable persistence when they addressed audiences in both the United States and the islands. According to Stuntz, the first Protestant sermon in the Philippines on March 2, 1899, which James Thoburn, a Methodist missionary visiting from India gave, set the tone by "trac[ing] the history of God's kingdom in Asia" and "show[ing] the providential character of American occupation."[75] Such rhetoric showed no signs of abating: "We are here," declared the revivalist George Pentecost, who visited the islands in 1902, "because in the mysterious providence of God the time had come for us to be here."[76] In a speech James Rodgers gave to the Evangelical Union in 1905, he recalled the "strange and unexpected turn of events" by which "the islands came under the care of the American people."[77] Baptist missionary Charles Briggs was still claiming in 1913 that "the battle of Manila Bay was an act in a drama of far greater design than the chief actors even guessed."[78] Even ten years after his departure from the Philippines in 1908, Episcopal missionary Mercer Johnston was emphasizing in his sermons in the United States that the American arrival in the Philippines had not happened "by chance," that Providence had guided McKinley, and that to suggest otherwise was "to defame God."[79]

The missionary reading of divine intervention in the Philippines was intimately linked to sweeping ideas about the historical import of the Pacific Ocean, which now supposedly cohered under American auspices. If the missionary community in Hawai'i was ambivalent about the idea that the United States was bringing the ocean together, supporters of the Philippine mission proved keen to situate the Philippine story in a broader history of how God and US empire were transforming the "island world." The Presbyterian magazine *Assembly Herald* produced articles on "the new Pacific" and "the outlook across the Pacific," declaring that "never in the history of the world has there been a greater opportunity."[80] Missionaries had to follow their nation across the ocean: "The peal of the trumpet rings out over the Pacific. The church must go where America goes."[81] Another article drew an analogy with Hawai'i, where the ABCFM had eighty years earlier "found natives as superstitious, degraded, and savage as any the Philippines to-day possess" but had effected remarkable changes.[82]

Women who supported missions also read significance into Pacific histories. The Congregationalist magazine *Life and Light for Woman* looked to nineteenth-century Pacific history as a source of hope for the Philippine enterprise, remembering evangelistic successes across the ocean.[83] The publication of Helen Barrett Montgomery's *Christus Redemptor* in 1906 further encouraged Christian women to conceive of the Pacific as an "island world" and as the site of historical missionary successes that pointed toward an important future. In this formulation, the Philippines was connected to the Society

Islands, Micronesia, Hawai'i, Fiji, New Zealand, and Malaysia, among others. Women's missionary societies issued study guides that coincided with the publication of Montgomery's book, suggested further reading, and started lending libraries on Pacific topics.[84] One book that was repeatedly recommended that offered a connected history of missionizing across the Pacific—*The Islands of the Pacific: From the Old to the New* (1895)—was authored by J. M. Alexander, the son of missionaries to Hawai'i.[85] This demonstrates how the perspectives of the descendants of missionaries in Hawai'i helped to frame understandings of the Pacific as a site of historical and religious significance in a new age of US imperialism. Articles that accompanied the publication of *Christus Redemptor* were also published in the periodicals. In one particularly fascinating essay in the Methodist magazine the *Woman's Missionary Friend*, Frances J. Dyer asked who had "right of jurisdiction" over the "island world," moving through time and considering in turn the historical claims of the Portuguese/Spanish, the Dutch, the British, and the Americans, each represented as a male character. Dyer elevated the US claim to the Pacific, arguing that it came about "not by right of discovery, not from . . . ambition to colonize" but because God "placed him in political control." She then brought onto the stage a fifth character, the missionary, "to typify Christ as the real ruler."[86] The colonization of the Philippines was situated in a sweeping and progressive oceanic history framed by a cast of colonial actors, but ultimately it was God's hand and his evangelistic purpose that was at its center.

Missionaries in the Philippines sought to instill in their Filipino students a divinely ordained, US-centric vision of Pacific and world history. In the March 1903 edition of *Silliman Truth*, the bilingual bulletin of David Hibbard's industrial school, an article appeared in both English and Tagalog entitled "The Future of the Pacific Ocean." Proclaiming at the outset that "westward the course of Empire has for centuries taken its way," it elaborated a sweeping historical schema that encompassed the dawn of civilization in Egypt, its movement through Greece and Rome, its improvement in Western Europe, and finally its settlement in the "New World of America," where "there is growing up a civilization" destined to be "the grandest the world has yet seen." The writer noted that each of these civilizations had grouped around a body of water: first the Mediterranean, then the Atlantic. The author proclaimed that "the attention of the world is slowly turning westward to this largest of all the Oceans, the Pacific," which was to be "the great theater of the world's history in the future." The signs were clear: the West Coast of the United States had become "the ruling force in the nation"; Japan and Korea had opened up; China was soon to awaken; Russia was seeking a Pacific outlet via the trans-Siberian railroad; Hawai'i had "developed rapidly under the care of the United States"; and Australia, Canada, and Alaska were all assuming importance. Moreover, in recent years, "by a sudden turn of history the Philippines [fell] under [the] care [of the United States] and[,] relieved from the oppression of the Friars of Rome[,] they will also take their place in this onward march of nations." The article concluded that contemporaries were "seeing history made rapidly" and asked: "Can we not see God's hand moving in history and guiding the affairs of nations for the accomplishment of his mighty purpose of extension for the kingdom of Christ in the world?"[87]

The notion that the United States and its missionaries had arrived in the Philippines as part of a grand providential design for the Pacific undoubtedly raised expectations for what would be accomplished by evangelistic work in the islands. Missionaries talked about the possibilities for their work as though they were limitless, seeing God as accelerating history in the islands away from a torpid Spanish Catholic past and opening the door for a spiritual change that could occur almost instantaneously. History, wrote one Presbyterian missionary in a letter to his board very early in his work, was now being made very rapidly.[88] Brent remarked on the difficulty of writing about spiritual conditions in the Philippines, given the rapidity with which "the old order" was "passing away to give place to the new. . . . What is true of to-day will not necessarily apply tomorrow."[89] After just five years in the islands, the Evangelical Union pronounced that the work that had been done amounted to fifty to seventy years' worth of work in other fields and that it would be "difficult to over estimate the vastness" of further opportunities.[90] "Events move quickly," wrote Presbyterian missionary Stealy Rossiter in January 1909, "when the times are ripe."[91]

Yet missionaries did not use the language of Providence to justify empire and swat away opposition in the same bombastic and confident terms as McKinley and Beveridge did. Instead, they profoundly felt the gravity of their belief in American providential appointment. In missionary hands, the ideas that Providence had used the United States to open up an important chance for evangelism and that the time was now ripe for a radical spiritual transformation were not straightforwardly causes for celebration. Missionaries insisted that the nature of divinely ordained enterprises was that the given windows of opportunity were narrow and that they only bore their promised fruit if those called by God earnestly accepted their spiritual duty. The consequences of failing to properly heed the call to arms in the Philippines would be ruinous for both the United States and its churches and for

Filipinos. The nation's chosen status was conditional and Providence was an inexorable force that could rapidly close the door it seemed to have opened so swiftly. Missionaries did not simply see themselves as actors driving forward an unfolding providential history but viewed history itself as an agent that could overtake and ruin them.

The Crisis of Mission and Empire

For missionary thinkers of the late nineteenth century, a crisis inhered in each divinely ordained opportunity. Arthur T. Pierson, the influential missionary leader, defined crisis in his 1886 book as "a combination of grand opportunity and great responsibility, the hour when the chance of glorious success and the risk of awful failure confront each other; the turning point of history and destiny." At the time Pierson wrote, he perceived "Satan's active agents" to be filling a gap missionaries needed to take advantage of.[92] Speaking from his theologically conservative standpoint, he saw the church in the United States as being preoccupied by a new theology that saw good in non-Christian religions, denied the reality of damnation, and downplayed the urgency of conversion. Consequently, those who subscribed to the new theology were not moving quickly enough to take advantage of the many doors Providence was opening around the world.[93] Christians needed to counter spiritual apathy with faith, prayer, and action to meet the opportunities they were being presented with, ensure that those opportunities did not pass by, and save the church at home and abroad from spiritual death.[94] Around the turn of the century, more theologically moderate leaders of the missionary movement such as Josiah Strong and John R. Mott also made clear their belief that the conversion of the world was not a task to be deferred; "the evangelization of the world in this generation" became the watchword of Mott and the Student Volunteer Movement.[95]

Charles Brent articulated similar ideas about crisis in relation to the Philippines to a laity in the United States. On the one hand, he shared Albert Beveridge's desire to turn to ideas about Providence in order to escape the confines of American history and precedent when justifying the US role in the islands. In his final sermon in Boston before leaving for the Philippines, he chastised those who were "bound up with the history of the past, who revere the Constitution as the sole safeguard of national life, who live in the aspirations & thoughts of the men of yesterday." He argued that a recognition that "there is a law higher than the Constitution" to which the United States was subjected—God's law—offered a way out of becoming "slaves" to historical precedent.[96]

On the other hand, in other sermons Brent wrote around the same time, he moved beyond Beveridge, not simply sanctioning US empire through the language of Providence but applying Pierson's notion of crisis to it, warning Americans of their solemn responsibilities when facing a God-given opportunity. Despite his ambivalence about the lessons to be drawn from historical precedent, Brent by no means abandoned the use of history altogether. Instead, he utilized a peculiar historical frame, infusing theories about the historical development of nations with a sacred purpose and, in a striking turn, imbuing patriotism with the imprimatur of Christ himself. The true purpose of the nation, said Brent, was to come to consciousness of a destiny to be a "universal servant."[97] This was the "higher patriotism" that was best exemplified historically by the "greatest Jewish patriot" Jesus Christ, who understood that "He was for the world & the world for Him."[98] Conversely, a turning inward and a failure to acknowledge the breadth of national destiny had led to the death of nations, from the Israelites to Rome to eighteenth-century Christendom.[99] In the United States, the "higher patriotism" was taking hold, manifesting itself in an imperial vision that recognized a duty "to lead the nations in a high flight of unselfishness." However, this vision was engaged in a struggle with a conceptualization of nationhood marked by "selfishness & cowardice" that threatened to send the United States the same way as the fallen empires that had preceded it.[100] White supremacist Democrats, older liberal Republicans, and anti-racist Black activists all opposed the seizure of overseas territory but for very different reasons, and some of these figures specifically decried the use of religious justifications for US imperialism.[101] Brent sought to counter their arguments by making clear that even though the US Constitution expressed ambivalence about empire, the broad sweep of global sacred history did not.

Brent's philosophy of history did not straightforwardly replicate McKinley's assertion of sudden providential interposition or Beveridge's vision of historical progress. Instead, it implied a specific soteriological purpose for US empire by styling the United States as the fulfillment of God's vision for the Jewish nation. He envisioned history not as progressive or teleological but as cyclical, marked by a repeating pattern of rise, decline, and fall that it was for the United States to transcend. Such cyclical conceptions of history were familiar to nineteenth-century Americans, and Brent's invocation of them demonstrates that they were still available at the dawn of the twentieth century, even as professional historians settled on a linear, historicist view of time.[102] In particular, Brent's formulation suggested a survival of the Puritan jeremiad, envisioning the United States on a knife edge between its destiny as the New Israel, on one side, and moral, spiritual, and physical ruin, on the other.[103] Ultimately, said Brent, US civilization, US institutions, and US Christianity were "at the bar of judgment" and swift action was necessary to avoid history recording the same "awful verdict which other civilizations and other religions have doomed themselves to hear:—*Weighed in the balances and found wanting.*"[104]

Brent was not the only prominent missionary figure to express such an idea in relation to the entry of the United States into the Philippines. Arthur Judson Brown identified the commencement of mission work in the islands as marking a "crisis" and an "emergency" in US history, issuing a jeremiad to the church in his 1902 report on his visit to the nascent Presbyterian mission. Americans had not lacked "martial courage" or "material resources," argued Brown, but the question still to be answered was whether the United States would lack "Christians of large hearts and broad vision, and holy purpose."[105] It was true, Brown wrote in his 1903 book, that a "new era" was dawning in the Philippines, but that did not automatically mean that "everything will be all right." It was down to Americans to "make it all right by honest, earnest, unselfish endeavor."[106] Brent's Episcopal colleague Mercer Johnston also found cause for trepidation in the idea that Providence had established the United States in the islands. Giving a sermon in Manila in June 1907, Johnston spoke of "the ways of God in this historical episode" but echoed Brent in calling for the United States to fulfill its grand role by showing patriotism greater than that of the biblical Israelites, whose punishment for their unfaithfulness served as a warning about the fate that might befall a nation ignorant of its divine purpose.[107]

It is clear that the boundaries between missionary discourse and a broader nationalist rhetoric regarding history were not firmly drawn. The notion of crisis and the possibility of ruin if Americans deviated from an imperial destiny were also inscribed in "secular" theories of the 1890s. Frederick Jackson Turner's frontier thesis, for example, understood the westward movement of the frontier as intrinsic to the character and democracy of Americans and feared for the implications of the frontier's "closure."[108] After 1893, the China-market lobby also deployed the idea of a crisis of overproduction to argue for Pacific expansion.[109] President Theodore Roosevelt, a prominent imperialist, also warned against the dangers of adopting a "life of ease" at the dawn of a twentieth century that loomed "big with the fate of many nations."[110] Even later, in 1910, the *Philippine Presbyterian* approvingly reprinted a Roosevelt speech in which he acknowledged that "assuredly, the dreams of golden glory in the future will not come true" unless "by our own mighty deeds we make them come true," citing the Mongols, Phoenicians, and Greeks as great civilizations that had failed to avert destruction by correctly embracing their world role.[111]

However, Brent's sermons demonstrated recourse to a particular missionary interpretation of history that was inflected with the sacred, the cyclical, and the global. By using the ancient Israelites as his key point of comparison, Brent emphasized the specifically spiritual nature of the work that was to be done if the United States was to take on the mantle that Providence intended for it instead of falling to ruin. US empire was not just chosen by God but was also accountable to him. In emphasizing this in sermons to the laity in the United States, Brent made clear that it was the responsibility of ordinary Christian Americans to lend their support to US empire and mission work in the Philippines, as much as it was the responsibility of Congress and the executive to legislate appropriately. He echoed other imperialist ideologues in arguing that US national history was not a large enough lens for apprehending these responsibilities, then turned specifically to the lessons offered by millennia of global sacred history. Such a qualification of the progressive and providential model indicated the peculiar kinds of attention missionaries might bring to questions of religion and temporality as they related to the United States and the Philippines.

During the course of their work in the Philippines, missionaries also frequently appealed to notions of crisis. They perceived a window of opportunity that Providence had opened only temporarily, underscoring the urgency of their work to US audiences that missionaries deemed to be supplying insufficient resources to take advantage of what was, in the words of Charles Briggs, a "tremendous possibility" that was "rapidly crystallizing into an impossibility and a forever lost opportunity."[112] They warned that history was not waiting for them and that the direction of Philippine religion was to be decided imminently one way or the other. In Brent's words, "the opportunity of reaching a primitive race" could last "but a brief season" before "world forces" caught up.[113] An Evangelical Union appeal for donations in 1904 demonstrated optimism that change would occur rapidly, stating that "the next few years are to definitely fix the religious status of the Filipino people," but it also warned that if Protestants failed to take advantage of that window by offering "liberal support" to evangelistic enterprise, it would become "impossible" to accomplish the same results "in a century."[114]

The sense of a narrow window did not pass away even as the missions entered their second and third decades. Briggs claimed in his 1913 book that the church in the United States stood at the "crossroads of history." It had a unique chance to win the "awakening Orient" for Protestantism, and its response thus far had been insufficient.[115] The future would be "an unsparing critic and judge."[116] Frank Laubach was particularly sensitive to the idea of a closing window, as he demonstrated when he made the case for the opening of new fronts for ABCFM work among the peoples of Mindanao. Writing to the board in March 1915 shortly after his arrival in the islands, he said that the field was "over-ripe. We have waited too long. . . . This hour is too critical for any dog-in-the-manger tactics."[117] At the end of 1915, he stressed that "we are not dealing with any slow moving China here. We are in the midst of one of the most rapid and thoroughgoing transformations in the history of the world."[118] Although the perceived acceleration of history in the Philippines, which he pointedly contrasted with the movement of history in a contemporary China perceived as stagnant and superstitious, might have been a positive sign for missionaries that God's hand was blessing their enterprise, inherent in this acceleration was the possibility of being overtaken by events. Later still, in the mid-1920s, Hibbard noted in his published work that "a time element enters into the mission work in the archipelago. . . . This is an open door and we cannot expect or ask that it remain open forever."[119]

Missionaries' exhortations about the need for urgency in the Philippines were strategic; they were well designed to rouse American Christians' support for mission work by impelling them to recognize the gravity of the providential opportunity and to respond accordingly. Indeed, the perpetual deferral of the closing of the window of opportunity allowed missionaries to sustain the sense of crisis for decades. The challenge of missionaries, in the words of Cornelia Moots, was to ensure that "Christians living so at ease in the faraway home land" were "burdened by the opportunities we felt ourselves weighted down with in these deep sea islands."[120] Invoking a sense of a crisis that was national as well as spiritual was one way of bridging the gap between comfortable distance and frontline evangelism.

That does not mean, however, that missionaries did not keenly feel a sense of crisis and the brevity of their opportunity. They were constantly plagued by the idea that their fellow Americans, and most obviously the US colonial administration in the Philippines, did not share their commitment to the cause of Protestantism in the archipelago. In this sense, they shared something with the missionary community in Hawai'i—a sense of intellectual distance from the mainstream of US imperial thought when working in Pacific islands that was engendered by the apparent unwillingness of Americans to properly examine religious histories. US policymakers may have used a language of providential appointment when they justified empire, but they seemed indifferent about the specific spiritual purpose missionaries clearly believed that God had ordained in prompting the US seizure of the islands. Missionaries also feared that the American nation might not be sufficiently invested in the colonial project that it had begun. When they reflected on the vicissitudes of US political opinion about the readiness of the Philippines for self-government and the appropriateness of empire, they perceived the United States to be exacerbating their sense of crisis. They were afraid that the American abandonment of the islands might in fact, if it happened, represent the slamming shut of the historic window of opportunity that they expected and feared.

The Spiritual Shortcomings of US Empire

Missionaries' belief that US empire was a providential instrument for ensuring Protestant triumph in the Philippines stood in tension with the US government's ambivalence about facilitating Protestant evangelism. Imperial administrators expressed a desire to break with Spanish precedent by underscoring the separation of church and state. Although such a separation was a broader American ideal, at least rhetorically, its importance in the archipelago was heightened by the US impulse to differentiate its empire from that of Spain.[121] If, as Americans wanted to believe, a key grievance of Filipinos against Spain had been that church and state were inextricably intertwined, then the United States had to convince Filipinos that its arrival in the islands did not automatically signify the coming of Protestantism. Although missionaries acknowledged the necessity of this course of action, they quickly became frustrated by their failure to benefit from it.[122] The US government broke with past precedent in one sense by establishing religious freedom as a governing principle, but in the eyes of missionaries, it did not then take the necessary next step of accepting the opportunity God had presented to radically reinvent Filipino Christianity. In fact, the government reached the conclusion that adhering to the principle of religious freedom in effect meant accepting that for Filipino Christianity, the Catholic past conditioned the future.

Successive officials in both Washington and Manila accepted that Filipinos were already Christian and advocated continuity over conversion. Although Protestants continued to heroize President McKinley for his role in opening the Philippines, he sought papal endorsement for his policy in the islands to smooth the transition to US governance.[123] When Albert Beveridge visited the archipelago in mid-1899, he had conversations with Filipino elites and mestizo businessmen who urged him "not to attack the prevailing religion which is Catholic & with which the people are satisfied."[124] Jacob Schurman, the first head of the Philippine Commission, heeded such advice, recommending that the question of religion be left alone lest Filipinos believe that Americans were destroying both their government and their faith and intensify their revolt.[125] The argument that the Philippines should remain Catholic was further amplified by Catholic voices in the United States, for example that of Archbishop John Ireland of St. Paul, Minnesota, the leader of the Americanization movement in the Catholic Church, and that of Representative Bourke Cochran of New York. In response to initial fears that US government in the islands would destroy the Philippine church, both men chose cooperation with the imperial project as the most effective tool for securing a Catholic future for the islands. They used the languages of religious freedom and providential design to carve out a role for Catholics in determining Philippine policy.[126]

When William Howard Taft became the first civilian American governor-general of the islands in July 1901, he did not envisage a Protestant future for the Philippines; he doubted that "any separation from the catholic church could be successful so as to include a very large part of the people."[127] Taft's Philippine Commission was convinced that Filipinos "love the Catholic Church. The solemnity and grandeur of its ceremonies appeal most strongly to their religious motives."[128] Himself a Unitarian and thus without much personal investment in the struggle between Protestantism and Catholicism, Taft expressed concerns that a break with Catholicism might see Filipinos "sink into fetichism and idolatry." He accordingly sought not only "to frame civil laws which shall accord with views conscientiously entertained by the Catholics" but also to "make the people better Catholics."[129] There was a racialized idea at work here that Catholicism was somehow the only religion suitable for Filipinos, an idea that operated hand in hand with a fundamental confidence in American civilization—the belief that anything from the United States would inevitably elevate anything Filipino and advance democracy, order, and freedom. In particular, Taft hoped that American bishops would fill clerical vacancies in the Philippines to "raise the tone of the religious teaching" and to ensure a Catholic leadership that was "loyal to the government," demonstrating to Filipinos that the United States was not overthrowing Philippine religion but reforming it.[130] The pope obliged by appointing four Americans to important sees, including Jeremiah Harty as archbishop of Manila in 1903.[131] President Roosevelt also saw an opportunity to bolster both his colonial policy and his electoral prospects by soliciting the cooperation of Catholics, selecting the Catholic Spanish-American War veteran James Francis Smith first as secretary of public instruction on the Philippine Commission in 1903 and then as governor-general in 1906.[132]

The attitude that their Catholic past determined the religious future of Filipinos persisted to a greater or lesser extent across successive US regimes. Initially, Protestant missionaries were asked not to conduct evangelistic work among Filipinos until the Philippine-American War was officially declared over for fear of adding further fuel to the conflagration, but government wariness of missionary efforts among Catholics endured after the war was over.[133] Leonard Wood, a leading military figure in the pacification of the Philippines who became the governor-general of the islands in the 1920s, advised ABCFM missionaries to confine their work to the non-Christian peoples that Spanish colonialism and evangelism had not reached instead of "interfering" with Catholicism.[134] W. Cameron Forbes, an official in the Philippines from 1904 and governor-general from 1909 to 1913, privately treated Protestant missionaries as an amusing sideshow in his journals. A man of little religious inclination, Forbes frequently described the hopelessness, infighting, and "biliousness" of missionaries and their unsuccessful attempts to solicit donations from him in his journals. He and other government officials attended Catholic processions and mixed socially with the Catholic hierarchy.[135] Although Taft, Roosevelt, Wood, and Forbes were not Catholic, they all accepted the continuity of Catholicism as best for the islands.

The unwillingness of the US government to offer any advantage to Protestantism in the islands was also apparent in its educational policy. The hundreds of teachers from the United States appointed by the colonial government after 1901 were the closest thing to state-sponsored missionaries in the Philippines.[136] A system of public education, conducted in English, was at the heart of the American vision of the colonial state, both as the fulfillment of a racial obligation to uplift the supposedly childlike people of the Philippines and as a form of pacification that complemented the violent discipline meted out during the Philippine-American War.[137] The Catholic hierarchy in both the United States and the Philippines, however, was attentive to the threat of public schools becoming the de facto centers of Protestant proselytism that they had been in the United States earlier in the century. Because their cooperation in the occupation of the Philippines was important in the smooth implementation of colonial governance, Catholics became key arbiters of educational policy, putting significant pressure on the insular government's Bureau of Education regarding issues such as the selection of teachers and history textbooks.[138] The result was an educational mission that was avowedly secular. Circulars from the Bureau of Education reminded teachers to say nothing of their personal faith even outside the classroom.[139] At the local level, teachers' reliance on the goodwill of local Catholic Filipino elites distanced them from missionaries, whom they became reluctant to engage with even in a social capacity.[140]

Missionaries felt that the ways the government implemented church-state separation and religious freedom did not allow for true liberty because it privileged Catholics. "The attitude of the government," complained one Presbyterian, "while theoretically impartial is really antagonistic to Protestantism."[141] Through such pandering, the government was entrenching Catholicism's historical advantage instead of accepting God's invitation to break further with the Spanish colonial past: "A considerable number of Americans both at home and abroad," observed an exasperated Arthur Judson Brown, "never tire of reminding us that the Filipinos had a form of the Christian religion before the Americans came, and that it is neither expedient or just to change it."[142] Missionaries argued that by being in thrall to the past, the government risked ruining the future. The free institutions of the United States were built on Protestant foundations, they argued, and to try to give Filipinos the former without the latter risked the development of an atheistic or "anti-Christian" educated class.[143] Moreover, discouraging individual religious expression would lead teachers, government officials, military men, and businessmen arriving from the United States to give up church attendance and instead involve themselves in a Manila society life of drinking, gambling, sex, and Sabbath-breaking, giving Filipinos the impression that Americans had no religion.[144] Cornelia Moots spoke of the need for missionaries to "establish every institution possible" to save Filipinos from the Catholic Church and from "evil Americans, many of whom are in Government employ."[145]

Taft and Roosevelt, among other contemporary Americans, began to reimagine Catholicism as a historical civilizing force that might turn its paternalistic authority to the purposes of Anglo-American hegemony.[146] Symbolic of this, Americans established a bronze statue of Andrés de Urdaneta, the first Augustinian friar to arrive in the Philippines in 1565, alongside another of the Spanish navigator Miguel López de Legazpi at the heart of the colonial capital in Manila early in the occupation.[147] Most missionaries, however, remained steeped in well-worn tropes of vehement anti-Catholicism, certain that Catholics were seeking to subvert the state. They argued that the new American Catholic hierarchy was no better than the hated Spanish friars. Although "Irish Yankee Romanist priests" paid lip service to religious freedom where it helped them make arguments that Americans should leave Catholicism alone, argued one Methodist missionary, at the same time they made a mockery of that ideal, embracing their heritage of deceitfulness, sedition, and aggression.[148] Insofar as Arthur Judson Brown acknowledged the need for a secular public education system, it was because he was certain that Catholics would otherwise manipulate the public schools.[149]

Mercer Johnston was particularly sensitive to what he perceived as ongoing Catholic attempts to claim a position as a de facto state religion. In a 1906 sermon, he noted Archbishop Jeremiah Harty's withdrawal from offering addresses at three successive inauguration ceremonies for governors-general, apparently in protest of the fact that he had been asked to speak alongside Protestant preachers.[150] Johnston also wrote an article expressing his discontent when Frederick Rooker, the bishop of Jaro, raised the US flag beneath that of the Vatican.[151] Johnston believed that the government was being naïve, and in his private correspondence he questioned its fitness. He expressed concern over the "Romewards" drift of US politics, going so far as to say that the "morally low grade government" almost disposed him "to speak peaceably with . . . anti-imperialists."[152] The only way around the influence of conniving Catholic lobbyists in Washington, suggested Stuntz in a letter to his Methodist sponsors, was to fight fire with fire. Taft's commission needed to be directed to American Protestant leaders who would speak up for the missionary cause and exercise "a legitimate amount of influence" in selecting officials.[153]

The US government's biggest crime was cowardice in the face of an opportunity to end four centuries of perceived historical stasis.[154] One of the strongest critiques along these lines came early in the US occupation in a manuscript Methodist missionary Arthur W. Prautch, one of the very first Protestants in the islands, sent to the United States. Prautch took umbrage at an order issued by the military governor, E. S. Otis, compelling a Filipino newspaper to retract an editorial demanding the removal of Spanish friars, after an episode in which a Catholic priest was alleged to have publicly humiliated a Filipino schoolboy. Prautch argued that Otis's deference to the Catholic hierarchy made "it difficult for the Filipinos to understand whether the R.C. Archbishop of Manila rules or . . . Otis." He continued by calling for "real American courage" to heed Providence's call to "break the spell and curse that has enslaved the people for 400 years."[155]

Missionaries spoke similarly of Taft's "sentimental" visit to Rome in 1902 to negotiate with the Vatican over the future of land in the Philippines previously held by Spanish friars. Those who had studied Catholic history "from a churchly standpoint," argued Stuntz, knew "how hopeless such an undertaking must be."[156] The Church was eventually deprived of these lands, which the US government purchased for over $7 million in 1903. The missionary argument, however, was that there should have been nothing to negotiate, given that friars had allegedly asserted ownership over the Philippines' most fertile land only through gross abuses of power.[157] In the eyes of missionaries, the government was again pandering to Rome's historical authority and buying into propaganda that falsely "dinned into their ears" Filipinos' love of Catholicism.[158]

In response, missionaries strove to point out why it was that Philippine religious history should have no weight in contemporary policy considerations. That history, Stuntz argued in his book, showed that Filipino allegiance to Catholicism could only be nominal and based on fear. Stuntz insisted that "no proof should be required that the friars are hated" and that because Philippine Catholic history was "unpleasant" to write about, "only so far as the interests of truthful history are concerned will Protestantism speak out on these matters."[159] He must have felt that "truthful history" was in jeopardy, however, because he went on to write in great detail about the supposed historical grievances of Filipinos against Catholicism. It was common knowledge, argued Stuntz, that friars had seized the best land for themselves, extorted money from the people, kept mistresses in contravention of their vows of celibacy, sought to keep Filipinos in ignorance by denying them education or the Bible, and stifled freedom of thought and speech through assassination, imprisonment, deportation, and intimidation.[160] The logical conclusion was that Filipinos could not know true spirituality or freedom of conscience and that Protestants would have to build religion from scratch.

Stuntz's arguments epitomized the fact that differences of opinion among Americans boiled down to how they perceived the utility of Philippine religious history. Although missionaries maintained that God had intervened in history to enable mass religious conversion, US colonial administrators seemed to believe that the past conditioned the future when it came to Filipino Christianity. Previous studies have argued that any hostility between missionaries and the government in the Philippines should not be overstated because a sense of mutual encouragement and a shared project remained, especially when writing for US audiences.[161] The evidence here, however, suggests that different perspectives on how the religious past should be treated marked a significant cleavage that was never fully overcome and prompted missionaries to view the United States as contributing to a crisis in Philippine history rather than as the instrument of Protestant triumph. In its failure to fully comprehend its spiritual duty, the United States risked failing to heed God's call and allowing a brief window of opportunity to close, with dire consequences for Americans and Filipinos alike.

Missionaries' concerns were further exacerbated by a sense that the United States might end up being responsible for the closing of the window of spiritual opportunity. Missionaries were haunted by fear, often driven by rumor, that US rule in the islands might prove to be temporary and that a change in the political winds in favor of a vocal anti-imperialist lobby could signal the end of the US national mission. Whatever missionaries' misgivings about the spiritual shortcomings of US empire may have been, they still recognized that they relied on that empire for their opening in the Philippines, and thus any sense that the United States might give up its duty was met with worry and opprobrium. Although Albert Memmi noted that the tendency to be "seized with worry and panic each time there is talk of changing the political status" was common to colonialists across imperial settings, missionaries imbued their fears with a particular spiritual weight.[162]

Uncertainty existed right from the start of evangelistic work in the islands. Indeed, a friend of Brent's advised him not even to accept the call to become bishop of Manila because "the Philippines may not be an American Colony by the time you are ready to go, but an independent Republic."[163] The anti-imperialist lobby remained a perceived threat well into the US occupation, and in a particularly scornful address Johnston gave on Memorial Day in 1906, extending his virulent criticism of New England anti-imperialists, he referred to a "devil's auction" in Washington that threatened to "substitute for the noble drama which is now in progress here, some opera bouffe of the Boston School of Scandal and Sentimentality." If the United States were to be "betrayed by sordid senators, cowardly congressmen, or sentimental scribblers . . . the beginning of the end of our national glory will be at hand."[164] There were signs that even arch-imperialists were getting cold feet when, under the presidency of Theodore Roosevelt and the governor-generalship of James Francis Smith, the Philippine Assembly was created in 1907 as an all-Filipino elected legislature under the oversight of the commission. Most missionaries deemed this move premature.[165] The insecurity continued for years afterward. One YMCA leader in Manila stated in October 1911 that "the big question of the future" was still "how long Uncle Sam will maintain sovereignty over the Archipelago."[166]

Missionaries complained that their Filipino proselytes were aware of the tentative nature of US sovereignty and that such awareness had implications for their evangelistic success. "It is often rumored that the Americans will leave here," wrote Robert Black to the ABCFM in May 1904, "and then [the Filipinos] think they will be left to the mercy of their oldtime oppressors." Because of this, they were disinclined to convert to Protestantism.[167] Such uncertainties particularly surfaced at climactic points of the US presidential election cycle because differences in opinion about the proper fate of the Philippines ran broadly along party lines. The anti-imperialist Democratic Party of William Jennings Bryan, Alton B. Parker, and Woodrow Wilson was seen to profoundly threaten the imperialistic vision of McKinley, Roosevelt, and Taft's Republicans. Black made his comment a few months before Roosevelt's victory over Parker in 1904, and in the immediate aftermath he expressed his relief that the result would stop the rumor mill from generating the belief that Americans were about to abandon the islands.[168] Overall, however, missionaries existed in a perpetual state of insecurity, fearing not only that the particular historic opportunity facilitated by US empire to transform Philippine religion would pass Americans by but that their nation's ambivalence about its spiritual as well as its secular responsibilities might be the direct cause of sudden and ruinous failure. Ultimately, as chapter 6 will show in more detail, Woodrow Wilson's victory in the presidential election of 1912 did indeed accelerate discussions about Philippine independence, and missionaries had to adjust to this new reality.

As the decades of American rule wore on, it became clear that the evangelistic project that God had inaugurated for Protestant missionaries in the Philippines through US empire was failing to live up to its apparently boundless potential. Fairly early on, Charles Briggs lamented the gap between "the romantic and ideal" and "the actual," finding that Filipinos were "disappointing" him. A Baptist colleague noted that "people are not coming to us by the dozens and hundreds as was first expected in the Philippine Islands."[169] Although the 105,000 converts won over to Protestant churches by 1925 represented a reasonable return, these numbers fell well short of initial expectations. Stuntz, for example, had predicted that 500,000 Filipino souls would be secured by the Methodist mission alone in its first twenty years.[170] These low numbers might have been seen as a confirmation of missionary fears—that the United States had wavered when presented with a God-given opportunity, that US empire's providential appointment did not automatically signify its enduring chosen status, and that Providence and history were inexorable forces that might overtake Americans, presenting openings but also rapidly taking them away. This chapter has shown that missionaries invoked history not simply to justify and heroize the US imperial project in the Philippines and to confirm Americans' starring role in a providential saga; rather, they wrestled with history as an external agent. Missionaries articulated a philosophy of history that not only raised expectations but also tempered them and supplied warnings, showing how history might index cowardice, stasis, and decline as much as progress.

The next chapter shows that when faced with a perpetual sense of crisis and disappointment, missionaries developed alternative ideas about the speed at which history moved. Instead of following their philosophies of Providence and crisis to their natural ends and blaming the ambivalence of Americans for the slow progress of their work, missionaries sought refuge in different conceptualizations of history that took the onus off the United States and revealed longer processes of development and change in the Philippines. First, like the missionary community in Hawai'i, missionaries to the Philippines engaged with social science, which in this case furnished a language that naturalized the slow progress of evangelistic work and placed the blame for it on Filipino racial capacity rather than on Americans' ambivalence. When borrowing from evolutionist models, missionaries often jarringly punctuated their persistent assertions of radical providential interventions in history with an emphasis on the need for patience. In doing this, they invested in a language, which US officials in the Philippines shared, of what the historian Michael Hawkins has termed "imperial historicism," whereby cultures could be placed on a scale of evolutionary progress and colonial interventions could be conceived of as leading them toward modernity.[171] Second, in paying attention to historical development, missionaries increasingly recognized that despite their grand expectations, the religious past of the Philippines was in fact inescapable. Hallmarks of Catholicism could not simply be cast aside but still had weight and had to be understood and negotiated. A few missionaries, notably Brent, even agreed with the US government that the proper and pragmatic course was to defer to and even appropriate elements of this past when conducting Protestant work. This viewpoint created tensions that were particularly evident in the ways missionaries responded to the built environment in the Philippines. In debating this issue, missionaries to the Philippines were, again like the missionary community in Hawai'i, drawn away from visions of a transformative American presence sweeping across the Pacific, instead being led to dwell upon the local past.

Chapter 5

"A Dark and Troubled Past"

Missionaries and Historicism in the Philippines

One missionary problematized the idea that Providence had presented an opportunity for rapid Protestant triumph in an American Philippines even before any formal mission had begun. Very soon after the United States annexed the islands, W. H. Lingle, a Presbyterian working in China, was commissioned by his board to investigate conditions in Manila. Perhaps because he was somewhat removed through his work in China from the hubristic language surrounding empire in the Philippines, the report he presented was qualified in its assessment of the prospects for radical change. Lingle warned that the opposition of Spanish priests endured and that conversions would be hard, as "the history of missions in all Roman Catholic countries" demonstrated. He praised Manila, noting its "refinement & elegance," in particular its "Roman Catholic churches & cathedrals which will rival any in Paris, London, or New York. . . . Any one coming to Manila may not think he is leaving all civilization behind." He also suggested that Filipinos had greatly benefited from the educational and benevolent institutions of the Catholic Church. Lingle's portrait of a dynamic, modernizing, and imposing city and of an entrenched Catholicism from which Filipinos had prospered somewhat undercut an idea that was the corollary of missionaries' belief in a providential intervention in Philippine history: that missionaries faced a stagnant Spanish Catholic culture that could be brushed aside in favor of a new Protestant and US history. Undeterred, the Presbyterian board's corresponding secretary simply annotated Lingle's report with the words "a fainthearted letter." The board proceeded to send a number of missionaries.[1]

Lingle was not the last missionary to suggest that understandings of US empire in the Philippines as a providential intervention in history only went so far and that the local past did in fact matter. When missionaries were on the ground in the Philippines, they frequently diluted a historical philosophy that thought in cycles of providential opportunity, crisis, and failure, instead locating US empire and missionary effort in the Philippines in more linear and progressive historical trajectories at the level of the archipelago. Recourse to these more gradual models of historical change gave missionaries an alternative way of contextualizing their work that staved off the fear that slow progress in converting the people of the Philippines to Protestantism was a sign that Americans were responsible for a ruinous failure to embrace a God-given opportunity. Instead, by locating their work on a historical continuum of development in the Philippines, missionaries deflected the blame for slow progress away from Americans and onto both their Spanish predecessors and the people of the islands who proved unable to escape their past quickly.

The theoretical underpinnings of missionaries' turn to historicism were furnished by the nascent social sciences and their notion of the stadial development of races. According to these evolutionary ideas, Filipinos could not be expected to transform into "civilized" Protestants overnight but needed time to emerge from the past their Spanish rulers had supposedly left them in, centuries behind the Anglo Saxon race. In this formulation, the slow progress of Protestant history in the islands was attributed both to the Spaniards' abdication of a colonial responsibility to drive Philippine history forward and to the inherent racial inferiority of Filipinos. In many ways, this idea brought missionaries into line with the epistemology of colonial administrators who were also heavily invested in evolutionary ideas, but in other ways, it was a language that allowed them to divorce their fortunes from ideas about the providential commission of US empire and to instead historicize their work.

Recognizing the supposed power of the past to limit the speed at which Filipinos could move forward also raised the possibility that missionaries would have to work within the constraints of Philippine history. Not least, it was not as easy as imperialists had hoped to yank the Philippines out of a "Spanish lake" and place it in a US Pacific. The Spanish Catholic past could not simply be dismissed as an impotent, medieval curio that Providence had blown away. Rather, it cast a long shadow. This was particularly clear in missionary discussions of the built environment. Even though missionaries saw architecture as the most visible evidence of the redundancy of the Spanish past, in their discussions of church buildings, missionaries showed that they recognized the need to adapt. Although they rhetorically equated Protestantism with a simpler, purer form of faith that would easily overpower a materialistic and empty Catholicism, missionaries simultaneously impressed on their American sponsors the need for churches that could compete with those standing on the Philippine landscape. This was an argument that combined missionaries' heavily racialized perceptions of Filipinos' proclivity toward "beautiful things" with a recognition that Catholicism was more than just a dead religion that Filipinos were either fundamentally ignorant about or deeply distrusted.[2]

The shaping of missionary work by Spanish precedent engendered tensions among evangelists. Although most missionaries still fundamentally believed they were in the Philippines to win them for Protestantism, some, notably the Episcopal missionary bishop Charles Brent, joined the US colonial government in arguing that Catholicism's historical legacy needed to be respected and that Protestants should not seek to win converts among Catholics. In other words, local history as Americans in the Philippines experienced it fractured the US project. It led to divergent perspectives on the purpose of empire and ensured that hopes for the rapid transformation of the archipelago, and indeed the Pacific Ocean, by Providence and US empire were punctuated by a more complex view of Philippine history. This view increasingly focused not on mission work in the Philippines as the culmination of God's historical plan for the Pacific but on the past of the islands.

Missionaries' supposed confidence in God's ability to intervene in and accelerate time, on the one hand, and their recourse to historicist conceptualizations, on the other, sat uneasily alongside one another. By drawing out this juxtaposition, this chapter complicates prior scholarship that has suggested that confident historical discourse gave rise to a coherent imperial project and that the rhetoric of Providence flowed easily and logically into the racialist and developmentalist notions with which Americans approached the Philippines.[3] Missionaries were good at rhetorically smoothing over the paradoxes in the way they thought about history, but the fluidity with which they moved between discourses of providentialism and historicism does not mean that these two conceptualizations fit neatly into a coherent whole. Different outlooks on history exposed fissures, contradictions, and the ever-shifting terrain on which Americans produced knowledge. The first half of this book argued that the missionary community in Hawai'i focused on the religious past in the islands to assert intellectual distance from the United States even as they invited US empire. In the Philippines, although the dynamics of the mission were very different from those in Hawai'i, the narration of local history through a religious lens again provided missionaries with a way of making sense of their shifting expectations and uncertain position on the ground.

The Slow Progress of Philippine History

Although for Nathaniel Emerson in Hawai'i, evolutionary ideas about the development of racial capacity supplied a scientific rationale for studying the intellectual production of Native Hawaiians, such ideas taught missionaries in the Philippines that island peoples could not be judged by the standards of contemporary Europe or North America. Instead, there were stages of historical development that every group had to pass through before reaching the pinnacle of modern civilization and gaining the capacity for self-governance in affairs of church and state. This form of historicism, which such theorists as the British anthropologist E. B. Tylor and his American counterpart Lewis Henry Morgan influentially posited, became a driving principle of the social sciences as they crystallized as professional disciplines and attained cultural authority in the late nineteenth and early twentieth centuries. In turn, it lent intellectual legitimacy to the tutelary project of the US state in the Philippines.[4] Leaning on these ideas, colonial administrators recognized Filipino capacity to move toward an unspecified future point of civilization without suggesting that it seemed imminently in reach.[5] They located the "non-Christian tribes" of the islands even farther back in time, justifying a more heavy-handed and nakedly paternalistic form of rule over the Muslim population of the southern islands of the Philippines, for example.[6]

According to Protestant missionaries, three and a half centuries of Spanish colonialism had done little to help Filipinos move along the evolutionary scale. "Has anything happened these past four hundred years?" asked the outspoken Episcopal missionary Mercer Johnston in one sermon that was reprinted for the benefit of American readers.[7] In this formulation, Spanish rule had done little more than place a veneer over the perceived follies and evils of a preexisting Philippine social order that was based on hereditary chieftainship, indolent serfdom, and pagan religious practice.[8] "A strang[e] mixture of paganism and Catholicism they have here," wrote one Presbyterian missionary in a letter to a sponsoring church in the United States. "You really can tell no difference between many of their beliefs and the pagan nations of the world."[9] Methodist evangelist Homer Stuntz added in his book that much of the supposedly superstitious practice found among Filipino Catholics represented survivals of idolatrous beliefs that predated the arrival of Catholic missionaries yet that were consonant with Catholicism. Catholic leaders had taken advantage of similarities, allowing Filipinos to believe that medallions of the Virgin Mary or the saints were new devices through which the protective influence of *anting-anting* (an amulet or charm) could be attained.[10] Baptist missionary Charles Briggs concurred, arguing that "crude *anitos*, or idols," had simply been exchanged for Catholic images, allowing Catholics to claim a raft of rapid conversions that demanded "no radical change of belief."[11] Arthur Judson Brown, secretary of the Presbyterian mission board, concluded that despite the claims that Spain had made to have Christianized the Philippines, Filipinos were nearly all "heathen with a thin veneer of Romanism of the mediaeval-Spanish type."[12] Wrapped up in this idea of a veneer were both long-standing tropes of Catholics as "insufficiently separate from the pagan Roman past" and racist notions that the missionary community in Hawai'i had applied to Native Hawaiians: that the Christianity of nonwhite others was necessarily superficial given their incapacity for true conversion.[13]

Brown's characterization of Spanish rule as "medieval" was frequently deployed to underscore the stagnancy of Spanish religious and political leadership, which Protestant missionaries implicitly contrasted with the self-evident virtues of being modern, farther forward on the scale of linear historical time. Not all Americans in the late nineteenth and early twentieth centuries were so convinced that being medieval was a bad thing—some found in their romanticized vision of the Middle Ages as a time of irrationality and primal impulse an antidote to the trappings of modernity—but there was consensus that the medieval was a precursor to the modern.[14] And, argued Mercer Johnston, the condition of Catholicism was such that without external stimulus, it would remain stuck in this precursory stage: "*This Italian idea must be killed.* Otherwise the future of these Islands will be but a repetition of the unhappy past."[15] The Spanish Inquisition was a particular historical point of reference. Missionaries styled the friars' abuses that the Filipinos had revolted against as the continuation of an unbroken, repetitious history of religiously motivated Spanish brutality that had roots in the fifteenth century. Brown remarked that Filipinos' "examples were the people who founded and maintained the Inquisition with all its bloody and fiendish cruelties," and Briggs argued that the friars had "enforc[ed] medieval ideals by means of the holy Inquisition."[16] One Baptist periodical offered Filipino students a direct comparison between the ways the people who "professed to be Christians" dealt with "heretics" in the "dark ages"—by means of an Inquisition—and those of Jesus, who showed that "if your brother does not believe in the truth, . . . it is your obligation to teach him."[17]

The association of Spanish Catholicism with stagnant medievalism was not unique to missionaries; policymakers and other US observers used similar rhetoric.[18] However, the response among missionaries was to invoke another historical marker: the Reformation. Regardless of the specifics of Philippine history, the European past told them everything they needed to know about how the future was about to unfold. The evangelistic project in the Philippines, as missionaries saw it, was akin to Martin Luther's project in sixteenth-century Europe of breaking the power of a church that was perceived to be corrupt and spiritually impoverished and distributing the Bible in vernacular languages to allow its message to touch the hearts of ordinary people.[19] Brown asserted that Filipinos were "on the eve of a religious revolution comparable only to that of the German and English revolt against Rome in the sixteenth century" and promised "better results" from the Protestant mission "in three decades than the Roman Catholics have produced in three centuries."[20] Spanish Catholicism had brought a cloistered form of Christianity, but now a widespread, deep, and democratic movement was about to burst forth.[21] Briggs dedicated a whole chapter of his book to "The Protestant Reformation in the Philippines," outlining the parallels between sixteenth-century Europe and the recent past in the islands with specific reference to ecclesiastical greed and inquisitorial repression. Although "the Spanish Church refused to learn the lessons its own history was so faithfully teaching," there had entered the Philippines "the spirit of the Renaissance, imported from the West, and belated by several centuries."[22] Into the 1920s, Frank Laubach of the ABCFM continued to convey to US audiences that "the Reformation which occurred in Europe four centuries ago began in the Philippines a quarter of a century ago and has been swifter and more thoroughgoing than in the days of Martin Luther."[23]

The notion of a new and condensed Reformation cutting through medieval torpor was compatible with the idea that US empire, directed by Providence, had opened the door to radical transformation. However, the racist and historicist ideas of contemporary evolutionary social scientists, which missionaries were well familiar with, gave pause for thought. If it was indeed true that Spanish colonialism had left a primitive Philippine people in the medieval European past, giving them nothing more than a veneer of civilization, then evolutionism seemed to warn that Americans would have to have the patience to guide Filipinos through multiple stages of development instead of expecting instantaneous results.

Although this emphasis on gradual, evolutionary process might seem jarringly juxtaposed with missionaries' ideas about providential opportunity and rapid transformation expressed elsewhere, it can be understood as a parallel language that missionaries retreated to in order to avoid directly suggesting that US empire was the source of their disappointments or that the United States risked ruinous failure because of its inadequate response to a providential opening. Despite the sense of missionaries that their nation's empire was too much in thrall to the Catholic past when handling questions of religion, their recourse to the language furnished by colonial racial science was emblematic of the fact that they always stopped short of wholehearted criticism of empire or of a disavowal of support. Although missionaries' ideas about Providence reminded Americans that supernatural issues were at stake in the Philippines, they fundamentally believed that the continuance of US empire was for the greater good because it could maintain order and dispel ignorance in the islands. They expressed this conviction in part by tempering their grave warnings about the immediate responsibility of the United States with calls for patience with the imperial project, using language borrowed from colonial racial science.

Rather than being due to American failure, then, slow progress could be attributed to natural laws and to the racial incapacity of the people of the Philippines. This idea was frequently evident in missionary writing for audiences in the United States, punctuating the more unbridled expressions of hope for a providentially ordained rapid Reformation. In his published report on the situation in the Philippines following his 1901 tour, Arthur Judson Brown wrote that "after their long and grievous bondage to cruel Spaniards," the only wonder was that Filipinos "are not worse." What they needed now were "some decades of fair treatment, of just laws, of American political and educational methods, and of a pure Protestant faith." Brown quoted the social evolutionist ideas of British sociologist Benjamin Kidd, emphasizing that even Western civilization was the product of organic development and that it was "irrational and foolish" to expect peoples to free themselves from their past in a single generation.[24] Medical missionary Alice Byram Condict agreed, reminding readers in the United States that Americans had taken 200 years to grow to a national maturity whereby they could form and sustain a constitutional government and that Filipinos too would need time.[25] After all, James Rodgers said in a sermon in Manila shortly after the opening of the Philippine mission field, the people of the islands had only just emerged from "semi-slavery" and Americans must not "forget the conditions of the past." The superimposition of forms of free government would "seem a failure for a long time and be a trying task."[26]

The true measure of Americans, therefore, would not be in the speed of their accomplishments but in their staying power. "We Americans are an impatient people," argued Homer Stuntz in his book, "but in this undertaking of making a nation we must count time by decades and generations, rather than by years."[27] Charles Briggs concurred: the "quick visible results" demanded "can only be had through the varnish and veneer of false reports. . . . Every American . . . in the Islands knows that a long and difficult undertaking has only just been entered upon." Only "generations of solid work" would suffice.[28]

Charles Brent deployed the language of evolutionism to temper expectations of dramatic transformation with particular frequency, seemingly to manage his own hopes as well as those of correspondents in the United States. Declaring himself particularly inspired by the US naturalist and founding president of Stanford University, David Starr Jordan, who was a preeminent Social Darwinist and eugenicist thinker, in a private diary entry Brent stressed the importance of not "contradicting nature" by "trying to make the poor chrysalis Filipino live as though he were a butterfly."[29] In another, he noted that Americans' enthusiasm had run ahead of the situation and made two historical allusions. First, he likened Filipinos to emancipated African Americans who "ought not to have had the franchise" and required uplift under "paternal gov[ernmen]t." This demonstrates that, just as Sereno Bishop argued that the Hawaiian franchise should be restricted using arguments about race relations in the South, Brent's perspective on the Philippines was informed partly by a Progressivist argument for Jim Crow segregation that focused on the need to manage racial others in order to maintain order. Second, Brent claimed that "democracy in the 15th Century [would] have been misrule." Because Filipinos had not left the fifteenth century behind, he said, they had "to learn that they are ignorant & inefficient" before they could be shepherded toward modernity and self-government.[30] In another diary entry, Brent added that "one hears much about the superstition of the natives, but I fail to see any thing beyond what has been found among other peoples at a similar stage of their development."[31] In Brent's analysis, "history tells of the steady progress of human life."[32]

Brent's vision of the slow and steady progress of civilization extended to his outlook on mission work. He wrote in his diary, for example, of the need for an unglamorous preparatory spiritual work akin to John the Baptist's ministry before Christ, arguing that spiritual change would not occur out of the blue.[33] He also sought to temper the enthusiasm of mission supporters back in the United States, writing to one donor that "we have accomplished very little, and those who think that we have done much are aided to their judgment through their confidence in the missionaries here and an exaggerated idea of the few achievements that have been reached."[34] He told another that "if the proverb is true that 'the Mills of the Gods grind slowly' it was also true that 'the Oriental Mills grind still more slowly.'"[35] James Rodgers agreed, telling an ecumenical world missionary conference in Edinburgh in 1910 that evangelistic work was predicated not on sweeping revivals and instantaneous transformation but on "natural development, seed time, growth and harvest."[36] Work was "necessarily slow," added an ABCFM missionary in a letter to his board, because foundations were being laid, not least among the non-Christian peoples of the Philippines, who could "only be reached by steady sure plodding."[37] For women's work, too, the mantra was "line upon line and precept upon precept."[38] These were formulations that significantly dialed down the sense of urgency and crisis inherent in the Student Volunteer Movement's drive toward "the evangelization of the world in a generation."

Some missionaries were frustrated and confused by the failure of the providential opening in the Philippines to yield results. One Presbyterian at Albay province on Luzon, Roy H. Brown, wrote to his board in 1904 that "these people are puzzling to me they are not [anxious] seemingly for the Gospel and do not seem to care much what happens in that line." Convinced that the people could not actually lack desire for God's word, he maintained that he had "no doubt that when I get down to really know the people I will find the deep longing."[39] However, a year later he reported to supporters in the United States that he had "gotten very blue," and was realizing "what must have been the great consecration of the early missionaries who had to wait years for one convert."[40] James Rodgers also to some extent recognized the paradox that missionaries created in simultaneously maintaining faith in the ability of Providence to radically intervene in the Philippines and a belief in the need for slow, steady, and careful work. He suggested in one letter that ultimate reliance on the latter model might in fact be indicative of "weak faith," thus showing that a lot was potentially at stake for missionaries who relied on historicist rather than providential ideas of development.[41] In some respects, Rodgers advocated a bolder approach and warned his colleagues of the dangers of excessive caution.[42] Regarding the question of handing over the responsibility of evangelizing Filipinos to local agents, for example, Rodgers retained a strong conviction that the Holy Spirit would miraculously intervene. He told the missionary gathering at Edinburgh that if Americans were to wait for the correct time, "then we should wait for a few more thousands of years." If the gospel was as potent as Christians believed, "then surely it is capable of caring for itself."[43]

Yet recourse to racialized ideas about historical development, borrowed at least in part from the social sciences, punctuated missionaries' grand ideas about Providence and rapid transformation. Although their calls for patience seem at odds with their sense that the United States was at a critical moment in its history that demanded urgent action, they show how anxieties could be palliated by racial prejudice and a stadial idea about history that indicated that there were stages that all societies had to pass through. When missionaries were uncomfortable with their own perceived failures or those of the US government to move Philippine religious history forward, they could fall back on the argument that it was no wonder that Filipinos could not immediately be brought into the light of Protestant modernity—their racial inferiority was such that they were still effectively living centuries in the past. By drawing on more than one of the different registers of historical thought they had available to them, missionaries found ways of managing their own stratospheric expectations and those of their supporters.

Another effect of missionaries' close attention to historical process when on the ground in the Philippines was their recognition that the Spanish past cast a long shadow and set precedents that profoundly shaped their evangelistic work. Missionaries found that the Spanish past was not dead in the Philippines and could not be cast off rapidly. To achieve success, they would have to reach an uneasy compromise with a past that they had come to realize was etched into the islands' religious traditions and built environment. A focus on the accommodations that missionaries made with the Spanish past further reveals the instability of a discourse in which the Philippines, and the Pacific more generally, were conceived of as a blank canvas for rapid transformation that the dual agencies of Providence and US empire presented.

The Indelibility of the Spanish Past

When it came to recognizing the power of the Spanish past and strategically building on it, US colonial administrators pointed the way forward. When William Howard Taft was governor-general of the islands, he spoke of his hope that government by the United States would escape "the influence of the evil customs of Spanish times upon our political organizations," but US officials got many of their ideas about colonial governance from Spanish precedent. Americans, as one Spanish general charged, were "without a history" in the islands, and they indeed struggled to establish themselves without reference to the past.[44] Not least, they inherited from their predecessors a bifurcated view of the people of the Philippines that translated into an idea that control of the islands was a "dual mandate" that required two distinct modes of rule. On the one hand, there was a Hispanicized Filipino population that US officials deemed fit for education and limited democracy. On the other, there were "non-Christian tribes" who had not been reached by Spanish evangelization, especially the animist hill peoples of the mountains of northern Luzon and the Muslim populations of the southern islands of Mindanao and Sulu. They were to be placed under paternalistic, militarized authority without representation.[45]

Even though they accused their government of being too deferential to Spanish colonial history in religious matters, missionaries also recognized how this history continued to shape spiritual practice and expectations. Beyond the persistence of their bombastic rhetoric about the scale of the opportunity presented by Providence, they understood that Catholicism in the Philippines was more than a medieval dead letter. Indeed, it was still ably adapting to new circumstances. The reality of the situation did not suggest, as David S. Hibbard had believed when he arrived in the Philippines in 1899, that the Catholic Church had "deteriorated" such that Protestantism would win easy acceptance.[46] Rather, according to missionaries, it continued to wield influence, propagandize, and even supposedly incite violence, notably in the key city of Cebu in the Visayas region where Presbyterians were attempting to conduct work.[47] Strengthened by an influx of American Catholic leaders, the Church was a meaningful rival in a new evangelistic climate. It made what one Presbyterian missionary referred to in 1910 as the "fight of her life" or a "death struggle," preaching far and wide, issuing tracts and pamphlets, and building schools and hospitals.[48]

This intractability could be a source of deep frustration. Arthur Judson Brown argued that the "erroneous and misleading conceptions" of the gospel that Catholicism had given Filipinos in fact made work harder than in "lands which were wholly heathen," and some missionaries sought historical blank canvases elsewhere in the islands among people who had not been touched by Catholicism.[49] On his first trip into rural areas of the islands in 1902, one Presbyterian missionary noted that he was "delighted . . . to find that Romanism has hardly touched" the people. Their minds were "like blank paper and their hearts, very open indeed."⁵⁰ An ABCFM worker similarly wrote that the Bagobo people in the areas around Davao were "untainted by most of the vices so prevalent on the coast." History was now being made, but "what that history will be must depend on the kind of a foundation that is laid." The ABCFM had to send workers before "civilization" swept in.⁵¹ If Americans could not remake history in the Catholic Philippines, they were excited to find that there were still places in the islands where they believed they could.

Another response among missionaries, however, was to look to Philippine history to reconfigure some of their ideas about Catholicism and to situate their own project within a story of religious development in the islands. The notion that missionaries needed to pay close attention to what local histories were telling them was baked into contemporary missionary thought. The 1886 book *The Crisis of Missions*, by leading missionary advocate Arthur Pierson, for example, implored Christians to search history for the signs that the divine was running ahead of his church and preparing the way for the world's evangelization: "To the attentive observer God is in history."⁵² The fact that "the pillar of God still moves before His people" was evident not only in the dramatic "removal or subsidence of barriers" but also "in the preparation of the field and workmen."⁵³ For missionaries in the Philippines, the search for preparatory signs meant reading Protestant significance into a Catholic history, undercutting the more polemical notion that Catholicism had done nothing but lay a veneer of corruption and cruelty over preexisting practice and the idea that God had used US empire to suddenly throw the Philippines open to a rapid Protestant transformation.

Homer Stuntz's book evinced missionaries' discomfort with the idea that a new mission field had been opened without preparation, noting that "the Holy Spirit never throws a land open to evangelistic effort until the burden of its salvation has been placed upon the hearts of his children." Stuntz showed how God had indeed been preparing the way for the Protestant evangelization of the Philippines. He pointed to events in recent history that suggested that this was the case, looking past the idea of a radical break when "the barred doors which shut out all evangelical truth were blown to shivers by the iron hail of Dewey's conquering fleet" and instead recognizing an intensification of evangelical interest in the years prior to 1898. In Stuntz's outline, James Thoburn, the Methodist missionary to India who entered the Philippines to survey conditions soon after the US occupation, had in fact had the "burden" of the islands laid on his mind as early as 1883. Stuntz saw similar signs of preparation in the 1889 attempts of Nicolas Lallave and Francisco

Castells, agents of the British and Foreign Bible Society, to bring portions of the Bible into the Philippines. The efforts of Castells and Lallave, the latter a convert from Catholicism who had previously served in the islands as a friar, were ill fated. Lallave died under mysterious circumstances (Stuntz suspected poisoning by the Spanish authorities) and Castells was imprisoned and subsequently banished. Although Dewey's victory at Manila Bay had stunned the world, Stuntz suggested that awareness of these preparatory episodes meant that missionaries were the one group of people who had not been surprised. Thoburn saw in the events of May 1898 "the fulfilment of the hopes and prayers of years." The one element he had supposedly not envisioned was that it would be his own United States rather than Japan, Russia, Britain, or Germany that would throw the islands open to the good news.[54]

The idea that the coming of Catholicism to the Philippines was actually a providential interposition that prefigured the sudden turn of the United States was common as missionaries sought signs of divine preparation. It may have been that the moral standard and true religiosity of the Catholic leadership had declined over the course of three centuries, but the evangelistic impulse that originally took Catholics to the islands could be lauded.[55] Charles Briggs, for example, outlined two "remarkable interventions" that indicated that the Philippines was a "strategic" site in the "Divine plans for the world's progress and regeneration." The first was the arrival of the Spaniards in the sixteenth century, which prevented the entirety of the archipelago from falling to Islam like the southern islands and prepared the ground over the course of three centuries for a second and greater intervention by the United States.[56] Charles Brent agreed that the friars had saved the Philippines from Islam and in Catholicism gave the peoples of the islands "the one unifying force they have ever had."[57] A YMCA worker also believed that "God entrusted the Christianization of this Archipelago and its religious destiny for nearly four hundred years" to the Catholic Church, "which won the people from paganism and Mohammedanism."[58] This was a blessing, argued one Christian periodical, because the Muslim populations of Mindanao and Sulu were located temporally even farther back than the "medieval" Spanish, "in the tenth century before Christ."[59] Other missionaries noted that Catholics had abolished idolatry and polytheism, introduced Filipinos to crude but valuable ideas of God, sin, and repentance, and established religious education through the University of Santo Tomas.[60] The ultimate result, said Rodgers, was that "during the last three centuries the Philippine Islands have been practically christianized, the only Eastern Asiatic people to adopt Christianity as a whole."[61] In acknowledging these signs of preparation, missionaries styled the United States as one player in a long-unfolding historical narrative that centered the Philippines.

Another outcome of such thought was that the emergence of an independent Filipino church led by Gregorio Aglipay, which broke with Rome in 1902, came to figure for some missionaries as a preparatory stage, a bridge from Spanish Catholicism to Protestantism. "Having first taken one step forward," wrote one Presbyterian missionary to his board shortly after Aglipay broke from the Catholic Church, "it will be much easier for them to take the next one."[62] Missionaries identified hallmarks of Protestantism or evangelicalism in Aglipayan churches—in their break with Rome, in their advocacy of Bible reading by ordinary people, and in the election of Aglipay as bishop by means of ecclesiastical council rather than according to ideas of apostolic succession.[63] Indeed, Aglipay seemed to have opened the door to Protestant success in some towns.[64] However, the retention of some Catholic practices and fears about the "political" nature of the church led another Presbyterian to feel there was still more work to be done to complete the transition to "an evangelical church in the truest sense of the word."[65] Such a formulation figured the Aglipayan movement as a stadial move toward the inevitable triumph of Protestantism. Stuntz wrote that "Aglipay loosens this fruit from the tree, and we gather it."[66]

The idea some missionaries expressed that Catholicism in both Spanish and Indigenous forms had prepared the ground for Protestantism somewhat diverged from the rhetoric of medievalism the very same evangelists used. Although on the one hand missionaries bought into the idea of a providentially ordained break in history, on the other hand they found further assurance only by situating their work within a longer historical trajectory that suggested that God had prepared the way for them through both distant and recent pasts. Missionaries thus thought carefully about what the Spanish Catholic past meant for them, and that past shaped their actions. The central idea of comity between different Protestant missions that the Evangelical Union represented, for example, was at least in part a response to the perceived homogeneity of Catholicism.[67] The Catholic hierarchy had supposedly characterized Protestants to Filipinos as divided over the smallest doctrinal points. "Roman priests," said Brown, "laud their external unity and emphasize the divisions of Protestantism." This was reason enough, Brown continued, to ensure that the mission field in the Philippines was kept unsectarian. Although comity was important "not simply to deprive Rome of a favorite argument, but because it is right," the emphasis on cooperation in the Philippines was clearly prompted by awareness of Catholicism's historical influence.[68] By

Brown's own admission, even the Evangelical Union's practice of placing denominational names in parentheses when naming churches, subordinate to the general designation "Iglesia Evangélica," mimicked the Catholic practice of bracketing the names of orders.[69] The use of Spanish as a lingua franca in this practice of naming churches indicates a further missionary concession to their local environment. This was despite Brown's stated initial belief that Spanish would be useless among many Filipinos due to failures of Spanish education (Brown said it was "associated with all that the natives hate") and that English would soon triumph.[70] Ultimately, the *Outlook* claimed in a review of Brown's 1903 book, "if Rome is learning something from the Protestants, the Protestants are also learning from Rome."[71]

Accommodation of local expectation was also evident in the social norms missionaries followed. Rodgers advocated adapting local "social habits . . . to our needs," arguing that there was biblical precedent for this in the evangelistic work of St. Paul.[72] Another Presbyterian missionary emphasized the urgency of establishing a school for girls alongside the Silliman Institute for boys in a letter to his board in February 1905. This, he argued, was because "the women of the Philippines are the ruling power in the homes" and Catholics had paid much better attention to this fact than Protestants, opening convents and girls' schools. Although he believed that many men had moved away from Catholicism, "in more than 95% of these cases" their wives were said to be "strong Roman Catholics" and to have "complete control of the children."[73] A similar argument prompted the ABCFM to encourage the Woman's Board of Missions to send single women into the field.[74] The concern missionaries expressed most often about Filipinas was that they were bastions of superstition, reflecting a long-standing missionary attitude toward women across the world.[75] They saw women as threatening to entrench and perpetuate medievalism in the Philippines, and arguments about the need to do missionary work for them were often shaped by this perception more than by any progressive concern for women's social status or welfare. Missionaries in the Philippines actually repeatedly suggested that Filipina women were doing well in terms of status. Charles Briggs praised Catholicism for having elevated the position and well-being of Filipina women beyond those in other "Oriental" nations.[76] Methodist women missionaries similarly encouraged women in the United States to imagine the Filipina as something other than the stereotype of the subjugated "oriental" woman. Although they styled the Filipinas they worked among as "naturally devout and mostly ignorant" and as "the most devoted adherents of the Roman Catholic Church," they also claimed that the Filipina was "unlike most of the orientals of her sex in that she has greater freedom."[77]

Missionaries also nodded to local historical precedent when thinking about the aesthetics of worship. On the one hand, missionaries were critical of the perceived spiritual emptiness of the Catholic fiesta in the Philippines.[78] On the other, one Methodist missionary argued at an Evangelical Union meeting in 1908 that Protestants should reorient traditional Catholic ceremonies toward Protestant ends. He noted that funerals, baptisms, marriages, and festival days presented excellent opportunities for evangelizing and believed that missionaries should join processions, holding banners emblazoned with biblical passages and preaching during the frequent stops on parade routes.[79] A Presbyterian colleague accepted this argument, writing in 1910 that the "pomp and oriental attractiveness" of the great processions of Easter week provided an excellent opportunity to show "that we believe in Christ and God." During Easter celebrations at Albay, he made sure that Protestant preachers were on hand to explain the meaning of Christ's passion as enacted in the processions.[80] Christmas presented another opportunity, as the Methodist missionary Winifred Spaulding noted: "Street parades, illuminations and music are [an] inevitable . . . accompaniment of religious holidays here. . . . The Protestants naturally reasoned that the Roman Catholics had no monopoly on these attractions, and so an elaborately illumined float was prepared."[81] The American Bible Society also took advantage of existing interest in the passion story as theatre, using stereopticon shows that depicted the life and suffering of Christ in their evangelism.[82]

The conversation between the Catholic past and a prospective Protestant future was particularly evident in the way that missionaries responded to the built environment of the archipelago. When they entered the islands, missionaries read Spanish colonial architecture, in particular Catholic churches, as striking evidence of Catholicism's anachronism, of its decay and spiritual emptiness. However, just as US authorities found themselves occupying old Spanish legislative buildings, offices, prisons, military barracks, forts, and schoolhouses, Protestant missionaries could not help but acknowledge that the built environment of Spanish colonial rule in the Philippines provided the concrete foundations of the islands' spiritual culture.[83] If they were to impose themselves on the religious landscape in the archipelago, they would have to respond to the dominance of Catholic heritage in the physical landscape.

Architecture and History in the Missionary Imagination

Alice Byram Condict's book *Old Glory and the Gospel* (1902) presents some of the best evidence for how the earliest US missionaries in the islands perceived local history when they encountered it. Reflecting on her first impressions of Manila on her arrival in 1899, Condict offered detailed descriptions of the history manifest in the built environment, complete with images for the benefit of the reader in the United States (figures 5.1 and 5.2). She wrote at length about Intramuros, the oldest part of Manila, where Spain had housed its finest buildings, its government officials, and its Catholic leadership in "wide, battlemented walls." For Condict, everything about this "Old Manila" evoked "mediaeval Europe." Its fortifications, no longer "of any value in modern warfare," suggested "a dark and troubled past" and stood as monuments to it. The city's "ancient churches of Rome" were "a relic of the past," as valuable as Pompeii had been to the student of history: "We have here unearthed a sample of the ancient Roman Church. We have suddenly come face to face with a very well preserved example of the power which reached its zenith in the Dark Ages."[84]

Condict's dismissal of the hallmarks of the Spanish past as a "relic," especially when coupled with apparent confidence that Providence was determining the direction of events in the islands, reduced Philippine history to little more than something to be viewed voyeuristically by the first Americans in the islands. In a modern Americanized world, there was little to be said for Spanish architecture in terms of defense, sanitation, aesthetics, or spirituality. The old transport infrastructure in Manila, other missionaries said, was so poor that it posed a barrier to evangelism and churchgoing.[85] It was therefore up to Americans to completely reimagine the urban landscape. Road building in particular became a motif that underscored the nature of the transition from Spanish to US governance.[86] Fifteen years after the start of the US occupation, Charles Briggs was able to write that "all things have become new in Manila," noting the filling in of "pest-breeding moats and swamps," the development of a consumer culture, and the modernization of housing, transportation, businesses, water systems, schools, universities, and churches.[87] The built environment was a potent marker of temporality for missionaries. They had entered a place that was out of its time, a place that belonged to a distant past, but the United States was writing a new history as it transformed the urban setting, marking a dramatic break with Spanish medievalism and freeing the Philippines from its influence.

Figure 5.1. *One of the Ten Gates of Old Manila Showing Moat and Bridge. Source*: Alice Byram Condict, *Old Glory and the Gospel in the Philippines: Notes Gathered during Professional and Missionary Work* (Chicago, IL: Fleming H. Revell Company, 1902), facing 37. Courtesy of the Library of Congress.

Figure 5.2. *The Cathedral in Old Manila. Source*: Alice Byram Condict, *Old Glory and the Gospel in the Philippines: Notes Gathered during Professional and Missionary Work* (Chicago, IL: Fleming H. Revell Company, 1902), facing 39. Courtesy of the Library of Congress.

Away from Manila, too, in provincial towns and more rural areas, the built environment attracted comments from missionaries. Church ruins supported their claims that an old world had been left behind and that a new one was beginning. "The old Romish churches in ruins," wrote Condict about a tour of the "provinces," "remind one that Old Glory and 'Americanos' have come to stay."[88] As late as 1915, Frank Laubach of the ABCFM noted that "no attempt was being made to repair" the Catholic cathedral at Baliangao on Mindanao with one side blown out. "No services were being held there now, and the priest had moved away from town."[89] Ruined churches symbolized both Spanish Catholic abandonment of their congregations and the resentment Filipinos supposedly felt toward Catholicism. Indeed, illustrating the destruction for her American audience, Condict suggested that Filipinos had themselves been responsible for damage to church buildings (figure 5.3). With this assertion, she erased the truth that during the Philippine-American War US troops who loathed Catholicism and deemed it a threat to their nation's sovereignty had caused great damage.[90]

Not all churches in cities or the provinces were ruined, however, and in any case they had long dominated the Philippine skyline, lending significant prestige to Catholicism with their stature and extravagance. Condict noted their prominence as she approached Manila Bay for the first time:

Figure 5.3. *All That Remains of a Romish Church Which Was Destroyed by Filipinos. Source*: Alice Byram Condict, *Old Glory and the Gospel in the Philippines: Notes Gathered during Professional and Missionary Work* (Chicago, IL: Fleming H. Revell Company, 1902), facing 64. Courtesy of the Library of Congress.

"We . . . see a low line of buildings, and towering above them, here and there, the domes of Roman Catholic churches."[91] In Manila, "a massive Roman Catholic church" was the centerpiece, towering over "a roomy plaza" that was the site of processions and evening torch displays.[92] The impact such conspicuous churches made on the missionary mind did not seem to decrease as the years went by. As Presbyterians conducted worship in a basement at Lucban in 1906, they noted that a 225-year-old church stood in the plaza outside, not crumbling or decaying but instead "as strong . . . as it ever was."[93] In his 1913 book, Briggs contrasted a "fine and imposing" Catholic church on Panay with surrounding buildings that he described as "humble shacks built entirely of bamboo" with grass roofs.[94]

Occupation of these "imposing" churches proved important during the first decade of US rule. The colonial government had allowed Gregorio Aglipay's independent Filipino Catholic church to occupy Roman Catholic churches under Governor-General Taft's "proclamation of peaceable possession." Local congregations could choose their allegiance and occupy their church on that basis. Under these conditions, Aglipay's movement expanded rapidly; it claimed that it had three million adherents in 1903 and four million in 1905. In 1906, however, the Philippine Supreme Court upheld a decision that all churches belonged to the Roman Catholics. After that, Aglipayans were no longer able to worship as Aglipayans in the churches their families had attended for generations, and the movement declined precipitously over the following decade or so before its numbers stabilized.[95] According to Laubach, the structures Aglipayans erected "were wretched, and failed to inspire the awe and reverence which the Filipinos had felt in their former magnificent churches."[96] This was clear evidence that the "medieval" built environment in the Philippines still held a great deal of spiritual significance for those Protestant missionaries sought to convert.

Although missionary reflections on church ruins suggested that there had been a parting of the ways between Filipinos and their Catholic history, it was harder for them to make the case to Americans that the intact, magnificent church buildings like those over which Aglipayans and Catholic authorities struggled were redundant. This task was made more difficult when Catholics returning from the Philippines to the United States, notably army chaplain William McKinnon, embarked on a campaign to heighten sympathy for the church among US audiences by emphasizing the architectural accomplishments he had seen on the islands.[97] Nonetheless, missionaries tried. They argued that even where churches and cathedrals were imposing monuments, they had been deserted; the people of the Philippines were craving a new form of worship that did not depend on elaborate buildings. Condict spoke of intense interest in open-air services in villages, noting that hostile curiosity gradually gave way to "unrestrained interest" as villagers realized they could "find God's temple" under "the shades of banana and bamboo."[98] Mrs. McLaughlin of the Methodist mission similarly noted that in her section of Manila, Protestants had "no fine or neat church by which the people are attracted from their wretched homes, so it must be from a higher motive that [Filipinos] come to the dilapidated old theatre building in which we meet."[99]

Arthur Judson Brown also reported at length on services drawing hundreds of Filipinos that were held in the open air or in plain, makeshift chapels. He illustrated his point with a striking photograph (figure 5.4), which depicts a throng of Filipinos apparently engaged in Protestant worship. In the background, a Catholic church looms over the assembled group but fails to draw their attention. Some Filipinos, Brown said, traveled four hours across the island of Panay to attend the Sunday service in the city of Iloilo, staying from Saturday to Monday in crowded rooms missionaries rented to them. Brown wished that Americans who believed that all Filipinos were Catholic and rejected Protestantism could "see that dense throng of people who have patiently trudged past stately Roman Catholic churches to a plain chapel where there are no altar lights, or gorgeous vestments, or fragrant incense, but only

Figure 5.4. *Protestant Outdoor Service: Roman Catholic Church in background. Source*: Arthur Judson Brown, *The New Era in the Philippines* (New York: Fleming H. Revell Company, 1903), facing 199. Courtesy of Cambridge University Library.

the preaching of the simple Gospel."[100] Indeed, Brown continued, "a surprisingly neat and commodious chapel can be cheaply built out of the bamboo and nipa of which the people construct their own houses." Charles Briggs agreed that this was enough to overcome the "ritual and tinsel [that] hypnotizes the native."[101] Briggs's formulation was clearly rooted in a racist disdain for what he perceived to be a childlike race that was easily attracted by shininess rather than substance. As subsequent parts of this chapter will show, Briggs was far from alone among missionaries in this contempt. Although Briggs asserted that the pure gospel was enough to triumph over racial incapacity, some of his peers proved less certain that it would be.

In provincial contexts, the idea that Filipino converts were rejecting Catholicism and building humble chapels, often without the prompts of Protestant missionaries, became a recurring motif of missionary writing. One Presbyterian noted as early as 1903 that in the towns of Leon and San Miguel, near Iloilo, "cane and nipa" chapels had been "neatly built" and that the local people had taken responsibility for the work and its costs.[102] Another told sponsoring churches stories of people in Laguna province on Luzon who had twice rebuilt a chapel that had burned down and of old washerwomen who had nothing but gave generously to building projects.[103] Seventeen Laguna congregations in fact built chapels within the first ten years of Presbyterian work there "without assistance from the mission."[104] Missionaries highlighted how locals persisted with construction projects despite natural disasters, financial difficulties, or the opposition of Catholics, who allegedly contested ownership of land and burned down churches.[105] For example, in his 1921 published collection of anecdotes from the Philippines, Bruce Kershner, a Disciples of Christ missionary, told the story of a makeshift place of worship being blown over in a storm as a meeting took place inside it. "This I supposed would end the meeting," he wrote. "It would have, with almost any congregation in America," but "not so with these earnest people. I scarcely knew what they were about before they had new poles brought, the shed reconstructed, and the meeting resumed."[106]

Such celebration reveals something peculiar about missionaries' sense of temporality when they thought about the built environment. They wrote off Spanish colonial architecture as being of the past but appropriated the image of the bamboo and nipa hut, which most Americans associated with a savagery that belonged to an even more distant past, as a symbol of Protestant innocence and resilience.[107] Historians have written of Americans' architectural projects in the Philippines in terms of their modernizing purpose, their efforts to bring history, culture, sanitation, order, and nationhood to spaces they perceived to be without these things.[108] Americans appropriated and modified local layouts, styles, and natural beauty, creating a "palimpsest of landscapes" but still fashioning something new, rhetorically characterizing the old as obsolete.[109] The missionary outlook on buildings for worship provides an interesting counterpoint. For missionaries, architectural projects taking place beyond the gaze of Americans that resulted in multiple architectural temporalities demonstrated that their message was taking root and that their converts had been liberated from the supposed spell of Catholic grandeur.

However, Protestant engagement with Catholic architecture was more complex than such missionary triumphalism suggested. Decades before the US occupation of the Philippines, Protestants in the United States had regarded Catholic churches with ambivalence. Even at the height of anti-Catholic sentiment in the mid-nineteenth century, Protestants began to embrace Gothic architecture, symbolic crosses, flowers, candles, robed choirs, feasts, and festivals in their churches. In the words of the historian Ryan K. Smith, "enthralled with the Catholic 'threat,' Protestant denominations adopted one of its most potent, yet seemingly superficial, components—its imposing physical presence." They did this in order to better compete in a religious marketplace by working to allay fears that Protestantism catered too exclusively to the intellect.[110]

Although Protestant missionaries might have regarded their work in the Philippines as an opportunity to begin anew, they were haunted by ghosts of the Catholic past and were thus drawn into forms of borrowing that were similar to those of their counterparts on the North American continent. They could never fully shake off the anxiety that Filipino understandings of Christianity were bound up with architectural splendor, especially in Manila. W. H. Lingle's report made this observation early on in the US occupation, as did General Adna Chafee, who counseled Arthur Judson Brown that any Protestant church in Manila had to be "large and handsome" because "the Filipinos are accustomed to see such churches."[111] Seemingly disregarding the US commitment to the separation of church and state in the Philippines, Chafee gave Brown some clear advice: he recommended a joint effort among mission boards instead of representation of different denominations with "little chapels of 15 or 20" that would leave "no impression."[112]

An interdenominational building project never came about—in fact, discourse surrounding church building sometimes retained a competitive edge—but missionaries nonetheless came to echo Lingle and Chafee's concerns.[113] Despite the high cost of building in the Philippines, Rodgers concluded as early as October 1899 that it was urgently necessary for Presbyterians to build a church in Manila.[114] Soliciting donations from Presbyterian congregants, the *Assembly Herald* asked: "Surrounded as they are by the cathedrals and churches of the friars, what impression can be made by a Presbyterian Mission," which had "only the use of a hospitable corner in a tent of the Y.M.C.A.?"[115] Homer Stuntz similarly noted in a 1903 Methodist pamphlet that to the "beauty-loving minds" of Filipinos, the "silent appeal" of the Catholic cathedral in Manila was "powerful, almost irresistible." Accordingly, "we ought not to build a shed here and call it a church." Although Stuntz insisted that he sought only a roomy and tasteful building befitting of a church in the United States, by tying his call for donations for a Methodist church-building project to a detailed discussion of the Catholic advantage in architectural affairs, he betrayed his anxiety that the Protestant message alone would not be enough to win over Filipinos. The architect C. B. Ripley was enlisted to design a building with "large effects and graceful lines" that could hold 2,000 people and had "perfect ventilation" and "ample exits."[116] A stone structure for the Methodist church was opened in November 1906 to Ripley's design. Interestingly, Ripley was best known for his work developing downtown Honolulu in Hawai'i, suggesting some pretensions to developing a US colonial architecture across Pacific environments.

Missionaries who worked outside Manila also felt the weight of the Spanish past in the built environment. Robert Black wrote to the ABCFM in 1905 of his work in the city of Davao on Mindanao: "I feel more and more the need of a chapel," he said. "The people cannot associate the idea of worship with an ordinary house," which lacked "the dignity of worship that means so much to these people."[117] The *Missionary Herald* conveyed Black's appeal to a broader US Christian audience, and Black began to consult C. B. Ripley about designing a chapel, though it was not completed until 1912.[118] Even in smaller provincial towns, Catholic churches, impressive in their "gray massiveness," rendered inferior the kind of building that one Presbyterian, Roy H. Brown, preached in at Camalig during a tour of the towns near his Albay mission station in 1906: a bamboo house that so many people crammed into for a service that the porch collapsed. Although the fact that there were enough congregants to collapse the porch might have been read as evidence of the ability of Protestantism to win listeners without resources, Brown concluded that "my heart aches for our people for I know even if you have the truth . . . , still you will think some of the worldly adornments such as an imposing church would not be amiss."[119] Missionaries also strategically built in cities to impress visitors traveling from rural areas, further undercutting claims that provincial Filipinos were perfectly happy with simple chapels.

Hibbard, for example, stated to the Presbyterian board that "the natives look for something at the capitols which will represent our work." If they were to arrive in cities to find that Protestant services were being conducted in "some nipa house or in a rented room," they would be left without "a feeling of permanence" and go back to their homes certain that Protestantism itself was not going to last in the islands.

Hibbard's desire for buildings that offered a "feeling of permanence" indicated that churches were also a counterpoint to missionary uncertainties. They were a decisive mark on the landscape that suggested the endurance of Protestantism, even as missionaries feared that their work was subject to the vicissitudes of US politics and Catholic backlash. Rodgers petitioned for a Presbyterian church that would be "substantial enough to show that it had come to stay."[120] The Methodist mission appealed to donors for a church building at San Isidro on the basis that "we must have a good substantial church which will last more than a few years which is the life time of such as we have now."[121] Colonial administrators who were committed to an ongoing US presence in the islands imprinted a hope for longevity onto church buildings: the cornerstone for the ABCFM's Davao chapel was laid in October 1911 at a ceremony at which District Governor Henry Gilsheuser celebrated the symbolic marking of the "firm and fixed determination of the American Protestant church to remain in these Islands."[122]

Undoubtedly, the concessions missionaries made to the historical built environment were also rooted in part in their assumptions about the racial proclivities of Filipinos. It was little wonder that the Spaniards had been so successful in the Philippines, claimed Stuntz, for "the Malay loves beautiful things" and equates "form and ceremony" with true religion. The Catholic images the Spaniards had brought had given Filipinos more attractive *anitos* (carved figures representing ancestral spirits) than the ones they already had and thus were bound to win them over.[123] Brent admired the figures Johannes Kirchmayer, one of the leading US craftsmen, had designed for St. Luke's Episcopal Church in Manila, stating that "the idea of coloring them is a good one" because Filipinos were "very fond of color."[124] In such statements, missionaries betrayed their ideas that Filipinos were inflexible and childlike in their love of aesthetics. These stereotypes played a key role in driving missionaries to temper their confidence that the unadulterated gospel would quickly bring Filipinos around to Protestantism.

Above all, the engagement of missionaries with the built environment in the Philippines provides a striking example of how they were forced to reckon with the weight of history. Even though they sometimes suggested that Providence had effected a radical break through US empire that would render the islands' past null and void, they recognized in the landscape that their victory was to be neither swift nor inevitable. Haunted by the specter of the Catholic past in the built environment, they were forced to think about their spiritual project in terms of space and aesthetics, undercutting their conviction that the unadorned gospel was enough. The built environment became emblematic both of the resistance of Filipinos to the radical religious transformation that missionaries hoped US empire would facilitate and their frustrated endeavors to make new history.

Compromise with the Spanish past did not occur without debate or controversy. Different answers to the question of how much attention should be paid to history in the Philippines opened profound fissures in the missionary enterprise. As it became clear how deep the legacy of the Philippines' Catholic past ran, there were doubts among both government officials and missionaries about how much responsibility the United States had to efface that legacy in favor of Protestantism. This was an age when some liberal Protestants reimagined the relationship between Protestantism and Catholicism and moved toward more expansive definitions of acceptable religious expression.[125] These more expansive definitions provided one response to the challenges biblical criticism, immigration, and modernism posed. That response was in tension with another response: holding fast to orthodoxy.[126] Missions were a particular fault line for this tension, which for the most part remained beneath the surface until after World War I and the fundamentalist-modernist controversy of the 1920s. However, a focus on Charles Brent indicates that more sympathetic attitudes toward Catholicism were creating difficulties in the mission field long before that decade.

Charles Brent and the Challenge of Philippine Catholicism

Some missionaries expressed discomfort that a fixation on the need for impressive churches represented a deviation from Protestant ideals. In 1899, even though James Rodgers stressed the urgent need for a Presbyterian church in Manila, he also argued that the "true" evangelistic method relied not on the pull of grand buildings but on "going from house to house and village to village with the simple Gospel gathering together into churches the Christians."[127] Over a decade later, in 1913, Charles Briggs again warned that missionaries must resist the temptation to build a "big chapel" in a central location, for there was no substitute for an itinerant work of "the New Testament type."

Figure 5.5. *Episcopal Church. Source*: Manila Merchants Association, *Manila, the Pearl of the Orient: Guide Book to the Intending Visitor* (Manila: Manila Merchants' Association, 1908), facing 24. Courtesy of the Library of Congress.

Briggs believed that instead of having Filipinos flock to an impressive church from miles around, missionaries had to take responsibility for touring their district. He also insisted that "church buildings must conform approximately to the standard of building materials used by the people . . . in their own homes."[128] For some missionaries, acquiescence to previous practice in the built environment was controversial.

Charles Brent in particular was scorned by colleagues for concessions to his surroundings. One flashpoint was the opening of a grand Episcopal cathedral in Manila (figure 5.5). Even though the cathedral was predominantly intended to serve American congregants, Brent argued he would be "seriously handicapped" without this "worthy symbol" of his work in a country such as the Philippines, the implication being both that Filipinos were taking notice of American architecture and that Americans' expectations were being reconfigured in the Philippine environment.[129] He consecrated the cathedral in February 1907 in a lavish and conspicuous ceremony, noting that "conditions here are such that it is necessary to lay emphasis on ceremony to which in America . . . I should be quite indifferent." Instead of rushing to the "opposite extreme" away from perceived Catholic materialism, wrote Brent, the prudent path in the Philippines was "to put the spiritual into the material."[130]

Brent's colleague Mercer Johnston, representing the more militantly Protestant wing of the Episcopal church, remained unconvinced.[131] He stated in his notebook that he became disillusioned "about the time of the laying of the cornerstone" of the cathedral in early 1905.[132] Although Johnston was not specific about what bothered him at this juncture, the consecration of the completed building certainly gave him cause for complaint. He wrote to a missionary friend in Japan of a "semi-barbaric occasion" at which Brent "'put it all on.' He had a real Roman Catholic pastoral staff, a cape that would have knocked the breath clear out of the Queen of Sheba."[133] Johnston's description of the "semi-barbaric" ceremonies to consecrate the cathedral implied that to some extent he understood Brent's ritualistic and aesthetic excess in foreign climes as a particular form of "going native," pandering to local tastes, but elsewhere he also accused the bishop of giving "form and color to the work in the Cathedral parish pleasing to himself, not to the congregation."[134] His suspicions were perhaps justified: Brent was indeed captivated by the materiality of Catholic worship when he visited Rome in 1905. He ordered the font for his cathedral, sculpted "on a beautiful Byzantine model," from a Roman manufacturer.[135] Brent was not an outlier among Episcopalians of his time. His coreligionists in the United States also enthusiastically engaged in contemporary forms of borrowing from Catholicism, as the historians Ryan K. Smith and T. J. Jackson Lears have described.[136] Yet the initial optimism about Protestants' ability to overwrite the history of a Philippine Catholicism that was seen as decadent and degraded meant that Brent's willingness to work within the confines of the Catholic past was especially disappointing to some of his fellow missionaries.

Brent's attitude might be explained by the fact that even though he argued that the United States should not be bound by its constitutional traditions in the Philippines, he was acutely sensitive to the ways his work was shaped by the past of the islands. He argued for the necessity of adapting to the conditions local Catholic history had created in a November 1902 letter to Filipino religious leaders: "Never have a body of men any justification for ignoring history and creating a so-called Church independent of tradition." Conversion between Christian denominations was "deeply serious a step" and not one to be taken lightly.[137] In making such a statement, Brent implicitly condemned Aglipay's schismatic Iglesia Filipina Independiente and cautioned his fellow Protestants, setting limits on what he believed Americans should seek to achieve in the islands with regard to historical precedent and continuity.

Brent believed that successful missions had an "elasticity" that allowed them to "bend to the . . . natural religious expression of the native" instead of stubbornly adhering to a particular tradition or institutional expression.[138] In the Philippines specifically, Brent resented attempts to win converts from Catholic churches rather than working among non-Christians or the "unshepherded."[139] His stance was certainly informed by his recognition of Catholicism not only as a valid expression of Christianity but also as having historical authority both locally and globally.[140] He even used the word "Catholic" to describe the Episcopal mission in the Philippines, asserting its place in a broad history of Christian endeavor and expressing "gratitude for our heritage which does not leave us a puny sect but part of the great Christian whole."[141] He argued that Protestantism must not disdain "Roman Catholicism or other Churches that lay great stress on historicity," for truth would be found only through a synthesis of Catholic claims to historical authority and Protestant claims to purity of worship.[142] Ultimately, Brent advocated true "Catholicity," which involved "fellowship with, and thinking in terms of the whole present" as well as "the whole past."[143]

In other words, Brent wrote elsewhere, "the past always more or less determines our future course," and attempts to break "from the Great Godly past of thought" were "eccentric" and isolating.[144] Historical continuity in religious affairs was especially necessary in the mission field. A foreign church would be viewed as an "offensive intruder if it goes abroad to daub its local color on people of foreign temperament." There was no reason to expect that "the mere translation of our liturgy or the exact reproduction of our ritual will suit any or every foreign people."[145] Years of experience did not change his conviction, and in 1918, shortly after leaving the islands, he reiterated that "the responsibility for [heavily Catholic] countries lies with the venerable Church which has always held exclusive sway."[146] In recognizing the weight of Philippine history, moreover, Brent saw an opportunity to ensure that the mistakes of the European past were not repeated in the islands. He refused to sign the Episcopal mission up to the Evangelical Union in the Philippines, seeking to move beyond its vision of Protestant comity and instead to attempt a rapprochement between Protestantism and Catholicism. Brent's heavily racialized argument was that the "primitive" nature of the Philippines called for a primitive Christianity that was free from great historical schisms.[147] In his words, "these simple people ought to know as little as possible of the competitive Christianity that tortures the outside world."

He added that "we are not in the Western world" that understood "the quarrels of five centuries ago."[148]

Nonetheless, Brent expressed some discomfort with the line that he and his church trod. Despite his insistence on a cathedral tailored to the local environment, he wrote to Johnston in the early stages of planning that he "would not consent to have the architectural plans marred by a local hand."[149] Moreover, when reflecting on the designs for St. Luke's Church in Manila in a letter to its architect, he claimed the vicar had "too great an inclination to bend to the whim of the people." Although it might have been right to "conform your architecture and your methods" to prevailing conditions and to "create the feeling of unity with any ancient historic church," there was a fine line between doing that and embracing "that which is actually debased"; in other words, "lowering one's whole tone and character in order to get into touch with a community." Brent concluded that he was not "by any means ready even in matters pertaining to architecture to pretend that there is no distinction between our Church and . . . the Church of Rome."[150]

Brent was also disillusioned by his first visit to Rome in 1902, remarking on the "material and scheming" nature of the church hierarchy and writing that "even the historical interest of Rome had largely faded away." The real had been replaced by the fake—"sham flowers, sham lace, altars painted to represent marble intarsia work"—in a manner that Brent felt was deeply symbolic of Catholicism's spiritual state.[151] Although he maintained, as he wrote in his diary in 1907, that God had designed one unbroken Christianity, he also accepted that history showed God adapting this over time. The thread of true Christianity, he suggested, was no longer with Roman Catholicism. The papacy had been consumed by "imperialism & tendency to political meddlesomeness" and was doomed to die.[152] Brent also admitted that the condition of Philippine Catholicism was "pitiable."[153] Although he would be greatly satisfied to see Catholicism in the islands "purify" itself, he was skeptical of its ability to do so given its "failure to acknowledge frankly painful facts" about its past behavior.[154]

Nonetheless, Brent continued to advocate concessions to local Catholic heritage, for example when discussing Episcopal work in the mountainous regions of northern Luzon. The people there were not Catholics; this work accorded with Brent's conviction that it was not the role of the Episcopal mission in the islands to win converts from Catholicism. Still, he assumed the suitability of an emphasis on Catholic ritual form for these people that was attributable both to the sporadic efforts of Catholic missionaries to win them over and their supposed racial proclivities.[155] He noted that it was good that the two men he had working in northern Luzon (one of whom was John S. Staunton, the Episcopalian missionary closest to wholehearted sympathy with Catholicism) were "high Churchmen and fond of ritual," because that would make them "of large service to a childlike people."[156] The most striking examples of Brent's accommodation of Catholic heritage came in a letter to a mission supporter in the United States in May 1909 in which Brent listed a number of ways that Episcopal practice in the mountains bent to what Brent deemed to be local expectation, which he defined as a heightened emphasis on Catholic nomenclature and ritual. Missionaries wore cassocks and distributed crosses. They were known as "'Padi' or 'Pachi,' a corruption from Padre," and called holy communion "Misa"—the Spanish word for Mass. Moreover, they had dedicated the church at Sagada on December 8, 1907, "the legendary date of the Conception of the Virgin Mary." Brent hastened to suggest that this was just coincidence—the church had not actually been dedicated to the Immaculate Conception, "as none of our Missionaries believe in it"—but the significance of the date was not lost on him, and his letter suggested that it may not have been lost on local proselytes either.[157]

Beyond Mercer Johnston's censure of the ceremonies surrounding the building of the cathedral, Brent's numerous manifestations of apparent respect for Philippine Catholic history drew criticism from other missionaries. One Episcopal colleague expressed frustration at Brent's failure to acknowledge staunch Catholic opposition to Episcopal work at Bontoc, while James Rodgers privately disparaged Brent's "attempt to assume name and habits of the Roman Church."[158] Baptist missionaries scorned Brent for accepting prior Catholic baptisms in the Philippines, confirming into the Episcopal Church those who had already received the Catholic rite instead of baptizing them again.[159] Johnston offered critiques in letters to family and to fellow missionaries. He accused Brent of looking "towards Rome with eyes . . . too sympathetic to behold her iniquity."[160] Although when he arrived in the Philippines in 1903, Johnston hoped that Protestantism might "help [its] erring old sister," he soon became convinced that Catholicism was so far morally degraded and steeped in idolatry that it deserved no more of a hearing than any non-Christian religion, and it was his "firm conviction" that "the policy of our Church here should be marked by aggressiveness" toward "the Church of Rome."[161]

Johnston's criticism of Brent's approach made the point that Catholicism's history was not enough to justify its continued supremacy. Even though "the history of these Islands contains a record of many heroic deaths" by Catholic martyrs, "if a latter-day friar asked for consideration on account of his spiritual ancestors, I would tell him that he ought to be ashamed to bring disgrace upon them by claiming to be descended from them."[162] Indeed, Johnston reflected in his notebook, Brent himself was vestigial and a barrier to progress. He stood "on the borderland between the Old Order and the New, rooted in the Old more deeply than I am, and somewhat more afraid of the New."[163] Even though he initially believed he would be in the Philippines for the rest of his life, Johnston left in 1908, just five years after arriving, citing his and Brent's divergent visions.[164]

The YMCA was the other missionary organization in the Philippines that gave most careful thought to the question of the Catholic past as it considered who should be admitted to membership and to leadership roles.[165] In the early 1910s, seeking to increase its appeal to Filipinos and to undercut alternative Catholic projects for young men, the association discussed whether Catholicism could legitimately be described as evangelical. Potential members of the YMCA in the islands were required to make an individual declaration of evangelical faith in accordance with the Paris Basis for membership.[166] By insisting on an individual proclamation, rejecting the Portland Basis that required prospective members to belong to churches the association regarded as evangelical, the YMCA sought to draw in Filipino Catholics who identified themselves as evangelical. In addition, the name of the Roman Catholic Church was explicitly written into the constitution of the Philippine YMCA as a church that members might be drawn from, and elite Filipino Catholics were appointed to its Board of Directors.[167]

Such concessions did not occur without debate among YMCA workers, but overall an acceptance of Catholics as legitimate potential evangelicals became an important tenet of YMCA work in the islands.[168] Indeed, one general secretary was swiftly dismissed from his post in early 1917 because he had proved "unable to make any allowances for the peculiar conditions that obtain" in a country "where the predominant thought is Catholic and where much of our support comes from independent, liberal, and broadminded Catholics."[169] The YMCA came under fire from supporters in the United States for its attitude. First, they accused it of attempting to unilaterally redefine evangelicalism, and second, when they contemplated appointing Manuel R. Camus, a Filipino Catholic and prominent judge, as their secretary for work among Filipinos in the late 1910s, US supporters deemed it to be out of touch with US Protestant attitudes toward Catholics.[170]

Brent and the YMCA put into practice something that other missionaries paid lip service to. Protestants often stated that they would be happy to see Catholicism in the islands reform, inspired by Protestant endeavor and facilitated by American Catholics in leadership roles. Current Philippine society showed the effect of "unrestrained" Catholic influence, wrote Arthur Judson Brown, but the experience of the United States, Britain, and Germany proved that good was to be found in Catholicism when it was tamed by "the example and competition of a dominant Protestantism."[171] In Stuntz's words, if "error and darkness" could be banished from Philippine Catholicism, "the leaders of Protestantism will rejoice with even a deeper gladness than over the mere swelling of their own lists of members."[172] For the most part, however, even where they paid lip service to the idea that a reformed Catholicism would be desirable, it was generally clear that missionaries' prejudice was too deeply rooted to seriously consider reform to be a possibility or to take Catholic efforts in good faith. History, missionaries argued, had already proven the church's failure to produce a true spiritual life, concerned as it was with temporal authority, superficial legalism, and the suppression of opposition.[173] Despite the centrality of the possibility of transformation through conversion in their world view, missionaries were skeptical about the ability of Catholics to truly change, and attempts from within missionary ranks to reconcile with the Catholic past were generally regarded with suspicion.

Missionaries' response to the Spanish colonial past in the Philippines, which was especially evident in the built environment, exemplified their complex relationship with history. On the one hand, the arrival of US empire in the islands was accompanied by a real sense that rapid transformation was on the horizon that would upend prior history in the Philippines and draw the islands into a Protestant US Pacific. On the other hand, however, the persistent raising of expectations was tempered by recourse to historicist models that reminded Americans that the islands' past carried great weight and placed significant constraints on the speed and nature of the change that US empire or Protestant missionaries would be able to bring about. A combination of Spanish rule and the racial inferiority of the people of the Philippines had allegedly left Filipinos in a feudal past, and the evolutionist theories of the social sciences taught that in those conditions, change would be gradual and slow. Moreover, Spanish Catholic heritage was etched into the islands' culture, particularly the built environment, and missionaries had to reckon with the past's long shadow, inserting themselves into a complex history instead of remaking that history wholesale. This reckoning created tensions. There was a fine line between pragmatically exploiting the conditions created by local history and showing excessive respect for Philippine religious heritage, thus indicating that one was governed by it. For most Protestant missionaries, Charles Brent, like the US government, fell on the wrong side of this line.

There was a strategic dimension discernible in how missionaries used history. In their communications with potential financial supporters in the United States, they sought to strike a fine balance by claiming that that their work was simultaneously special, urgent, and demanding of patience. The language of historicism gave them a way of managing expectations. Providence might have used US empire to indicate that the Philippines was of world-historic significance in a scheme to evangelize the world, but there were other historical laws that Americans had to pay attention to when gauging what to expect in the islands. For missionaries, historicism also provided a way out of following their view of the crisis engendered by providential opportunities to its logical end. It allowed them to stop short of suggesting that the United States was responsible for slow progress in the evangelization of the Philippines and that it faced ruinous failure in not adequately responding to a providential opportunity. They were clearly worried that their nation was not doing enough, and in the process they complicated their use of religion as a justification for empire in the Philippines. Yet their ambivalence never manifested as a wholehearted criticism of US empire or as a disavowal of support. Instead, missionaries focused on Filipinos' supposed racial incapacity and on the stubborn persistence of the Spanish Catholic past. Missionaries were drawn away from a vision of a radically transformative US empire in the Pacific without ever becoming its opponents.

Even where they were influenced by the past, missionaries defined the boundaries of the history that might shape them, for the most part engaging only with Spanish Catholic history, which could be described in terms of corrupted European civilization and Christianity. In so doing, they elided the historical narratives of Filipino intellectuals who sought to tell stories of a rich precolonial Philippine society and spirituality that was buried under the weight of Spanish historical understandings. As chapter 6 will show, Indigenous articulations of history provided an important backdrop for missionaries' employment of historical discourse, just as in Hawai'i, and furnished source material that could be both eschewed and appropriated according to need. Although for the first two decades of their work in the Philippines, missionaries chose to comprehend the people of the islands through the lens of anthropology rather than history, denying the historical relevance of the precolonial past in order to reinforce a colonial agenda, there was a remarkable shift in their attitudes as the 1920s began. As missionaries increasingly accepted that Filipino autonomy in political and religious affairs offered the best prospects for Protestantism in the islands and began to doubt the moral superiority of Europe and North America in the aftermath of World War I, they turned to echo Filipino nationalist historians. They articulated a long Philippine past to demonstrate that God had been preparing the archipelago to undertake a pivotal role in the evangelization of the world for centuries. In the process, they completed their turn away from seeing the Philippines through the lens of the American Pacific, instead viewing US empire as one instrument in a larger narrative that Filipinos represented the potential fulfilment of.

Chapter 6

"A Chosen People"

Filipino Nationalism, Protestant Missionaries, and the Long Philippine Past

Apolinario Mabini was one of the most significant intellectual influences behind the Filipino revolution against Spain that preceded the entry of the United States into the Philippines. Trained as a lawyer at Manila's oldest university, the University of Santo Tomas, Mabini did not leave the islands for Europe like many of his contemporaries but steeped himself in what he could of European revolutionary thought from within the Philippines. Although he struggled with illness throughout his life, he involved himself in the revolutionary campaigns against Spain and was briefly arrested in 1896 before becoming one of Emilio Aguinaldo's closest advisers by 1898. Mabini authored the constitution of the Philippine Republic that Aguinaldo declared at Malolos after Spain's defeat, before becoming the first prime minister of the republic in January 1899. He resigned months later, rejecting attempts to reach an agreement with Americans who he did not believe were negotiating in good faith. Captured by the US military in December 1899 and refusing to pledge allegiance to the new colonial administration, Mabini was exiled to Guam, another of the new imperial possessions of the United States, in 1901. He did not return to the Philippines until very shortly before his death in April 1903 at the age of just 38.

While in Guam, Mabini penned a "manifesto," parts of which attracted the attention of Americans because it apparently vindicated their ideas about the moral shortcomings of Filipino revolutionaries. It seemed to show that these figures were plagued by factionalism and murderous intrigue, had lost the support of the people, and were deemed to have failed even by Mabini, one of their most incorrigible partisans. James A. LeRoy, William Howard Taft's secretary, who during the early years of the US occupation became perhaps the best-known authority on Philippine history in the United States, offered a translation and commentary for the *American Historical Review* in 1906. He focused on a chapter in which Mabini detailed the conflicts within the Republic's leadership, which culminated in the notorious assassination of General Antonio Luna, supposedly at Aguinaldo's behest. LeRoy also reproduced the introduction to the manifesto, disparaging the "egotism" and "childishness" that he believed characterized Mabini's political theory but seeing his words nonetheless as constituting a valuable "expression of Filipino racial sentiment" that might help Americans better understand their colonial responsibilities.[1]

Mabini elsewhere translated the entirety of the manifesto into English himself; another American historian of the Philippines, James A. Robertson, donated a copy of this translation to the Library of Congress in 1916. The full manifesto shows that Mabini not only commented on the internal politics of the recent Philippine Revolution but also pointed the way toward a decolonized vision of a much broader sweep of Philippine history that could provide a rallying point for Filipino nationalism. Mabini spoke of how the Spaniards had arrived in a nascent Philippine society in the sixteenth century, branded the people ignorant and indolent, and destroyed the local religion and songs that stored information about the origin and culture of the islands' people. For these traditions, Spanish colonists had substituted "creeds and practices contrary to [Filipinos'] education and habitual life," which explains why the Philippines had "turned back to the cradle and lived unconscious of itself for three long centuries." Far from simply laying a veneer over existing practice, as missionaries sometimes suggested, in Mabini's formulation the coming of Spanish Catholicism marked a "radical and violent" change and a "painful apprenticeship" that divorced Filipinos from their art, spirituality, and historical consciousness. In making this argument, Mabini picked up on an idea generated by some of the educated Filipinos, or *ilustrados*, who engaged with European intellectual cultures in the final decades of the nineteenth century: that a nation needed a history and a sense of shared traditions. Thus, the separation of Filipinos from their precolonial history and the perpetuation of the myth that real history in the Philippines did not begin until the advent of Spanish rule were vital weapons in the colonial arsenal. As Filipinos roused from their "protracted sleep," a different view became possible and even necessary: that of a rich cultural and spiritual precolonial heritage that proved that Filipinos had existed and could exist again outside the framework of European or US colonialism.[2]

The previous two chapters have shown that missionaries' vision of the United States as a divinely ordained agent for rapid transformation in the Philippines and the Pacific was complicated by their articulation of a number of other ideas when they were faced with the realities of work in the islands. None of these conceptualizations took seriously the ways Filipinos thought about their own history. Even though missionaries increasingly recognized the need to engage with the Spanish past, their elision of any Indigenous history outside the colonial framework endured for longer, mirroring an inability to conceive of Filipinos as fit for the self-government nationalists sought in politics and religion. For the first two decades of US rule, missionaries joined many other imperialists in continuing to read and write Philippine history exclusively through a colonial lens, comprehending the people of the archipelago chiefly through anthropology instead of regarding them as historical actors. In the process, they tried out a range of ways of typologizing the people of the islands that revealed the instability of the idea that the Philippines was a Pacific place.

The period following Woodrow Wilson's election as president of the United States, which was marked both by a heightened US commitment to ultimate Philippine independence and the outbreak of World War I, precipitated a remarkable shift. As the US presence in the islands increasingly felt temporary and the claims of Europeans and Americans to moral leadership were undermined by the Great War, missionaries completed their turn away from grandiose historical designs that placed Providence and US empire at the center of the frame. Books that Frank Laubach of the ABCFM and Presbyterian missionary David S. Hibbard published for audiences in the United States instead appeared to echo the Filipino nationalist historiographical trope that insisted on the deep past of Filipino spirituality and concomitantly on the capacity of Filipinos to govern their nation and church or even to take on a leadership role in the evangelization of the world. This new formulation made sense of changes in American, Philippine, and global politics and implied that the leadership of Americans was no longer needed to ensure material and spiritual progress in the archipelago.

A consideration of missionaries' engagements with competing historical traditions in the Philippines demonstrates that, as in Hawai'i, missionary perspectives on the island groups their nation had colonized and the historical knowledge they produced about them were ultimately contingent on local conditions rather than on a sense of US hegemony projected across Pacific space. Missionaries' historical perspectives were devised at the intersection of American observation, Spanish legacy, imperial need, and local agency and were defined in significant ways by all four. At the same time, even when Americans integrated Filipino viewpoints into their narratives, it was always clear that missionaries would make use of them only insofar as they helped render the projects of US mission and empire legible. Thus, apparent discontinuities and contradictions can be explained in terms of a fundamental continuity: the ongoing search for justification through historical narration. This narration, even when it appeared to accept local outlooks on history, always privileged the scientific, paternalistic, and Protestant voice and failed to acknowledge missionaries' prior complicity in suppressing Filipino perspectives. New historiographical insights were explained as the result not of dialogue but of Americans' evolving ability to make sense of the Philippines through objective observation. Missionaries thus strategically and authoritatively employed historical narratives to offer a veneer of coherence as American approaches to the islands shifted, failing to explicitly acknowledge the paradoxes they were creating or the voices they were suppressing and appropriating.

The Historical Thought of Filipino Nationalists

Beginning in the late nineteenth century, as they developed the intellectual underpinnings of a revolutionary movement against Spanish and then US rule, Filipino nationalists sought a frame through which to comprehend their history that would transcend colonial narratives and provide a basis for understanding the Philippines as an independent nation. Their historical conceptualizations acted as direct counterpoints to colonists' claims to have a monopoly on providential purpose, political maturity, and civilization. For example, Filipino revolutionaries suggested that they had a divinely ordained historic destiny when they made war against Spain and then against the United States.[3] The revolutionary leader Emilio Aguinaldo used providential language to motivate Filipinos to continue the fight against the United States in early 1899 despite their comparative military weakness: "Providence has means in reserve and prompt help for the weak in order that they may not be annihilated by the strong, that justice may be done and humanity progress."[4] Another revolutionary manifesto laid out an even grander vision, stating that "divine Providence has put us in these circumstances within reach of our independence, and under the freest form to which every individual, every people, every country can aspire."[5] The ideas that God had brought Filipinos to the brink of independence and that Philippine autonomy would have profound global ramifications furnished a counterclaim to the vision of US empire as a providential instrument. It also demonstrated a clear Filipino expression of belief, undercutting the idea that their Catholicism was nominal, imitative, or based only on fear.

Another historical strategy Filipino revolutionaries used was to expose the hypocrisy of US empire with reference to its own vaunted founding principles. Americans wanted Filipinos to understand US history through a particular lens, evident in the first celebration of George Washington's birthday in the islands in February 1901. Medical missionary Alice Byram Condict described the "American fiesta" that took place in Manila to mark the occasion. This was emblematic of a "fiesta politics" Americans engaged in from early in the occupation that sought to win over Filipino elites by courting them at social events in order to establish mutual respect, deflect attention from the violence that underpinned US colonialism, and generate legitimacy for their nation's empire in the Philippines.[6] Americans cultivated relationships with local political elites, leaving them to govern provincial affairs. At the insular level, many of the *ilustrados* who had provided the intellectual foundations for the revolution against Spanish rule responded positively to American overtures, including Benito Lagarda, Felipe Buencamino, Trinidad Pardo de Tavera, and Cayetano Arellano.[7] These men formed the core of the Partido Federalista, a pro-United States political party, and collaborated with the US colonial state in the hope of achieving recognition and, ultimately, statehood. Their cooperation enabled them to fulfill personal ambitions and win high official positions.[8] Condict recorded a string of speeches such politicians made during the celebration of Washington. The local mayor announced that "Washington is not dead, but lives to-day in the principles of liberty of the great Republic, whose father he was."[9] The mayor was followed by Pardo de Tavera, the leader of the Partido Federalista, who declared that "*a people who venerates as its hero*" such a man as Washington could not "plant its sovereignty in any part of the world with the object to dominate, but only to fulfill its historic *mission of extending among men the blessings of liberty*."[10] A vision of continuity emerged between the supposed founding ideals of the United States and an imperialist United States of the early twentieth century that had extended the benefits of Washington's radical democratic experiment to the Philippines.

This was the mythologized idea of US history that the United States hoped Filipinos would embrace, but it was one that proved unwieldy for colonial administrators and educators whose Filipino pupils picked up on its potentially subversive implications for those who did not yet have representative government.[11] In an 1899 memorandum addressed to US secretary of state John Hay, lawyer Felipe Agoncillo pointed out the gap between Filipinos' experience of American rule and the ideals Americans outlined. Agoncillo laid out the Philippines' long history of anticolonial struggle, which was marked by false promises from external powers, beginning with the 1565 "blood compact" that ostensibly sealed a reciprocal relationship between Spanish explorer Miguel López de Legazpi and Datu Sikatuna, the chieftain of Bohol. For the last hundred years or so of these centuries of struggle, Agoncillo stated, Filipinos had "been largely influenced and controlled in their hopes, aspirations and actions by the Declaration of Independence of the American people." The constitution of the Philippine Republic had drawn on the same principles, and according to Agoncillo, the republic had been true to that constitution. It was the United States that had broken its promises by failing to recognize the national autonomy the creation of such a constitution laid claim to.[12]

Agoncillo continued to subvert the idea that US empire in the Philippines was consistent with US principles by outlining to Hay the precedents his predecessors as secretary of state had set. He showed that John Adams, Henry Clay, Edward Livingston, James Buchanan, and Daniel Webster had all addressed the question of whether or not to recognize de facto governments that declared independence from a parent state and had reached the decision that such claims were to be recognized. Agoncillo concluded that because US "history of more than one hundred years" declared "the absolute right of all nations to rule themselves, free from the control of alien masters," he could submit to Hay, "with entire confidence, the right of the Filipinos to their self government."[13] For Americans to deny Filipinos their claim would be to break with their own venerated traditions.

In his manifesto, Apolinario Mabini, the author of the republic's constitution that had drawn so heavily on the Declaration of Independence, concurred with Agoncillo. He asked whether any policy for the Philippines that went "against the spirit of American institutions" could even be "held as valid" and argued that "if the United States government has been able to lead the Union on the path of prosperity and greatness, it is because its practices have not gone astray from the theory embodied in the [Declaration] of Independence."[14] Like Agoncillo, Mabini initially upheld faith that the United States could not possibly violate its promises because of its pride in its reason, lore, and history; surely Americans would recognize the Philippines as a nation born of an emancipatory revolution, just as the United States had been.[15] Although it appeared that such faith was soon to be dashed,

Mabini and others still hoped that "Americans [would] neither forget the father of their country, nor frustrate his cherished hopes." After all, Mabini continued provocatively, by their own admission Americans were not experienced in colonial governance and could not be deemed any more qualified to undertake it than Filipinos were to govern themselves.[16] Like Queen Liliʻuokalani's supporters in Hawaiʻi, Filipino revolutionaries were prepared to use the history of the United States to hold Americans to account, albeit with little success. Filipinos also recognized that the history of liberty and democracy had never been for all in the United States but was built on the back of a history of overriding Indigenous claims to sovereignty and domestic racial violence.[17] It seemed that this would be the heritage US empire in the islands most obviously drew on. Meanwhile, imperialists such as Albert Beveridge and Charles Brent turned to ideas about the providential duty of the United States in order to avoid having to justify American actions toward the Philippines in terms of any historical or legal precedent.[18]

Mabini's manifesto also exemplified a continuation of the historical work Filipino *ilustrados* had engaged in during the final decades of the nineteenth century. By narrating a precolonial history, they sought to escape the constraints on national consciousness that came with viewing the history of the Philippines only as that of the Spanish colonial era.[19] The reclamation of a precolonial past of religious life and prosperity was thus an important philosophical underpinning of Filipino calls for independence. The pioneer of such work was the famed Filipino writer José Rizal.[20] Beginning in the 1880s while studying in Europe, Rizal became increasingly aware that all histories of the Philippines were written or influenced by Spanish colonialists who believed, in the words of one mid-nineteenth-century Spanish writer, that everything prior to Legazpi was "chaos, ignorance, nothing!"[21] Rizal's time immersed in the European intellectual milieu also made clear to him the links between historical scholarship and the invention of traditions that were fundamental for aspiring nations, and he and other *ilustrados* thought about how scholarly disciplines that were often used to provide bolstering arguments for colonial rule—linguistics, folklore, and ethnology, for example—could be turned to anticolonial purposes.[22] Rizal expressed his desire "to do something for science and the history of my native country" and corresponded extensively with the European scholar Ferdinand Blumentritt, who was from the part of the Austrian empire that is now the Czech Republic.[23] Rizal attempted to convince Blumentritt to write an impartial history that would offer Filipinos a way of understanding themselves outside the Spanish gaze.[24] Although Blumentritt was a friend and a supporter of Rizal, he did not believe himself to be the best person to undertake such a work, so Rizal began his own monumental research project in European archives, aiming to construct a new historiography.[25]

One of the outcomes of Rizal's efforts was an unrealized proposal for a congress on Philippine history to be held at the Paris Exposition of 1889 at which discussion would be based on a tripartite division of this history, beginning with the period "before the arrival of the Spaniards (before 1521)."[26] Rizal promulgated his vision of history in various pamphlets and essays, and it bled into the fiction writing for which he was most famous.[27] His greatest historiographical achievement, however, was his annotated edition of the early seventeenth-century Spanish chronicle *Sucesos de las Islas Filipinas* by Antonio de Morga. Rizal used Morga to show that if it were indeed true that Filipinos were indolent and superstitious, this was not because they were incapable but rather because the Spaniards had enervated a Philippine society that was thriving in manufacturing, agriculture, and trade.[28]

Other Filipino nationalists expressed similar ideas about history, notably Pedro Paterno and Isabelo de los Reyes. These men did not always agree with one another. De los Reyes was a journalist (and later a pioneering trade unionist) who engaged with folklore. Through his studies, he sought to bring a Filipino perspective to a new Spanish metropolitan science and thus to demonstrate that the Philippines could contribute to humankind's store of knowledge. He also developed the idea that the nascent Filipino nation had rich traditions that lent it historical legitimacy.[29] De los Reyes was less celebratory about the precolonial past than Rizal and Paterno; he sought simply to create a sense of Filipino identity through a quest for knowledge of history and folklore.[30] Paterno focused on religion and glorified the past far more. His argument, about which Rizal was highly skeptical but which de los Reyes adopted, was that prior to the coming of the Spaniards, Filipinos worshipped a single supreme deity, Bathalà, in a manner similar to the way Christians worship God.[31]

In his formulation of Paterno's argument, de los Reyes believed that inherent in Filipino worship of Bathalà was an understanding of the Trinity, the afterlife, and evolution; that Jesus was an incarnation of Bathalà as much as of the Christian God; and that all religions were fundamentally the same because they pointed toward the same God and the same morality.[32] He also argued that the ancestor worship found in precolonial Philippine culture was not "rude polytheism" but an acknowledgement of Bathalà's presence everywhere.[33] The way forward for Filipinos, de los Reyes concluded, was not to accept the doctrines of foreign religions but to regain the "purity" of their own.³⁴ Precolonial knowledge of a single God proved that Filipinos had innate spiritual genius, that they had not merely imitated the Spaniards, and that they had the ability and right to form their own churches. This vision of history found religious expression through Gregorio Aglipay's independent church.³⁵ Aglipay rejected papal leadership partly on the grounds that before the coming of the Spaniards, Filipinos had "worshipped God according to the dictates of their own conscience."³⁶ This was a spiritual argument that complemented a fight for political freedom.

There are limits to what the work of the *ilustrados* can tell us about history and historical narration in the Philippines. *Ilustrado* historiography was somewhat exclusive, reflecting what Paul Kramer has termed a "nationalist colonialism."³⁷ Although Rizal and others sought to emphasize shared traditions between groups the US colonialists insisted were too divided to form a nation, a significant part of the islands' population—animist hill tribes and Muslim groups in the southern islands—were conspicuously and deliberately left out of the vision for a Filipino nation with a shared history.³⁸ As *ilustrados* sought recognition by Europeans and spent time immersed in European intellectual traditions, they imbibed historicist ideas, telling a story based on linear development and hegemonic colonial conceptions of time that has cast a shadow over Philippine historiography ever since.³⁹ In fact, they founded their vision of the Philippine past on the kinds of evolutionist racial science that Protestant missionaries and other US colonialists used to suggest that Filipinos were not ready for self-government. Specifically, they drew on Blumentritt's idea that the islands had been populated by three migratory waves in the distant past—first primitive "Negritos," then a group of "barbarous" Malayans, and then a higher class of Malayans. The Hispanicized, "civilized" Filipino of the late nineteenth century was said to be a product of the last of these three waves, which was distinct from the descendants of the first two waves, who were still present in remote regions of the islands.⁴⁰ The boundaries of the Filipino or Tagalog civilization that emerged in *ilustrado* histories were somewhat elastic, and de los Reyes in particular found closer kinship to non-Christian hill peoples than some of his counterparts.⁴¹ Nevertheless, all *ilustrados* asserted a fundamentally hierarchical view of the people of the Philippines and were especially keen to assert historical distance from Muslim populations.⁴²

On the one hand, some evidence suggests that movements that touched a broader segment of the Philippine population were influenced to some extent by *ilustrado* historiography. For example, the Katipunan revolutionary society that Andrés Bonifacio founded converted ideas about a glorious pre-Hispanic past into a popular poetic form as a part of its rallying cry.⁴³ On the other hand, *ilustrado* historicism obscured some alternative conceptions that were fundamental to Philippine cosmology, for example genealogies that were not dissimilar to those found in Hawai'i. According to the historian Vicente L. Rafael, genealogy for Southeast Asian peoples traditionally "acted as a provisional, revisable marker rather than as an unassailable organizing principle of authority." It did more than merely chart lines of descent; it also tracked shifting status and kinship alliances and provided evidence of ritual, agricultural, commercial, or military prowess that might raise a claimant to the status of ancestor who had been able to effectively mediate the reciprocal relationship between earth and cosmos.[44] The *awit*—a song or romance that enshrined genealogical linkages—was an alternative historical source that was equivalent to the *mele* the Board of Genealogy and Nathaniel Emerson studied in Hawai'i.[45] The Muslim populations of the southern Philippines also pushed back against hegemonic historical narratives using genealogies. These told the story of how Islamic traditions and political structures were shaped in the islands and connected the history of these populations to the wider Philippine archipelago by remembering shared cultural origins in the Indo-Malay world, the continuation of which colonialism interrupted.[46] Tagalog nationalist dramas of the early twentieth century presented another mode of historical narration whose "meanings eluded the imperial logic of benevolent assimilation and the surveying gaze of the archive," writes Rafael. These plays presented Philippine history as punctuated by waves of anticolonial struggle, with colonial agents appearing as "figures disruptive of reciprocal obligations." They foregrounded the vernacular, the agency of women, and kinship ties, countering Americans' attempts to impose classificatory order, for example through the 1903 census, and to prescribe "manly discipline."[47]

Nonetheless, *ilustrado* historiography was significant, and it provides the context we might read missionaries' historical writings against. For the first two decades of Protestant mission work in the islands, missionaries' narratives acknowledged but rejected the *ilustrados'* alternative histories. Instead, they continued to view the history of the Philippines, insofar as they recognized that it was important at all, only through the lens of Spanish colonialism. They portrayed Filipinos as gaining agency only in reaction to the Spaniards and as best understood through the lens of anthropology rather than history. Despite the ostensible aim of the United States to liberate Filipinos from the ignorance that Spanish rule had supposedly fostered, missionaries joined with other US imperialists to perpetuate the sense of Filipinos as a people without proper history and thus without the capacity for self-governance.

Missionaries' Elision of Filipino Nationalist Historiography

For the first two decades of their work in the Philippines, missionaries' historical overviews in their printed works, which constituted significant sources of knowledge about the archipelago for their fellow Americans, often began with the "discovery" of the islands by Portuguese explorer Ferdinand Magellan, who landed at Cebu in 1521 and was subsequently killed.[48] Missionaries were also repeatedly drawn back to this moment of discovery in their correspondence. Hibbard wrote that the site of Magellan's landing was "highly venerated by the inhabitants," but it provoked missionary fascination too.[49] When discussing Cebu, missionaries noted that it was the site of Magellan's discovery, of the first Mass, and of the first European settlement.[50] Charles Brent marveled at the heroism of Magellan in undertaking an oceanic voyage under conditions of sixteenth-century seafaring, and the frontispiece of Stuntz's book showed a statue of Captain Cano, a sailor in Magellan's fleet who made it back to Spain, labeling him "the man who did what Columbus failed to do."[51] In frequently returning to this particular historical moment, which they felt haunted a particular place on the Philippine landscape, missionaries showed that they were compelled by the idea of a founding or discovery that had brought the archipelago into history.

Missionaries' potted histories, found in the published works of Arthur Judson Brown, Homer Stuntz, and Charles Briggs, continued from Magellan along a familiar trajectory that was entirely framed by Spanish rule. Miguel López de Legazpi swiftly followed, setting sail in 1564 not only backed by the Spanish state but accompanied by five Augustinian friars, thus beginning the long and inextricably connected histories of Spanish colonialism and Catholic hegemony in the Philippines.[52] Recurrent struggles ensued, both between Spanish religious and temporal authorities and between the Spaniards and various foreign powers, during which the welfare of the people was neglected, beyond a "mechanical" desire to see them all baptized.[53] There were consequent insurrections by the people of the archipelago, but these were never a concerted bid for independence; rather, they were "a blind, striking out against glaring injustice and pitiless inhumanity."[54] A crisis of Spanish hegemony after the Seven Years' War opened the door to the possibility of a new imperial policy, but the promise of proper representation, which was made multiple times over the course of the nineteenth century, only ever proved to be a false dawn. Against this backdrop, beginning with the Cavite insurrection of 1872, which was precipitated in particular by debates over the status of Filipino clergy, an awakened Filipino populace struck, still not for independence, supposedly, but rather for justice, paving the way for the decisive uprising in 1896.[55] In this history of Spanish neglect and cruelty, it was really the friars who held the power all along, constituting a permanent outpost of Spanish influence as governors came and went.[56]

Although missionary narratives appeared sympathetic to Filipinos, their framing continued to suggest that it was only through Spanish agency that Filipinos had a history at all and that both the good and bad in them had been forged in reaction to the Spaniards. The implication was that because they lacked inherent racial capacity in the first place and had furthermore been denied the ability to think by the Spaniards, they could not possibly set out a coherent vision for self-governance, create anything meaningful, or hold individual faith in ways that might register as being worth the attention of the historian. Homer Stuntz suggested in his book that any attempts to reconstruct a history of the people of the Philippines outside the colonial frame were futile; such an enterprise would have required written sources, and the stocks of such knowledge were "meager." What little was known about that precolonial past, Stuntz contended, suggested a world view based on "an idolatrous form of demon-worship."[57] Stuntz's assessment of the impossibility of reconstructing a precolonial past was not due to a lack of awareness of the work of the *ilustrados*. Stuntz acknowledged that this work existed, but he clearly did not see it as worth integrating into his own historical understandings.[58] Although Filipino nationalists also recognized that the self-consciousness of the islands' people had been suppressed under Spanish rule and that many useful repositories of historical knowledge had been destroyed, they took an alternative approach to addressing the consequent void by issuing a rallying call for a project of historical rediscovery by trawling European archives or engaging in the study of folklore.

Stuntz, along with some of the key architects of US governance in the Philippines, turned to the social sciences and became fascinated with the ways the archipelago's people might be taxonomized.[59] Stuntz stressed that it was "a fundamental mistake to think of the inhabitants of the Philippine Islands as one people." He outlined an overarching distinction between "non-Christian tribes" and the "Christianized Filipino," noting that "both of these classes again subdivide along ethnological and linguistic lines of cleavage" until "we have heterogeneity raised to its highest power." There were in fact "sixty-nine sorts of people, speaking thirty-four languages." Stuntz described the key divisions in "chronological" order, by which he meant the order in which each of the groups were believed to have arrived in the islands, each apparently more civilized than the last.[60] The classifications Stuntz devised were emblematic of the interimperial dimension of Americans' knowledge about the Philippines. Not only was the overarching distinction between non-Christian and Christianized peoples derived from the Spaniards, but Stuntz's main textual source was *The Philippine Islands* by John Foreman, a British scholar and a fellow of the Royal Geographical Society. Foreman had collected information about the islands while working for British manufacturers of agricultural machinery in the 1880s. He published his book first in Hong Kong and then in London.[61] In the damning verdict of James LeRoy: "No other writer on the Philippines has been so often quoted in the United States since 1898 as John Foreman. Certainly no other has so often been made sponsor for garbled versions of Philippine history and . . . downright inaccuracies."[62]

Stuntz turned to social science to deny any unity among the peoples of the archipelago and thus to rebut any claims they made to nationhood. He drew on many of the same core ideas as the *ilustrados* but reached very different conclusions. *Ilustrados* had turned to the techniques of European social science in order to assert the fundamental unity of a Filipino people, although they engaged in some imperial historicism of their own along the way with their argument that "civilized" Filipinos represented the most recent of three migratory waves. Stuntz, in contrast, explicitly made the point that the "distrust and dislike" between the "racial and linguistic subdivisions" of the Philippines made it "impossible to speak of 'the Filipino people'" as having "common aspirations or . . . sympathies."[63] Instead, the islands' people as a whole were rendered "childlike" and "tribal," just as American Indians had been described by white settlers.[64] To be "tribal," according to stadial models of civilizational development, was to be far away from the goal of nationhood.[65] It was also, as Charles Brent noted in a sermon on US national purpose around the time he left the United States for the Philippines, to be without history, which he argued begins when "the nation emerges from tribal chaos" and "shakes itself from the garments of legend."[66] The compression of Philippine history into the period of Spanish rule and the understanding of the islands' people through anthropology rather than history were arguments against Filipino self-governance just as much as the reclamation of a longer history was an argument for independence. By defining the boundaries of history, Americans were defining the boundaries of civilization.

The language of racial or religious categorization allowed missionaries to emphasize Filipinos' lack of unity at an archipelagic level. At a different level, racial and religious classifications helped missionaries understand exactly why

God might have led them to the Philippines. By placing the people of the islands in a broad, preexisting racial or religious category instead of recognizing them as a national group with a particular history, missionaries could portray their work in this archipelago, about which most Americans had supposedly known little or nothing before May 1898, as being of worldhistoric importance. Stuntz, for example, turned to British naturalist Alfred Wallace's theories of the geological and cultural unity of the "Malay Archipelago" to suggest that "whatever is done for the Philippines will inevitably affect the destinies of millions who, like the Filipinos, are Malayan in blood and speech."[67] Ideas about the unusual benefits of Philippine geography and about the pathbreaking nature of evangelism among this "Oriental" people became tropes in missionary writing in the early twentieth century. Stuntz wrote of God having "swung . . . America out on the highway of the seas between the two great continents upon which live the . . . thousand millions of our fellow-beings who are yet unevangelized."[68] The general secretary of the YMCA in Manila noted in 1920 that the Philippines stood at the "gateway of the Orient" and that India, China, and Japan were "observing Christian America."[69] In his foreword to Frank Laubach's *The People of the Philippines* (1925), prominent missiologist Daniel Johnson Fleming wrote that "the Philippines can serve as a window through which we can think out to India, the Far East and the islands of the sea."[70] This vision of a work in the Philippines that would radiate across Asia was very much dialed in to a broader imperialist rhetoric that emphasized the strategic location of the Philippines, like that of Hawai'i, as a nodal point from which American civilization and commerce could spread.[71]

The perspectives of some missionaries undercut this United States–centric vision of Asia and the Pacific too, though. For Methodists, the Philippine mission was closely linked to older evangelistic work in Asia. James Thoburn, who first scoped out the Philippines, was a missionary to India, and the islands were subsequently brought into a South Asian bishopric alongside India and Malaysia that was overseen by the British-American bishop William F. Oldham. Oldham's wife Marie told women in the United States that evangelistic efforts in the Philippines were the "children" of the Indian mission, and Oldham argued that the Philippines was geographically a part of Malaysia.[72] In this formulation, the Philippines was not an outpost of the United States from which Asia could be evangelized but instead a satellite of other missions in Asia that had longer histories.

In a different way, a broader historical and geographical perspective also allowed missionaries to figure US efforts in the Philippines as the stage God had set for a world-historic battle between Protestantism and Catholicism or, in the case of the southern island groups of Mindanao and Sulu, between Protestantism and Islam.[73] Presbyterian missionary James Rodgers, for example, linked the "strange and unexpected turn of events" that had brought the islands under US control to his previous mission work in Brazil. Although he had initially been skeptical of the need to evangelize in "the Latin countries," he had seen in Brazil that those who had fallen under the sway of Catholicism had only "a dim knowledge of the truths of Scripture" hidden by "a mass of superstition" and believed that God was sending Protestantism into places where the gospel was "obscured by the traditions of men."[74] The Philippines thus represented a new front in this wider battle. It was this sense that the Philippines was above all situated in a "Latin" Catholic world and that there were cultural and linguistic similarities across this world that prompted the Presbyterian board to send Rodgers straight from Brazil to conduct work in the Philippines in the first place; this world view also prompted the Baptist mission to transfer Eric Lund from his work in Spain.[75] In a different way, this idea of the Philippines as a typological meeting ground for Protestantism and "Latin" Catholicism also colored the work of the YMCA, whose decision to include Catholics in its evangelical organization was made in part with reference to precedents set in other Latin American contexts the association had worked in.[76] According to Frank Laubach, who was working in Mindanao, US rule in the islands had also created "the one weak spot in Mohammedanism to be found in the entire world today."[77] The peculiar opportunity to combat both Catholicism and Islam in one nation no doubt underscored the islands' uniqueness for Protestant missionaries, even if relatively few took up the call to evangelize the Muslim population.

The various typologies missionaries deployed to portray the Philippines as a crucial point of entry for winning an entire race or religion—Malay, Oriental, or Latin peoples; Catholics or Muslims—over to the Protestant Christ reveal the ways the archipelago defied any single cultural or cartographical characterization. These multiple connective frames the islands might be placed in further undercut the pretensions that a US Pacific connected the West Coast to Asia via Hawai'i and the Philippines. Missionaries were implicitly recognizing that Philippine history connected the islands to South America across a "Spanish lake" and to Malayan and Islamic worlds across the Indian Ocean and that all of these conceptualizations were more meaningful when thinking about their work on the ground than any sense that the archipelago was connected to the United States across the North Pacific.[78] Nonetheless, just as much as typologies that asserted the tribal nature of the people of the Philippines, the large-scale schemes that attempted to locate the Philippines in broader global spiritual struggles obscured the actual agency of Filipinos as historical actors and the attempts of José Rizal and other *ilustrados* to build a nation with reference to a particular kind of historical narrative.

The final insult was that missionaries were complicit in an American project to appropriate Rizal's legacy without acknowledging the implications of his intellectual work. As a thinker who embraced the modern and spoke out against the Catholic regime and who was martyred in 1896 for this crime, the late Rizal could transition to being a Filipino who would have welcomed the United States. Such a transition was made easier by the statements in some of his earlier intellectual work that he did not seek independence for the Philippines because of the violence that such a struggle would engender; he only wanted to assert the rights of Filipinos under colonial governance.[79] US government officials thus appropriated Rizal as a suitable hero. They buried his bones in the heart of the colonial capital, established memorial parks and monuments, and acknowledged the day of Rizal's martyrdom—December 30—as a public holiday, continuing a practice the Philippine Republic had instituted.[80] The educator Austin Craig contributed an extensive English-language biography of Rizal in 1913.[81] Americans' perspective on Rizal constituted a false dichotomy between the reformism of Rizal and the revolutionary traditions that directly opposed Spanish and US colonial rule. This dichotomy became widely accepted, even among subsequent Filipino nationalist historians writing in the mid-twentieth century.[82]

Rizal was similarly eulogized in missionary writings as an exemplar for the future Filipino under US rule. They remembered him as a visionary and as the greatest victim of the cruel Spanish regime.[83] What was particular about the missionary perspective was an attempt to imbue Rizal with a decidedly Protestant significance despite his self-declared Catholicism. When the revivalist George Pentecost visited the islands in 1902, he used Rizal Day as an opportunity to address a mass meeting. Presbyterian missionaries expected great results from such a strategy because "anything connected with Rizal Day will interest the people . . . throughout the islands."[84] Writing in 1905, James Rodgers did not mention Rizal specifically but celebrated Filipino intellectuals who had traveled to Hong Kong and Europe, had visited Protestant churches there, and had supposedly "longed for a similar service and for the unknown things of the Gospel."[85] Mercer Johnston stated that Filipinos would be "false to the memory of Rizal" if they allowed Catholicism to persist in the islands, while Hibbard called Rizal the "George

Washington of the Filipinos" before stating that "as sin goes out that wonderful emotional enthusiasm of the Filipino nature becomes available for deeper Christian life. . . . It was this that made Rizal write and die."[86] In a particularly evocative article, the Presbyterian missionary Charles R. Hamilton, whose field included Rizal's birthplace of Calamba, imagined a young Rizal standing on the shores of Laguna de Bay, staring out across it in search of a better future for his people. Were Rizal "able to see the freedom and progress of religion in his beloved land and the material improvement of his people, he would feel that the millennium of which he dreamed . . . was almost at hand."[87]

Although Frank Laubach criticized the Aglipayan church for viewing Rizal as a saint or a messiah, Protestants competed for his legacy and were attentive to where, in their view, it was misused.[88] One ABCFM worker criticized plans to place a statue of Rizal outside the Catholic church in Davao, given that Catholicism's "representatives were responsible for his death."[89] In 1936, Laubach wrote a celebratory biography.[90] Missionaries presented a Protestant, US-friendly Rizal with some enduring success, as is indicated by the repetition of the notion that Rizal was Protestant even in recent scholarship.[91] In so doing, they overlooked his Catholic background and the fact that his project of historical reclamation was a key philosophical underpinning of the movement against colonial rule.

Missionaries ignored innovations in Philippine historiography in ways that suited their denial of Filipinos' capacity to govern themselves in spiritual or political affairs. The next section of this chapter, however, argues that a remarkable shift happened moving into the 1920s. As the political context changed, missionaries began to tell a different history that echoed nationalist narrations of a long Philippine past of spiritual and material accomplishment. Just as previous missionary histories had made the case for Americans remaining in the islands, these new narratives paved the way for them to leave and for Filipinos to become those who would evangelize the world. A history emerged that centered the Philippines and viewed the world from the archipelago outward instead of representing the islands as the farthest reaches of a new US Pacific.

The Missionary Turn to the Long Philippine Past

Woodrow Wilson's election to the US presidency in 1913 marked the first time since Philippine annexation that the executive branch had been controlled by a Democratic Party that was seen as the anti-imperialist counterpoint to Republicans McKinley, Roosevelt, and Taft. It would be too strong to say that Wilson was a committed anti-colonialist on any principled grounds (he had spoken in the past about Filipinos' incapacity for self-government), but his party was ready to begin steps to relieve the United States of the Philippine burden.[92] Soon the question no longer seemed to be whether the islands would be granted independence, but when. Wilson immediately appointed Francis Burton Harrison, a fellow Democrat and an anti-imperialist, to the position of governor-general, and Harrison pursued a policy of Filipinization, prompting US civil servants to leave the islands in droves while Filipino nationalist politicians, especially Manuel Quezon, gained stature. Harrison replaced several American members of the Philippine Commission almost immediately after his arrival in the islands, leading to a Filipino majority on the Commission for the first time. More broadly, when Harrison assumed the governor-generalship in 1913, Americans constituted 29 percent of the colonial bureaucracy in the Philippines. Six years later, they made up only 6 percent. A first formal commitment to decolonization by the United States was made in the Jones Law of 1916, which created a bicameral elected legislature in which a Philippine Senate replaced the Philippine Commission and promised independence, albeit only when US overseers deemed the Filipino population sufficiently orderly.[93]

For missionaries, it seemed as though their fears that the providential window of opportunity would at some point snap shut were finally being realized and that the US imperial and missionary projects faced failure. "Looming up in the future is the independence of the islands, an unavoidable fact, which no thinking man can ignore," wrote Hibbard in 1917. "The years which are ours for work are few."[94] Motivated by this heightened sense that their time was short, missionaries desperately sought to foster awareness among both colonial officials and mission supporters of the dangers their evangelistic project faced due to lukewarm US imperialism. Brent warned Harrison of the "undue speed" with which the experiment of Filipinization was being undertaken and emphasized to co-religionists in the United States that he believed history would judge Wilson's actions.[95] A Presbyterian missionary in 1916 articulated more specific concerns about what might happen in the event of independence: "I greatly fear that Romanism would regain its lost hold in a few years and the old regime be here in full force again with Spanish instead of English."[96] In 1919, an ABCFM worker wrote that as thousands of Americans began to leave the islands, the rapid evangelization of young mestizos who were about to enter political office became even more imperative: "To wait five years would mean the lost opportunity of training the American mestizos in a Christian school."[97]

Halfway through Wilson's first term, World War I broke out in Europe. Missionaries recognized this as a further blow to their project that was predicated on the notion that Europeans and Americans were fit to lead the world in spiritual and material progress.[98] Charles Brent noted the significant setback that war in Europe represented to the missionary enterprise, referencing a Chinese correspondent in a Philippine newspaper who questioned "how Christians could explain the war" and "by what right we invaded the Orient professing to hold in our gift the blessings of peace and righteousness."[99] Brent's own impulse, he wrote in another letter, was "to go off into the wilds and live with the so called savages whose worst atrocities are mild compared with this storm of destruction."[100] According to Frank Laubach, who arrived in the Philippines in 1915 as the war raged, it was becoming clear that Europe and North America themselves needed a "thoroughgoing religious reconstruction."[101] Just as the brutality of World War I pushed influential anthropologists, including Ruth Benedict and Margaret Mead, to bring the idea of cultural relativism to the center of their discipline, it also paved the way for some missionaries in the Philippines to begin to view the islands' history and culture in more relativistic terms and to emphasize human sameness over human difference.[102]

Wilson's presidency, Harrison's governor-generalship, and the moral crisis of World War I all took place in the context of an increasingly vocal and influential Filipino nationalist movement that had an ability to make pariahs of Americans who continued to suggest that Filipinos were not ready to go it alone in affairs of church and state. The election of the Philippine Assembly in 1907 brought to the fore a new generation of nationalist politicians, including Quezon, to replace those of the Partido Federalista who had been the Americans' key collaborators in the early years of colonial rule.[103] Nationalist intellectuals began to push back more forcefully against the tribal interpretation of the Philippine past that the zoologist and US government official Dean Conant Worcester had articulated and Homer Stuntz had amplified. Because to suggest that the people of the Philippines were tribal was to suggest that they had no common national aims, it was crucial to continue the *ilustrados'* project of identifying a long, shared history that could provide the basis for a nation.

The Lake Mohonk Conference on the Indians and Other Dependent Peoples of 1912 provided good examples both of how Filipino intellectuals directly challenged an American audience's presumptions about the nature of Philippine history and how missionaries became wrapped up in controversies surrounding the presentation of the islands' people. First, Maximo Kalaw spoke at the conference. Kalaw was a Filipino law student at Georgetown who had come to the United States as private secretary to Quezon; in 1912, he was the Philippines' resident commissioner in the US Congress. He articulated a vision of a primordial Filipino unity forged through both precolonial and colonial cultures.[104] Presbyterian missionary James Rodgers spoke at the same gathering, offering a paper that focused on a syncretic religious sect in Cavite province. To nationalists who were invested in a nationalist colonialism that distanced Filipinos from hill peoples and Muslims and increasingly asserted the capacity of Filipinos to rule over non-Christians, Rodgers's focus seemed to perpetuate the very stereotype of the Philippines Kalaw spoke out against—that the people of the islands were tribal and that they held onto primitive beliefs.[105] Americans' choice to have non-Christian peoples represent the Philippines at the World's Fair in St. Louis in 1904 had similarly horrified Filipino elites seeking recognition by the United States who feared the damage done by the primary association of the archipelago with people both they and US audiences deemed to be savages.[106] Rodgers fell afoul of these nationalist colonialist sensitivities, supposedly to the great detriment of mission work. J. M. Groves of the YMCA attributed a schism from the Presbyterian mission to the fallout from this speech, noting that this tension added to the difficulties Methodists faced because of the "unguarded utterances" of Homer Stuntz regarding Filipino incapacity for self-government and Bishop William F. Oldham's involvement in the pro-imperialist Philippine Society.[107]

In fact, since as early as 1905, when the Cristianos Vivos Metodistas led by Manuel Aurora left the Methodists, missionaries from across denominations had been facing divisions within their congregations. One of the most prominent examples was the Iglesia Evangélica Metodista, which was founded in 1909 by Nicolas Zamora, a man whom Methodists had previously held up as the exemplary Filipino convert and preacher. The Cristianos Filipinos left the Presbyterians in 1911, allegedly supported by leading nationalist politicians. Schisms also plagued the Presbyterians, the Disciples of Christ, the Christian and Missionary Alliance, and the Seventh-day Adventists from 1905 to 1915. Although it is not certain that these schisms were all motivated by nationalism, the only denominations that avoided such ruptures were the apolitical Baptists and the anti-imperialist United Brethren, both of whom made more substantial efforts to develop an Indigenous church leadership than their counterparts from other missions.[108]

Missionaries were thus well aware of the potential religious ramifications of taking the retentionist stance on political issues before promises of independence and the moral turpitude of World War I gave further impetus to the nationalist movement. In the subsequent period, Quezon led the first of a number of missions to the United States in 1919 to push Americans to honor the commitment set out in the Jones Law.[109] Large-scale student protests in the Philippines against perceived insults by the colonial government increased in number and became increasingly explicit in demands for independence.[110] Filipinos residing in the United States published tracts for US audiences outlining the arguments for self-government, including direct rebuttals of the "insidious" characterization of the Philippine people as tribal.[111] Again, the narration of history was a particular battleground. The Philippine Women's University that Francisca Tirona Benitez and Paz Marquez Benitez founded in 1919 stressed as part of its curriculum the importance of Philippine history being taught by Filipinos, and the University of the Philippines under its president Jorge Bocobo promoted a cultural revival of Filipino folklore and customs.[112] The writings of the journalist Manuel Artigas y Cueva and the work of the new Philippine Historical Association sought to continue the work of the *ilustrados* by rooting Filipino nationality in a deep past.[113]

Philippine independence had a strange career. There was no straight line from the Jones Law to self-government, which would not take its complete and final form until 1946. In the 1920s, Republicans returned to dominance in US domestic politics, as did a resurgence of retentionist sentiment regarding the Philippines, beginning with a report produced by colonial old hands Leonard Wood and W. Cameron Forbes reaffirming Filipino unreadiness for self-government. Between 1921 and 1927, Governor-General Wood, convinced of Filipino incapacity for self-governance, walked back Filipinization by once again expanding the number of Americans in the colonial bureaucracy and increasing his executive power. The combination of a report by the Ohio Republican Carmi Thompson in the 1920s and a sensationalist account by the journalist Katherine Mayo further underscored the arguments for retention to US audiences: that the consequences of the United States leaving the Philippines would be an outbreak of chaos due to the incapability of Filipinos and a wave of violent oppression and exploitation due to the contempt of Filipinos for "non-Christian tribes." When the Tydings-McDuffie Act of 1934 finally inaugurated an autonomous Philippine Commonwealth and promised complete independence in ten years, it did not represent the triumph of Filipino nationalism and of the principle of self-determination. Instead, it was the triumph of protectionist and nativist sentiments in the United States that demanded an end to the flow of Philippine goods and Filipino laborers into the country: by the terms of the Act, Filipinos became "aliens" subject to stringent immigration quotas.[114]

Nonetheless, there was still a sense in which the events surrounding Wilson's presidency and World War I represented a point of no return and that the middle ground between outright nationalism and outright retentionism had disappeared.[115] Against this backdrop, in the 1910s and the 1920s, missionaries increasingly embraced support for Philippine independence as the best way forward for Protestantism in the islands, recognizing the continuing growth of nationalism among their congregations and the ability of nationalist opposition to derail their work.[116] This represented a significant evolution from a missionary perspective that had previously seen US empire as a necessary precondition of Protestant evangelistic success and that had initially seen Wilson's commitment to Filipinization as spelling disaster for the missionary enterprise. Presbyterians moved quite early to adjust their religious work, establishing an independent Filipino synod in 1914 on the grounds that in an increasingly nationalistic climate, "anything Filipino appeals very strongly to the hearts of the people and anything foreign is not well received."[117] By the mid-1920s, Arthur Judson Brown was arguing on behalf of the Presbyterian board that "independence should not be deferred," and by the early 1930s Methodist missionaries had adopted an official resolution that supported nationalist ambitions.[118]

In the late 1910s and the 1920s, retentionists, including Forbes and Wood, with whom most missionaries had previously shared sympathies, deployed history to argue that the islands had "always been a dependent group under the influence of a stronger power" and that US interest in the Philippines far predated 1898.[119] They thus sought to naturalize US governance in the Philippines as a product of history in order to counter arguments for decolonization. Alongside their embrace of the independence movement, missionaries developed alternative ways of dealing with Philippine history. Much like their turn to historicism and social science, these conceptualizations allowed them to avoid the conclusion that the United States had abjectly failed in its providential duty to effect rapid religious transformation in the Philippines. Instead, at least some missionaries began to read history in ways that suggested that the historical fate of world Christianity was in the hands of the coming Filipino nation. Reframing the meaning of US intervention, they began to take more seriously an idea that Filipino nationalist intellectuals dating back to the *ilustrados* had argued for all along: that there was a long history of Philippine civilization that far predated colonial interventions and that this history had profound spiritual significance.

In the mid-1920s, two missionary texts for US audiences—*Making a Nation* (1926) by the long-serving David S. Hibbard and *The People of the Philippines* (1925) by Frank Laubach—used this idea of a long Philippine past as the foundation for a somewhat surprising conclusion. Both works argued that the chosen nation in the imperial relationship between the United States and the Philippines might be the latter rather than the former. Certainly the United States was the instrument that had opened the archipelago to Protestantism, they said, but the important role for the future, in uplifting themselves and evangelizing those around them, was for Filipinos. Hibbard noted that although there was a tendency to attribute Philippine progress, which was greater than that of any other colony in the world, to their American overseers, "much of the real work and real progress have been by the Filipinos themselves."[120] Laubach wrote that the Filipino was "capable of a far more profound *religious insight* than the Spaniards ever suspected." Masculinizing his idealized Filipino, Laubach argued that he had "the talent, and is on the point of receiving the opportunity which may easily make him the spiritual leader of the Far East." He would not merely be "a replica of America," but would be "something better than an imitation—he will express his own fine genius."[121]

Both Hibbard and Laubach presented evidence for their convictions with reference to history. Hibbard presented a Filipino subject with a long history of profound spiritual life who was prepared to take on a leadership role of international proportions in spreading Protestantism.[122] Laubach wrote that "one may see in the history of the Philippines a vast meaning, pregnant with wonderful possibilities for the future."[123] The first step toward identifying meaningfulness in Philippine history was to acknowledge that it was possible and worthwhile to reconstruct the past beyond the Spanish colonial period. Hibbard's book began, as so many of its predecessors had, with the "discovery" of the islands by Magellan. However, it then consciously took a turn that earlier works had not: "The discovery of the Philippines by Magellan marks the beginning of the Islands' history for most writers, but the history really dates from far earlier times." Among other things, Hibbard suggested that there was a Philippine commerce with China dating back to before Christopher Columbus was even born, a period when the Philippines was under the sway of "the powerful rulers of Borneo" and a strong Hindu influence.[124] This formulation transcended the hermetically sealed, teleological narrative from Magellan to McKinley most missionaries had previously relied on and used a broader source base to suggest that there were alternative ways of narrating Philippine history.

Laubach, who had a PhD in sociology from Columbia, moved beyond these general ideas about precolonial Philippine civilization and commercial prosperity in his book. He sketched out "religion before 1000 A.D."[125] He first considered the "Negritos," the islands' aboriginal inhabitants. Laubach believed that because of this group's relative isolation, some of their "ancient customs" were extant and identified remnants of their animistic world view among peoples of the contemporary Philippines. Among later arrivals in the islands ("Indonesians" and "Malays"), Laubach identified more substantial belief systems that were still evident among the Bagobos of Mindanao and the Tinguians and Igorots of Luzon. These involved elaborate creation narratives, a belief in various spirits who dwelled in the landscape, knowledge of an afterlife, awareness of a single supreme being, and religious specialists who conducted ceremonies, saw visions, and practiced medicine. Laubach not only acknowledged such precolonial religious awareness but suggested that it showed a peculiar and valuable spiritual sensitivity. He praised the attention of these "primitive people" to the "unseen world" that was greater than that of the "average civilized man" and their religion's restraining influence against various vices. Laubach also considered the influence of India and China on Philippine spirituality from the year 1000 to Magellan's arrival. He sketched out the expansion of Hindu influence through the Srivijaya and Majapahit empires, which dominated Southeast Asia from the eighth to the fourteenth centuries, and ongoing commercial contacts with China from as early as 982. He lamented that the Spaniards had destroyed any evidence of such contacts and believed that there must previously have been a "very considerable literature" demonstrating that the people of the Philippines "were semi-civilized, and not savages, as the Spaniards pictured them."[126]

All in all, Laubach concluded, Philippine history "reminds one of a Chosen People millenniums ago." Having blended "Indonesian and Mongoloid blood" and maintained contact with India and China, Filipinos were in prime position to "know the Orient a thousand times better than any Occidental," but they also knew "Europe and America a thousand times better than any other Oriental nation" through their experience of Spanish and US rule. It was "the first time in history the four greatest streams of civilization the world has known, Northern and Southern Asia, and Northern and Southern Europe, have merged, in one nation. . . . It would be surprising if some of the great international prophets of the future . . . should not come from the Philippines." On top of this, the Philippines was the only nation in the East that called itself Christian. It promised to overturn the assumption "that the Occident . . . always must lead in everything" and gave rise to hope that "the Orient may be able to do what the Occident has so signally failed to accomplish": complete the world's evangelization.[127] Laubach spoke approvingly of Aguinaldo's use of providential language and historical argument and offered a positive reassessment of Aglipay's church, by contrast noting that "the chief contribution that Europe and America have made to Christianity is to lead it into a slough of theological despond."[128] He startlingly shifted the center of gravity of global Christian history to the Philippines, with US agency receding into the background.

Another hallmark of this shift was that whereas Stuntz had drawn on anthropological knowledge to emphasize the disunity of the people of the Philippines, missionaries increasingly came to stress their unity. This shift was evident in Charles Briggs's 1913 book *The Progressing Philippines*, which was published before Hibbard and Laubach's books and indeed not long after James Rodgers fell afoul of nationalist sentiment at the 1912 Lake Mohonk Conference. Briggs became an early missionary proponent of the idea that differences between the people of the islands were not inherent but cultural, based on class rather than ethnicity. Although his private views of Filipinos remained fairly negative, Briggs wrote in his book that as class consciousness broke down, the "fundamental" unity of Filipinos through blood and language would overcome differences.[129] Briggs argued that the anthropological idea of distinct ethnic groups or tribes was "quite unreliable," based on the "unscientific" writings of Spanish friars. According to Briggs, all of the "tribes" were in fact Malayan, with the exception of the Negrito inhabitants of remote mountainous regions, who were the aboriginal people.[130] Briggs wrote that "the present-day Filipino is of predominating Malayan characteristics, in something the same way that the American is an American, despite the fact that his ancestry and many of his institutions originated in various parts of Europe."[131] This idea echoed the contention of Pablo Ocampo, the Philippines' resident commissioner in the United States, at Lake Mohonk in 1908 that any differences between Filipinos were no greater than those between the different colonies that had composed the United States; the Filipino population was no more diverse than the colonial population of North America in class and religion.[132] Of course, in both cases, ideas of national unity were founded as much upon exclusion as inclusion. The Filipino was to the Philippines what the Anglo-Saxon was to the United States—an ethnic and national identity constructed to the detriment of proximate others deemed less civilized. Nonetheless, Hibbard went a step beyond the nationalist colonialism of Filipino thinkers in his book by arguing that even the Muslims of the southern Philippines shared ancestry with other peoples of the archipelago and that any differences in character they had were attributable more to religion than to anything essential.[133] Frequent risings against Spanish rule, Hibbard added, had moreover "tended to unite the tribes and to develop a national consciousness."[134] Although missionaries had different ideas about exactly how expansive the Philippine nation was, they shifted toward claiming that the people of the Philippines had a shared history, a concept that implied that they could be treated as a nation.

Ideas about the long and harmonious history of Philippine spirituality and about the crucial historical role of the Philippines for the global spread of Protestantism also came to be part of the self-conception of Filipino converts to Christianity. In a book published in Ohio in 1931 by the United Brethren, prominent politician Camilo Osías and his wife Avelina Lorenzana, both self-proclaimed evangelicals, argued against the prevailing perception that Philippine culture and spirituality dated only to the US occupation. "Such impressions are clearly contrary to facts," they wrote, seeking to demonstrate that the earliest inhabitants of the archipelago had "culture and civilization" that provided "fertile ground" for Christianity.[135] They invoked Tagalog creation myths as well as precolonial evidence of sexual morality, family values, respect for women, literature, trade, agriculture, and manufacturing.[136] They pointed to an ancient religion based on worship of the *anito*, or ancestral spirit, that was also influenced by Hinduism, Buddhism, and Islam.[137] Finally, they argued that all three branches of Christianity in the Philippines—Catholicism, Aglipayanism, and Protestantism—had contributed to a rich evangelical strain of religious life in the islands.[138] This evidence demonstrated that there was a mold that evangelical Christianity naturally fit into.

Osías and Lorenzana were unabashed Filipino nationalists. They held Americans to account for the fact that more than three decades after 1898, "the Philippines still continues to be dependent despite the promises made and the continuous and insistent demand" for "a final settlement." Fortunately, they wrote, it appeared that a resolution was imminent, and they were confident that the end of US occupation would lead to "a new spiritual reawakening which will culminate in the Filipinos fulfilling more adequately than possible at present the mission which Providence has for them."[139] As at other sites across the globe, recourse to the deep past allowed nationalists to transcend the colonial, antinationalist origins of their Protestant faith, insist that that faith had always somehow inhered in them, and express confidence about its future flourishing as a Filipino religion.[140]

Missionaries' support for Philippine independence in the 1920s was somewhat overdetermined. On a local level, they contended with the impact of changing attitudes in the United States toward the idea that the Philippines should remain a US colony and with the conviction of nationalist Filipino Protestants that Filipinos were ready for autonomous governance of their nation and their churches. Against this local backdrop, it is easy to see why missionaries might have believed themselves to be smoothing the path for the survival of Philippine Protestantism by vocally backing decolonization. However, we might equally think that the currents of missionary thought in the Philippines were being dictated by broader phenomena, in particular by what the historian Michael G. Thompson has called "Christian internationalism." This was a vision that repudiated ideas of American superiority or Christian nationhood in the aftermath of World War I and shaped a new conception of mission that was palatable to liberal-modernist Protestants as they moved away from an older evangelical consensus and split from fundamentalist counterparts. In the new formulation, the purpose of missions was to help nations become independent from Americans' tutelage and to establish an equal relationship with them.[141]

That missionaries adopted historical narratives that were amenable to Filipino nationalists in the 1920s suggests more about what they drew from these global currents and what was formulated at a local level in the missionary imagination. Missionaries in the Philippines were clearly aware of the weakened claims of Europeans and Americans to spiritual and moral leadership in the aftermath of World War I. They also were not acting in isolation in shifting toward a more liberal basis for their mission. Whatever the broader forces were that reshaped missionary perspectives, however, their historical narratives show that the ways they chose to express their sympathy for Philippine independence were drawn from local knowledge traditions. Philippine nationalist historiographies gave missionaries a language for expressing a vision of history centered on the Philippines and for making the case for decolonization not in terms of general moral principles but as an argument drawn from their observation of the specific situation in the islands. This alerts us to the fact that there was a kaleidoscopic array of forms Americans' Christian internationalism might take as it was reshaped and rearticulated at a local level.

A more critical perspective on the work of Hibbard and Laubach would be that they were seamlessly reframing the goal of US empire in the Philippines as imperial enthusiasm waned and Filipino nationalism grew instead of actually amplifying Filipino historiographical traditions. As much as their conclusions resonated with a perspective Filipino nationalist intellectuals had been articulating for five decades, from Rizal through Mabini and Kalaw to Osías and Lorenzana, Hibbard and Laubach attributed the discovery of a long Philippine past to white Americans. Hibbard said that his conclusions had been made possible by the discoveries of collectors from the United States who had uncovered ancient "curiosities" dating back to "the early centuries of the Christian era," and Laubach attributed his arguments to a body of evidence that had been "accumulating during the past twenty years," firmly in the era of US rule.[142] They may both have been thinking of the work of scholars including H. Otley Beyer, Austin Craig, and James A. Robertson. From early in the US occupation, such men had appropriated and watered down the *ilustrado* vision of the past to serve particular and various American purposes. For instance, they sought to undermine the legitimacy of Spanish rule by showing that Filipino culture was not a creation of Spanish colonialism or by styling US colonialism as the fulfillment of a narrative of continuous Philippine progress.[143] Pardo de Tavera, one of the closest collaborators with the US regime, produced a similar narrative to accompany the Philippine census of 1903, demonstrating that histories of a precolonial past could be marshaled to bolster the colonial state's knowledge-gathering projects.[144]

Missionaries found their own use for such historical perspectives. Although in the aftermath of 1898, missionaries would have seen the departure of the United States from the islands as a dereliction of a providentially ordained, world-historic duty that threatened national ruin, the longer frame for Philippine spiritual history allowed Americans to feel that their work was done. Writing for Christians back home, Hibbard and Laubach sought to help their supporters understand that Americans had reawakened a people with a rich history of both spiritual endeavor and commercial prosperity and could now recede into the background with their honor intact, leaving Filipinos to fulfil their important global role as Christians and capitalists. In making a historiographical turn to this end, Hibbard and Laubach failed to acknowledge the work of Filipino nationalist historians. Laubach even denigrated the studies of Paterno and de los Reyes as "unhistorical" and "inadequate."[145] They also failed to mention the prior complicity of missionaries in presenting the Philippine past as marked by tribalism and given shape only by colonialism. Instead, Hibbard and Laubach presented the discovery of Filipino spiritual history as the result of Americans' observation and intellectual labor.

The suggestion that the Philippines was ready to lead in the global spread of Protestantism removed the United States from the center of the historical frame in a way that would have seemed alien to Americans, missionary and nonmissionary alike, when US imperialists first entered the islands. For missionaries, however, who had always been attentive to the meaning of Philippine history, the shift toward a broad historical conception that marginalized the United States marked evolution rather than radical change. Even though on one level they amplified an imperialist confidence that US empire in the Pacific was providentially ordained, missionaries had long recognized that centering the United States in a global sacred history was not to be taken for granted. In conducting their work, they had qualified grandiose visions of the role of the United States with notions of crisis, social scientific concepts, and recourse to both Spanish Catholic and, later, Filipino histories. In each case, they decentered the transformative power of the United States and figured US empire as incidental in a longer history of spiritual development. They came to share with the missionary community in Hawai'i a sense that as much as their work might be facilitated by the projection of US power across the Pacific, it was local religious histories that most profoundly shaped their thoughts and actions, over and above any sense of existing in an "American lake."

In charting the ways missionaries narrated history, we see the contingency of knowledge production. The shifting frame missionaries used to describe Philippine history to US audiences suggests the malleability of their perspective in response to local conditions. As in Hawai'i, there was always a relationship between local ideas about history and the ideas of missionaries. For the first two decades of the US occupation of the Philippines, the two sets of ideas were in tension. Missionaries either deemed Providence to have rendered local history irrelevant or they resisted the idea that Filipinos had any self-governing ability beyond that which Americans and, to a lesser extent, Spanish Catholics, gave them. They argued that uplift was a slow process that demanded generations of US intervention. Accordingly, missionary retellings of history for the most part suppressed Filipino agency, instead relying on Spanish sources and ethnological taxonomies. As political concerns swamped and threatened the work of evangelization, however, missionary needs were drawn into line with local conceptions, and missionaries began disseminating different kinds of knowledge.

On the one hand, we might identify in this shift evidence that local agency influenced US actors. Hibbard and Laubach's texts displayed what appeared to be genuine sympathy with the people of the Philippines, suggesting that cultural encounter had hybridized the perspectives of some missionaries. This expression of sympathy might seem all the more remarkable when placed against the backdrop of the anti-Filipino nativism in the United States in the 1920s and 1930s that spilled over into violence, most famously in Watsonville, California, in early 1930, when white mobs attacked Filipino laborers and killed twenty-two-year-old Fermin Tobera.[146] Through the work of Hibbard and Laubach, Indigenous historiographical perspectives and arguments for decolonization infiltrated mainstream thought in the United States, a clear instance of what the historian David Hollinger calls the "boomerang" effect of Protestant mission.[147] Laubach appears in Hollinger's work as exemplifying this effect: his decision to stop proselytizing in 1930, after fifteen frustrating years in the Philippines, in order to engage sympathetically with Mindanao Muslims and promote literacy among them, constituted an effort to challenge racism and to try to make American Protestants "more comfortable with other faiths."[148]

On the other hand, however, historians should also note the limits of the boomerang, which are visible in the ways Americans sought to retain control of historical narrative. Assertions of ancient spiritual capacity among the peoples of the Philippines still left actual local intellectual agency conspicuously absent. Its discovery was framed as the fruit of the labor of white observers from the United States who were able to study the situation scientifically. Moreover, prior to this, even though they were aware of *ilustrado* historical narratives, missionaries chose to focus on the Spanish Catholic past in a manner that implicitly justified a continued US presence by indicating that Filipinos lacked historical agency or spiritual capacity. By appropriating a long Philippine history without acknowledging its nationalist origins and by presenting it as new knowledge on their own terms, Americans were able to orient historical narrative toward a specific Protestant purpose and a vindication of US intervention and thus to uphold the fantasy of their nation's benign governance in a fraught political landscape. In the process, they found themselves drawn away from imagining US power radiating outward across the Pacific and toward a vision of history centered on the Philippine Islands.

Conclusion

The Purposes and Ambivalences of Missionary Knowledge Production

A comparison of the intellectual production of US Protestant missionaries in Hawai'i and the Philippines complicates understandings of the role that both history and Protestantism played in rendering the emergence of US empire legible to Americans. Historical narratives and philosophies of history did more than simply help Americans make sense of their new overseas imperial world and assert control over it. History could index disappointment, retrogression, crisis, and stasis as much as imperial optimism, order, and progress. The peoples the United States colonized deployed it as a tool of resistance to empire and as an assertion of independence or sovereignty, and it was etched into the landscapes, oral traditions, and cultural practices of the different Pacific locales Americans encountered. In attempting to effect a transformative reorientation of Pacific histories and cultures, missionaries found their own epistemologies remolded by the local.

In addition, despite the grandiose ideas about the divine historical purpose of the United States that accompanied the American seizure of territory across the ocean in 1898, those on the front lines of religious efforts in the Pacific betrayed ambivalence about the idea of a connected ocean under US control. Missionaries certainly were not opponents of US colonialism, and in fact for the most part were vocal supporters, but they increasingly articulated ideas about history that suggested that empire was only useful or interesting to them insofar as it served their purposes on a local scale. By understanding history writing as part of a constant process of negotiation and adjustment, we can look past the confident spatial-temporal rhetoric that accompanied oceanic colonialism toward the potency of islands in shaping the cultures of US empire and mission.

In the Hawaiian case, annexation represented the fulfillment of a "missionary" vision that took advantage of the US turn toward formal empire but did so with recourse to arguments about an incomplete history of local mission work. As was particularly clear in Nathaniel Emerson's story, descendants of missionaries styled themselves as liminal to both the United States and Hawai'i, sensing their distance from the nation their ancestors had departed from decades before and appropriating a Hawaiian cultural identity to undercut the sovereignty of the Indigenous people of the islands. This sense of liminality shaped the perspectives on Hawaiian history and culture that the children and grandchildren of missionaries relayed to US audiences even after annexation.

In the Philippines, the shared ideas of missionaries and US politicians about the providential appointment of US empire soon gave way. As they conducted their work on the ground in the archipelago, missionaries struggled with the entrenched nature of Catholicism, with Filipino resistance to US rule, and with the US government's lack of commitment to Protestantism in the Philippines. They increasingly deemphasized US empire as an agent of radical historic transformation, turning instead to read meaning into the history of the islands and ultimately conceptualizing change as a gradual process that God had long ago initiated in the Philippine past and through the Philippine people.

By comparing the missionary community's uses of history in the Hawaiian and Philippine cases, we understand that even as the United States quickly secured a territorial empire in 1898, Americans' attempts to forge a cohesive imperial epistemology that enabled them to make sense of their new territories or of Pacific space as a totality were limited. Rhetorical assertions of a "Greater United States," of an "American lake," or of a grand providential design were not only undermined by the sheer cultural diversity of the territories that fell under these rubrics but also often meant little to Americans who were engaging with these diverse locales on the ground and producing knowledge about them for US audiences.[1] In failing to explicitly acknowledge and systematically deconstruct this difference between rhetoric and reality, historians have missed an opportunity to take up Paul Kramer's call to look beyond what has previously been characterized as the "rigid, determined, and determining character" of US empire, framed by "a tone of bombastic confidence," and instead "pay attention to empire's vulnerabilities" when "the extension of control failed to live up to expectations."[2] By recognizing such vulnerabilities in the context of the Pacific, we might write histories that do greater justice to island spaces instead of privileging visions of the ocean from the continent outward.

In many ways, similar impulses underpinned the missionary community's uses of history in Hawai'i and the Philippines. In both cases, they deployed history to demonstrate that the divine will was to use the United States to secure the triumph of Protestantism, even as definitions of acceptable religious expression began to pluralize. Also, at both sites missionaries sought to make sense of local history for US audiences, encouraging support for evangelistic projects by situating them within meaningful historical trajectories. Finally, in both island groups, missionaries encountered potent local histories and traditions of historical narration that they felt compelled to engage and incorporate as they sought legitimacy for their work and that of empire.

The differences that emerged in the engagements of missionary communities with history in Hawai'i and the Philippines, however, are explained by the diversity of historical conditions that structured American interactions with the Pacific. Different histories of missionary involvement with different parts of the US empire served to fragment any sense of what bound that empire together. The missionary community in Hawai'i, a group that had long been separated from the United States, was in many ways anachronistic, the legacy of an early nineteenth-century New England Calvinist project to convert the "heathen." Even though this community was central to a settler-colonial project that invited US annexation, it was divorced from both the Student Volunteer Movement that was characteristic of a new and more ambitious age of missions and from the clamor that motivated US engagement with the Philippines. New engagements with the Pacific by Americans that emerged in the late nineteenth century, like those in the Philippines, were instigated instead by a generation that had witnessed the completion of continental expansion and that could conceive of the ocean as the next logical step in an imperial vision in a way that the missionary community in Hawai'i historically had not.

The genealogies of Hawaiian monarchs demonstrated both their people's indigeneity to the islands and a heritage that stretched across an island world, and Native Hawaiians laid claims to sovereignty on this basis. Filipinos had endured over three centuries of Spanish colonial rule that had situated them in a Pacific world connected to Latin America. They also had a prior history of trade and migration that linked them to Asia in ways that nationalist historians of the late nineteenth century sought to demonstrate as part of their claims to Filipino nationhood. Other peoples of the Philippines were not part of the Hispanicized population and held onto animistic or Islamic world views in ways that confounded and reshaped colonial states. It is not surprising that these diverse Pacific worlds and their different pasts ultimately fragmented missionary ideas about what was of historical importance and caused them to lose sight of notions of a divinely ordained US imperial hegemony over oceanic space. The history writing and knowledge production of missionaries was influenced by their need to negotiate their own position between the imperial and the local rather than by totalizing imperial visions of the ocean. In this way, we understand what the historian Sujit Sivasundaram means about the Pacific, which was long characterized as a laboratory in which European and North American knowledge was produced: "When searching questions were asked in this region, the Pacific had a role to play in the answers that emerged."[3]

At the same time, for the most part, missionaries were able to appropriate and marshal competing perspectives and obscure tensions and paradoxes in the missionary and imperial projects. They styled the knowledge they conveyed to US audiences as cohesive and authoritative, and it was received that way. Missionary-descendant memoirists in Hawai'i deployed their childhood memories to convince audiences in the United States that Hawai'i was a safe space of racial and religious harmony after annexation, despite the invective they had unleashed against Native Hawaiians just a few years earlier. Nathaniel Emerson obscured his sense of distance from the United States, his romanticism, and the historical and political meanings of Hawaiian tradition by labeling his work as science. Missionaries in the Philippines devised an array of contradictory conceptions of history in their bids to secure donations from the United States without acknowledging the paradoxes they were creating. David S. Hibbard and Frank Laubach sympathetically centered the Philippines in their historical narratives but failed to give voice to the nationalist historians who had long predated them in drawing the same conclusions or acknowledge the complicity of missionaries in the prior suppression of Filipino perspectives. The missionary knowledge about the Pacific that emerged in the United States thus bore many of the hallmarks of colonial knowledge. It obscured its own idiosyncrasies and insecurities, styling itself as authoritative while frequently effacing precolonial histories and Indigenous traditions of knowledge, featuring racial others as little more than ciphers, and failing to problematize the concept or practice of a US colonialism that was marked by tremendous violence and resistance on the part of diverse populations.

The intellectual paths missionary producers of history forged in both Hawai'i and the Philippines had echoes that reached deeper into the twentieth century. The notion that the "missionary" memoir was an authoritative vehicle for narrating Hawaiian history was perpetuated into the 1930s and beyond with the posthumous publication of three volumes of Lorrin Thurston and Sanford Dole's recollections of the Hawaiian "revolution" of the 1890s. According to the historian Tom Coffman, these writings, which privileged the voices and perspectives of white settlers, "set the tone" for the production of Hawaiian history for most of the rest of the century.[4] Nathaniel Emerson's negotiation of his status within Hawai'i as expressed through his "scientific" treatment of Hawaiian traditional narratives also found echoes in later twentieth-century writing. We might consider, for example, the ways the folklorist Martha Warren Beckwith presented her 1951 translation of the genealogical text *The Kumulipo: A Hawaiian Creation Chant*. Beckwith was the daughter of white settlers—in this case schoolteachers who became sugar planters—who had come to the islands in the 1870s because of their ties to the Thurston missionary family. Like Emerson, Beckwith established herself as an expert at the expense of Indigenous authorities. She overlooked the fact that Queen Lili'uokalani had translated the same text in the 1890s and cited the Indigenous people she claimed to have engaged with only minimally. The Native Hawaiian scholar Brandy Nālani McDougall notes that, again like Emerson, Beckwith "aestheticize[d] to depoliticize" and "domesticated the Kumulipo for an American settler readership," purporting to be engaged in an objective act of preservation while dismissing the utility of *The Kumulipo* as a political history.[5] Similar things might be said of Mary Kawena Pukui's 1963 translation of John Papa 'Ī'ī's discourses on Hawaiian history from late nineteenth-century newspapers, gathered and published as *Fragments of Hawaiian History*. Marie Alohalani Brown argues that, as Emerson's approach to traditional narratives also did, this translation appropriated 'Ī'ī's authority but overwrote his Native Hawaiian ways of knowing, repackaging material "in accordance with a Western lens that sharply distinguishes between *legend* and *history*."[6]

In the Philippines, although it perhaps cannot be said that Protestantism constituted a significant part of the American legacy in the islands given Filipinos' continued overwhelming adherence to Catholicism, missionary individuals still made an impact on intellectual culture. From the mid-1950s onward, Episcopal missionary William Henry Scott greatly expanded on the interest Hibbard and Laubach had shown in precolonial Philippine history, becoming one of the foremost experts in the field. He worked among the people of the Cordillera on Luzon, exposing the tribal view of the Philippine people as a colonial construction, becoming a citizen of the Philippines and a Filipino nationalist, and opposing both the brutal regime of the dictator Ferdinand Marcos and ongoing US involvement in the islands.[7] In both Hawai'i and the Philippines, albeit in very different ways and for very different reasons, missionary-connected individuals continued to voice local histories in the Pacific, finding meaning and historical interest in island spaces.

However, as the twentieth century wore on, the idea of a collapsible Pacific space defined by the nations on its rim gained further potency in the minds of both missionary and nonmissionary Americans. In February 1925, for example, the YMCA held a Christian Conference of the Pacific Area in Honolulu. Although Hawai'i was chosen as the venue because of its "tradition of inter-racial good will" and "missionary background," the key nations in the vision of the Pacific that were presented at this conference were China, India, Japan, and the United States.[8] Hawai'i was thus reduced to a stepping-stone from which the United States could access the Asian nations on the other side of the ocean, and the Philippines receded from view altogether. The Institute for Pacific Relations, an influential nongovernmental organization, emerged from this conference, further institutionalizing a particular vision of which places in the Pacific mattered.

After World War II, when the ocean had been recast as "the Pacific theater," the idea of the "American Pacific" arguably reached its zenith, as the US occupation of Japan and seizure of strategic territories across the ocean seemingly created the conditions for US military dominance and, ultimately, neoliberal order that stretched across the water.[9] Although the United States finally ended its formal colonial presence in the Philippines in 1946, its fingerprints remained all over the archipelago. Trumpeting the anticommunist and democratic credentials of a decolonized Philippines, the United States legitimized the perpetuation of an authoritarian police state whose tactics of surveillance and violence borrowed directly from the US colonial state, while an expansive American economic and military presence remained in the islands through the Bell Trade Act of 1946 and the Military Bases Agreement of 1947.[10] Also against the backdrop of the Cold War, the United States recognized the strategic advantages of coopting Hawai'i's "montage of minorities"—East Asian migrants who had made the archipelago into both a geographical and cultural midpoint between the United States and Asia. When Hawai'i became a US state in 1959, it was the first majority nonwhite territory to be admitted into the union.[11] It continues to be the site of the largest US naval base in the Pacific—the headquarters of the United States

Pacific Fleet and the Pacific Air Forces.[12] In both island groups, American militarization and tourism proved to be two sides of the same coin as military presence enabled and protected Americans crossing the ocean in search of paradise.[13] US colonialism was not always viewed in the same way in the two archipelagoes. Scholars and activists have sought to bridge a gap between a fairly positive perception of American presence among Filipinos and Filipino migrants to Hawai'i on the one hand and an ongoing sense of an illegal and unwanted occupation by the United States among Native Hawaiians on the other hand.[14] In any case, in meaningful ways that are often overlooked from the perspective of the continent, the United States has entrenched itself as "an oceanic and archipelagic nation," not least through its ongoing engagements with Hawai'i and the Philippines.[15]

Missionaries were complicit in many ways in efforts to render the Pacific to US audiences as a place where Americans belonged and as a place where they could assert moral leadership, but at the same time the perspectives they conveyed from Hawai'i and the Philippines also demonstrated how island spaces could reorient Americans' vision of geography and history. The contradictions and contestations that haunted an imperialist world view might be appreciable only if we examine the missionary or colonial archive at a granular level, but historians should be alert to them if they seek to more effectively challenge empire's claims to control and to comprehend vast and diverse spaces. Although the Pacific is a place of many pasts and many peoples, it is too often talked about as an "American" unit and is seen as a site for geopolitical wrangling or tourist escape.[16] Thinking instead about how Americans have been reshaped at different points within the ocean gives us a way of appreciating the limits of the US imperial vision and of doing greater justice to the dynamism and power of the vast Pacific.

Notes

Introduction

1. "Statement on the Death of Dr. James A. Graham and Dr. George W. Wright."
2. Letter of September 7, 1907, *Travel Letters*, October 1907, 1.
3. Beveridge, "The March of the Flag."
4. On the idea of the China market as a driver of American expansion across the Pacific, see Young, *The Rhetoric of Empire*.
5. Whitelaw Reid quoted in Connery, "Pacific Rim Discourse," 41.
6. Beveridge, "The March of the Flag."
7. Bancroft, *The New Pacific*, 12–13.
8. Weinberg, *Manifest Destiny*, chap. IX.
9. Cronon, *Nature's Metropolis*, 41–46.
10. On the key role of missionaries in producing knowledge about the world for Americans, see Conroy-Krutz, *Christian Imperialism*, 4; Hollinger, *Protestants Abroad*, 4; and Oliver et al., "Special Issue," 1023–24.
11. One of the most influential works in this vein is Kramer, *The Blood of Government*.
12. For an argument that missionaries in particular developed their own priorities and strategic visions of the world independent of the imperatives of US colonialism, see Conroy-Krutz, "Foreign Missions and Strategy, Foreign Missions as Strategy," 324.
13. Connery, "Pacific Rim Discourse"; Dirlik, *What Is in a Rim?*; Eperjesi, *The Imperialist Imaginary*; Geiger, *Facing the Pacific*, 5; Wilson, *Reimagining the American Pacific*, 57–65. For an echo of the "stepping-stone" view of islands in recent historiography, see Green, *By More than Providence*, 70.
14. For an example of a study that takes the "American Pacific" as a normative unit of analysis, see Dudden, *The American Pacific*.
15. Armitage and Bashford, "Introduction," 9.

16. Arvin, *Possessing Polynesians*, 35–39; Geiger, *Facing the Pacific*, 3–4; Jolly, "Imagining Oceania," 516.

17. Salmond, *Aphrodite's Island*, 20; Smith, *European Vision and the South Pacific*, 91.

18. Bashford, "The Pacific Ocean," 80–81; Sivasundaram, "Science," 237–38; Thomas, *Islanders*, 14–26; Thompson, "Heuristic Geographies," 60.

19. Bashford, "The Pacific Ocean," 63; Iriye, "A Pacific Century?," 97–101; Teaiwa, "Reading Paul Gauguin's *Noa Noa* with Epeli Hau'ofa's *Kisses in the Nederends*," 252.

20. Dvorak, "Oceanizing American Studies," 614.

21. On Indigenous visions of the Pacific, see Hau'ofa, "Our Sea of Islands"; Lyons and Tengan, "Introduction"; Salesa, "The Pacific in Indigenous Time," 31–38. On the long history of overlapping empires and Christian missions in the Pacific, see Bashford, "The Pacific Ocean," 73, 79–80. For recent attempts to develop a transpacific perspective appreciating the complexity of the ocean see Choy and Wu, "Gendering the Trans-Pacific World," 3–4; Kurashige, Hsu, and Yaguchi, "Introduction."

22. Matsuda, "AHR Forum," 758; Salesa, "The Pacific in Indigenous Time," 44; Igler, *The Great Ocean*; Matsuda, *Pacific Worlds*; Armitage and Bashford, "Introduction," 6–16; Bashford, "The Pacific Ocean," 68–71; Dening, "History 'in' the Pacific," 134–35; Wilson, *Reimagining the American Pacific*, 103–6.

23. Geiger, *Facing the Pacific*, 51; Cumings, *Dominion from Sea to Sea*, 142. On the connections between Mahan's religion and his views about naval strategy, see Geissler, *God and Sea Power*.

24. Eperjesi, *The Imperialist Imaginary*, 61; Hoganson, *Fighting for American Manhood*.

25. Williams, "The Frontier Thesis and American Foreign Policy," 379–80; Clark, "Manifest Destiny and the Pacific."

26. Drinnon, *Facing West*; Hixson, *American Settler Colonialism*.

27. Cumings, *Dominion from Sea to Sea*; Dudden, *The American Pacific*; Eperjesi, *The Imperialist Imaginary*, chap. 1; Grimshaw, *Paths of Duty*; Horne, *The White Pacific*; Iriye, *Across the Pacific*; Kauanui, "Imperial Ocean," 627; Lyons, *American Pacificism*, 29; Schulz, *Hawaiian by Birth*; Shoemaker, *Pursuing Respect in the Cannibal Isles*; Thigpen, *Island Queens and Mission Wives*.

28. Gonzalez, *Securing Paradise*, 3–4, 9–12. On Filipino migration to Hawai'i, see also Poblete, *Islanders in the Empire*.

29. Gin Lum, *Heathen*, 184–86.

30. Roberts, *Borderwaters*, 9.

31. Roberts, *Borderwaters*, 1–5, 11.

32. Lyons and Tengan, "Introduction," 550; Roberts, *Borderwaters*, 5–13; Roberts and Stephens, "Introduction," 29–30.

33. Roberts, *Borderwaters*, 25, 36–37; Roberts and Stephens, "Introduction," 14.

34. McDougall, "'We Are Not American.'"

35. Hau'ofa, "Our Sea of Islands."

36. Thompson, *Imperial Archipelago*, 1–13.

37. Aikau, *A Chosen People, a Promised Land*, 12; Cook, *Return to Kahiki*, 7; Williams, "'Ike Mōakaaka," 69. The most influential examples of scholarship accused of replicating these imperialist perspectives are Daws, *Shoal of Time*; and Kuykendall, *The Hawaiian Kingdom*.

38. Knight Lozano, *California and Hawai'i Bound*.

39. Trask, *From a Native Daughter*, 2.

40. Trask, *From a Native Daughter*, 114–21.

41. Nogelmeier, *Mai Pa'a I Ka Leo*, chap. 3; Silva, *Aloha Betrayed*, chap. 2; Silva, *The Power of the Steel-Tipped Pen*.

42. On the perception of consensual colonization, see Imada, *Aloha America*, 9–10. On strategies of resistance, see Beamer, *No Mākou ka Mana*, 230.

43. On the perception of Hawai'i as a "fait accompli" after 1898, see Eperjesi, *The Imperialist Imaginary*, 92, italics in original. See also Chang, *The World and All the Things upon It*, viii. On the links between the perception of consensual colonization and American business and tourism, see Imada, *Aloha America*, 10. The idea that the post-1898 story is that of Asian immigrants and not of Native Hawaiians is apparent in Fuchs, *Hawaii Pono*; and Takaki, *Pau Hana*. For critical readings of the presence of Asian migrants in Hawai'i, see Fujikane and Okamura, *Asian Settler Colonialism*. On Hawaiian statehood, see Miller-Davenport, *Gateway State*.

44. Chang, *The World and All the Things upon It*; Cook, *Return to Kahiki*; Rosenthal, *Beyond Hawai'i*.

45. Arista, *The Kingdom and the Republic*; Banner, *Possessing the Pacific*, chap. 4; Beamer, *No Mākou ka Mana*, 3–4; Kame'eleihiwa, *Native Land and Foreign Desires*, 13–14; Osorio, *Dismembering Lāhui*, 44–49; Silva, *Aloha Betrayed*, 15–16.

46. Chang, *The World and All the Things upon It*, ix–x; Kauanui, *Hawaiian Blood*, 16–21; Rohrer, *Staking Claim*, 3.

47. Okihiro, *Island World*, 2, 5.

48. On this apology and its limitations, see Kauanui, "A Sorry State."

49. Osorio, *Dismembering Lāhui*, 3. On disease, see Archer, *Sharks upon the Land*; Inglis, *Ma'i Lepera*; and Stannard, *Before the Horror*. On law, see Merry, *Colonizing Hawai'i*.

50. Chang, *The World and All the Things upon It*, xi.

51. Rohrer, *Staking Claim*, 9. For more on the nineteenth-century history and historiography of Hawai'i, see Smith, "Hawaiian History and American History."

52. D'Arcy, "Sea Worlds," 23–24. For another essay that explicitly situates the Philippines in a Southeast Asian rather than a Pacific world, see Clymer, "Southeast Asia."

53. Buschmann, Slack, and Tueller, *Navigating the Spanish Lake*. On the multitude of imperial "Pacifics" that we might identify, see Dvorak, "Oceanizing American Studies," 615.

54. Mawson, *Incomplete Conquests*.

55. Blanco, *Frontier Constitutions*; Ileto, *Pasyon and Revolution*; Rafael, *Contracting Colonialism*.

56. CuUnjieng Aboitiz, *Asian Place, Filipino Nation*.

57. Anderson, *Under Three Flags*, 244–69; Mojares, *Brains of the Nation*; Ocampo, "Rizal's Morga and Views of Philippine History"; Schumacher, "The 'Propagandists" Reconstruction of the Philippine Past"; Thomas, *Orientalists, Propagandists, and Ilustrados*.

58. The idea of a Pacific "highway" from the United States to Asia was articulated by Mark Twain, quoted in Lyons, *American Pacificism*, 27. "At the gates of Asia" is from Beveridge, "The March of the Flag."

59. On benevolence as an imperial fantasy, see Mendoza, *Metroimperial Intimacies*, 9.

60. On transimperial connections, see Go, "Introduction"; and Kramer, "Empires, Exceptions, and Anglo-Saxons." On Spanish precedent, see Kramer, *The Blood of Government*, 5. On US imperialists in the Philippines as "prolific producers of social categories," see Mendoza, *Metroimperial Intimacies*, 3.

61. For a neat conceptualization of how scholars in American studies can productively engage with Native Pacific studies, see Dvorak, "Oceanizing American Studies," 616.

62. Hutchison, *Errand to the World*, 1.

63. Curtis, *Holy Humanitarians*, 9–10; Mislin, *Saving Faith*, 6–9.

64. Sutton, *American Apocalypse*, 14; Wacker, "The Holy Spirit and the Spirit of the Age in American Protestantism," 58.

65. Preston, *Sword of the Spirit, Shield of Faith*, 178–79; Hutchison, *Errand to the World*, 103; Oliver et al., "Special Issue," 1025–26.

66. Hollinger, *Protestants Abroad*, 10–11; Sutton, *American Apocalypse*, 82; Thompson, *For God and Globe*, 1–18.

67. For a classic study of anti-imperialism, see Beisner, *Twelve against Empire*. On the role of racism in anti-imperialism, see Love, *Race over Empire*.

68. Bemis, *A Diplomatic History of the United States*, chap. XXVI. On waning enthusiasm for empire, see Love, *Race over Empire*, epilogue. For examples of scholarship emphasizing that contrary to Bemis's exceptionalism, imperialism is ubiquitous in US history, see Go, *Patterns of Empire*; Kaplan, "'Left Alone with America'"; Kramer, "Power and Connection"; and Stoler, *Haunted by Empire*.

69. Preston, *Sword of the Spirit, Shield of Faith*, 180–82; Tyrrell, *Reforming the World*, 50–51.

70. Tyrrell, *Reforming the World*, 51.

71. Hutchison, *Errand to the World*, 91–93; Tyrrell, *Reforming the World*, 67.

72. There is a wide literature on this debate outside the American missionary context. For scholarship that is defensive of missionaries, downplaying their relationship to empire and emphasizing their efforts to transform it, see Porter, *Religion versus Empire?*; and Stanley, *The Bible and the Flag*. For literature that views missionaries as an integral part of the imperial apparatus, see Comaroff and Comaroff, *Of Revelation and Revolution*.

73. Hutchison, *Errand to the World*, 2.

74. Harris, "Cultural Imperialism and American Protestant Missionaries"; Rosenberg, *Spreading the American Dream*, 28–33; Comaroff and Comaroff, *Of Revelation and Revolution*, xi.

75. McCoy, Scarano, and Johnson, "On the Tropic of Cancer," 32. For evidence of missionary influence on US foreign policy, see Fairbank, *The Missionary Enterprise in China and America*; Grabill, "The 'Invisible' Missionary"; Grabill, *Protestant Diplomacy and the Near East*; and Reed, "American Foreign Policy, the Politics of Missions and Josiah Strong."

76. Campbell, "'To Make the World One in Christ Jesus'"; Oliver et al., "Special Issue," 1026; Preston, *Sword of the Spirit, Shield of Faith*, 184–85; Tyrrell, *Reforming the World*, 6–7, 38, 59–60.

77. Clymer, *Protestant Missionaries in the Philippines*, 8; Dunch, "Beyond Cultural Imperialism"; Hollinger, *Protestants Abroad*, 288–92; Preston, *Sword of the Spirit, Shield of Faith*, 183–84; Robert, "Introduction," 4–6; Tyrrell, *Reforming the World*, chaps. 6–7.

78. For this argument in relation to US missionaries, see McAlister, *The Kingdom of God Has No Borders*, 3–4; Oliver et al., "Special Issue," 1032–37.

79. Dunch, *Fuzhou Protestants and the Making of a Modern China*; Jones, *Christian Missions in the American Empire*, 248–55; Sanneh, *Translating the Message*; Walls, *The Missionary Movement in Christian History*.

80. Hutchison, *Errand to the World*, chap. 4; Tyrrell, *Reforming the World*, 4, 43; Preston, *Sword of the Spirit, Shield of Faith*, 188.

81. Clymer, *Protestant Missionaries in the Philippines*, 154; Harris, *God's Arbiters*, 13–14; McCullough, *The Cross of War*; Stephanson, *Manifest Destiny*, 67.

82. Clymer, *Protestant Missionaries in the Philippines*, 4–7.

83. Clymer, *Protestant Missionaries in the Philippines*, 155, 161.

84. Conroy-Krutz, *Christian Imperialism*, 5–11.

85. Trask, *From a Native Daughter*, 6; Wood, *Displacing Natives*, 38.

86. Maffly-Kipp, "Eastward Ho!"

87. Williams, "Claiming Christianity."

88. For more on the need to understand religion in order to fully understand empire, see Wenger and Johnson, "Introduction," 7–8.

89. Memmi, *The Colonizer and the Colonized*, part 1.
90. For a recent expression of this argument in the context of the British empire, see Satia, *Time's Monster*.
91. Ross, "Historical Consciousness in Nineteenth-Century America," 916.
92. Hawkins, *Making Moros*, 5.
93. Allen, *A Republic in Time*, chap. 1; Bendroth, "Time, History, and Tradition in the Fundamentalist Imagination," 335; Shalev, *Rome Reborn on Western Shores*.
94. Bendroth, *The Last Puritans*; Morgan, *A Nation of Descendants*, chap. 1; O'Brien, *Firsting and Lasting*; Drinnon, *Facing West*, 277.
95. Guyatt, *Providence and the Invention of the United States*; Koenig, *Providence and the Invention of American History*; Stephanson, *Manifest Destiny*; Weinberg, *Manifest Destiny*.
96. Novick, *That Noble Dream*, 65.
97. On "imperial historicism," see Hawkins, *Making Moros*. On Providence and the Spanish-American and Philippine-American Wars, see Harris, *God's Arbiters*, 18–19; and McCullough, *The Cross of War*, chap. 3.
98. "The Missionary Convention," *Woman's Missionary Friend*, July 1905, 258.
99. Speer, *Missions and Modern History*.
100. Hasinoff, "The Missionary Exhibit."
101. Gin Lum, "The Historyless Heathen and the Stagnating Pagan."
102. McCullough, *The Cross of War*, 62.
103. Silva, *Aloha Betrayed*, chap. 3.
104. Blanco, *Frontier Constitutions*, 104–5, 244–69; Ileto, "Tagalog Poetry and the Image of the Past during the War against Spain"; Kramer, *The Blood of Government*, 8–9; Ocampo, "Rizal's Morga and Views of Philippine History"; Rafael, *White Love and Other Events in Filipino History*, 39–51; Schumacher, "The 'Propagandists' Reconstruction of the Philippine Past."
105. Hixson, *American Settler Colonialism*, 11–12; O'Brien, *Firsting and Lasting*.
106. Blight, *Race and Reunion*.
107. Thigpen, *Island Queens and Mission Wives*. On the suppression of Hawaiian traditions of women's leadership across the nineteenth century, see Silva, *Aloha Betrayed*, 44.
108. Reeves-Ellington, Sklar, and Shemo, "Introduction," 2; Moots, *Pioneer "Americanas."*
109. Hill, *The World Their Household*, 3–4. See also Hunter, *The Gospel of Gentility*; Seat, "Providence Has Freed Our Hands"; and Tyrrell, *Reforming the World*, chap. 2.
110. For works that emphasize how women's "domestic vision" was essential to imperial meaning making, see Rafael, *White Love and Other Events in Filipino History*, chap. 2; and Wexler, *Tender Violence*.
111. Gin Lum, *Heathen*, 17–18. For another argument questioning the supposed differences between European and North American history writing and other traditions, see Borofsky, "An Invitation," 7–8.
112. Comaroff and Comaroff, *Ethnography and the Historical Imagination*, 35.
113. Stoler, *Along the Archival Grain*, 53.
114. Gonzalez, *Securing Paradise*, 18.

Part I. Hawai'i

1. Moore, *American Imperialism and the State*, 52–57, 61–62.
2. Arista, *The Kingdom and the Republic*, 5; Takaki, *Pau Hana*.

3. "Annexation at Last," *The Friend*, July 1898, 61.
4. Conroy-Krutz, *Christian Imperialism*, 10–11; Gin Lum, *Heathen*, 12; Hixson, *American Settler Colonialism*, viii.
5. Stratford, "Imagining the Archipelago," 79; Merry, *Colonizing Hawai'i*, 28.
6. Smith, "Hawaiian History and American History."
7. Silva, *Aloha Betrayed*, 145–59.
8. Coffman, *Nation Within*, 2–5.

1. "Venerated Fathers"

1. "Early Missionary Days," *Pacific Commercial Advertiser*, June 15, 1895, clipping, vol. 25, no. 66, Hawaiian Islands Mission, Papers of the American Board of Commissioners for Foreign Missions, Houghton Library, Harvard University, Cambridge, Massachusetts (hereafter Hawaiian Islands Mission).
2. Pierson, *The Crisis of Missions*, 239.
3. "Early Missionary Days." For a powerful refutation of the idea that Native Hawaiian society was feudal, see Trask, *From a Native Daughter*, 115–17.
4. "Early Missionary Days."
5. For an example of a study that reduces religion to little more than a general sense of moral superiority, see Schulz, *Hawaiian by Birth*. Laavanyan M. Ratnapalan also argues that we should take the religion of descendants of missionaries more seriously; Ratnapalan, "'This Greater Issue of Light against Darkness,'" 4.
6. For a classic work that makes this argument, see Memmi, *The Colonizer and the Colonized*, part 1.
7. Rufus Anderson to Sandwich Islands Mission, *General Letter to the Sandwich Islands Mission*, October 27, 1852, italics in original.
8. Hutchison, *Errand to the World*, 77–78.
9. Harris, *Nothing but Christ*, 79.
10. Gin Lum, *Heathen*, 80.
11. Anderson, *The Hawaiian Islands*; Anderson, *A Heathen Nation Evangelized*.
12. "Annual Meeting of the Board," *Missionary Herald*, November 1870, 356–58.
13. "The Missions in the Sandwich Islands," *New York Daily Tribune*, May 26, 1860, 9.
14. Twain, "Our Fellow Savages of the Sandwich Islands"; Twain, *Roughing It*, 464. For Twain's most famous critique of missionaries, see "To the Person Sitting in Darkness."
15. Gin Lum, "The Historyless Heathen and the Stagnating Pagan," 59–60; Bingham, *A Residence of Twenty-One Years in the Sandwich Islands*; Dibble, *History and General Views of the Sandwich Islands' Mission*; Conroy-Krutz, *Christian Imperialism*, 37.
16. Arista, *The Kingdom and the Republic*, 73.
17. Brain, *The Transformation of Hawaii*, 64; Chang, *The World and All the Things upon It*, 83–92; Maffly-Kipp, "Eastward Ho!" 128.
18. Arista, *The Kingdom and the Republic*; Banner, *Possessing the Pacific*, chap. 4; Beamer, *No Mākou ka Mana*; Chang, *The World and All the Things upon It*; Kame'eleihiwa, *Native Land and Foreign Desires*; Osorio, *Dismembering Lāhui*, chap. 3.
19. Brown, *Facing the Spears of Change*, 21, 23. See also the analysis of David Malo in Osorio, *Dismembering Lāhui*, 14–17, 22.
20. Brown, *Facing the Spears of Change*, 28, 69–71.
21. Robert, *Occupy until I Come*, vii; Pierson, *The Crisis of Missions*, 159.

22. Pierson, *The Crisis of Missions*, 159–60.
23. Pierson, *The Crisis of Missions*, 239.
24. Pierson, *The Crisis of Missions*, 273.
25. Phelps, "Introduction," vii. On Strong's missionary connections, see Reed, "American Foreign Policy, the Politics of Missions and Josiah Strong."
26. For an overview of different estimates of the scale of Native Hawaiian population decline, see Stannard, *Before the Horror*, chap. I. On the range of diseases that blighted the Indigenous population, see Trask, *From a Native Daughter*, 6.
27. Brantlinger, *Dark Vanishings*; Dippie, *The Vanishing American*.
28. Schulz, *Hawaiian by Birth*, 44.
29. Schulz, *Hawaiian by Birth*, 146.
30. Moore, *American Imperialism and the State*, 55–57.
31. The Bayonet Constitution was so called because of the involvement of an armed militia in pressuring Kalākaua to sign away many of the Hawaiian monarchy's executive powers. For more on this Constitution and the backdrop to it, see Osorio, *Dismembering Lāhui*, chap. 7.
32. Sereno Bishop quoted in Schulz, *Hawaiian by Birth*, 42.
33. "Correspondence," *Hawaii Holomua*, January 6, 1894, 3.
34. "Samuel Pua Speaks," *Hawaii Holomua*, March 20, 1894, 3.
35. James H. Blount to Walter Q. Gresham, July 17, 1893, in *Intervention of United States Government in Affairs of Foreign Friendly Governments*, 34.
36. Love, *Race over Empire*, 79–80; McWilliams, "James H. Blount, the South, and Hawaiian Annexation."
37. Schulz, "Birthing Empire," 923; Wetmore, "Extract from *Sounds from Home and Echoes of a Kingdom*," 284.
38. Putney, *Missionaries in Hawai'i*, 98.
39. Putney, "The Legacy of the Gulicks."
40. Hollinger, *Protestants Abroad*, 139–42.
41. "Copy in Liliuokalani's handwriting of C. T. Gulick's disquisition," 1894, box 19, folder 151, document S79, Lili'uokalani Papers, Hawai'i State Archives, Honolulu (hereafter Lili'uokalani Papers).
42. Lili'uokalani, *Hawaii's Story by Hawaii's Queen*, 391.
43. "Liliuokalani's comments respecting C. O. Berger's vote in turning out the Brown Cabinet," undated, box 18, folder 146, document S17, Lili'uokalani Papers; Williams, "To Raise a Voice in Praise," 27.
44. Fish Kashay, "Agents of Imperialism"; Maffly-Kipp, "Eastward Ho!" 140–41.
45. Allardyce, *Society, Politics and Religion in the Hawaiian Islands*, 3–37.
46. On the *Herald*'s earlier defense of missionaries to Hawai'i, see Smith, "American Protestant Missionaries, Native Hawaiian Authority, and Religious Freedom in Hawai'i."
47. *Missionary Herald*, June 1894, 229.
48. Hiram Bingham II [to *Pacific Commercial Advertiser*], June 21, 1894, series II, box 13, folder 171, MS 81, Bingham Family Papers, Manuscripts and Archives, Yale University Library, New Haven, Connecticut, emphasis in original.
49. *The Friend*, February 1890, 12.
50. William DeWitt Alexander to G. E. Curtis, March 10, 1898, William DeWitt Alexander Papers, Hawaiian Historical Society, Honolulu; Frank W. Damon to Judson Smith, June 11, 1885, vol. 22, no. 220, Hawaiian Islands Mission.
51. Quoted in Schulz, *Hawaiian by Birth*, 163.
52. Schulz, *Hawaiian by Birth*, chaps. 2–3.

53. Taylor, "Report of the Corresponding Secretary," 7–9.
54. "Recapitulation."
55. University of Hawai'i at Mānoa Library, "Hawai'i—Censuses: Historical Censuses," accessed June 29, 2023, https://guides.library.manoa.hawaii.edu/c.php?g=105181&p=684171.
56. "Constitution," 22.
57. Smith, "Address of the Retiring President," 35.
58. Dole, "Address of the Retiring President, Hon. S. B. Dole," 36.
59. Williams, "Claiming Christianity," 8, 18.
60. "Officers and Members of the Board of the Hawaiian Evangelical Association for 1879–80"; "Officers and Members of the Board of the Hawaiian Evangelical Association, 1898–99."
61. Jared K. Smith and Juliette Smith, "The Hawaiian Islanders: Their Present Condition and Needs," [1887], vol. 22, no. 64, Hawaiian Islands Mission.
62. William DeWitt Alexander, Walter Frear, and Sereno Bishop to Hawaiian Mission Children's Society, April 5, 1893, vol. 25, no. 43, Hawaiian Islands Mission.
63. Judd, "Introductory Note."
64. Judd, *Honolulu*, v.
65. Judd, *Honolulu*.
66. Judd, *Honolulu*, v.
67. Wexler, *Tender Violence*.
68. Bonura and Day, *An American Girl in the Hawaiian Islands*.
69. Thigpen, *Island Queens and Mission Wives*.
70. Bederman, *Manliness and Civilization*, 4.
71. Bingham, *A Residence of Twenty-One Years in the Sandwich Islands*, 78.
72. Anderson, *Kapiolani*, 8.
73. "For Young People: A Heroine of Hawaii," *Missionary Herald*, January 1883, 41–44; "For Young People: Keopuolani, Queen and Christian," *Missionary Herald*, February 1886, 77–80.
74. Rosenthal, *Beyond Hawai'i*, 5.
75. Kauanui, *Paradoxes of Hawaiian Sovereignty*, 39, 143–47; Silva, *Aloha Betrayed*, 44.
76. "Patriotic Work," *Washington Evening Star*, July 19, 1894, 9.
77. "The Deposed Queen," *Washington Evening Star*, October 27, 1894, 13. For more on the misogynistic overtones of critiques of Lili'uokalani and "heathen" women more generally, see Gin Lum, *Heathen*, 179.
78. "Constitution," 22; Damon, "Report of the Recording Secretary."
79. "Early Missionary Days."
80. The influence of descendants of missionaries as founding members and officers in the early years of the Honolulu YMCA is evident in "Constitution and By-Laws of the Young Men's Christian Association of Honolulu, Hawaiian Islands," 1897, box 1, Hawaii: Constitution and By-Laws, Local Association Files, Kautz Family YMCA Archives, Elmer L. Andersen Library, University of Minnesota, Minneapolis (hereafter Local Association Files); "Larger Family, Larger House," [1937], box 2, Hawaii: Printed Material (2), Local Association Files.
81. Charles Hyde to N. G. Clark, November 22, 1880, vol. 23, no. 5; Charles Hyde to Judson Smith, November 15, 1888, vol. 23, no. 202. Both in Hawaiian Islands Mission.
82. Peter Gulick to John Thomas Gulick, May 27, 1859, vol. 1, John T. Gulick Papers, Bancroft Library, University of California, Berkeley; Daniel Dole to George Dole, October 15, 1877, Daniel Dole Letters to His Sons, Bancroft Library, University of California, Berkeley (hereafter Daniel Dole Letters to His Sons); Daniel Dole to Sanford B. Dole, November 19, 1877, Daniel Dole Letters to His Sons; Daniel Dole to George Dole, November 23, 1877, Daniel Dole Letters to His Sons; Richard Armstrong to Reuben Chapman, February 27, 1844, Family Cor-

respondence 1840–44, Richard Armstrong Papers, Manuscript Division, Library of Congress, Washington, DC.

83. "Officers for 1879–80"; "Officers for 1884–5."

84. Charles Hyde to Judson Smith, April 21, 1891, vol. 26, no. 61, Hawaiian Islands Mission.

85. Charles Hyde to Judson Smith, June 28, 1894, vol. 26, no. 138, Hawaiian Islands Mission.

86. Judd, "Introductory Note," iii–iv.

87. Coan, *Life in Hawaii*, ii.

88. On the importance of the Bayonet Constitution as a trigger, see Williams, "Claiming Christianity," 14.

89. Quoted in Gulick and Gulick, *The Pilgrims of Hawaii*, 304.

90. W. B. Oleson to Judson Smith, September 24, 1885, vol. 24, no. 192, Hawaiian Islands Mission.

91. Hawaiian Mission Children's Society, *Jubilee Celebration of the Arrival of the Missionary Reinforcement of 1837*, 16.

92. Hawaiian Evangelical Association, "Report of Special Committee of Hawaiian Board," 1887, vol. 22, no. 9, Hawaiian Islands Mission; Gin Lum, *Heathen*, 95–96.

93. Hawaiian Mission Children's Society, *Jubilee Celebration of the Arrival of the Missionary Reinforcement of 1837*, 17.

94. Nathaniel Emerson to Judson Smith, August 28, 1887, vol. 22, no. 251, Hawaiian Islands Mission.

95. Sereno Bishop to Judson Smith, April 11, 1887, vol. 22, no. 154, Hawaiian Islands Mission.

96. Schulz, *Hawaiian by Birth*, 153–58; Walther, "'The Same Blood as We in America.'"

97. Armstrong, "Lessons from the Hawaiian Islands," 211–13, 217–18.

98. Beyer, "Manual and Industrial Education for Hawaiians during the 19th Century," 16.

99. Charles Hyde to E. K. Alden, November 1, 1884, vol. 23, no. 76, Hawaiian Islands Mission; James M. Alexander to Samuel Chapman Armstrong, August 24, 1887, James M. Alexander Papers, Children of the Mission Collection, Hawaiian Mission Children's Society Archives, Honolulu; Nathaniel Bright Emerson to Joseph S. Emerson, November 7, 1881, EMR 793, Nathaniel Bright Emerson Papers, Huntington Library, San Marino, California.

100. Elias Bond to N. G. Clark, December 8, 1880, vol. 22, no. 156, Hawaiian Islands Mission.

101. Lorenzo Lyons to Judson Smith, September 5, 1885, vol. 24, no. 154, Hawaiian Islands Mission.

102. Hawaiian Mission Children's Society to the Constituency of the American Board of Commissioners for Foreign Missions, 1887, vol. 22, no. 31, Hawaiian Islands Mission.

103. Smith and Smith, "The Hawaiian Islanders."

104. On the letter to the American Board of Commissioners for Foreign Missions, see Williams, "Claiming Christianity," 56.

105. Oleson, "Address of the Retiring President Rev. W. B. Oleson," 32.

106. Clara Bingham to Judson Smith, May 29, 1889, vol. 22, no. 149, Hawaiian Islands Mission.

107. Hawaiian Mission Children's Society, "Report of the Committee," 1887, vol. 22, no. 30, Hawaiian Islands Mission.

108. Hawaiian Evangelical Association, "Report," n.d., vol. 25, no. 10, Hawaiian Islands Mission.

109. Williams, "Claiming Christianity," 57–63.
110. William D. Westervelt to Judson Smith, May 7, 1889, vol. 24, no. 257, Hawaiian Islands Mission.
111. William D. Westervelt to Judson Smith, September 25, 1889, vol. 24, no. 264, Hawaiian Islands Mission.
112. William D. Westervelt to Judson Smith, November 29, 1889, vol. 24, no. 266A, Hawaiian Islands Mission.
113. William D. Westervelt to Judson Smith, February 10, 1890, vol. 26, no. 254, Hawaiian Islands Mission.
114. For examples of HEA board members complaining to the ABCFM about Westervelt, see Oliver Emerson to Judson Smith, August 22, 1890, vol. 25, no. 223; Charles Hyde to Judson Smith, January 23, 1891, vol. 26, no. 52; and Charles Hyde to Judson Smith, February 16, 1891, vol. 26, no. 54. All in Hawaiian Islands Mission.
115. Nathaniel Emerson to William D. Westervelt, April 24, 1891, vol. 25, no. 39, Hawaiian Islands Mission.
116. On the idea that the financial clout and high profile of the American Board of Commissioners for Foreign Missions were necessary for bringing workers into the field, see Charles Hyde to Judson Smith, March 23, 1891, vol. 26, no. 59, Hawaiian Islands Mission.
117. Charles Hyde to Judson Smith, July 2, 1888, vol. 23, no. 190A, Hawaiian Islands Mission.
118. Charles Hyde to Judson Smith, July 5, 1889, vol. 23, no. 222, Hawaiian Islands Mission.
119. Charles Hyde to Judson Smith, August 7, 1889, vol. 23, no. 225, Hawaiian Islands Mission.
120. William D. Westervelt to Judson Smith, February 16, 1891, vol. 26, no. 262, Hawaiian Islands Mission.
121. William D. Westervelt to Judson Smith, September 23, 1891, vol. 26, no. 273, Hawaiian Islands Mission, emphasis in original.
122. William DeWitt Alexander, Sereno Bishop, and William Richards Castle to Nathaniel Emerson, January 9, 1892, vol. 25, no. 13; Hawaiian Evangelical Association, "Report of Committee on Appropriations from the American Board," 1892, vol. 25, no. 17. Both in Hawaiian Islands Mission.
123. John Leadingham to Judson Smith, August 13, 1897, vol. 26, no. 228; John Leadingham to Judson Smith, November 12, 1898, vol. 26, no. 230. Both in Hawaiian Islands Mission.
124. On Emerson, see Sereno Bishop to Judson Smith, August 27, 1888, vol. 22, no. 155, Hawaiian Islands Mission. On Gulick, see Sereno Bishop to Judson Smith, October 11, 1892, vol. 25, no. 193, Hawaiian Islands Mission.
125. Oliver Emerson to Judson Smith, May 2, 1890, vol. 25, no. 216, Hawaiian Islands Mission.
126. Oliver Emerson to Judson Smith, October 19, 1892, vol. 25, no. 250, Hawaiian Islands Mission.
127. Williams, "Claiming Christianity," 64.
128. Williams, "To Raise a Voice in Praise."
129. "A Missionary Disgrace," [*New York Evening Post*, February 27, 1895,] clipping, vol. 25, no. 65, Hawaiian Islands Mission.
130. "In Mid Pacific," *Washington Evening Star*, April 6, 1895, 19; "A Letter from 'Mother Rice,'" *New York Sun*, April 20, 1895, 6. Coan's letter is mentioned alongside Hall's own rebuttal in William W. Hall to Judson Smith, April 11, 1895, vol. 26, no. 18, Hawaiian Islands Mission.

131. Charles Hyde to E. K. Alden, November 20, 1886, vol. 23, no. 135; Charles Hyde to Judson Smith, November 17, 1886, vol. 23, no. 136; Charles Hyde, "Hawaiian Annexation—Its Necessity and Its Urgency," 1893, vol. 25, no. 42. All in Hawaiian Islands Mission.

132. 26 Cong. Rec., part 2, 1849 (1893–94).

133. James H. Blount to Walter Q. Gresham, July 17, 1893, in *Intervention of United States Government in Affairs of Foreign Friendly Governments*, 60.

134. Charles Hyde to Judson Smith, November 17, 1886, vol. 23, no. 136, Hawaiian Islands Mission.

135. "In Mid Pacific"; "Afraid of Japan," *Washington Evening Star*, April 27, 1895, 9; "Her Real Character," *Washington Evening Star*, July 7, 1897, 11; "Japan's Intention," *Washington Evening Star*, August 10, 1897, 11.

136. Sereno Edwards Bishop to J. Elizabeth Hillebrand, December 23, 1896, Sereno Bishop Papers, Children of the Mission Collection, Hawaiian Mission Children's Society Archives, Honolulu (hereafter Sereno Bishop Papers, Children of the Mission Collection).

137. Williams, "'Aole Hoohui ia Hawaii.'"

138. For Cleveland's address, see 26 Cong. Rec., part 1, 4 (1893–94). On Emerson's speech, see Williams, "Claiming Christianity," 108–110.

139. "A Talk on Hawaii," *Washington Evening Star*, December 18, 1893, 9.

140. "A Talk on Hawaii."

141. Charles Hyde to Judson Smith, November 17, 1886, vol. 23, no. 136, Hawaiian Islands Mission.

142. Smith and Smith, "The Hawaiian Islanders."

143. Sereno Bishop to Judson Smith, April 11, 1887, vol. 22, no. 154, Hawaiian Islands Mission.

144. Ratnapalan, "'This Greater Issue of Light against Darkness,'" 5; Sereno Bishop to Gorham D. Gilman, January 26, 1893, Sereno Bishop Papers, Children of the Mission Collection.

145. Nathaniel Emerson to Judson Smith, August 28, 1887, vol. 22, no. 251; and Charles Hyde to N. G. Clark, March 10, 1883, vol. 23, no. 46. Both in Hawaiian Islands Mission. On Kalākaua's plans for a state church, see Williams, "Claiming Christianity," 28–29.

146. James Bicknell to Judson Smith, August 23, 1888, vol. 22, no. 95; Sereno Bishop, "Statement to Hawaiian Board, January 18, 1887," vol. 22, no. 153. Both in Hawaiian Islands Mission.

147. For some of Hyde's examples of supposed Hawaiian apostasy, see Charles Hyde to N. G. Clark, September 27, 1880, vol. 23, no. 1; Charles Hyde to N. G. Clark, March 11, 1882, vol. 23, no. 30; Charles Hyde to N. G. Clark, September 25, 1882, vol. 23, no. 39; Charles Hyde to N. G. Clark, February 12, 1883, vol. 23, no. 45; and Charles Hyde to Judson Smith, May 3, 1894, vol. 26, no. 133. All in Hawaiian Islands Mission.

148. Charles Hyde to Judson Smith, July 25, 1886, vol. 23, no. 161; Charles Hyde to Judson Smith, June 21, 1892, vol. 26, no. 92. Both in Hawaiian Islands Mission.

149. Charles Hyde to Judson Smith, January 17, 1890, vol. 26, no. 27, Hawaiian Islands Mission.

150. Charles Hyde to Judson Smith, March 29, 1892, vol. 26, no. 85, Hawaiian Islands Mission.

151. Oliver Emerson to Judson Smith, April 17, 1894, vol. 25, no. 265, Hawaiian Islands Mission.

152. "Aloha! Hawaii!" *Missionary Herald*, March 1893, 91–93.

153. Williams, "Claiming Christianity," 52; Chang, *The World and All the Things upon It*, 208–24; Silva, *Aloha Betrayed*, 139–40.

154. Williams, "Claiming Christianity," 74–88.

155. Williams, "Claiming Christianity," 222–30, chaps. 3–4.

156. Hawaiian Patriotic League petition to President Cleveland, in *Relations with Hawaii*, 2.

157. Liliʻuokalani, *Hawaii's Story by Hawaii's Queen*, 367. See also Gin Lum, *Heathen*, 184.

158. Clara Bingham to Judson Smith, February 5, 1891, vol. 25, no. 189, and Charles Hyde to Judson Smith, February 9, 1891, vol. 26, no. 53, both in Hawaiian Islands Mission; Sereno Bishop to John Thomas Gulick, October 5, 1891, Sereno Bishop Papers, Children of the Mission Collection; "The New Queen of the Hawaiian Islands," *Missionary Herald*, March 1891, 97–99.

159. Quoted in *Kalākaua Dead*.

160. Ida May Pope to Lois Prosser and others, February 2, 1891, HM 47012, Ida May Pope Papers, Huntington Library, San Marino, California; Castle, *Hawaii*, 48.

161. See also Williams, "Claiming Christianity," 6.

162. Williams, "To Raise a Voice in Praise," 27.

163. "Matter of Control," *Washington Evening Star*, July 18, 1896, 19; Coffman, *Nation Within*, 251.

164. Coffman, *Nation Within*.

165. Williams, "'Aole Hoohui ia Hawaii,'" 178; "Feeling of Security," *Washington Evening Star*, October 27, 1897, 7.

166. Love, *Race over Empire*, 106.

167. Coffman, *Nation Within*, chap. 14.

168. "Honolulu Agog," *Washington Evening Star*, May 12, 1894, 17; "Afraid of Japan"; "Why Hawaii Hopes," *Washington Evening Star*, August 27, 1895, 8; "Hawaii's Future," *Washington Evening Star*, November 21, 1895, 15; "Hawaii Distraught," *Washington Evening Star*, April 7, 1897, 11; Thurston, "Preface and a Brief Biography of Sereno Edwards Bishop," 9.

169. Brain, *The Transformation of Hawaii*, 17.

170. Brain, *The Transformation of Hawaii*, 9.

171. On anti-annexation petitions, see Silva, *Aloha Betrayed*, 145–59.

2. "From the Beginning of the World"

1. Charles Hyde to Judson Smith, February 11, 1888, vol. 23, no. 173, Hawaiian Islands Mission, Papers of the American Board of Commissioners for Foreign Missions, Houghton Library, Harvard University, Cambridge, Massachusetts (hereafter Hawaiian Islands Mission).

2. Bicknell, *Hoomanamana—Idolatry*; Sereno Bishop to Judson Smith, October 11, 1892, vol. 26, no. 193, and Oliver Emerson to Judson Smith, September 21, 1892, vol. 26, no. 249, both in Hawaiian Islands Mission.

3. Gin Lum, *Heathen*, 182.

4. Karpiel, "Notes & Queries," 205, 208.

5. Hale Nauā, *Constitution and By-Laws of the Hale Naua*, 5.

6. Silva, *Aloha Betrayed*, 89.

7. Karpiel, "Notes & Queries," 204–5.

8. Gin Lum, *Heathen*, 181.

9. Emerson's notes in Malo, *Hawaiian Antiquities*, 262–63.

10. Karpiel, "Notes & Queries," 205–6.

11. Bicknell, *Hoomanamana—Idolatry*, 3.

12. On the missionary community's broader fears about the supposed appropriation of Christian ritual, see Gin Lum, *Heathen*, 182–83.
13. Gin Lum, "The Historyless Heathen and the Stagnating Pagan," 53–54, 57–59.
14. Chang, *The World and All the Things upon It*; Kameʻeleihiwa, *Native Land and Foreign Desires*; Nogelmeier, *Mai Paʻa I Ka Leo*; Silva, *Aloha Betrayed*; Trask, *From a Native Daughter*; Young, *Rethinking the Native Hawaiian Past*.
15. Silva, *Aloha Betrayed*, 105.
16. *Report of the Board of Genealogy of Hawaiian Chiefs*, 11–26; Hale Nauā, *Constitution and By-Laws of the Hale Naua*, 5.
17. Silva, *Aloha Betrayed*, 94–97.
18. *Report of the Board of Genealogy of Hawaiian Chiefs*, 14.
19. Quoted in Silva, *Aloha Betrayed*, 107.
20. Daggett, "Hawaiian Legends," 65.
21. Kameʻeleihiwa, *Native Land and Foreign Desires*, 19; Smith, "Islanders, Protestant Missionaries, and Traditions Regarding the Past in Nineteenth-Century Polynesia," 76–77.
22. Cook, *Return to Kahiki*, chap. 3; Gonschor, *A Power in the World*, chaps. 3–4.
23. Smith, "Islanders, Protestant Missionaries, and Traditions Regarding the Past in Nineteenth-Century Polynesia," 75; Kauanui, *Hawaiian Blood*, 38.
24. Smith, "Islanders, Protestant Missionaries, and Traditions Regarding the Past in Nineteenth-Century Polynesia," 71–72.
25. Smith, "Islanders, Protestant Missionaries, and Traditions Regarding the Past in Nineteenth-Century Polynesia," 80–82; Kauanui, *Hawaiian Blood*, 52.
26. Kamakau, *Ka Poʻe Kahiko*, 4.
27. "Six Election Broadsides Issued by Kalakaua and Queen Emma."
28. Silva, *Aloha Betrayed*, 103.
29. Baker, *A Reply to the Ministerial Utterances*, 6; italics in original.
30. *The Coronation of King Kalakaua*, 8–10.
31. Liliʻuokalani, "Liliuokalani's history of her family, exhorting them, and refuting Bush's insinuations in Ka Leo belittling them," n.d., box 19, folder 151, document S62, Liliʻuokalani Papers, Hawaiʻi State Archives, Honolulu.
32. Kameʻeleihiwa, *Native Land and Foreign Desires*, 19.
33. Quoted in Silva, *Aloha Betrayed*, 104.
34. Silva, *Aloha Betrayed*, 105.
35. Rohrer, *Staking Claim*, 9, 12–13.
36. On the initial Mormon lack of interest in preaching to Native Hawaiians, see Aikau, *A Chosen People, a Promised Land*, 16.
37. Henry W. Bigler journal, 1896, box 2, FAC 1341, Henry W. Bigler Diaries, Huntington Library, San Marino, California. This journal consists of typescripts of portions published in newspapers relating to Bigler's 1849 trip to California and the Hawaiian mission.
38. Aikau, *A Chosen People, a Promised Land*, 3–14.
39. Woods, "A Most Influential Mormon Islander," 136.
40. Church of Jesus Christ of Latter-Day Saints, "Facts and Statistics," accessed June 8, 2021, https://newsroom.churchofjesuschrist.org/facts-and-statistics/state/hawaii; Williams, "Claiming Christianity," 52.
41. Entry for April 28, 1853, John Stillman Woodbury Diaries, FAC 507, Huntington Library, San Marino, California.
42. On the religious competition that the Mormons provided, see Charles Hyde to Judson Smith, September 21, 1888, vol. 22, no. 198; and John Leadingham to Judson Smith, October 17,

1896, vol. 26, no. 224. Both in Hawaiian Islands Mission. For the missionary community's views on Gibson, see Thrum, *The Shepherd Saint of Lanai*.

43. Kuykendall, *The Hawaiian Kingdom*, 2:91–97; Staley, *A Pastoral Address*; Alexander, *A Review of A Pastoral Address by the Right Rev. T. N. Staley*.

44. *Hawaiian Church Mission*, 2–3.

45. "A Warning Voice," *Anglican Church Chronicle*, November 6, 1886, 162.

46. "The Church of England," *Anglican Church Chronicle*, January 2, 1886, 22–23.

47. Willis, *The Principles of Government of the Anglican Church in Hawaii*.

48. Alexander, *A Brief History of the Hawaiian People*, 168.

49. Fish Kashay, "Savages, Sinners, and Saints," 296–313, 336–41.

50. Bingham, *A Residence of Twenty-One Years in the Sandwich Islands*, 414.

51. Dibble, *History and General Views of the Sandwich Islands' Mission*, 110.

52. Bingham, *A Residence of Twenty-One Years in the Sandwich Islands*, 535.

53. Armstrong, "Lessons from the Hawaiian Islands," 209–10; Brain, *The Transformation of Hawaii*, 107–8.

54. Chang, *The World and All the Things upon It*, 210.

55. "Dedication of the New Church at Waialua," *The Friend*, January 1891, 2.

56. For a "missionary" perceptive on heightened Catholic activity in the late nineteenth century, see W. B. Oleson to Judson Smith, June 11, 1885, vol. 24, no. 149, Hawaiian Islands Mission.

57. For a reprint of Hyde's letter, see Hyde, *Father Damien and His Work for the Hawaiian Lepers*.

58. Robert Louis Stevenson, "Father Damien: An Open Letter to the Reverend Dr. Hyde of Honolulu," *Elele*, May 10, 1890, newspaper clipping, Hawaiian and Pacific Collections, Hamilton Library, University of Hawai'i, Mānoa. On Stevenson's time in Hawai'i and friendship with Kalākaua, see Ratnapalan, "Sereno Bishop, Robert Louis Stevenson and 'Americanism' in Hawai'i."

59. "A Missionary Disgrace," [*New York Evening Post*, February 27, 1895,] clipping, vol. 25, no. 65, Hawaiian Islands Mission; Stoddard, *Father Damien*.

60. Sereno Bishop to Artemas Bishop, January 30, 1871, box 6, BSH 652, Sereno Edwards Bishop Papers, Huntington Library, San Marino, California (hereafter Bishop Papers, Huntington).

61. Merry, *Colonizing Hawai'i*, 28.

62. Coffman, *Nation Within*, 46; Daws, *Shoal of Time*, 114–20, 133–34.

63. On the arrival of British and Tahitian missionaries, see Chang, *The World and All the Things upon It*, 92–99.

64. Daws, *Shoal of Time*, 292.

65. Nathaniel Emerson, "A Page from Hawaiian History!" 1893, box 3, EMR 80, Nathaniel Bright Emerson Papers, Huntington Library, San Marino, California (hereafter Emerson Papers).

66. "Her Real Character," *Washington Evening Star*, July 7, 1897, 11.

67. Alexander, *Kalakaua's Reign*, 34.

68. Imada, *Aloha America*, 32.

69. Silva, *Aloha Betrayed*, 110–12.

70. Imada, *Aloha America*, 33.

71. Alexander, *Kalakaua's Reign*, 34.

72. Nick Fielding, "The Life of Alatau Tamchiboulac Atkinson," *Siberian Steppes: A blog about Thomas Witlam Atkinson and Lucy Atkinson, the 19th Century Explorers of Siberia and Central Asia*, accessed November 28, 2018, https://siberiansteppes.com/2017/02/15/the-life-of-alatau-tamchiboulac-atkinson.

73. Forbes, *Hawaiian National Bibliography*, 223–24.
74. Atkinson, "A Stranger Asks Bliff about the Historical Procession," 10.
75. Alexander, *Kalakaua's Reign*, 32–33; Sereno Bishop, "Statement to Hawaiian Board, January 18, 1887," vol. 22, no. 153, and Charles Hyde, "Idolatry among Hawaiians," n.d., vol. 23, no. 238, both in Hawaiian Islands Mission.
76. Karpiel, "Notes & Queries," 207.
77. Silva, *Aloha Betrayed*, 144.
78. James H. Blount to Walter Q. Gresham, July 17, 1893, in *Intervention of United States Government in Affairs of Foreign Friendly Governments*, 40, 43.
79. Schulz, *Hawaiian by Birth*, 126–28.
80. Schulz, *Hawaiian by Birth*, 1, 34.
81. "Thurston at Home," *Washington Evening Star*, June 22, 1895, 14.
82. Message of the President, December 18, 1893, in *Intervention of United States Government in Affairs of Foreign Friendly Governments*, 12–14.
83. 26 Cong. Rec, part 3, 2288 (1893–94).
84. *Our Relations with Hawaii*, 5–6.
85. Richard F. Pettigrew to Joseph Oliver Carter, September 1, 1891, box 3, HM 76674, Joseph Oliver Carter Papers, Huntington Library, San Marino, California (hereafter Carter Papers). For evidence of Pettigrew's racist arguments, see Love, *Race over Empire*, 122–24.
86. Julius A. Palmer to Joseph Oliver Carter, August 18, 1896, box 3, HM 76637, Carter Papers.
87. "Broadside regarding Hawaiian-U.S. Relations," [1893], box 3, EMR 63, Emerson Papers. Kathryn Gin Lum also writes about this document with a slightly different focus in Gin Lum, *Heathen*, 175–77.
88. Williams, "Claiming Christianity," 100–101.
89. Quoted in Ratnapalan, "'This Greater Issue of Light against Darkness,'" 24.
90. See also Moore, *American Imperialism and the State*, 60–61.
91. "Royalty Retarded," *Washington Evening Star*, May 19, 1894, 13.
92. "Favors Annexation," *Washington Evening Star*, November 9, 1894, 9; "Affairs in Hawaii," *Washington Evening Star*, May 18, 1895, 16; "Kate Field's Death," *Washington Evening Star*, June 11, 1896, 11.
93. "State of Hawaii," *Washington Evening Star*, October 3, 1896, 21.
94. "Hawaii Is Waiting," *Washington Evening Star*, February 8, 1898, 6.
95. Coffman, *Nation Within*, 124, 174; "Honolulu Agog," *Washington Evening Star*, May 12, 1894, 17.
96. For an article that makes this argument with reference to settler colonies in the British empire, see Lester, "British Settler Discourse and the Circuits of Empire."
97. Moore, *American Imperialism and the State*, 61–62.
98. Minutes for June 13, 1887, vol. 2, Social Science Association Papers, Hawai'i State Archives, Honolulu (hereafter Social Science Association Papers).
99. Sanford Ballard Dole, "Hawaii Under Annexation," draft, n.d., box 2, folder 13, Sanford Ballard Dole Papers, Hawai'i State Archives, Honolulu (hereafter Dole Papers).
100. William DeWitt Alexander to J. J. Morgan, February 17, 1894, William DeWitt Alexander Papers, Hawaiian Historical Society, Honolulu.
101. Excerpt from the *Hawaiian Star*, January 18, 1894, in *Message from the President of the United States*, 11.
102. Lorrin Thurston and F. M. Hatch, "Argument in Support of Enactment by the Hawaiian Legislature of an Act Effectuating Annexation," 1898, box 2, folder 5, Dole Papers.

103. Lepore, *These Truths*, 6.
104. Bingham, *A Residence of Twenty-One Years in the Sandwich Islands*, 18.
105. McDougall, "Moʻokūʻauhau versus Colonial Entitlement," 752, 759.
106. Klein, *Frontiers of the Historical Imagination*, 3.
107. Ratnapalan, "Science and Politics in the Hawaiian Kingdom," 140.
108. Gin Lum, *Heathen*, 84.
109. Emerson, "Chairman's Address," 4.
110. Emerson, "Chairman's Address," 4–5.
111. Alexander, "Report of the Corresponding Secretary," 9.
112. Alexander, "Corresponding Secretary's Report."
113. Burbank, "Annual Report of the Librarian of the Hawaiian Historical Society," 7.
114. Hyde, "Minutes of the Annual Meeting," 4; "Officers—1901."
115. Alexander, *A Brief History of the Hawaiian People*, chaps. ii–iii; Thurston, "Preface and a Brief Biography of Sereno Edwards Bishop," 10. On Gulick, see Schulz, *Hawaiian by Birth*, 274–93. For an overview of the wide-ranging scientific interests of descendants of missionaries, see Kay, "Missionary Contributions to Hawaiian Natural History," 31.
116. Ratnapalan, "Science and Politics in the Hawaiian Kingdom," 140; Sereno Bishop to Alexander Winchell, April 12, 1879, box 9, BSH 707, Bishop Papers, Huntington.
117. For example, John Thomas Gulick to George John Romanes, March 7, 1891, vol. 2, John T. Gulick Papers, Bancroft Library, University of California, Berkeley (hereafter Gulick Papers).
118. Coffman, *Nation Within*, 89–90.
119. Kay, "Missionary Contributions to Hawaiian Natural History," 28; Ratnapalan, "'This Greater Issue of Light against Darkness,'" 9.
120. Williams, "Claiming Christianity," 209.
121. Alexander S. Twombly to the Prudential Committee of the ABCFM, November 21, 1894, vol. 25, no. 49, Hawaiian Islands Mission.
122. For the tensions between Gulick and his father over his pursuit of a scientific career, see John Thomas Gulick to father, April 1, 1854, vol. 1, Gulick Papers. For Gulick's attempts to reconcile Christianity and science, see John Thomas Gulick to George John Romanes, March 7, 1891, vol. 2, Gulick Papers; and John Thomas Gulick to George John Romanes, May 19, 1891, vol. 2, Gulick Papers.
123. Bishop, *Reminiscences of Old Hawaii*, 38.
124. Wood, *Displacing Natives*, 69–70.
125. Ratnapalan, "Science and Politics in the Hawaiian Kingdom," 141.
126. Allen, *A Republic in Time*, 151.
127. Arvin, *Possessing Polynesians*, 3.
128. Silva, *Aloha Betrayed*, chap. 2.
129. Brown, *Facing the Spears of Change*, chap. 5; Nogelmeier, *Mai Paʻa I Ka Leo*, 81.
130. Kualapai, "The Queen Writes Back," 58.
131. Kualapai, "The Queen Writes Back," 47–51. On Native Hawaiian interest in life writing, see Brown, *Facing the Spears of Change*, 17–19.
132. Kualapai, "The Queen Writes Back," 51–55.
133. Sereno Bishop to Gorham D. Gilman, July 19, 1898, Sereno Bishop Papers, Children of the Mission Collection, Hawaiian Mission Children's Society, Honolulu.
134. "No Value as History," *Washington Evening Star*, March 1, 1898, 11.
135. Ross, "Historical Consciousness in Nineteenth-Century America"; Novick, *That Noble Dream*.

136. Morgan, *A Nation of Descendants*, chap. 1; Wulf, "Bible, King, and Common Law"; Bendroth, *The Last Puritans*; Balmer, *Mine Eyes Have Seen the Glory*, 93.
137. O'Brien, *Firsting and Lasting*.
138. Gin Lum, "The Historyless Heathen and the Stagnating Pagan," 71.
139. Arista, *The Kingdom and the Republic*, 102–3.
140. Bingham, *A Residence of Twenty-One Years in the Sandwich Islands*, 17–28.
141. Alexander, *A Brief History of the Hawaiian People*, 20.
142. Blight, *Race and Reunion*, chap. 3; Marshall, *Creating a Confederate Kentucky*, chap. 4.
143. Bendroth, *The Last Puritans*, 73–78, 118–25.
144. William DeWitt Alexander to R. R. Hoes, May 6, 1895, W. D. Alexander Letters to R. R. Hoes, Bancroft Library, University of California, Berkeley.
145. Nathaniel Emerson, "Comrades of the Grand Army of the Republic," 1891, speech, final draft, box 11, EMR 388, Emerson Papers.
146. Schulz, *Hawaiian by Birth*, 113–15, 124.
147. "Thurston at Home."
148. Wood, *Displacing Natives*, 41; Rohrer, *Staking Claim*, 10.
149. Silva, *Aloha Betrayed*, 101.
150. Julius A. Palmer to Joseph Oliver Carter, December 30, 1896, Box 3, HM 76638, Carter Papers.
151. Message of the President, December 18, 1893, in *Intervention of United States Government in Affairs of Foreign Friendly Governments*, 12.
152. James H. Blount to Walter Q. Gresham, July 17, 1893, in *Intervention of United States Government in Affairs of Foreign Friendly Governments*, 55.
153. Petition of the Hawaiian Patriotic League to President Cleveland, in *Intervention of United States Government in Affairs of Foreign Friendly Governments*, 4.
154. "Royalists' Claims," *Washington Evening Star*, June 2, 1894, 2. On the tendency of settlers to emphasize the immigrant pasts of Indigenous peoples, see Arvin, *Possessing Polynesians*, 41. For a classic text on the rise of Americans' anti-immigrant nativism in this period, see Higham, *Strangers in the Land*.
155. "Royalists' Claims."
156. "Affairs in Hawaii."
157. On "playing Indian" see Deloria, *Playing Indian*.
158. Lott, *Love and Theft*, 9.
159. "Affairs in Hawaii."
160. "Japan's New Claim," *Washington Evening Star*, August 2, 1897, 3.
161. On the representation of Polynesians as close to Blackness, see Arvin, *Possessing Polynesians*, 4.
162. Orramel Hinckley Gulick to N. G. Clark and Judson Smith, April 16, 1894, vol. 26, no. 1, Hawaiian Islands Mission.
163. Emerson, "A Page from Hawaiian History!"
164. "Early Missionary Days," clipping from *Pacific Commercial Advertiser*, June 15, 1895, vol. 25, no. 66, Hawaiian Islands Mission.
165. "Clippings related to the fiftieth anniversary of the mission in 1887 [sic]," vol. 22, no. 65, Hawaiian Islands Mission.
166. Charles Hyde to Judson Smith, November 22, 1889, vol. 23, no. 234, Hawaiian Islands Mission; "Oahu College," 1891, vol. 24, no. 38, Hawaiian Islands Mission; "The Island City," *Washington Evening Star*, December 6, 1895, 11.

167. Nathaniel Emerson to Samuel Alexander, November 14, 1901, EMR 1315, Emerson Papers; Lyman, "Recollections of Kamehameha V."
168. *A Sketch of Recent Events*, 15.
169. Kauanui, *Hawaiian Blood*, 40.
170. "The Island City."
171. On Bishop's embarrassment, see Williams, "Claiming Christianity," 103–4.
172. Minutes for December 13, 1886, vol. 2, Social Science Association Papers.
173. Gulick and Gulick, *The Pilgrims of Hawaii*, 54.
174. Quotation from Kauanui, *Hawaiian Blood*, 12.
175. Linnekin, "The Politics of Culture in the Pacific," 155.
176. Schulz, *Hawaiian by Birth*, 145.
177. Kauanui, *Paradoxes of Hawaiian Sovereignty*, chap. 3.
178. Quoted in Kauanui, *Hawaiian Blood*, 46.
179. Coffman, *Nation Within*, 70.
180. For example, "Afraid of Japan," *Washington Evening Star*, April 27, 1895, 9.
181. "Hawaiian Rebellion," *Washington Evening Star*, February 12, 1895, 9.
182. "Hawaii Is Waiting."

3. "A Past That Is Often Noble"

1. Nishimoto, "The Progressive Era and Hawai'i," 174–77.
2. Untitled clipping from *Pacific Commercial Advertiser*, February 8, 1911, box 10, EMR 370, Nathaniel Bright Emerson Papers, Huntington Library, San Marino, California (hereafter Emerson Papers).
3. Untitled clipping from *Pacific Commercial Advertiser*, February 10, 1911, box 10, EMR 370, Emerson Papers.
4. Untitled clipping from *Pacific Commercial Advertiser*, February 8, 1911.
5. Untitled clipping from *Pacific Commercial Advertiser*, February 8, 1911.
6. Untitled clipping from *Pacific Commercial Advertiser*, February 8, 1911.
7. Untitled clipping from *Pacific Commercial Advertiser*, February 10, 1911.
8. Damon quoted in Beamer, *No Mākou ka Mana*, 197.
9. Gonzalez, *Securing Paradise*, 45.
10. Eperjesi, *The Imperialist Imaginary*, 92.
11. Sereno Bishop to Gorham D. Gilman, March 31, 1899, Sereno Bishop Papers, Children of the Mission Collection, Hawaiian Mission Children's Society, Honolulu.
12. Oliver Emerson to Judson Smith, February 13, 1901, vol. 27, no. 112, Hawaiian Islands Mission, Papers of the American Board of Commissioners for Foreign Missions, Houghton Library, Harvard University, Cambridge, Massachusetts (hereafter Hawaiian Islands Mission).
13. "Rev. Oliver Pomeroy Emerson," *The Friend*, November 1906, 12.
14. O. H. Gulick speech at Broadway Tabernacle, April 23, 1900, box 3, folder 7, Ecumenical Conference on Foreign Missions Records, 1900-04–1900-05, Burke Library, Union Theological Seminary, Columbia University, New York.
15. "The Christianization of Hawaii," *Missionary Herald*, December 1904, 512–18; "Special Providences in the Christianization of Hawaii," *Missionary Herald*, January 1905, 15–19; "Special Providences in the Christianization of Hawaii," *Missionary Herald*, February 1905, 61–65.
16. Frear, *Memory's Silver Screen of Hawaii's Social Life*, 24; Daughters of Hawai'i, "About Us," accessed January 6, 2021, https://daughtersofhawaii.org/about-us.

17. Frear, *Memory's Silver Screen of Hawaii's Social Life*, 24.
18. Gulick and Gulick, *The Pilgrims of Hawaii*, 335.
19. Hiram Bingham II to Judson Smith, July 22, 1903, vol. 27, no. 34; Oliver Emerson to Judson Smith, February 13, 1901, vol. 27, no. 112; Orramel Gulick to Judson Smith, November 10, 1903, vol. 27, no. 129. All in Hawaiian Islands Mission.
20. "Impressions from a Recent Journey to Mexico and Hawaii," *Missionary Herald*, July 1903, 324–25; Orramel Gulick to Judson Smith, James L. Barton, and Charles H. Daniels, March 2, 1900, vol. 27, no. 128, Hawaiian Islands Mission.
21. Hawaiian Mission Centennial, *Official Program for the Events of Centennial Week*, 3.
22. Frear, "A Century of Achievement," 5–6.
23. Frear, "A Century of Achievement," 14; Erdman, "A Brief Historical Sketch of the Hawaiian Board of Missions," 78.
24. Thrum, "The Native Leaders of Hawaii."
25. Restarick, "The Story of the Mission," 56.
26. Perry, "The Catholic Church in Hawaii"; Anderson, "The Protestant Episcopal Church in Hawaii"; Trent, "The Methodist Episcopal Church in Hawaii."
27. Untitled article (report of a sermon by Henry Bond Restarick), *Anglican Church Chronicle*, January 2, 1904, 33; Restarick, *Hawaii, 1778–1920, from the Viewpoint of a Bishop*.
28. Lewis, "Minutes of Meeting of Hawaiian Historical Society, held at the Library, August 20, 1908 at 7:30 P.M.," 7; Yzendoorn, "The Introduction of the Algaroba."
29. *Hawaiian Missions Centennial*, 3–4.
30. Hawaiian Mission Centennial, *Official Program for the Events of Centennial Week*, 64–66.
31. Hawaiian Mission Centennial, *Official Program for the Events of Centennial Week*.
32. *Hawaiian Missions Centennial*, 7–9.
33. Hawaiian Mission Centennial, *Official Program for the Events of Centennial Week*, 14–39.
34. Kenny, "The World Day of Prayer," 142.
35. Hawaiian Mission Centennial, *Official Program for the Events of Centennial Week*, 16–36.
36. *Hawaiian Missions Centennial*, 3.
37. Gulick and Gulick, *The Pilgrims of Hawaii*, 323.
38. "The Island City," *Washington Evening Star*, December 6, 1895, 11.
39. Adams, *Education for Extinction*.
40. Castle, *Hawaii*, chap. III.
41. Albert W. Palmer quoted in Emerson, *Pioneer Days in Hawaii*, 255–56.
42. Gulick and Gulick, *The Pilgrims of Hawaii*, 337–39, chap. XXIV.
43. Gulick and Gulick, *The Pilgrims of Hawaii*, 311, chap. VII.
44. Barton, "Introduction."
45. Kualapai, "The Queen Writes Back," 32.
46. Schulz, "Empire of the Young," 86.
47. Thurston, "Preface and a Brief Biography of Sereno Edwards Bishop," 3.
48. Sereno Bishop to Gorham D. Gilman, March 26, 1902, Sereno Edwards Bishop Letters to Gorham D. Gilman, Hawaiian Historical Society, Honolulu.
49. Castle, *Hawaii*, vii.
50. Castle, *Hawaii*, 228–29.
51. Trask, *From a Native Daughter*, 120.
52. Roosevelt, "The Strenuous Life."
53. Thurston, "Preface and a Brief Biography of Sereno Edwards Bishop," 5.
54. Bishop, *Reminiscences of Old Hawaii*, 18.
55. Bishop, *Reminiscences of Old Hawaii*, 13.

56. Rosenthal, *Beyond Hawai'i*, 3; Bishop, *Reminiscences of Old Hawaii*, 12–13.
57. Bishop, *Reminiscences of Old Hawaii*, 47.
58. Slotkin, *Gunfighter Nation*, 10–13.
59. Bishop, *Reminiscences of Old Hawaii*, 13, 16.
60. Bishop, *Why Are the Hawaiians Dying Out?*, 3–14. On the idea among settlers in Hawai'i and elsewhere that Indigenous peoples were responsible for their own decline, see Archer, "Remedial Agents," 544; Dippie, *The Vanishing American*, 34–38; and Metaxas, "'Licentiousness Has Slain Its Hundreds of Thousands.'"
61. Lyman, *Hawaiian Yesterdays*, 10–11.
62. Whitaker, "Foreword."
63. Gulick and Gulick, *The Pilgrims of Hawaii*, chap. XI.
64. Emerson, *Pioneer Days in Hawaii*, 2, 7–8.
65. Emerson, *Pioneer Days in Hawaii*, 161–68.
66. Engleman, *A Peep into Paradise*, 7.
67. "The Civilization of the Hawaiian Islands," *Pacific Commercial Advertiser*, November 14, 1902, 9.
68. Castle, *Hawaii*, 13.
69. Gulick and Gulick, *The Pilgrims of Hawaii*, 18.
70. Castle, *Hawaii*, 8.
71. Castle, *Hawaii*, 26–27.
72. Castle, *Hawaii*, 21–24, 217–19.
73. Castle, *Hawaii*, 121–22.
74. Castle, *Hawaii*, 119–20, 138, 142, 151, 156.
75. Castle, *Hawaii*, 149, 178–79, 183.
76. Indigenous scholars have emphasized the connections between history and place in Hawaiian and Pacific cosmologies in Chang, *The World and All the Things upon It*, 197–204; Oliveira, *Ancestral Places*; Rohrer, *Staking Claim*, 9; and Salesa, "The Pacific in Indigenous Time," 43.
77. For an overview of the patterns of labor migration to Hawai'i from the mid-nineteenth century onward, see Takaki, *Pau Hana*. On Filipino and Puerto Rican migration to and labor in Hawai'i, see Poblete, *Islanders in the Empire*.
78. Nathaniel Emerson, "Hawaii's Race Problem," n.d. (after 1906), box 13, EMR 435, Emerson Papers.
79. Chang, *The World and All the Things upon It*, viii–ix; Jacobs, "Seeing Like a Settler Colonial State," 262.
80. On the work of the Hawaii Promotion Committee, see Bryan, "Report of the Corresponding Secretary for the Year Ending Nov. 28, 1905," 11–13; and Moser, "The Hawaii Promotion Committee and the Appropriation of Surfing."
81. Whitney, *The Hawaiian Guide Book*.
82. "In the Land of Poi," *Washington Evening Star*, August 2, 1895, 9; "Touring Hawaii," *Washington Evening Star*, February 21, 1896, 11; "State of Hawaii," *Washington Evening Star*, October 3, 1896, 21; "Japan Is Friendly," *Washington Evening Star*, June 7, 1897, 11; Ratnapalan, "'This Greater Issue of Light Against Darkness,'" 22.
83. Coffman, *Nation Within*, 144.
84. W. C. Rodgers and E. D. Kilburne, "Obituary of Nathaniel Bright Emerson," [1915], EMR 22, Emerson Papers.
85. Barrow, "Introduction to the New Edition," xviii–xix.
86. For a statement of Emerson's motivation of collecting Hawaiian folklore while it was still possible to do so, see Emerson, *Unwritten Literature of Hawaii*, 12–13.

87. Christian, "Preface," xix.

88. Nathaniel Emerson to Titus Munson Coan, August 6, 1905, EMR 1316, Emerson Papers.

89. Emerson, "Biographical Sketch of David Malo," ix, xiv; Nathaniel Emerson to Titus Munson Coan, April 9, 1907, EMR 1316, Emerson Papers.

90. Emerson, *Unwritten Literature of Hawaii*, 263.

91. Nathaniel Emerson, "A Myth of Kane and Kanaloa," n.d., box 9, EMR 344; Nathaniel Emerson, "The House, the Family and Home-Life among the Ancient Hawaiians," n.d., box 13, EMR 451. Both in Emerson Papers.

92. Emerson, "Biographical Sketch of David Malo," viii–ix.

93. Emerson, "A Myth of Kane and Kanaloa."

94. Nathaniel Emerson, "General Remarks on Translation," n.d., box 12, EMR 425, Emerson Papers.

95. Nathaniel Emerson, "Hawaii's Response to Environment," n.d., box 13, EMR 437, Emerson Papers.

96. Nathaniel Emerson, "The Myth of Pele, the Volcanic Goddess of Hawaii," n.d., box 7, EMR 285, Emerson Papers; Emerson, *The Long Voyages of the Ancient Hawaiians*. For twentieth-century scholarship that questions the possibility of long-distance navigation by canoe, see Sharp, *Ancient Voyagers in Polynesia*. For more recent interpretations reaffirming Indigenous knowledge, see Finney, *Sailing in the Wake of the Ancestors*; Lewis, *We, the Navigators*; and Turnbull, *Masons, Tricksters, and Cartographers*.

97. Nathaniel Emerson, "The Growth of Insanity," 1891, box 5, EMR 163; Nathaniel Emerson, "The Key to Eugenics," n.d., box 14, EMR 464. Both in Emerson Papers.

98. Nathaniel Emerson, "Ethnic Factors in Civilization," 1905, box 12, EMR 415, Emerson Papers.

99. Nathaniel Emerson to Joseph Emerson and Dorothea Lamb Emerson, September 24, 1898, box 20, EMR 878, Emerson Papers.

100. Nathaniel Emerson to K. Hofmann, January 26, 1907, EMR 1316, Emerson Papers.

101. For evidence of Emerson's wavering, see Nathaniel Emerson to the *New York Tribune*, December 26, 1891, box 18, EMR 670, Emerson Papers.

102. Nathaniel Emerson, "Notes regarding Hawaiian Annexation," n.d., box 3, EMR 72, Emerson Papers.

103. Nathaniel Emerson, "A Page from Hawaiian History!" 1893, box 3, EMR 80; Nathaniel Emerson, "The Function of the White Man in Hawaiian Affairs," 1893, box 12, EMR 424; Emerson, "Notes regarding Hawaiian Annexation." All in Emerson Papers.

104. For evidence that Emerson struggled in private to neatly taxonomize Hawaiian folklore, see Nathaniel Emerson, "Classification of Hawaiian Poetry," n.d. [1900], box 9, EMR 308, Emerson Papers. For scholarship that suggests the intertwining of mythological, traditional, and genealogical elements, see Silva, *Aloha Betrayed*, 94–95.

105. Nathaniel Emerson to W. C. Morrow, December 7, 1904, EMR 1316, Emerson Papers.

106. Nathaniel Emerson, "Biographical Information regarding Davida Malo," n.d., box 2, EMR 45, Emerson Papers.

107. Nathaniel Emerson, "The Story of Hiiaka" (additional draft pages), n.d. [1911], box 8, EMR 297, Emerson Papers. For Emerson's appreciation of the importance of the nonverbal in Hawaiian tradition, see Emerson, *Unwritten Literature of Hawaii*, chap. XXII.

108. Emerson, *Unwritten Literature of Hawaii*, 12.

109. Emerson, *Unwritten Literature of Hawaii*, 260.

110. Nathaniel Emerson, "The Date of Hawaii's Period of Maritime Activity in Ancient Times," n.d. [1890], box 4, EMR 115, Emerson Papers.

111. Emerson, *Unwritten Literature of Hawaii*, 7, 263.
112. Emerson, *Unwritten Literature of Hawaii*, 27.
113. Emerson, *Unwritten Literature of Hawaii*, 262.
114. Emerson, *Unwritten Literature of Hawaii*, 8.
115. Emerson, *Unwritten Literature of Hawaii*, 82.
116. See, for example, Fornander, *An Account of the Polynesian Race*, 160.
117. Smith, "Islanders, Protestant Missionaries, and Traditions Regarding the Past in Nineteenth-Century Polynesia," 75, 88–89; Arvin, *Possessing Polynesians*, 53.
118. Doty, "Introduction to the New Edition," x–xi; Silva, *Aloha Betrayed*, 71.
119. Frear, "Minutes of Annual Meeting, Held January 14, 1907," 7; Emerson, "The Date of Hawaii's Period of Maritime Activity in Ancient Times"; Charles Hyde to H. M. Hagen, January 14, 1882, vol. 23, no. 26, Hawaiian Islands Mission; Alexander, *A Brief History of the Hawaiian People*, iv.
120. Fornander, *An Account of the Polynesian Race*, vi.
121. Fornander, *An Account of the Polynesian Race*, ix; Bryan, "Report of the Corresponding Secretary for the Year Ending Nov. 28, 1905," 14.
122. Alexander, "Report of the Corresponding Secretary for the Year Ending November 28, 1901," 7, 9; Alexander, "Report of the Corresponding Secretary for the Year Ending November 28, 1899," 10.
123. Nathaniel Emerson, "Catalogue of Ethnological Objects," 1884–1915, box 11, EMR 385; Nathaniel Emerson to S. Percy Smith, August 5, 1892, box 23, EMR 1144; Abraham Fornander to Nathaniel Emerson, January 5, 1883, box 23, EMR 1171; S. Percy Smith to Nathaniel Emerson, December 10, 1892, box 24, EMR 1278; S. Percy Smith to Nathaniel Emerson, July 28, 1894, box 24, EMR 1279. All in Emerson Papers.
124. Lyon, "Davida Malo, Nathaniel Emerson, and the 'Sins' of Hawaiians," 118; Weir, "'White Man's Burden,' 'White Man's Privilege,'" 283.
125. Nathaniel Emerson to Titus Munson Coan, June 16, 1902, EMR 1315, Emerson Papers.
126. McGregor, *Nā Kua'āina*; Williams, "Claiming Christianity," 264.
127. Chang, *The World and All the Things upon It*, 254–56.
128. Castle, *Hawaii*, 228.
129. Bingham, *A Residence of Twenty-One Years in the Sandwich Islands*, 559.
130. Brown, *Facing the Spears of Change*, 89–91; Schulz, "Empire of the Young," 244; Silva, *Aloha Betrayed*, 62–63, 81.
131. Nathaniel Emerson, "Lonomuku: The Woman in the Moon," [1880], box 14, EMR 479; Nathaniel Emerson to Joseph Emerson, July 15, 1889, box 20, EMR 852; Nathaniel Emerson to Joseph Emerson, August 20, 1894, box 20, EMR 866; Nathaniel Emerson to Joseph Emerson, October 22, 1894, box 20, EMR 867. All in Emerson Papers. See also Emerson, "The Mythical Story of Maui," 290; and Emerson, *Unwritten Literature of Hawaii*, 227.
132. Albert Francis Judd [Jr.] to Nathaniel Emerson, January 15, 1901, box 23, EMR 1186; Nathaniel Emerson to Titus Munson Coan, April 9, 1902, EMR 1315; Nathaniel Emerson to George Wilcox, September 24, 1900, EMR 1315; Nathaniel Emerson to George Wilcox, April 11, 1901, EMR 1315; Nathaniel Emerson to Albert Wilcox, April 11, 1901, EMR 1315. All in Emerson Papers.
133. Nathaniel Emerson, "The Hula Pele," undated, box 9, EMR 332, Emerson Papers.
134. For a later twentieth-century example, see Gin Lum, *Heathen*, 195–97.
135. Tony Ballantyne has shown this in the case of ethnologists studying the Māori in Ballantyne, *Orientalism and Race*, 118–20.

136. Gin Lum, *Heathen*, 198.
137. Gin Lum, *Heathen*, 207.
138. Lears, *No Place of Grace*.
139. Nathaniel Emerson, "The Last of His Line" (second draft of a short story), n.d. [1904], box 14, EMR 472; Nathaniel Emerson, "The Prick of Honor" (final draft of a short story), 1904, box 15, EMR 537. Both in Emerson Papers.
140. Daniel M. Murphy to Nathaniel Emerson, December 13, 1906, box 24, EMR 1229, Emerson Papers.
141. Nathaniel Emerson to W. C. Morrow, July 24, 1905, EMR 1316, Emerson Papers.
142. Nathaniel Emerson to W. C. Morrow, July 24, 1905, EMR 1316, and Nathaniel Emerson to W. H. Holmes, February 5, 1908, EMR 1316, both in Emerson Papers; Emerson, *Unwritten Literature of Hawaii*, 261; Emerson, "General Remarks on Translation."
143. Nathaniel Emerson, "Unwritten Literature of Hawaii," n.d. [1908], EMR 1316, Emerson Papers.
144. McGregor, *Nā Kuaʻāina*, 187.
145. Emerson, *Pele and Hiiaka*, xxi–xxii.
146. Nathaniel Emerson, "A Hawaiian Chap Book" (third draft), 1907, box 13, EMR 430, Emerson Papers, emphasis in original.
147. Emerson, *Unwritten Literature of Hawaii*, 9.
148. Emerson, *Unwritten Literature of Hawaii*, 226–27, 231.
149. Emerson, *Unwritten Literature of Hawaii*, 113, 120, 230, 233.
150. Silva, *Aloha Betrayed*, 76.
151. Nathaniel Emerson, "The Voyages of the Ancient Hawaiians," n.d. [1890], box 4, EMR 147, Emerson Papers.
152. Nathaniel Emerson to George Wilcox, September 24, 1900, EMR 1315. For Emerson's suggestion that annexation resulted in improved opportunities for extracting lore from Native Hawaiians, see Nathaniel Emerson to Dorothea Lamb Emerson, November 20, 1898, box 18, EMR 732. Both documents in Emerson Papers.
153. Nachman, "Lies My Informants Told Me," 538. For evidence that the payment of money to extract narratives was a broader phenomenon across Pacific contexts, see Ballantyne, *Orientalism and Race*, 121.
154. Barrow, "Introduction to the New Edition," xvii–xviii.
155. Gin Lum, *Heathen*, 202; McDougall, "Moʻokūʻauhau versus Colonial Entitlement," 755. For evidence that Emerson made use of newspaper accounts himself, see Emerson, *Pele and Hiiaka*, xxi.
156. Lyon, "Davida Malo, Nathaniel Emerson, and the "Sins" of Hawaiians."
157. Nathaniel Emerson, "Comrades of the Grand Army of the Republic" (final draft of speech), 1891, box 11, EMR 388; Nathaniel Emerson, "Programme for Decoration Day" (speech), 1884, box 15, EMR 538; Isaac P. Gragg to Nathaniel Emerson, July 24, 1911, box 23, EMR 1173. All in Emerson Papers.
158. Emerson, "The Prick of Honor."
159. Nathaniel Emerson to W. C. Morrow, October 5, 1903, EMR 1315, Emerson Papers.
160. Schulz, *Hawaiian by Birth*, 110–13, 134–35.
161. Quoted in Schulz, *Hawaiian by Birth*, 155.
162. Schulz, *Hawaiian by Birth*, chap. 2.
163. Memmi, *The Colonizer and the Colonized*, 60–64.
164. Emerson, "The Mythical Story of Maui"; Emerson, "Unwritten Literature of Hawaii" (*American Anthropologist*).

165. Nathaniel Emerson to G. P. Putnam's Sons, December 14, 1901, EMR 1315; Nathaniel Emerson to Harper and Brothers, December 16, 1901, EMR 1315; Nathaniel Emerson to Titus Munson Coan, June 16, 1902, EMR 1315. All in Emerson Papers.

166. On deepening divisions between science and literature in the late nineteenth century and the unsuccessful attempts of certain American authors to continue drawing the two together, see Vandome, "American Scientists and Their Fictions."

167. Harriet Christiana Peirce to Arthur Webster Emerson, December 20, 1920, box 24, EMR 1239, Emerson Papers.

168. "Hula-Hula Dances Scientifically Investigated at Last," *New York Daily Tribune*, January 23, 1910, 3.

169. Barrow, "Introduction to the New Edition," xi–xii.

170. On the links between certain presentations of *hula*, the myth of Native Hawaiian passivity, and the commodification of Hawaiian culture, see Imada, *Aloha America*, 9–15.

Part II. The Philippines

1. Coffman, *Nation Within*, 289–93, 300.
2. Sereno Bishop to Gorham D. Gilman, June 16, 1898, Sereno Bishop Papers, Children of the Mission Collection, Hawaiian Mission Children's Society, Honolulu (hereafter Sereno Bishop Papers, Children of the Mission Collection).
3. Coffman, *Nation Within*, 295.
4. Coffman, *Nation Within*, 307.
5. Gonzalez, *Securing Paradise*, 41–42.
6. Sereno Bishop to Gorham D. Gilman, February 27, 1899, Sereno Bishop Papers, Children of the Mission Collection.
7. "Hawaii's Responsibilities to the Philippines," *The Friend*, October 1898, 77.
8. Alexander, "Report of the Corresponding Secretary for the Year Ending November 28, 1899," 8; Sewall, "Part of a Paper on the Partition of Samoa and the Past Relations between that Group and the United States"; "A Letter from Prof. Townsend"; Alexander, "President's Address," 8.
9. Alexander, "Report of the Corresponding Secretary for the Year Ending November 28, 1904," 11.
10. Chakrabarty, "The Time of History and the Times of Gods," 36.
11. Clymer, *Protestant Missionaries in the Philippines*, 191.

4. "A Sudden Turn of History"

1. Beveridge, "The March of the Flag."
2. Love, *Race over Empire*, 166–67, 181–94.
3. Kramer, *The Blood of Government*, 164–65.
4. "Interview with President William McKinley," *Christian Advocate*, January 22, 1903, 17.
5. McKinley quoted in Brown, *The New Era in the Philippines*, 296; Guyatt, *Providence and the Invention of the United States*, 6.
6. For the longer history of Providence in American thought, see Guyatt, *Providence and the Invention of the United States*. On "Christian nationalism" and its role in stoking US empire,

see McCullough, *The Cross of War*, 4–5. On the role of Protestant thought more broadly, see Hudson, "Protestant Clergy Debate the Nation's Vocation"; Miller, *"Benevolent Assimilation,"* 17–19; Smylie, "Protestant Clergymen and American Destiny"; Welch, *Response to Imperialism*, chap. VI.

7. Hofstadter, *The Paranoid Style in American Politics and Other Essays*, 177–78; Weinberg, *Manifest Destiny*, chap. IX.
8. Harris, *God's Arbiters*, 18–19, 30.
9. Clymer, *Protestant Missionaries in the Philippines*, 5.
10. Pease et al., *Mahlon Johnson Family of Littleton, New Jersey*, 49.
11. Clymer, *Protestant Missionaries in the Philippines*, 6.
12. Rodgers, *Forty Years in the Philippines*.
13. Brown, *The New Era in the Philippines*, 207; "Presbyterian Work in the Philippines, 1899–1912," *Assembly Herald*, October 1912, 525.
14. Prieto, "'Stepmother America,'" 360.
15. Moots, *Pioneer "Americanas,"* 5–12; "Woman's Work in the Philippines," *Woman's Missionary Friend*, November 1906, 386.
16. "Fellowship in the Philippines," *Woman's Missionary Friend*, May 1924, 169.
17. "II. The Ellinwood School for Girls," *Assembly Herald*, July 1908, 319–20; Prieto, "'New Women,' American Imperialism and Filipina Nationalism," 87.
18. Prieto, "'Stepmother America,'" 348; "Woman's Work in the Philippines," *Woman's Missionary Friend*, July 1906, 234.
19. Clymer, *Protestant Missionaries in the Philippines*, 5–8.
20. Welch, *Response to Imperialism*, 97–98.
21. Clymer, *Protestant Missionaries in the Philippines*, 6.
22. Norbeck, "The Legacy of Charles Henry Brent."
23. Clymer, *Protestant Missionaries in the Philippines*, 6–7.
24. "Abstract of Proceedings of the Executive Committee," *Baptist Missionary Magazine*, January 1900, 60.
25. Clymer, *Protestant Missionaries in the Philippines*, 29, 81–84.
26. "Eighty-Ninth Annual Meeting," *Baptist Missionary Magazine*, July 1903, 252.
27. Clymer, *Protestant Missionaries in the Philippines*, 7.
28. Hollinger, *Protestants Abroad*, 253–57.
29. Prieto, "'Stepmother America,'" 343.
30. Moots, *Pioneer "Americanas,"* 15.
31. Brown, *The New Era in the Philippines*, chap. XI.
32. Brown, *The New Era in the Philippines*, chaps. XVII–XVIII.
33. Brown, *The New Era in the Philippines*, 190–92.
34. "Mission to the Philippines," *Missionary Herald*, November 1903, 486–87.
35. On Episcopal work in northern Luzon, see Jones, *Christian Missions in the American Empire*. On Brent's work in Mindanao and Sulu, see Spencer, *What the Golden Rule Has Accomplished among the Moros*.
36. Rafael, *White Love and Other Events in Filipino History*, chap. 2; Moots, *Pioneer "Americanas,"* 35.
37. Moots, *Pioneer "Americanas,"* 45–46.
38. "Snapshots from the Mary Johnston Hospital," *Woman's Missionary Friend*, January 1920, 3–6.
39. Prieto, "'Stepmother America.'"

40. Warne, "Prefatory Note."
41. Montgomery, *Christus Redemptor.*
42. "United Study of Missions," *Woman's Missionary Friend*, April 1906, 126–27.
43. Waterbury et al., "Foreword."
44. "The Awakening of a Missionary Society," *Life and Light for Woman*, July 1899, 330.
45. Quoted in Moots, *Pioneer "Americanas,"* 13.
46. Stuntz, *The Philippines and the Far East*, 136.
47. Brown, *Report of a Visitation of the Philippine Mission of the Board of Foreign Missions of the Presbyterian Church*, 85.
48. Brown, *The New Era in the Philippines*, 301.
49. Brown, *The New Era in the Philippines*, 155–56.
50. Charles Brent, text of final sermon in Boston, n.d. [1902], box 25, Sermon Notes 1901–2, Charles Henry Brent Papers, Manuscript Division, Library of Congress, Washington, DC (hereafter Brent Papers).
51. Stuntz, *The Philippines and the Far East*, 509.
52. 33 Cong. Rec., part 1, 710–12 (1900).
53. Eperjesi, *The Imperialist Imaginary*, 155–56.
54. Kramer, *The Blood of Government*, 130–57.
55. Kramer, *The Blood of Government*, 42–63.
56. On the exclusivity of the Propagandists' "nationalist colonialism," see Kramer, *The Blood of Government*, 73.
57. Kramer, *The Blood of Government*, 73–81.
58. Kramer, *The Blood of Government*, 92–111.
59. Hudson, "Protestant Clergy Debate the Nation's Vocation," 118; McCullough, *The Cross of War*, 8.
60. Francis M. Price speech, April 23, 1900, box 3, folder 12, Ecumenical Conference on Foreign Missions Records, 1900-04–1900-05, Burke Library, Union Theological Seminary, Columbia University, New York.
61. Alidio, "'When I Get Home, I Want to Forget,'" 114–15.
62. "What Will the United States Do with the Philippines?," *Woman's Missionary Friend*, June 1908, 194–95; "How Are We Treating Our Little Brown Brother?," *Life and Light for Woman*, March 1907, 101–5.
63. Miller, *"Benevolent Assimilation,"* 248; Stuntz, *The Philippines and the Far East*, 150.
64. Brown, *The New Era in the Philippines*, 297.
65. Johnson, "The Legacy of Arthur Judson Brown."
66. Responses from numerous boards to Arthur Judson Brown's proposal for a conference on opening foreign mission work in Cuba, Puerto Rico, and the Philippines, 1898, vol. 259, no. 1, Board of Foreign Missions Correspondence and Reports, National Archives of the Presbyterian Church of the United States of America, Presbyterian Historical Society, Philadelphia, Pennsylvania (hereafter Board of Foreign Missions Correspondence and Reports).
67. "Action of a Conference of Representatives of the Boards of Foreign Missions of the U.S. and Canada, Touching Missionary Work in Cuba, Porto Rico, the Philippine Islands, etc.," n.d. [1898], vol. 259, no. 2, Board of Foreign Missions Correspondence and Reports.
68. David S. Hibbard to F. F. Ellinwood, May 31, 1899, vol. 259, no. 20, Board of Foreign Missions Correspondence and Reports.
69. Charles Brent to Bishops Potter, Doane, Satterlee, and Leonard, October 26, 1901, box 5, Brent Papers.

70. H. Y. Satterlee to Charles Brent, October 15, 1901, box 5, Brent Papers.

71. Joshua Kimber to Mercer Johnston, January 20, 1903, box 38, Mercer Green Johnston Papers, Manuscript Division, Library of Congress, Washington, DC (hereafter Johnston Papers).

72. Presbyterian Board of Foreign Missions to Philippine Mission, April 9, 1920, RG 85, box 4, folder 8, Board of Foreign Missions Correspondence and Reports.

73. Homer Stuntz to H. W. Warren, January 5, 1905, reel 24, Methodist Episcopal Church Missionary Correspondence 1846–1912, United Methodist Church General Commission on Archives and History, Madison, New Jersey (hereafter Methodist Episcopal Church Missionary Correspondence).

74. C. H. Daniels to Arthur Judson Brown, June 23, 1898, in Responses from numerous boards to Arthur Judson Brown's proposal for a conference.

75. Stuntz, *The Philippines and the Far East*, 421.

76. Pentecost, *Protestantism in the Philippines*, 20.

77. James B. Rodgers, "Lessons from Five Years of Protestant Work in the Philippine Islands," 1905, vol. 263, no. 37, Board of Foreign Missions Correspondence and Reports.

78. Briggs, *The Progressing Philippines*, 163.

79. Mercer Johnston, "America's Duty in the Far East," n.d. [1918], box 83, folder 129, Johnston Papers.

80. "Strategic Points—California," *Assembly Herald*, April 1902, 146; "The Outlook Across the Pacific," *Assembly Herald*, January 1901, 6–7.

81. "Presbyterian Imperialism," *Assembly Herald*, January 1899, 6.

82. "Our Island Possessions," *Assembly Herald*, January 1900, 342.

83. "Scraps from Our Work Basket," *Life and Light for Woman*, February 1899, 68–69.

84. "United Study of Missions 1906–1907," *Woman's Missionary Friend*, July 1906, 249; "For the Study of the Island World," *Woman's Missionary Friend*, October 1906, front matter; "Twenty Helpful Books in the Study of 'Christus Redemptor,'" *Woman's Missionary Friend*, October 1906, 352–53; "Our Loan Library," *Woman's Missionary Friend*, January 1907, 31; "The Reference Library," *Life and Light for Woman*, November 1906, 483.

85. Alexander, *The Islands of the Pacific*.

86. "The Island World," *Woman's Missionary Friend*, December 1906, 420–22.

87. "The Future of the Pacific Ocean," *Silliman Truth*, March 1903, 3.

88. J. Andrew Hall to F. F. Ellinwood, November 22, 1899, Philippine Letters—Outgoing, February 27, 1899 to October 7, 1902, no. 15, Board of Foreign Missions Correspondence and Reports.

89. Brent, *Religious Conditions in the Philippine Islands*.

90. Evangelical Union, "Statement," 1904, vol. 1, no. 9, Philippine Islands Mission, Papers of the American Board of Commissioners for Foreign Missions, Houghton Library, Harvard University, Cambridge, Massachusetts (hereafter Philippine Islands Mission).

91. Stealy B. Rossiter, "The Philippines: Before and After the Occupation, May 1, 1898," n.d. [1909], supplement to Stealy B. Rossiter to Arthur Judson Brown, January 31, 1909, vol. 267, no. 14, Board of Foreign Missions Correspondence and Reports.

92. Pierson, *The Crisis of Missions*, 273–74.

93. Pierson, *The Crisis of Missions*, 292–94.

94. Pierson, *The Crisis of Missions*, chaps. XXVII–XXXV.

95. Mott, *The Evangelization of the World in This Generation*. On Strong's view of history, see Stephanson, *Manifest Destiny*, 79–80.

96. Brent, text of final sermon in Boston.

97. Charles Brent, "With God in the Nation," n.d., box 25, Sermon Notes 1901–2; Charles Brent, "The Growth of the Higher Patriotism," n.d., box 25, Sermon Notes 1901–2. Both in Brent Papers.
98. Brent, "The Growth of the Higher Patriotism."
99. Brent, "With God in the Nation."
100. Brent, "The Growth of the Higher Patriotism."
101. Kramer, *The Blood of Government*, 116–20; Bell, *Dreamworlds of Race*, 92–93.
102. On cyclical understandings of history in the United States and the American relationship with historicism, see Allen, *A Republic in Time*, chap. 1; Bendroth, *The Last Puritans*, chap. 5; Bendroth, "Time, History, and Tradition in the Fundamentalist Imagination," 335; Marsden, *Fundamentalism and American Culture*, 225–26; Ross, "Historical Consciousness in Nineteenth-Century America"; and Shalev, *Rome Reborn on Western Shores*.
103. Bercovitch, *The American Jeremiad*.
104. *Official Journal of the Second Annual Convention of the Missionary District of the Philippine Islands*, 19, italics in original.
105. Brown, *Report of a Visitation of the Philippine Mission of the Board of Foreign Missions of the Presbyterian Church*, 89.
106. Brown, *The New Era in the Philippines*, 5–6.
107. Johnston, *Plain American Talk in the Philippines*, 179, 189–90.
108. Turner, "The Significance of the Frontier in American History."
109. Eperjesi, *The Imperialist Imaginary*, chaps. 2–3.
110. Roosevelt, "The Strenuous Life."
111. "The World Movement," *Philippine Presbyterian*, July 1910, 2.
112. "VII. Missions in the Philippine Islands," *Baptist Missionary Magazine*, July 1904, 507.
113. Charles Brent report, n.d., box 6, folder 9, World Missionary Conference Records 1883–1910, Burke Library, Union Theological Seminary, Columbia University, New York.
114. Evangelical Union, "Statement."
115. Briggs, *The Progressing Philippines*, 169.
116. Briggs, *The Progressing Philippines*, 172.
117. Frank Laubach to James L. Barton, March 4, 1915, vol. 2, no. 227, Philippine Islands Mission.
118. Frank Laubach to James L. Barton, December 15, 1915, vol. 2, no. 243, Philippine Islands Mission.
119. Hibbard, *Making a Nation*, 119–20.
120. Moots, *Pioneer "Americanas,"* 31.
121. Wenger, *Religious Freedom*, 16–17.
122. For missionary acknowledgements of the importance of church-state separation, see F. F. Ellinwood to Presbyterian Alliance, October 20, 1899, vol. 259, no. 35, Board of Foreign Missions Correspondence and Reports; Brown, *The New Era in the Philippines*, 147; Brown, *Report of a Visitation of the Philippine Mission of the Board of Foreign Missions of the Presbyterian Church*, 33–34.
123. Miller, *"Benevolent Assimilation,"* 139.
124. Diary entry for May 25, 1899, box 418, Philippines Notebook & Related Papers, Albert J. Beveridge Papers, Manuscript Division, Library of Congress, Washington, DC.
125. James B. Rodgers to F. F. Ellinwood, May 5, 1899, vol. 259, no. 19, Board of Foreign Missions Correspondence and Reports.
126. Moran, *The Imperial Church*, 194–200; Wenger, *Religious Freedom*, 40–41; "Speech of Congressman Bourke Cochran at Banquet of Archbishop of Manila Jeremiah J. Harty, printed in *The Cablenews*, August 19, 1905," box 4, W. Cameron Forbes Papers, Houghton Library, Har-

vard University, Cambridge, Massachusetts. See also Reuter, *Catholic Influence on American Colonial Policies*.

127. William Howard Taft to Elihu Root, January 29, 1901, series 8, Philippine Commission vol. 1, William Howard Taft Papers, Manuscript Division, Library of Congress, Washington, DC (hereafter Taft Papers).

128. Quoted in Brown, *Report of a Visitation of the Philippine Mission of the Board of Foreign Missions of the Presbyterian Church*, 71.

129. Addendum (October 13, 1900) to William Howard Taft to Elihu Root, October 10, 1900, series 8, Philippine Commission vol. 1, Taft Papers; Brown, *The New Era in the Philippines*, 148.

130. Addendum (October 13, 1900); William Howard Taft to Elihu Root, October 29, 1902, series 8, Philippine Commission vol. 1, Taft Papers.

131. Raferty, "Textbook Wars," 150.

132. Raferty, "Textbook Wars," 144–46.

133. James B. Rodgers to F. F. Ellinwood, July 17, 1899, vol. 259, no. 26, Board of Foreign Missions Correspondence and Reports.

134. Robert F. Black to Judson Smith, March 30, 1906, vol. 1, no. 83, Philippine Islands Mission.

135. There are multiple examples of Forbes's attitudes toward missionaries in his journal entries for April 27, 1906 to April 16, 1908, in Journal of W. Cameron Forbes, vol. 2, W. Cameron Forbes Papers, Manuscript Division, Library of Congress, Washington, DC.

136. For descriptions of US teachers as "missionaries," see Kramer, *The Blood of Government*, 169; and Steinbock-Pratt, *Educating the Empire*, 1.

137. Kramer, *The Blood of Government*, 199–205; Steinbock-Pratt, *Educating the Empire*, 213.

138. Steinbock-Pratt, *Educating the Empire*, 30–31; Raferty, "Textbook Wars."

139. For example, see David P. Barrows, "Religious Teaching Forbidden," Bureau of Education Circular No. 32, March 11, 1908, vol. 267, no. 27, Board of Foreign Missions Correspondence and Reports.

140. Steinbock-Pratt, *Educating the Empire*, 232–33.

141. Supplement to Lewis B. Hillis to Arthur Judson Brown, August 26, 1903, vol. 261, no. 67, Board of Foreign Missions Correspondence and Reports.

142. Brown, *The New Era in the Philippines*, 152.

143. George W. Wright to Arthur Judson Brown, April 3, 1905, vol. 263, no. 43, Board of Foreign Missions Correspondence and Reports; Marvin A. Rader to A. B. Leonard, May 6, 1911, reel 24, Methodist Episcopal Church Missionary Correspondence; Brown, *The New Era in the Philippines*, 163.

144. Supplement to James B. Rodgers to F. F. Ellinwood, October 4, 1899, vol. 259, no. 36, and Charles E. Rath to Arthur Judson Brown, May 16, 1904, vol. 262, no. 53, both in Board of Foreign Missions Correspondence and Reports; Brown, *The New Era in the Philippines*, chap. X; Pentecost, *Protestantism in the Philippines*, 17; Stuntz, *The Philippines and the Far East*, 352–55, 479.

145. Moots, *Pioneer "Americanas,"* 24.

146. On the reimagining of Catholic history in US imperial contexts, including the Philippines, see Moran, "Catholicism and the Making of the U.S. Pacific"; and Moran, *The Imperial Church*.

147. Kramer, *The Blood of Government*, 211.

148. Oscar Huddleston to A. B. Leonard, July 26, 1909, reel 24, Methodist Episcopal Church Missionary Correspondence.

149. Brown, *The New Era in the Philippines*, 260.

150. Johnston, *Plain American Talk in the Philippines*, 170–74.

151. Johnston, *Plain American Talk in the Philippines*, 84–85.
152. Mercer Johnston to Cyrus L. Pickett, December 4, 1907; Mercer Johnston to Ernest A. Rayner, March 2, 1908. Both in box 39, letterbook 1, Johnston Papers.
153. Homer C. Stuntz to A. B. Leonard, December 24, 1903, reel 24, Methodist Episcopal Church Missionary Correspondence.
154. Clymer, *Protestant Missionaries in the Philippines*, 171.
155. Arthur W. Prautch, "A Crime, Not a Blunder," [1899], reel 24, Methodist Episcopal Church Missionary Correspondence.
156. Johnston, *Plain American Talk in the Philippines*, 11; Stuntz, *The Philippines and the Far East*, 290.
157. Stuntz, *The Philippines and the Far East*, 284.
158. Stuntz, *The Philippines and the Far East*, 351.
159. Stuntz, *The Philippines and the Far East*, 91, 109, 360.
160. Stuntz, *The Philippines and the Far East*, 364–72, chaps. VI–VII.
161. Clymer, *Protestant Missionaries in the Philippines*, 161–62.
162. Memmi, *The Colonizer and the Colonized*, 61–62.
163. Edith to Charles Brent, [1901], box 5, Brent Papers, emphasis in original.
164. Johnston, *Plain American Talk in the Philippines*, 128–30.
165. Clymer, *Protestant Missionaries in the Philippines*, 138.
166. William A. Tener to Bayard W. Christy, October 24, 1911, box 1, Correspondence 1910–11, International Work in the Philippines, Kautz Family YMCA Archives, Elmer L. Andersen Library, University of Minnesota, Minneapolis.
167. Robert F. Black to Judson Smith, May 10, 1904, vol. 1, no. 62, Philippine Islands Mission.
168. Robert F. Black to Judson Smith, November 11, 1904, vol. 1, no. 69, Philippine Islands Mission.
169. "The Philippine Islands," *Baptist Missionary Magazine*, July 1903, 520; "VII. Missions in the Philippine Islands," *Baptist Missionary Magazine*, July 1905, 513.
170. Clymer, *Protestant Missionaries in the Philippines*, 94.
171. Hawkins, *Making Moros*, 4, 24.

5. "A Dark and Troubled Past"

1. W. H. Lingle to F. F. Ellinwood, January 17, 1899, vol. 259, no. 6, Board of Foreign Missions Correspondence and Reports, National Archives of the Presbyterian Church of the United States of America, Presbyterian Historical Society, Philadelphia, Pennsylvania (hereafter Board of Foreign Missions Correspondence and Reports).
2. Stuntz, *The Philippines and the Far East*, 383.
3. Hawkins, *Making Moros*, 5; Harris, *God's Arbiters*, 18–19.
4. Kramer, *The Blood of Government*, 200–201.
5. Kramer, *The Blood of Government*, 191–92.
6. Hawkins, *Making Moros*. For a comprehensive history of US governance among Muslims in the southern Philippines, see Charbonneau, *Civilizational Imperatives*.
7. Johnston, *Plain American Talk in the Philippines*, 28–29.
8. Briggs, *The Progressing Philippines*, chap. III; Stuntz, *The Philippines and the Far East*, chap. III.

9. Roy H. Brown to Mr. Comstock, August 17, 1905, vol. 263, no. 87, Board of Foreign Missions Correspondence and Reports.

10. Stuntz, *The Philippines and the Far East*, 389–91.

11. Briggs, *The Progressing Philippines*, 93–94.

12. Brown, *Report of a Visitation of the Philippine Mission of the Board of Foreign Missions of the Presbyterian Church*, 1.

13. Gin Lum, *Heathen*, 12, 180.

14. Lears, *No Place of Grace*, chaps. 4–5.

15. Johnston, *Plain American Talk in the Philippines*, 121–22, emphasis in original.

16. Brown, *The New Era in the Philippines*, 52; Briggs, *The Progressing Philippines*, 95.

17. "What Jesus Christ Did with Heretics," *Filipino Student's Companion*, January 1908, 5.

18. Fred Simpich, "Some Features of Manila Life," April 30, 1903, newspaper clipping, series VIII, box 175, folder 2978, John R. Mott Papers, Special Collections, Yale Divinity School, New Haven, Connecticut; Theodore Roosevelt in Kaplan, *The Anarchy of Empire*, 13; Daniel Williams in Go, "Introduction," 1.

19. On the importance of Bible translation and distribution to missionaries, see Briggs, *The Progressing Philippines*, 125–28; Brown, *The New Era in the Philippines*, 216–18; Stuntz, *The Philippines and the Far East*, chap. XXII.

20. Brown, *The New Era in the Philippines*, 143; Brown, *Report of a Visitation of the Philippine Mission of the Board of Foreign Missions of the Presbyterian Church*, 78.

21. Brown, *The New Era in the Philippines*, 163.

22. Briggs, *The Progressing Philippines*, 106–7.

23. Laubach, *The People of the Philippines*, viii.

24. Brown, *Report of a Visitation of the Philippine Mission of the Board of Foreign Missions of the Presbyterian Church*, 2–3.

25. Condict, *Old Glory and the Gospel in the Philippines*, 92.

26. Supplement to F. F. Ellinwood to Presbyterian Alliance, October 20, 1899, vol. 259, no. 35, Board of Foreign Missions Correspondence and Reports.

27. Stuntz, *The Philippines and the Far East*, 215.

28. Briggs, *The Progressing Philippines*, 170.

29. Entry for September 6, 1906, box 1, Diary for 1906, Charles Henry Brent Papers, Manuscript Division, Library of Congress, Washington, DC (hereafter Brent Papers).

30. Entry for October 15, 1903, box 1, Diary for 1903, Brent Papers.

31. Entry for February 6, 1903, box 2, Diary for 1903, Brent Papers.

32. Entry for December 13, 1903, box 1, Diary for 1903, Brent Papers.

33. Entry for December 18, 1902, box 1, Diary for 1902, Brent Papers.

34. Charles Brent to John W. Wood, February 11, 1907, box 6, Brent Papers.

35. Charles Brent to Mrs. Frederick Greeley, January 29, 1915, box 10, Brent Papers.

36. James B. Rodgers report, box 6, folder 9, World Missionary Conference Records 1883–1910, Burke Library, Union Theological Seminary, Columbia University, New York.

37. Charles T. and A. E. Sibley to James L. Barton, April 19, 1910, vol. 2, no. 13; Charles T. Sibley to James L. Barton, October 30, 1911, vol. 2, no. 339. Both in Philippine Islands Mission, Papers of the American Board of Commissioners for Foreign Missions, Houghton Library, Harvard University, Cambridge, Massachusetts (hereafter Philippine Islands Mission).

38. "Our Work in Manila," *Woman's Missionary Friend*, July 1910, 231.

39. Roy H. Brown to Arthur Judson Brown, August 13, 1904, vol. 262, no. 83, Board of Foreign Missions Correspondence and Reports.

40. Roy H. Brown to Mr. Comstock, August 17, 1905, vol. 263, no. 87, Board of Foreign Missions Correspondence and Reports.

41. James B. Rodgers to F. F. Ellinwood, September 21, 1900, vol. 259, no. 93, Board of Foreign Missions Correspondence and Reports.

42. James B. Rodgers, "Lessons from Five Years of Protestant Work in the Philippine Islands," 1905, vol. 263, no. 37, Board of Foreign Missions Correspondence and Reports.

43. Rodgers report.

44. General Basilio Augusti y Davila quoted in Laubach, *The People of the Philippines*, 120.

45. Kramer, *The Blood of Government*, 208–14.

46. David S. Hibbard to F. F. Ellinwood, June 6, 1899, vol. 259, no. 21, Board of Foreign Missions Correspondence and Reports.

47. Robert F. Black to Judson Smith, April 13, 1903, vol. 1, no. 30, Philippine Islands Mission; Edward A. Sibley to Charles Brent, August 25, 1916, box 11, Brent Papers; P. F. Jansen to F. F. Ellinwood, December 23, 1902, vol. 260, no. 119, Board of Foreign Missions Correspondence and Reports; F. J. Purcell to Arthur Judson Brown, September 9, 1903, vol. 261, no. 71, Board of Foreign Missions Correspondence and Reports; Lilian Holmes Graham to Arthur Judson Brown, December 16, 1907, vol. 265, no. 94, Board of Foreign Missions Correspondence and Reports.

48. C. N. Magill to Arthur Judson Brown, July 7, 1910, vol. 268, no. 43, Board of Foreign Missions Correspondence and Reports; Communication sent by the Philippine Mission to the ABCFM, received July 19, 1915, n.d. [1915], vol. 2, no. 55, Philippine Islands Mission; Laubach, *The People of the Philippines*, chap. XXXI.

49. Brown, *The New Era in the Philippines*, 211.

50. J. Andrew Hall to F. F. Ellinwood, February 4, 1902, vol. 260, no. 82, Board of Foreign Missions Correspondence and Reports.

51. Frank J. Woodward to James L. Barton, August 3, 1917, vol. 2, no. 422, Philippine Islands Mission.

52. Pierson, *The Crisis of Missions*, 19.

53. Pierson, *The Crisis of Missions*, 5, 12.

54. Stuntz, *The Philippines and the Far East*, 409–12.

55. On the idea of Catholic declension, see Brent, *Religious Conditions in the Philippine Islands*; Hibbard, *Making a Nation*, 92; Moran, "Catholicism and the Making of the U.S. Pacific," 454.

56. Briggs, *The Progressing Philippines*, 160–63.

57. Brent, *Religious Conditions in the Philippine Islands*.

58. J. M. Groves, "Annual Report, October 1, 1910 to September 30, 1911," 1911, box 5, Administrative Reports 1910–12, International Work in the Philippines, Kautz Family YMCA Archives, Elmer L. Andersen Library, University of Minnesota, Minneapolis (hereafter International Work in the Philippines).

59. "Slavery in the Sulu Archipelago," *The Outlook*, December 2, 1899, 765.

60. Brown, *The New Era in the Philippines*, 168, 210; Stuntz, *The Open Door in the Philippines*, 7; Stuntz, *The Philippines and the Far East*, 88–90.

61. Rodgers report.

62. P. F. Jansen to F. F. Ellinwood, December 23, 1902, vol. 260, no. 119, Board of Foreign Missions Correspondence and Reports.

63. Roy H. Brown to Mr. Comstock, April 8, 1907, vol. 265, no. 29, Board of Foreign Missions Correspondence and Reports; Laubach, *The People of the Philippines*, 141–42.

64. C. N. Magill to Arthur Judson Brown, December 22, 1908, vol. 266, no. 70, Board of Foreign Missions Correspondence and Reports.

65. Roy H. Brown to Mr. Comstock, April 8, 1907, vol. 265, no. 29, Board of Foreign Missions Correspondence and Reports.

66. Stuntz, *The Philippines and the Far East*, 495.

67. On the broader Protestant tendency to view Catholicism as monolithic, see Smith, *Gothic Arches, Latin Crosses*, 14–15.

68. Brown, *The New Era in the Philippines*, 170.

69. Brown, *The New Era in the Philippines*, 195.

70. Brown, *The New Era in the Philippines*, 275–76.

71. "New Era in the Philippines," *The Outlook*, December 5, 1903, 862.

72. Quoted in Brown, *Report of a Visitation of the Philippine Mission of the Board of Foreign Missions of the Presbyterian Church*, 44.

73. H. W. Langheim to Arthur Judson Brown, February 25, 1905, vol. 263, no. 22, Board of Foreign Missions Correspondence and Reports.

74. Prieto, "'Stepmother America,'" 343.

75. For expressions of this idea in relation to the Philippines, see Brent, *Religious Conditions in the Philippine Islands*; Briggs, *The Progressing Philippines*, 94, 140; Condict, *Old Glory and the Gospel in the Philippines*, 96; Stuntz, *The Philippines and the Far East*, 93, 476. For evidence that this was a broader missionary attitude, see Mrs. McLaren's statement, April 26, 1900, in box 2, folder 4, Ecumenical Conference on Foreign Missions Records, 1900-04–1900-05, Burke Library, Union Theological Seminary, Columbia University, New York. For evidence that these perceptions of women were present among missionaries almost a century before, see Gin Lum, *Heathen*, 109–10.

76. Briggs, *The Progressing Philippines*, 150.

77. "Bible Training for Filipina Women," *Woman's Missionary Friend*, May 1907, 161; "The Filipina Woman a Comerciante," *Woman's Missionary Friend*, March 1910, 79; Prieto, "'New Women,' American Imperialism and Filipina Nationalism," 84.

78. "Candles and Clouds," *Woman's Missionary Friend*, March 1922, 90–91.

79. James B. Rodgers to Arthur Judson Brown, March 6, 1908, vol. 266, no. 21, Board of Foreign Missions Correspondence and Reports.

80. Roy H. Brown to Arthur Judson Brown, March 30, 1910, vol. 268, no. 23, Board of Foreign Missions Correspondence and Reports.

81. "Christmas in the Philippines," *Woman's Missionary Friend*, December 1907, 419.

82. Advertisement for a "Passion Play," October 17, 1905, box 21, Misc. Pamphlets 1902–9, International Work in the Philippines. For more on the Filipino relationship with the narrative of Christ's passion, see Blanco, *Frontier Constitutions*, chap. 3; Ileto, *Pasyon and Revolution*, 11–16.

83. Kramer, *The Blood of Government*, 209; Steinbock-Pratt, *Educating the Empire*, 19.

84. Condict, *Old Glory and the Gospel in the Philippines*, 36–49.

85. Brent, *Religious Conditions in the Philippine Islands*; supplement to Lewis B. Hillis to Arthur Judson Brown, August 26, 1903, vol. 261, no. 67, Board of Foreign Missions Correspondence and Reports; "Thanksgiving in Manila," *New York Observer*, May 4, 1905, 567.

86. Gonzalez, *Securing Paradise*, 52–53.

87. Briggs, *Progressing Philippines*, 25.

88. Condict, *Old Glory and the Gospel in the Philippines*, 95.

89. Frank Laubach to James L. Barton, August 23, 1915, vol. 2, no. 233, Philippine Islands Mission.

90. Condict, *Old Glory and the Gospel in the Philippines*, 64. On the US army's looting and destruction of churches, see Mancini, *Art and War in the Pacific World*, chap. 5.

91. Condict, *Old Glory and the Gospel in the Philippines*, 20.

92. Condict, *Old Glory and the Gospel in the Philippines*, 22.

93. C. N. Magill to friends, January 1, 1906, vol. 264, no. 1, Board of Foreign Missions Correspondence and Reports.

94. Briggs, *The Progressing Philippines*, 202.

95. Wenger, *Religious Freedom*, 73–74, 79–80.

96. Laubach, *The People of the Philippines*, 149.

97. Mancini, *Art and War in the Pacific World*, 148.

98. Condict, *Old Glory and the Gospel in the Philippines*, 33–34.

99. "Our Post-Office Box," *Woman's Missionary Friend*, March 1905, 93.

100. Brown, *The New Era in the Philippines*, 197–200.

101. Brown, *The New Era in the Philippines*, 231; Briggs, *The Progressing Philippines*, 112–13.

102. J. Andrew Hall to George F. Pentecost, November 9, 1903, vol. 261, no. 87, Board of Foreign Missions Correspondence and Reports.

103. Brown, *Letters and Greeting to You*, 13–14.

104. "Ten Years' Advance at Laguna," *Assembly Herald*, October 1912, 532.

105. On Catholic opposition, see Lilian Holmes Graham to Arthur Judson Brown, August 21, 1907, vol. 265, no. 68, Board of Foreign Missions Correspondence and Reports.

106. Kershner, *The Head Hunter and Other Stories of the Philippines*, 17.

107. On the association of the hut with savagery, see Brody, "Building Empire," 124–25.

108. Anderson, *Colonial Pathologies*, 126; Brody, "Building Empire," 138–39; Lico, *Arkitekturang Filipino*, 244; McKenna, *American Imperial Pastoral*, 11; Morley, *Cities and Nationhood*; Robin, *Enclaves of America*, 23–25.

109. McKenna, *American Imperial Pastoral*, 19. On the adoption and modification of existing local styles and layouts in US colonial architecture, see Brody, "Building Empire," 128; Doeppers, "Manila's Imperial Makeover," 490–92; Lico, *Arkitekturang Filipino*, 198–99; Robin, *Enclaves of America*, 25–26. On the prevailing characterization of old Manila and its architecture as obsolete, see Mancini, *Art and War in the Pacific World*, 216–23.

110. Smith, *Gothic Arches, Latin Crosses*, 5, 8–10, 18.

111. W. H. Lingle to F. F. Ellinwood, January 17, 1899, vol. 259, no. 6, Board of Foreign Missions Correspondence and Reports; Chafee quoted in Brown, *The New Era in the Philippines*, 122.

112. September 23, 1901, series II, box 11, folder 16, book IIX, Arthur Judson Brown Papers, Special Collections, Yale Divinity School, New Haven, Connecticut.

113. For examples of competitive language, see Lewis B. Hillis to Arthur Judson Brown, August 26, 1903, vol. 261, no. 67, Board of Foreign Missions Correspondence and Reports; and "Monthly Survey," *Baptist Missionary Magazine*, November 1902, 674.

114. James B. Rodgers to F. F. Ellinwood, October 4, 1899, vol. 259, no. 36, Board of Foreign Missions Correspondence and Reports.

115. "An Urgent Call from Manila," *Assembly Herald*, December 1899, 300.

116. Stuntz, *Wanted: A Filipino Church in Old Manila*.

117. Robert F. Black to Judson Smith, February 1, 1905, vol. 1, no. 71; Robert F. Black to Judson Smith, January 4, 1905, vol. 1, no. 70. Both in Philippine Islands Mission.

118. "Mission to the Philippine Islands," *Missionary Herald*, June 1905, 295; Robert F. Black to Judson Smith, December 4, 1905, vol. 1, no. 81, and Robert F. Black to James L. Barton, July 26, 1912, vol. 2, no. 129, both in Philippine Islands Mission.

119. Supplement to Roy H. Brown to Arthur Judson Brown, March 30, 1910, vol. 268, no. 23; Roy H. Brown [to home church], November 6, 1906, vol. 264, no. 82. Both in Board of Foreign Missions Correspondence and Reports.

120. Supplement to James B. Rodgers to F. F. Ellinwood, October 4, 1899, vol. 259, no. 36, Board of Foreign Missions Correspondence and Reports.

121. Supplement to Harry Farmer to A. B. Leonard, n.d., reel 24, Methodist Episcopal Church Missionary Correspondence 1846–1912, United Methodist Church General Commission on Archives and History, Madison, New Jersey.

122. Henry Gilsheuser, untitled article (speech when laying cornerstone of Davao chapel, 1911), vol. 2, no. 81, Philippine Islands Mission.

123. Stuntz, *The Philippines and the Far East*, 383, 476.

124. Charles Brent to R. C. Sturgis, February 9, 1915, box 11, Brent Papers.

125. Mislin, *Saving Faith*, chap. 3.

126. Mislin, *Saving Faith*, 2–9.

127. Supplement to F. F. Ellinwood to Presbyterian Alliance, October 20, 1899, vol. 259, no. 35, Board of Foreign Missions Correspondence and Reports.

128. Briggs, *The Progressing Philippines*, 145, 149.

129. Charles Brent to H. H. Montgomery, January 26, 1907, box 6, Brent Papers.

130. Charles Brent to Silas McBee, February 22, 1907, box 6, Brent Papers.

131. Clymer, *Protestant Missionaries in the Philippines*, 27.

132. Entry for June 19, 1907, box 3, Notebook 1905, Mercer Green Johnston Papers, Manuscript Division, Library of Congress, Washington, DC (hereafter Johnston Papers).

133. Mercer Johnston to Irvin H. Correll, July 10, 1907, box 39, letterbook 1, Johnston Papers.

134. Mercer Johnston to Arthur Selden Lloyd, March 19, 1908, box 39, letterbook 1, Johnston Papers.

135. Charles Brent to A. C. A. Hall, February 22, 1905, box 6, Brent Papers.

136. Lears, *No Place of Grace*, 184; Smith, *Gothic Arches, Latin Crosses*, 12.

137. Charles Brent to Manuel Gregorio, Ladislao Alcantara, Gregorio Lorenzano, and others, November 16, 1902, box 6, Brent Papers.

138. Charles Brent to A. C. A. Hall, February 22, 1905, box 6, Brent Papers; Charles Brent, "Introduction to Dr Hall's Lectures," box 25, Sermon Notes ca. 1909 (1), Brent Papers; *Official Journal of the Second Annual Convention of the Missionary District of the Philippine Islands*, 26–28.

139. Charles Brent, untitled document (report for first year in the Philippines, 1903), box 1, Diary for 1903, Brent Papers; *Official Journal of the Second Annual Convention of the Missionary District of the Philippine Islands*, 23.

140. Charles Brent to James B. Rodgers, November 10, 1905, box 6, Brent Papers.

141. Charles Brent to Howard Mellish, August 19, 1914, box 10, Brent Papers.

142. Charles Brent to S. G. Inman, September 2, 1915, box 11, Brent Papers.

143. "The True Perspective," *The Churchman*, May 1, 1915, 565.

144. Entry for August 28, 1903, box 1, Diary for 1903, Brent Papers; Charles Brent, notes for sermon entitled "Where the Spirit of the Lord is, there is liberty," box 1, Diary for 1903, Brent Papers.

145. Charles Brent to S. G. Inman, September 2, 1915, box 11, Brent Papers.

146. Charles Brent to William Lawrence, January 21, 1918, box 14, Brent Papers.

147. Charles Brent, "Race Prejudice; Notes on Mediaeval History," n.d., box 28, Brent Papers.

148. Charles Brent to Howard Mellish, August 19, 1914, box 10, Brent Papers.

149. Charles Brent to Mercer Johnston, November 2, 1904, box 38, Johnston Papers.

150. Charles Brent to R. C. Sturgis, February 9, 1915, box 10, Brent Papers.

151. Charles Brent to A. C. A. Hall, July 25, 1902, box 5, Brent Papers.
152. Entry for March 27, 1907, box 68, Diary for 1907, Brent Papers.
153. Charles Brent to A. C. A. Hall, March 16, 1903, Box 6, Brent Papers.
154. Brent, report for first year in the Philippines.
155. Brent, report for first year in the Philippines. On Staunton, see Clymer, *Protestant Missionaries in the Philippines*, 51.
156. Charles Brent to David H. Greer, March 5, 1906, box 6, Brent Papers.
157. Charles Brent to Mr. McCorkell, May 6, 1909, box 8, Brent Papers.
158. Edward A. Sibley to Charles Brent, September 23, 1916, box 11, Brent Papers; James B. Rodgers to Robert E. Speer, December 3, 1917, box 5, folder 7, no. 50, United Presbyterian Church in the U.S.A. Commission on Ecumenical Mission and Relation Secretaries' Files: Philippine Mission, National Archives of the Presbyterian Church of the United States of America, Presbyterian Historical Society, Philadelphia, Pennsylvania.
159. "Editorial," *Baptist Missionary Magazine*, February 1904, 59.
160. Mercer Johnston to James S. Johnston, August 27, 1904, box 39, letterbook 1, Johnston Papers.
161. Mercer Johnston to Homer Stuntz, December 9, 1903; Mercer Johnston to James S. Johnston, August 27, 1904. Both in box 39, letterbook 1, Johnston Papers.
162. Mercer Johnston to Irvin H. Correll, July 10, 1907, box 39, letterbook 1, Johnston Papers.
163. Entry for August 1, 1908, box 3, Notebook 1905, Johnston Papers.
164. Mercer Johnston to Irvin H. Correll, July 10, 1907, box 39, letterbook 1, Johnston Papers.
165. Clymer, *Protestant Missionaries in the Philippines*, 103–4; Smith, "American Missionaries and the Boundaries of Evangelicalism in the Philippines."
166. The "Paris Basis" for YMCA membership was adopted at a conference in Paris in 1855 and stated that membership was open to any young men who "regarding Jesus Christ as their God and Saviour, . . . desire to be his disciples." In 1869, however, the YMCA in the United States adopted the "Portland Basis" at a conference in Portland, Maine—a more rigorous test demanding that members held to a set of conservative evangelical theological principles. See University of Minnesota Libraries, "YMCA religious work records," accessed January 5, 2024, https://archives.lib.umn.edu/repositories/7/resources/993.
167. J. M. Groves, "The Basis of Membership in the Young Men's Christian Association in the Philippine Islands," box 1, Correspondence 1910–11, International Work in the Philippines.
168. "Answers to Questions Regarding the Basis of Membership of the Young Men's Christian Association in Manila," n.d. [1918], box 1, Correspondence & Reports 1918, International Work in the Philippines. For further evidence of debate among missionaries on this point, see A. T. Morrill, "Report to the International Committee of Young Men's Christian Association by City Department, Manila, Young Men's Christian Association of the Philippine Islands," 1916, and E. S. Turner, "First Annual Report Ending September 30, 1916." Both in box 5, Administrative Reports 1914–16, International Work in the Philippines.
169. R. M. Shearer to John R. Mott, February 23, 1917, box 1, Correspondence & Reports 1917, International Work in the Philippines.
170. J. M. Groves to L. Wilbur Messer, April 14, 1913, box 1, Correspondence & Reports 1913; E. C. Jenkins to Elwood S. Brown, February 6, 1919, box 1, Correspondence & Reports 1919. Both in International Work in the Philippines.
171. Brown, *The New Era in the Philippines*, 161.
172. Stuntz, *The Philippines and the Far East*, 363–64.

173. Briggs, *The Progressing Philippines*, 103; Brown, *Report of a Visitation of the Philippine Mission of the Board of Foreign Missions of the Presbyterian Church*, 75; Johnston, *Plain American Talk in the Philippines*, 109–10; Stuntz, *The Philippines and the Far East*, 363–64.

6. "A Chosen People"

1. LeRoy, "Apolinario Mabini on the Failure of the Filipino Revolution."
2. Apolinario Mabini, "Manifesto Regarding the American Occupation and the Philippine Insurrection," 1916, translated typescript, Manuscript Division, Library of Congress, Washington, DC.
3. Weinberg, *Manifest Destiny*, 291.
4. Emilio Aguinaldo to the Philippine people, February 5, 1899, Letters Received by the Commission, 1898–1899, entry 1032, RG 59, Department of State Central Files, National Archives and Records Administration, College Park, Maryland.
5. "Mğa Kababayan," undated, box 5, Miscellany: Printed Matter, Rounsevelle Wildman and Edwin Wildman Papers, Library of Congress, Washington, DC, my translation (hereafter Wildman Papers).
6. Kramer, *The Blood of Government*, 185–95.
7. Kramer, *The Blood of Government*, 112–13.
8. Kramer, *The Blood of Government*, 173.
9. Quoted in Condit, *Old Glory and the Gospel in the Philippines*, 88.
10. Quoted in Condit, *Old Glory and the Gospel in the Philippines*, 91, italics in original.
11. Steinbock-Pratt, *Educating the Empire*, 203–4.
12. Felipe Agoncillo, "Memorandum Relative to the Right of the Philippine Republic to Recognition, Accompanying Letter to the Honorable the Secretary of State, of date January 11, 1899," box 5, Miscellany: Printed Matter Undated, Wildman Papers.
13. Agoncillo, "Memorandum Relative to the Right of the Philippine Republic to Recognition."
14. Mabini, "Manifesto Regarding the American Occupation and Philippine Insurrection."
15. Kramer, *The Blood of Government*, 136.
16. Mabini, "Manifesto Regarding the American Occupation and Philippine Insurrection."
17. Kramer, *The Blood of Government*, 104.
18. Harris, *God's Arbiters*, 25.
19. Mojares, *Brains of the Nation*, 480–89.
20. Blanco, *Frontier Constitutions*, 244–69; Kramer, *The Blood of Government*, 8–9; Schumacher, "The 'Propagandists" Reconstruction of the Philippine Past," 269–77.
21. José Rizal to Ferdinand Blumentritt, August 16, 1886, in Alzona, *The Rizal-Blumentritt Correspondence*, 1:9; Ricardo de Puga quoted in Blanco, *Frontier Constitutions*, 237.
22. Kramer, *The Blood of Government*, 63; Thomas, *Orientalists, Propagandists, and Ilustrados*, 2–7.
23. José Rizal to Ferdinand Blumentritt, November 22, 1886, in Alzona, *The Rizal-Blumentritt Correspondence*, 1:21.
24. José Rizal to Ferdinand Blumentritt, April 13, 1887, in Alzona, *The Rizal-Blumentritt Correspondence*, 1:71–74.
25. Ocampo, "Rizal's Morga and Views of Philippine History," 186–88; Schumacher, "The 'Propagandists" Reconstruction of the Philippine Past," 270–71. For an example of Rizal working in European archives, see José Rizal to Ferdinand Blumentritt, October 12, 1888, in Alzona, *The Rizal-Blumentritt Correspondence*, 1:203.

26. José Rizal to Ferdinand Blumentritt, January 14, 1889, in Alzona, *The Rizal-Blumentritt Correspondence*, 1:231–32; Ocampo, "Rizal's Morga and Views of Philippine History," 209–10.

27. Blanco, *Frontier Constitutions*, 252–54; Ocampo, "Rizal's Morga and Views of Philippine History," 209–11; Schumacher, "The 'Propagandists'' Reconstruction of the Philippine Past," 276.

28. Blanco, *Frontier Constitutions*, 249–52, Kramer, *The Blood of Government*, 64; Ocampo, "Rizal's Morga and Views of Philippine History"; Schumacher, "The 'Propagandists'' Reconstruction of the Philippine Past," 272–74; Thomas, *Orientalists, Propagandists, and Ilustrados*, 174.

29. Anderson, *Under Three Flags*, chap. 1; Kramer, *The Blood of Government*, 64–65.

30. De los Reyes, *El folk-lore filipino*; Dizon and Imson, "Preface," xi; Ocampo, "Rizal's Morga and Views of Philippine History," 205–8; Schumacher, "The 'Propagandists'' Reconstruction of the Philippine Past," 267–68.

31. Paterno, *El Cristianismo en la Antigua Civilización Tagalog*; Mojares, *Brains of the Nation*, 46–56, 295–331; Schumacher, "The 'Propagandists'' Reconstruction of the Philippine Past," 268–69. On Rizal's skepticism, see José Rizal to Ferdinand Blumentritt, March 29, 1887, in Alzona, *The Rizal-Blumentritt Correspondence*, 1:70; José Rizal to Ferdinand Blumentritt, April 17, 1890, in Alzona, *The Rizal-Blumentritt Correspondence* 2:350–51; and Mojares, *Brains of the Nation*, 14–15.

32. De los Reyes, *The Religion of the Katipunan*, part 1.

33. De los Reyes, *The Religion of the Katipunan*, 31.

34. De los Reyes, *The Religion of the Katipunan*, 77–81.

35. On the connections between de los Reyes's theology and the Aglipayan church, see Achútegui and Bernad, *Religious Revolution in the Philippines*, 170–71.

36. Gregorio Aglipay to William Howard Taft, March 4, 1903, box 6, Charles Henry Brent Papers, Manuscript Division, Library of Congress, Washington, DC (hereafter Brent Papers).

37. Kramer, *The Blood of Government*, 65–73.

38. Schumacher, "The 'Propagandists'' Reconstruction of the Philippine Past," 274–75.

39. Ileto, "Outlines of a Nonlinear Emplotment of Philippine History."

40. Aguilar, "Tracing Origins."

41. On de los Reyes's sympathy with the "primitive" peoples of his home region in northern Luzon, see Anderson, *Under Three Flags*, 17

42. Thomas, *Orientalists, Propagandists, and Ilustrados*, chap. 2, 174–75.

43. Kramer, *The Blood of Government*, 77; Schumacher, "The 'Propagandists'' Reconstruction of the Philippine Past," 277–78.

44. Rafael, *Contracting Colonialism*, 14.

45. Ileto, "Outlines of a Nonlinear Emplotment of Philippine History," 123; Ileto, "Tagalog Poetry and the Image of the Past during the War against Spain."

46. Tan, *Filipino Muslim Perceptions of Their History and Culture*, 14.

47. Rafael, *White Love and Other Events in Filipino History*, 39–51.

48. Briggs, *The Progressing Philippines*, 52, 160–63; Brown, *The New Era in the Philippines*, chap. I; Farmer, *The Philippine Mission of the Methodist Episcopal Church*, 17; Stuntz, *The Philippines and the Far East*, 60–62.

49. David S. Hibbard to F. F. Ellinwood, November 28, 1899, vol. 259, no. 41, Board of Foreign Missions Correspondence and Reports, National Archives of the Presbyterian Church of the United States of America, Presbyterian Historical Society, Philadelphia, Pennsylvania (hereafter Board of Foreign Missions Correspondence and Reports).

50. Robert F. Black to Judson Smith, July 17, 1903, vol. 1, no. 38, Philippine Islands Mission, Papers of the American Board of Commissioners for Foreign Missions, Houghton Library,

Harvard University, Cambridge, Massachusetts (hereafter Philippine Islands Mission); C. N. Magill to friends, February 7, 1907, vol. 265, no. 11, Board of Foreign Missions Correspondence and Reports.

51. Charles Brent to Evelyn [sister], January 22, 1911, box 9, Brent Papers; Stuntz, *The Philippines and the Far East*, frontispiece.

52. Brown, *The New Era in the Philippines*, 124–25; Stuntz, *The Philippines and the Far East*, 65–67.

53. Briggs, *The Progressing Philippines*, 53–61; Stuntz, *The Philippines and the Far East*, 67–71, 80.

54. Stuntz, *The Philippines and the Far East*, 74.

55. Stuntz, *The Philippines and the Far East*, 73–78; Briggs, *The Progressing Philippines*, 63–69, chap. VIII.

56. Briggs, *The Progressing Philippines*, 62; Farmer, *The Philippine Mission of the Methodist Episcopal Church*, 17–19; Stuntz, *The Philippines and the Far East*, 85–86.

57. Stuntz, *The Philippines and the Far East*, 379.

58. Stuntz, *The Philippines and the Far East*, 56.

59. Clymer, *Protestant Missionaries in the Philippines*, chap. 4. On Dean Conant Worcester's influential anthropological work, see Drinnon, *Facing West*, chap. XX.

60. Stuntz, *The Philippines and the Far East*, 31–40.

61. Foreman, *The Philippine Islands*.

62. LeRoy, "Reviews of Books: *The Philippine Islands*," 388.

63. Stuntz, *The Philippines and the Far East*, 39.

64. Clymer, *Protestant Missionaries in the Philippines*, 73–74; Drinnon, *Facing West*, 291–92; Hixson, *American Settler Colonialism*, 169, 180.

65. Kramer, *The Blood of Government*, 121–24.

66. Charles Brent, "With God in the Nation," n.d., box 25, Sermon Notes 1901–2, Brent Papers.

67. Stuntz, *The Philippines and the Far East*, 19–20.

68. Stuntz, *The Open Door in the Philippines*, 2.

69. H. W. Love to friends, September 10, 1920, box 1, Correspondence & Reports 1920, International Work in the Philippines, Kautz Family YMCA Archives, Elmer L. Andersen Library, University of Minnesota, Minneapolis (hereafter International Work in the Philippines).

70. Fleming, "Foreword," v.

71. Briggs, *The Progressing Philippines*, 165–68.

72. "South India Jubilee Items," *Woman's Missionary Friend*, October 1906, 348; "Beginnings in Malaysia," *Woman's Missionary Friend*, May 1914, 161–62.

73. Wenger, *Religious Freedom*, 21–22; Walther, *Sacred Interests*, 166.

74. James B. Rodgers, "Lessons from Five Years of Protestant Work in the Philippine Islands," 1905, vol. 263, no. 37, Board of Foreign Missions Correspondence and Reports.

75. Clymer, *Protestant Missionaries in the Philippines*, 5–6; "Notes from the Wide Field," *Missionary Herald*, January 1906, 41–42.

76. J. M. Groves to John R. Mott, June 28, 1911, box 1, Correspondence 1910–11, International Work in the Philippines; John Ireland to Carlos J. Findlay, December 10, 1910, box 6, Catholic Church 1910–29, International Work Subject Files, Kautz Family YMCA Archives, Elmer L. Andersen Library, University of Minnesota, Minneapolis (hereafter International Work Subject Files); "Summary of the Results of the Inquiry as to the Membership Basis of Various Latin American Associations," 1919, box 10, Membership Base 1891–1935 (1), International Work Subject Files; Sotomayor, "The Triangle of Empire," 501.

77. Frank Laubach to Frank W. Carpenter, September 23, 1921, General Correspondence: February 20, 1921 to September 20, 1922, Frank W. Carpenter Papers, Manuscript Division, Library of Congress, Washington, DC.

78. See Buschmann, Slack, and Tueller, *Navigating the Spanish Lake*.

79. José Rizal to Ferdinand Blumentritt, January 26, 1887, Alzona, *The Rizal-Blumentritt Correspondence*, 1:44.

80. For US government celebrations of Rizal, see William Howard Taft to Elihu Root, August 18, 1900, series 21, vol. 2, William Howard Taft Papers, Library of Congress, Washington, DC (hereafter Taft Papers); William Howard Taft to Elihu Root, August 31, 1900, series 21, vol. 2, Taft Papers; entries for December 30, 1910 and February 10, 1911 in Journal of W. Cameron Forbes, vol. 4, W. Cameron Forbes Papers, Library of Congress, Washington, DC; "Rizal Day in the Philippines: The Day the Filipinos Celebrate," *Baptist Missionary Magazine*, July 1909, 238–39; Doeppers, "Manila's Imperial Makeover," 491; Kramer, *The Blood of Government*, 333–38; Morley, *Cities and Nationhood*, 15.

81. Craig, *Lineage, Life and Labors of José Rizal*.

82. Schumacher, "Rizal and Filipino Nationalism," 549–52, 562.

83. Briggs, *The Progressing Philippines*, 104; Condit, *Old Glory and the Gospel in the Philippines*, 71–74; Stuntz, *The Philippines and the Far East*, 99–101; Clymer, *Protestant Missionaries in the Philippines*, 80.

84. J. Andrew Hall to F. F. Ellinwood, January 13, 1903, vol. 261, no. 4, Board of Foreign Missions Correspondence and Reports.

85. Rodgers, "Lessons from Five Years of Protestant Work in the Philippine Islands."

86. Johnston, *Plain American Talk in the Philippines*, 122; Hibbard, *Making a Nation*, 13.

87. "Ten Years' Advance at Laguna," *Assembly Herald*, October 1912, 533.

88. Laubach, *The People of the Philippines*, 156.

89. Julius S. Augur, "Annual Report: Evangelical and Educational Department," 1918, vol. 2, no. 30, Philippine Islands Mission.

90. Laubach, *Rizal*.

91. Hollinger, *Protestants Abroad*, 255.

92. Kramer, *The Blood of Government*, 344–45.

93. Kramer, *The Blood of Government*, 352–55.

94. "Is the Filipino Ready for Independence?," *Assembly Herald*, August 1917, 380.

95. Charles Brent to Francis Burton Harrison, June 5, 1914; Charles Brent to J. T. Addison, December 2, 1915. Both in box 10, Brent Papers.

96. J. Andrew Hall to Arthur Judson Brown, March 29, 1916, box 5, folder 6, no. 16, United Presbyterian Church in the U.S.A. Commission on Ecumenical Mission and Relation Secretaries' Files: Philippine Mission, National Archives of the Presbyterian Church of the United States of America, Presbyterian Historical Society, Philadelphia, Pennsylvania.

97. Julius S. Augur to Enoch F. Bell, July 10, 1919, vol. 2, no. 95, Philippine Islands Mission.

98. Clymer, *Protestant Missionaries in the Philippines*, 89.

99. Charles Brent to E. D. Brandegee, September 18, 1914, box 10, Brent Papers.

100. Charles Brent to Bishop Lawrence, September 18, 1914, box 10, Brent Papers.

101. Frank Laubach to James L. Barton, May 2, 1918, vol. 2, no. 288, Philippine Islands Mission.

102. On cultural relativism, see Brown, "Cultural Relativism 2.0," 364.

103. Kramer, *The Blood of Government*, 287.

104. Kramer, *The Blood of Government*, 286–87.

105. Clymer, *Protestant Missionaries in the Philippines*, 140–46; Kramer, *The Blood of Government*, 369–82.
106. Kramer, *The Blood of Government*, chap. 4.
107. J. M. Groves to G. Sherwood Eddy, June 29, 1914, box 1, Correspondence & Reports 1914, International Work in the Philippines.
108. Clymer, *Protestant Missionaries in the Philippines*, 124–30.
109. Kramer, *The Blood of Government*, 385–87.
110. Steinbock-Pratt, *Educating the Empire*, 265–88.
111. Melencio, *Arguments against Philippine Independence and Their Answers*.
112. Steinbock-Pratt, *Educating the Empire*, 205–6.
113. Kramer, *The Blood of Government*, 305–8.
114. Kramer, *The Blood of Government*, 388–93.
115. Kramer, *The Blood of Government*, 390–91.
116. Clymer, *Protestant Missionaries in the Philippines*, 146–50. On the continued rise of nationalism in the Methodist and Presbyterian churches across the 1920s, see Apilado, *Revolutionary Spirituality*, 254.
117. "The Great Advance in the Philippines: The New Synod," *Assembly Herald*, October 1914, 546.
118. Brown, "Foreword," 5; Osías and Lorenzana, *Evangelical Christianity in the Philippines*, xvi.
119. Leonard Wood and W. Cameron Forbes, "Report of the Special Mission on Investigation to the Philippine Islands," n.d., box 2; John G. Russell, "American Trade with the Philippines: Beginnings and Early Growth, 1796–1897," n.d. [1920s], box 2; W. Cameron Forbes, "Our China Trade," 1919, box 3. All in W. Cameron Forbes Papers, Houghton Library, Harvard University, Cambridge, Massachusetts.
120. Hibbard, *Making a Nation*, 18–19.
121. Laubach, *The People of the Philippines*, xv, italics in original.
122. Laubach, *The People of the Philippines*, 96.
123. Laubach, *The People of the Philippines*, xv.
124. Laubach, *The People of the Philippines*, 8.
125. Hollinger, *Protestants Abroad*, 254.
126. Laubach, *The People of the Philippines*, 24–43.
127. Laubach, *The People of the Philippines*, 458–61.
128. Laubach, *The People of the Philippines*, 121, 461, chap. IX.
129. Briggs, *The Progressing Philippines*, 49–50.
130. Briggs, *The Progressing Philippines*, 26–27.
131. Briggs, *The Progressing Philippines*, 37–38.
132. Kramer, *The Blood of Government*, 323.
133. Hibbard, *Making a Nation*, 89.
134. Hibbard, *Making a Nation*, 12.
135. Osías and Lorenzana, *Evangelical Christianity in the Philippines*, 23–25.
136. Osías and Lorenzana, *Evangelical Christianity in the Philippines*, 7–9, 13–16, 24–26, 201–2.
137. Osías and Lorenzana, *Evangelical Christianity in the Philippines*, 61–62, 137–39.
138. Osías and Lorenzana, *Evangelical Christianity in the Philippines*, chap. IX.
139. Osías and Lorenzana, *Evangelical Christianity in the Philippines*, 20–21.
140. J. D. Y. Peel makes a similar argument about Christianity, cultural nationalism, and historical narrative among the Yoruba of West Africa, in Peel, *Religious Encounter and the Making of the Yoruba*, 295–98.

141. Thompson, *For God and Globe*, 1–4, 17–18.
142. Hibbard, *Making a Nation*, 7–8; Laubach, *The People of the Philippines*, xv.
143. Schumacher, "The 'Propagandists" Reconstruction of the Philippine Past," 279–80; Kramer, *The Blood of Government*, 336–37.
144. Mojares, *Brains of the Nation*, 178–80.
145. Laubach, *The People of the Philippines*, 43, 153.
146. On anti-Filipino nativism, see Kramer, *The Blood of Government*, 397–423; Ngai, *Impossible Subjects*, chap. 3; Steinbock-Pratt, *Educating the Empire*, 250.
147. Hollinger, *Protestants Abroad*, 1–2.
148. Hollinger, *Protestants Abroad*, 253–57.

Conclusion

1. On the "Greater United States," see Immerwahr, *How to Hide an Empire*.
2. Kramer, "Power and Connection," 1382–83.
3. Sivasundaram, "Science," 238.
4. Dole and Thurston, *Memoirs of the Hawaiian Revolution*; Coffman, *Nation Within*, 321.
5. McDougall, "Moʻokūʻauhau versus Colonial Entitlement."
6. Brown, *Facing the Spears of Change*, 7–8, italics in original.
7. For Scott's deconstruction of the tribal view of Philippine history, see Scott, "An Historian Looks into the Philippine Kaleidoscope."
8. "Suggestive Notes on Proposed Pan Pacific Young Men's Christian Association Conference, Discussed at the Portschach Meeting, May 31, 1923"; Fletcher S. Brockman, "Program Suggestions," n.d. Both in box 2, Hawaii: Christian Conference of the Pacific Area 1924–25, Local Association Files, Kautz Family YMCA Archives, Elmer L. Andersen Library, University of Minnesota, Minneapolis.
9. On the "Pacific theater" see Kauanui, "Imperial Ocean," 626. On the rise of the "American Pacific" idea after World War II, see Wilson, *Reimagining the American Pacific*, 68, 106.
10. For historians who examine these legacies of US rule in the Philippines, see Capozzola, *Bound by War*, chaps. 7–11; McCoy, *Policing America's Empire*, part 2; Woods, *Freedom Incorporated*; and Compoc, "Weaving Our Sovereignties Together," 318.
11. Miller-Davenport, *Gateway State*, 13.
12. Gonzalez, *Securing Paradise*, 20; Stratford, "Imagining the Archipelago," 79.
13. Gonzalez, *Securing Paradise*.
14. Compoc, "Considerations from the U.S.-Occupied Pacific"; Compoc, "Weaving Our Sovereignties Together"; Gonzalez, *Securing Paradise*, 2–3.
15. Roberts, *Borderwaters*, 24.
16. For a recent critical journalistic articulation of the "American lake" idea, see "The American Lake."

Bibliography

Archival Sources

Bancroft Library, University of California, Berkeley
    Daniel Dole Letters to His Sons
    John T. Gulick Papers
    W. D. Alexander Letters to R. R. Hoes
Burke Library, Union Theological Seminary, Columbia University, New York
    Missionary Research Library Archives
        Ecumenical Conference on Foreign Missions Records, 1900-04–1900-05
        World Missionary Conference Records, 1883–1910
Elmer L. Andersen Library, University of Minnesota, Minneapolis
    Kautz Family YMCA Archives
        International Work in the Philippines
        International Work Subject Files
        Local Association Files
Hamilton Library, University of Hawai'i, Mānoa
    Hawaiian and Pacific Collections
Hawai'i State Archives, Honolulu
    Lili'uokalani Papers
    Sanford Ballard Dole Papers
    Social Science Association Papers
Hawaiian Historical Society, Honolulu
    Sereno Edwards Bishop Letters to Gorham D. Gilman
    William DeWitt Alexander Papers

Hawaiian Mission Children's Society, Honolulu
   Children of the Mission Collection
      James M. Alexander Papers
      Sereno Bishop Papers
Houghton Library, Harvard University, Cambridge, Massachusetts
   Papers of the American Board of Commissioners for Foreign Missions
      Hawaiian Islands Mission
      Philippine Islands Mission
   W. Cameron Forbes Papers
Huntington Library, San Marino, California
   Henry W. Bigler Diaries
   Ida May Pope Papers
   John Stillman Woodbury Diaries
   Joseph Oliver Carter Papers
   Nathaniel Bright Emerson Papers
   Sereno Edwards Bishop Papers
Library of Congress, Washington, DC
   Manuscript Division
      Richard Armstrong Papers
      Albert J. Beveridge Papers
      Charles Henry Brent Papers
      Frank W. Carpenter Papers
      W. Cameron Forbes Papers
      Mercer Green Johnston Papers
      Apolinaro Mabini, "Manifesto Regarding the American Occupation and Philippine Insurrection"
      William Howard Taft Papers
      Rounsevelle Wildman and Edwin Wildman Papers
National Archives and Records Administration, College Park, Maryland
   Department of State Central Files (RG 59)
      Letters Received by the Commission, 1898–1899
National Archives of the Presbyterian Church of the United States of America, Presbyterian Historical Society, Philadelphia, Pennsylvania
   Board of Foreign Missions Correspondence and Reports
   United Presbyterian Church in the U.S.A. Commission on Ecumenical Mission and Relation Secretaries' Files: Philippine Mission
United Methodist Church General Commission on Archives and History, Madison, New Jersey
   Methodist Episcopal Church Missionary Correspondence 1846–1912
Yale Divinity School Library, New Haven, Connecticut
   Special Collections
      Arthur Judson Brown Papers (RG 2)
      John R. Mott Papers (RG 45)

Yale University Library, New Haven, Connecticut
   Manuscripts & Archives
      Bingham Family Papers (MS 81)

Periodicals

Anglican Church Chronicle
Assembly Herald
Baptist Missionary Magazine
Christian Advocate
Congressional Record
Filipino Students' Companion
General Letter to the Sandwich Islands Mission
Hawaii Holomua
Life and Light for Woman
Missionary Herald
Philippine Presbyterian
Silliman Truth
The Churchman
The Friend
The Outlook
Travel Letters
Woman's Missionary Friend

Newspapers

New York Daily Tribune
New York Observer
New York Sun
Pacific Commercial Advertiser
Washington Evening Star

Printed Primary Sources

Alexander, James M. *The Islands of the Pacific: From the Old to the New.* New York: American Tract Society, 1895.

Alexander, W. D. *A Brief History of the Hawaiian People.* New York: American Book Company, 1891.

Alexander, W. D. "Corresponding Secretary's Report." In *First Annual Report of the Hawaiian Historical Society, Honolulu, H.I.,* 7–8. Honolulu: Hawaiian Gazette Company, 1893.

Alexander, W. D. *Kalakaua's Reign: A Sketch of Hawaiian History.* Honolulu: Hawaiian Gazette Company Publishers, 1894.

Alexander, W. D. "President's Address." In *Fifteenth Annual Report of the Hawaiian Historical Society for the Year Ending December 31, 1907,* 7–9. Honolulu: Hawaiian Gazette Co., 1908.

Alexander, W. D. "Report of the Corresponding Secretary." In *Fifth Annual Report of the Hawaiian Historical Society, Honolulu, H.I.,* 7–9. Honolulu: Robert Grieve, 1898.

Alexander, W. D. "Report of the Corresponding Secretary for the Year Ending November 28, 1899." In *Seventh Annual Report of the Hawaiian Historical Society with a Paper on the Partition of Samoa, and the Past Relations between that Group and the United States, by Hon. H. M. Sewall,* 7–10. Honolulu: The Robert Grieve Publishing Company, 1900.

Alexander, W. D. "Report of the Corresponding Secretary for the Year Ending November 28, 1901." In *Ninth Annual Report of the Hawaiian Historical Society with a Paper on Some Hawaiian Beliefs Regarding Spirits by J. S. Emerson and a Report on a Find of Human Bones Exhumed in the Sands of Waikiki by N. B. Emerson,* 7–9. Honolulu: Hawaiian Gazette Company, 1902.

Alexander, W. D. "Report of the Corresponding Secretary for the Year Ending November 28, 1904." In *Twelfth Annual Report of the Hawaiian Historical Society for the Year Ending Dec. 31, 1904,* 9–11. Honolulu: N.p., 1905.

Alexander, W. D. *A Review of a Pastoral Address by the Right Rev. T. N. Staley, D. D., Reformed Catholic Bishop of Honolulu, Containing a Reply to Some of His Charges against the American Protestant Mission to the Hawaiian Islands.* Honolulu: H. M. Whitney, 1865.

Allardyce, John C. *Society, Politics and Religion in the Hawaiian Islands.* San Francisco, CA: Published for the Author, 1881.

Alzona, Encarnación, ed. *The Rizal-Blumentritt Correspondence.* 2 vols. Translated by Encarnación Alzona. Manila: National Historical Institute, 1992.

Anderson, Robbins B. "The Protestant Episcopal Church in Hawaii." In Hawaiian Mission Centennial, *The Centennial Book: One Hundred Years of Christian Civilization in Hawaii, 1820–1920,* 70–71. Honolulu: Central Committee of the Hawaiian Mission Centennial, 1920.

Anderson, Rufus. *The Hawaiian Islands: Their Progress and Condition under Missionary Labors.* Boston, MA: Gould and Lincoln, 1864.

Anderson, Rufus. *A Heathen Nation Evangelized: History of the Sandwich Islands Mission.* Boston, MA: Congregational Publishing Society, 1870.

Anderson, Rufus. *Kapiolani: Heroine of Hawaii.* New York: Charles Scribner & Co., 1866.

Armstrong, Samuel Chapman. "Lessons from the Hawaiian Islands." *Journal of Christian Philosophy* 111 (1884): 200–229.

Atkinson, Alatau T. "A Stranger Asks Bliff about the Historical Procession." In Atkinson, *Gynberg Ballads,* 9–11. San Francisco, CA: Schmidt Lithograph Company, 1887.

Baker, Robert Hoapili. *A Reply to the Ministerial Utterances.* [Honolulu]: N.p., 1880.

Bancroft, Hubert Howe. *The New Pacific*. New York: The Bancroft Company, 1900.
Barrow, Terence. "Introduction to the New Edition." In Nathaniel B. Emerson, *Pele and Hiiaka: A Myth from Hawaii*, xi–xx. 1915; repr., Rutland, VT: Charles E. Tuttle Company, 1978.
Barton, James L. "Introduction." In Orramel Hinckley Gulick and Ann Eliza Clark Gulick, *The Pilgrims of Hawaii: Their Own Story of Pilgrimage from New England and Life Work in the Sandwich Islands, Now Known as Hawaii, with Explanatory and Illustrative Material Compiled and Verified from Original Sources*, 5–6. New York: Fleming H. Revell Company, 1918.
Beveridge, Albert J. "The March of the Flag (September 16, 1898)." Accessed August 18, 2020. Voices of Democracy: The U.S. Oratory Project. https://voicesofdemocracy.umd.edu/beveridge-march-of-the-flag-speech-text/.
Bicknell, James. *Hoomanamana—Idolatry*. [Honolulu]: N.p., n.d. [1888].
Bingham, Hiram. *A Residence of Twenty-One Years in the Sandwich Islands, or the Civil, Religious, and Political History of Those Islands*. Hartford, CT: Hezekiah Huntington, 1847.
Bishop, Sereno Edwards. *Reminiscences of Old Hawaii*. Honolulu: Hawaiian Gazette Co., Ltd., 1916.
Bishop, Sereno Edwards. *Why Are the Hawaiians Dying Out?* [Honolulu]: N.p., 1888.
Bonura, Sandra, and Deborah Day, eds. *An American Girl in the Hawaiian Islands: Letters of Carrie Prudence Winter, 1890–1893*. Honolulu: University of Hawaiʻi Press, 2012.
Brain, Belle M. *The Transformation of Hawaii: How American Missionaries Gave a Christian Nation to the World . . . Told for Young Folks*. New York: Fleming H. Revell Company, 1898.
Brent, Charles Henry. *Religious Conditions in the Philippine Islands*. New York: The Domestic and Foreign Missionary Society of the Protestant Episcopal Church, 1905.
Briggs, Charles W. *The Progressing Philippines*. Philadelphia, PA: Griffith & Rowland Press, 1913.
Brown, Arthur Judson. "Foreword." In David S. Hibbard, *Making a Nation: The Changing Philippines*, 5–6. New York: Board of Foreign Missions of the Presbyterian Church in the United States of America, 1926.
Brown, Arthur Judson. *The New Era in the Philippines*. New York: Fleming H. Revell Company, 1903.
Brown, Arthur Judson. *Report of a Visitation of the Philippine Mission of the Board of Foreign Missions of the Presbyterian Church in the United States of America*. New York: Board of Foreign Missions of the Presbyterian Church in the United States of America, 1902.
Brown, Roy H. *Letters and Greeting to You*. [Milwaukee, WI]: Forward Movement Committee of Immanuel Presbyterian Church, n.d. [1905].
Bryan, William Alanson. "Report of the Corresponding Secretary for the Year Ending Nov. 28, 1905." In *Thirteenth Annual Report of the Hawaiian Historical Society with a Paper on the Development of Hawaiian Statute Law by Chief Justice W. F. Frear*, 9–14. Honolulu: Hawaiian Gazette Co., 1906.

Burbank, Mary A. "Annual Report of the Librarian of the Hawaiian Historical Society." In *Fifth Annual Report of the Hawaiian Historical Society, Honolulu, H.I.*, 6–7. Honolulu: Robert Grieve, 1898.

Castle, William R., Jr. *Hawaii: Past and Present*. New York: Dodd, Mead and Company, 1914.

Coan, Titus. *Life in Hawaii: An Autobiographic Sketch of Missions Life and Labors, 1835–1881*. New York: Anson D. F. Randolph & Company, 1882.

Condict, Alice Byram. *Old Glory and the Gospel in the Philippines: Notes Gathered during Professional and Missionary Work*. Chicago, IL: Fleming H. Revell Company, 1902.

"Constitution." In *Annual Report of the Hawaiian Mission Children's Society, Presented May 21st, 1853*, 22–24. Honolulu: Government Press, 1853.

The Coronation of King Kalakaua (February 12th, 1883) and Unveiling Ceremonies of the Statue of Kamehameha I and Grand State Dinner etc. (February 14th, 1883). Honolulu: Hawaiian Gazette Print, 1883.

Craig, Austin. *Lineage, Life and Labors of José Rizal, Philippine Patriot: A Study in the Growth of Free Ideas in the Trans-Pacific American Territory*. Manila: Philippine Education Company, 1913.

Daggett, R. M. "Hawaiian Legends: Introduction." In Kalākaua, *The Legends and Myths of Hawaii: The Fables and Folk-Lore of a Strange People*, edited by R. M. Daggett, 11–65. New York: Charles L. Webster & Company, 1888.

Damon, Samuel M. "Report of the Recording Secretary." In *Annual Report of the Hawaiian Mission Children's Society*, 5. Honolulu: H. M. Whitney, 1865.

De los Reyes y Florentino, Isabelo. *El folk-lore filipino*. Vol. 1. Translated by Salud C. Dizon and Maria Elinora P. Imson. Quezon City: University of the Philippines Press, 1994.

De los Reyes y Florentino, Isabelo. *The Religion of the Katipunan: or, The Old Beliefs of the Filipinos*. Translated by Joseph Martin Yap. Quezon City: University of the Philippines Press, 2002.

Dibble, Sheldon. *History and General Views of the Sandwich Islands' Mission*. New York: Taylor & Dodd, 1839.

Dole, Sanford B. "Address of the Retiring President, Hon. S. B. Dole." In *Thirty-Sixth Annual Report of the Hawn. Mission Children's Society, Presented May 26, 1888*, 29–36. Honolulu: Press Publishing Company Steam Print, 1888.

Dole, Sanford B., and Lorrin A. Thurston. *Memoirs of the Hawaiian Revolution*. 3 vols. Edited by Andrew Farrell. Honolulu: Advertiser Publishing Co., 1936.

Emerson, J. S. "Chairman's Address." In *First Annual Report of the Hawaiian Historical Society, Honolulu, H.I.*, 4–7. Honolulu: Hawaiian Gazette Company, 1893.

Emerson, Nathaniel B. "Biographical Sketch of David Malo." In David Malo, *Hawaiian Antiquities (Moolelo Hawaii)*, vii–xv. Translated by Nathaniel B. Emerson. 1903; repr., Honolulu: Bishop Museum Press, 1951.

Emerson, Nathaniel B. *The Long Voyages of the Ancient Hawaiians*. Honolulu: Hawaiian Historical Society, 1893.

Emerson, Nathaniel B. "The Mythical Story of Maui, the Prometheus of Polynesia." In *The International Folk-Lore Congress of the World's Columbian Exposition, Chicago, July, 1893*, 288–93. Chicago, IL: Charles H. Sergel Company, 1898.

Emerson, Nathaniel B. *Pele and Hiiaka: A Myth from Hawaii*. 1915; repr., Rutland, VT: Charles E. Tuttle Company, 1978.

Emerson, Nathaniel B. "Unwritten Literature of Hawaii." *American Anthropologist*, n.s., 8, no. 2 (1906): 271–75.

Emerson, Nathaniel B. *Unwritten Literature of Hawaii: The Sacred Songs of the Hula*. Washington, DC: Government Printing Office, 1909.

Emerson, Oliver Pomeroy. *Pioneer Days in Hawaii*. Garden City, NY: Doubleday, Doran & Company, 1928.

Engleman, Harry. *A Peep into Paradise: Reminiscences from the Islands of Kauai, Oahu, Maui and Hawaii*. Los Angeles, CA: Tribune Press, 1929.

Erdman, John P. "A Brief Historical Sketch of the Hawaiian Board of Missions." In Hawaiian Mission Centennial, *The Centennial Book: One Hundred Years of Christian Civilization in Hawaii, 1820–1920*, 77–79. Honolulu: Central Committee of the Hawaiian Mission Centennial, 1920.

Farmer, Harry. *The Philippine Mission of the Methodist Episcopal Church*. New York: Board of Foreign Missions of the Methodist Episcopal Church, 1910.

Fleming, Daniel Johnson. "Foreword." In Frank Charles Laubach, *The People of the Philippines: Their Religious Progress and Preparation for Spiritual Leadership in the Far East*, v–vi. New York: George H. Doran Company, 1925.

Foreman, John. *The Philippine Islands: A Historical, Geographical, Ethnographical, Social and Commercial Sketch of the Philippine Archipelago and Its Political Dependencies*. London: S. Low, Marston, Searle & Rivington, 1890.

Fornander, Abraham. *An Account of the Polynesian Race, Its Origin and Migrations, and the Ancient History of the Hawaiian People to the Times of Kamehameha I*. Vol. 1. 1878; repr., Rutland, VT: Charles E. Tuttle Company, 1969.

Frear, Mary Dillingham. *Memory's Silver Screen of Hawaii's Social Life*. Honolulu: N.p., n.d.

Frear, Walter F. "A Century of Achievement." In Hawaiian Mission Centennial, *The Centennial Book: One Hundred Years of Christian Civilization in Hawaii, 1820–1920*, 5–16. Honolulu: Central Committee of the Hawaiian Mission Centennial, 1920.

Frear, Walter F. "Minutes of Annual Meeting, Held January 14, 1907." In *Fourteenth Annual Report of the Hawaiian Historical Society for the Year Ending Dec. 31st, 1906*, 6–7. Honolulu: Hawaiian Gazette Co., 1907.

Gulick, Orramel Hinckley, and Ann Eliza Clark Gulick. *The Pilgrims of Hawaii: Their Own Story of Pilgrimage from New England and Life Work in the Sandwich Islands, Now Known as Hawaii, with Explanatory and Illustrative Material Compiled and Verified from Original Sources*. New York: Fleming H. Revell Company, 1918.

Hale Nauā. *Constitution and By-Laws of the Hale Naua, or Temple of Science*. San Francisco, CA: The Bancroft Company, 1890.

Hawaiian Church Mission (Sandwich Islands). [Honolulu]: N.p., n.d. [1887].

Hawaiian Mission Centennial. *Official Program for the Events of Centennial Week.* [Honolulu: Centennial Committees, 1920.]

Hawaiian Mission Children's Society. *Jubilee Celebration of the Arrival of the Missionary Reinforcement of 1837, Held April 9th, 10th, and 11th, 1887.* Honolulu: Daily Bulletin Steam Print, 1887.

Hawaiian Missions Centennial, Honolulu, April 11 to 19, 1920. Honolulu: Star-Bulletin Press, 1920.

Hibbard, David S. *Making a Nation: The Changing Philippines.* New York: Board of Foreign Missions of the Presbyterian Church in the United States of America, 1926.

Hyde, Charles M. *Father Damien and His Work for the Hawaiian Lepers: A Careful and Candid Estimate.* Boston, MA: Thomas Todd, 1890.

Hyde, Charles M. "Minutes of the Annual Meeting." In *Fourth Annual Report of the Hawaiian Historical Society, Honolulu, H.I.*, 3–4. Honolulu: Robert Grieve, 1896.

Intervention of United States Government in Affairs of Foreign Friendly Governments. 53rd Congress, 2nd Session, House of Representatives Report No. 243. Washington, DC: Government Printing Office, 1893.

Johnston, Mercer Green. *Plain American Talk in the Philippines.* Manila: John R. Edgar & Co., 1907.

Judd, Albert Francis. "Introductory Note." In Laura Fish Judd, *Honolulu: Sketches of Life Social, Political, and Religious in the Hawaiian Islands from 1828 to 1861*, iii–iv. New York: Anson D. Randolph & Company, 1880.

Judd, Laura Fish. *Honolulu: Sketches of Life Social, Political, and Religious in the Hawaiian Islands from 1828 to 1861.* New York: Anson D. Randolph & Company, 1880.

Kalākaua Dead: The King Dies on a Foreign Shore, Passes Away at the Palace Hotel at San Francisco, Cal., January 20, 1891. Honolulu: Bulletin Publishing Company, 1891.

Kamakau, Samuel M. *Ka Poʻe Kahiko: The People of Old.* Edited by Dorothy B. Barrère. Translated by Mary Kawena Pukui. Honolulu: Bishop Museum Press, 1964.

Kershner, Bruce L. *The Head Hunter and Other Stories of the Philippines.* Cincinnati, OH: Powell & White, 1921.

Laubach, Frank Charles. *The People of the Philippines: Their Religious Progress and Preparation for Spiritual Leadership in the Far East.* New York: George H. Doran Company, 1925.

Laubach, Frank Charles. *Rizal: Man and Martyr.* Manila: Community Publishers, Inc., 1936.

LeRoy, James A. "Apolinario Mabini on the Failure of the Filipino Revolution." *American Historical Review* 11, no. 4 (1906): 843–61.

LeRoy, James A. "Reviews of Books: *The Philippine Islands.* By John Foreman." *American Historical Review* 12, no. 2 (1907): 388–91.

"A Letter from Prof. Townsend." In *Eleventh Annual Report of the Hawaiian Historical Society for the Year Ending Dec. 31st, 1903*, 10–11. Honolulu: [Hawaiian] Gazette, 1904.

Lewis, A., Jr. "Minutes of Meeting of Hawaiian Historical Society, Held at the Library, August 20, 1908 at 7:30 P.M.." In *Sixteenth Annual Report of the Hawaiian Historical Society and Papers for the Year Ending December 31st, 1908*, 5–7. Honolulu: Hawaiian Gazette Co., 1909.

Lili'uokalani. *Hawaii's Story by Hawaii's Queen.* Boston, MA: Lothrop, Lee & Shepard Co., 1898.

Lyman, Henry M. *Hawaiian Yesterdays: Chapters from a Boy's Life in the Islands in the Early Days.* Chicago, IL: A. C. McClurg & Co., 1906.

Lyman, R. A. "Recollections of Kamehameha V." In *Third Annual Report of the Hawaiian Historical Society,* 12–19. Honolulu: Robert Grieve, 1895.

Malo, David. *Hawaiian Antiquities (Moolelo Hawaii).* Translated by Nathaniel B. Emerson. 1903; repr., Honolulu: Bishop Museum Press, 1951.

Manila Merchants' Association. *Manila, the Pearl of the Orient: Guide Book to the Intending Visitor.* Manila: Manila Merchants' Association, 1908.

Melencio, Jose P. *Arguments against Philippine Independence and Their Answers.* [Washington, DC: Philippine Press Bureau, 1919].

Message from the President of the United States, In Answer to the Senate Resolution of February 16, 1894, and Transmitting Copies of Additional Dispatches, and Exhibits Thereto, Relating to Hawaii. Washington, DC: Government Printing Office, 1894.

Montgomery, Helen Barrett. *Christus Redemptor: An Outline Study of the Island World of the Pacific.* New York: The Macmillan Company, 1906.

Moots, Cornelia Chillson. *Pioneer "Americanas," or, First Methodist Missionaries in the Philippines.* [Bay City, MI,]: N.p., 1903.

Mott, John R. *The Evangelization of the World in This Generation.* New York: Student Volunteer Movement for Foreign Missions, 1901.

"Officers—1901." In *Annual Report of the Hawaiian Historical Society with a Paper on the History of the Honolulu Fort by Dr N. B. Emerson,* 2. Honolulu: The Robert Grieve Publishing Company, 1900.

"Officers and Members of the Board of the Hawaiian Evangelical Association for 1879–80." In *Annual Report of the Hawaiian Evangelical Association: Presented at the Meeting Held at Honolulu, June 3–10, 1879,* 2. Honolulu: J. H. Black, 1879.

"Officers and Members of the Board of the Hawaiian Evangelical Association, 1898–99." In *Thirty-Fifth Annual Report of the Hawaiian Evangelical Association,* 2. Honolulu: Hawaiian Board, 1898.

"Officers for 1879–80." In *Twenty-Seventh Annual Report of the Hawaiian Mission Children's Society, Presented June 7th, 1879,* 2. Honolulu: J. H. Black, 1880.

"Officers for 1884–5." In *Thirty-Third Annual Report of the Hawaiian Mission Children's Society, Presented June 8, 1885,* 2. Honolulu: Hawaiian Gazette Publishing Company, 1885.

Official Journal of the Second Annual Convention of the Missionary District of the Philippine Islands, Held in S. Stephen's Church Manila, Wednesday, Thursday, and Friday January 27, 28, 29 1904. Manila: Methodist Publishing House, 1904.

Oleson, W. B. "Address of the Retiring President Rev. W. B. Oleson." In *Thirty-Seventh Annual Report of the Hawaiian Mission Children's Society, Presented June 8, 1889,* 30–38. Honolulu: Press Publishing Company Print, 1889.

Osías, Camilo, and Avelina Lorenzana. *Evangelical Christianity in the Philippines.* Dayton, OH: United Brethren Publishing House, 1931.

Our Relations with Hawaii: Speech of Hon. J. F. Stallings, of Alabama, in the House of Representatives, Tuesday, February 6, 1894. Honolulu: Holomua Publishing Co., 1894.
Paterno, P. A. *El Cristianismo en la Antigua Civilización Tagalog*. Madrid: Imprenta Moderna, 1892.
Pentecost, George F. *Protestantism in the Philippines: Its Relation to the State, to the Roman Catholic Church, and to the People*. Manila: American Bible Society, 1903.
Perry, Antonio. "The Catholic Church in Hawaii." In Hawaiian Mission Centennial, *The Centennial Book: One Hundred Years of Christian Civilization in Hawaii, 1820–1920*, 65–69. Honolulu: Central Committee of the Hawaiian Mission Centennial, 1920.
Phelps, Austin. "Introduction." In Josiah Strong, *Our Country: Its Possible Future and Its Present Crisis*, iii–vii. New York: Baker & Taylor Co., 1885.
Pierson, Arthur T. *The Crisis of Missions; Or, The Voice Out of the Cloud*. New York: Robert Carter and Brothers, 1886.
"Recapitulation." In *Forty-Third Annual Report of the Hawaiian Mission Children's Society, Presented June 1, 1895, with the Constitution and By-Laws and Full List of Members*, 83. Honolulu: Press Publishing Company Print, 1895.
Relations with Hawaii: Message of the President of the United States dated January 22, 1894, Transmitting Additional Correspondence Relating to the Hawaiian Islands. 53rd Congress, 2nd Session, House of Representatives Ex. Doc. No. 79. Washington, DC: Government Printing Office, 1894.
Report of the Board of Genealogy of Hawaiian Chiefs. Honolulu, 1884.
Restarick, Henry Bond. *Hawaii, 1778–1920, from the Viewpoint of a Bishop: Being the Story of English and American Churchmen in Hawaii, with Historical Sidelights*. Honolulu: Paradise of the Pacific, 1924.
Restarick, Henry Bond. "The Story of the Mission: A Statement of Values." In Hawaiian Mission Centennial, *The Centennial Book: One Hundred Years of Christian Civilization in Hawaii, 1820–1920*, 53–56. Honolulu: Central Committee of the Hawaiian Mission Centennial, 1920.
Rodgers, James B. *Forty Years in the Philippines: A History of the Philippine Mission of the Presbyterian Church in the United States of America 1899–1939*. New York: Board of Foreign Missions of the Presbyterian Church in the United States of America, 1940.
Roosevelt, Theodore. "The Strenuous Life." 1899. Accessed June 22, 2021. Voices of Democracy: The U.S. Oratory Project. https://voicesofdemocracy.umd.edu/roosevelt-strenuous-life-1899-speech-text/.
Sewall, H. M. "Part of a Paper on the Partition of Samoa and the Past Relations between that Group and the United States, Read before the Hawaiian Historical Society, May 11, 1900, by Hon. H. M. Sewall." In *Seventh Annual Report of the Hawaiian Historical Society with a Paper on the Partition of Samoa, and the Past Relations between that Group and the United States, by Hon. H. M. Sewall*, 11–27. Honolulu: The Robert Grieve Publishing Company, 1900.
"Six Election Broadsides Issued by Kalakaua and Queen Emma." n.d. [1874]. In *Kalakaua's Hawaii, 1874–1891: A Collection of Pamphlets Dealing with the Political, Social and Economic History of Hawaii during the Reign of King Kalakaua and the Many Controversies of the Period*. Microfilm. Honolulu: Hawaiian Historical Society, 1968.

A Sketch of Recent Events, Being a Short Account of the Events which Culminated on June 30, 1887, Together with a Full Report of the Great Reform Meeting, and the Two Constitutions in Parallel Columns. Honolulu: A. M. Hewett, 1887.

Smith, William O. "Address of the Retiring President." In *Thirtieth Annual Report of the Hawaiian Mission Children's Society, Presented June 17th, 1882,* 35–44. Honolulu: R. Grieve & Co., Hawaiian Gazette, 1882.

Speer, Robert E. *Missions and Modern History: A Study of the Missionary Aspects of Some Great Movements of the Nineteenth Century.* 2 vols. New York: Fleming H. Revell Company, 1904.

Spencer, Caroline S. *What the Golden Rule Has Accomplished among the Moros.* New York: National Committee for Upbuilding the Wards of the Nation in the Philippines, 1915.

Staley, T. N. *A Pastoral Address, by the Right Reverend the Bishop of Honolulu, Delivered in His Church on New Year's Day, 1865, in Reply to Certain Mis-Statements in a Recent Report of the American Board of Commissioners for Foreign Missions.* Honolulu: Hawaiian Gazette Office, 1865.

"Statement on the Death of Dr. James A. Graham and Dr. George W. Wright." In *Minutes of the Executive Committee of the Philippine Mission of the Board of Foreign Missions, Presbyterian Church in the U.S.A,* 26. Manila: N.p., 1940.

Stoddard, Charles Warren. *Father Damien: The Martyr of Molokai.* San Francisco, CA: Catholic Truth Society, 1901.

Stuntz, Homer C. *The Open Door in the Philippines.* New York: Missionary Society of the Methodist Church Rindge Literature Department, 1903.

Stuntz, Homer C. *The Philippines and the Far East.* Cincinnati, OH: Jennings and Pye, 1904.

Stuntz, Homer C. *Wanted: A Filipino Church in Old Manila.* [Manila]: N.p., 1903.

Taylor, Persis G. "Report of the Corresponding Secretary." In *Annual Report of the Hawaiian Mission Children's Society, Presented May 21st, 1853,* 7–10. Honolulu: Government Press, 1853.

Thrum, Thomas G. "The Native Leaders of Hawaii: Their Contribution to the Cause of Christian Civilization, The Kuhina-Nui and Privy Council." In Hawaiian Mission Centennial, *The Centennial Book: One Hundred Years of Christian Civilization in Hawaii, 1820–1920,* 17–23. Honolulu: Central Committee of the Hawaiian Mission Centennial, 1920.

Thrum, Thomas G. *The Shepherd Saint of Lanai: Rich "Primacy" Revelations, Gathered from Various Sources and Produced in Historical Form for the First Time, in the "Saturday Press," Dec. 24, 1881 to Jan. 21, 1882.* Honolulu: Thomas G. Thrum, 1882.

Thurston, Lorrin. "Preface and a Brief Biography of Sereno Edwards Bishop." In Sereno Edwards Bishop, *Reminiscences of Old Hawaii,* 3–11. Honolulu: Hawaiian Gazette Co., Ltd., 1916.

Trent, Richard H. "The Methodist Episcopal Church in Hawaii." In Hawaiian Mission Centennial, *The Centennial Book: One Hundred Years of Christian Civilization in Hawaii, 1820–1920,* 72–73. Honolulu: Central Committee of the Hawaiian Mission Centennial, 1920.

Turner, Frederick Jackson. "The Significance of the Frontier in American History." In *Proceedings of the State Historical Society of Wisconsin*, 79–112. Madison: Democrat Printing Co., 1894.
Twain, Mark. "Our Fellow Savages of the Sandwich Islands." n.d. [1869–70.] Accessed November 20, 2020. https://twain.lib.virginia.edu/onstage/savlect.html.
Twain, Mark. *Roughing It*. Hartford, CT: American Publishing Company, 1872.
Twain, Mark. "To the Person Sitting in Darkness." *North American Review*, February 1901: 161–76.
Warne, Frank W. "Prefatory Note." In Alice Byram Condict, *Old Glory and the Gospel in the Philippines: Notes Gathered during Professional and Missionary Work*, 5–6. Chicago, IL: Fleming H. Revell Company, 1902.
Waterbury, Mrs. Norman Mather, E. Harriet Stanwood, Ellen C. Parsons, Mrs. J. T. Gracey, Mrs. Decatur Sawyer, and Clementina Butler. "Foreword." In Helen Barrett Montgomery, *Christus Redemptor: An Outline Study of the Island World of the Pacific*, v. New York: Macmillan Company, 1906.
Wetmore, Mary B. "Extract from *Sounds from Home and Echoes of a Kingdom* (Cincinnati, OH: The Editor Publishing Co., 1898)." In *Glimpses of Hawaiian Daily Life and Culture*, ed. Gary Dean Best and Mary Lani Best, 283–85. New York: American Heritage Custom Publishing, 1994.
Whitaker, Robert. "Foreword." In Orramel Hinckley Gulick and Ann Eliza Clark Gulick, *The Pilgrims of Hawaii: Their Own Story of Pilgrimage from New England and Life Work in the Sandwich Islands, Now Known as Hawaii, with Explanatory and Illustrative Material Compiled and Verified from Original Sources*, 11–12. New York: Fleming H. Revell Company, 1918.
Whitney, Henry M. *The Hawaiian Guide Book, Containing Brief Description of the Hawaiian Islands, Their Harbors, Agricultural Resources, Plantations, Scenery, Volcanoes, Climate, Population, and Commerce*. Honolulu: Henry M. Whitney, 1875.
Willis, Alfred. *The Principles of Government of the Anglican Church in Hawaii, Traced to Their Source, for the Settlement of Certain Controversial Questions; To Which Is Added a Review of the Present Position of the Anglican Church in the Kingdom of Hawaii*. Honolulu: Robert Grieve, 1890.
Yzendoorn, Reginald. "The Introduction of the Algaroba." In *Eighteenth Annual Report (Nineteenth Year) of the Hawaiian Historical Society for the Year 1910*, 29–34. Honolulu: Paradise of the Pacific Print, 1911.

Secondary Sources

Achútegui, Pedro S. de, and Miguel A. Bernad. *Religious Revolution in the Philippines: The Life and Church of Gregorio Aglipay, 1890–1906*. 2nd ed. Vol. 1, *From Aglipay's Birth to His Death, 1860–1940*. Manila: Ateneo de Manila, 1961.
Adams, David Wallace. *Education for Extinction: American Indians and the Boarding School Experience, 1875–1928*. Lawrence: University Press of Kansas, 1995.

Aguilar, Filomeno V., Jr. "Tracing Origins: *Ilustrado* Nationalism and the Racial Science of Migration Waves." *Journal of Asian Studies* 64, no. 2 (2005): 605–37.
Aikau, Hokulani K. *A Chosen People, a Promised Land: Mormonism and Race in Hawai'i.* Minneapolis: University of Minnesota Press, 2012.
Alidio, Kimberley. "'When I Get Home, I Want to Forget': Memory and Amnesia in the Occupied Philippines, 1901–1904." *Social Text* 59 (1999): 105–22.
Allen, Thomas M. *A Republic in Time: Temporality and Social Imagination in Nineteenth-Century America.* Chapel Hill: University of North Carolina Press, 2008.
"The American Lake: A Brief History of America in the Pacific." *The Economist,* April 20, 2017. Accessed July 7, 2021. https://www.economist.com/special-report/2017/04/20/a-brief-history-of-america-in-the-pacific.
Anderson, Benedict. *Under Three Flags: Anarchists and the Anti-Colonial Imagination.* London: Verso, 2005.
Anderson, Warwick. *Colonial Pathologies: American Tropical Medicine, Race, and Hygiene in the Philippines.* Durham, NC: Duke University Press, 2006.
Apilado, Mariano C. *Revolutionary Spirituality: A Study of the Protestant Role in the American Colonial Philippines, 1898–1928.* Quezon City: New Day Publishers, 1999.
Archer, Seth. "Remedial Agents: Missionary Physicians and the Depopulation of Hawai'i." *Pacific Historical Review* 79, no. 4 (2010): 513–44.
Archer, Seth. *Sharks upon the Land: Colonialism, Indigenous Health, and Culture in Hawai'i, 1778–1855.* New York: Cambridge University Press, 2018.
Arista, Noelani. *The Kingdom and the Republic: Sovereign Hawai'i and the Early United States.* Philadelphia: University of Pennsylvania Press, 2018.
Armitage, David, and Alison Bashford. "Introduction: The Pacific and Its Histories." In *Pacific Histories: Ocean, Land, People,* ed. David Armitage and Alison Bashford, 1–28. Basingstoke: Palgrave Macmillan, 2014.
Arvin, Maile. *Possessing Polynesians: The Science of Settler Colonial Whiteness in Hawai'i and Oceania.* Durham, NC: Duke University Press, 2019.
Ballantyne, Tony. *Orientalism and Race: Aryanism in the British Empire.* Basingstoke: Palgrave, 2002.
Balmer, Randall. *Mine Eyes Have Seen the Glory: A Journey into the Evangelical Subculture in America.* New York: Oxford University Press, 1989.
Banner, Stuart. *Possessing the Pacific: Land, Settlers, and Indigenous People from Australia to Alaska.* Cambridge, MA: Harvard University Press, 2007.
Bashford, Alison. "The Pacific Ocean." In *Oceanic Histories,* ed. David Armitage, Alison Bashford, and Sujit Sivasundaram, 62–84. New York: Cambridge University Press, 2017.
Beamer, Kamanamaikalani. *No Mākou ka Mana: Liberating the Nation.* Honolulu: Kamehameha Publishing, 2014.
Bederman, Gail. *Manliness and Civilization: A Cultural History of Gender and Race in the United States, 1880–1917.* Chicago, IL: University of Chicago Press, 1995.
Beisner, Robert L. *Twelve against Empire: The Anti-Imperialists, 1898–1900.* New York: McGraw-Hill, 1968.

Bell, Duncan. *Dreamworlds of Race: Empire and the Utopian Destiny of Anglo-America.* Princeton, NJ: Princeton University Press, 2020.
Bemis, Samuel Flagg. *A Diplomatic History of the United States.* New York: Henry Holt and Company, 1936.
Bendroth, Margaret. *The Last Puritans: Mainline Protestants and the Power of the Past.* Chapel Hill: University of North Carolina Press, 2015.
Bendroth, Margaret. "Time, History, and Tradition in the Fundamentalist Imagination." *Church History* 85, no. 2 (2016): 328–42.
Bercovitch, Sacvan. *The American Jeremiad.* Madison: University of Wisconsin Press, 1978.
Beyer, Carl Kalani. "Manual and Industrial Education for Hawaiians during the 19th Century." *Hawaiian Journal of History* 38 (2004): 1–34.
Blanco, John D. *Frontier Constitutions: Christianity and Colonial Empire in the Nineteenth-Century Philippines.* Berkeley: University of California Press, 2009.
Blight, David W. *Race and Reunion: The Civil War in American Memory.* Cambridge, MA: Harvard University Press, 2001.
Borofsky, Robert. "An Invitation." In *Remembrances of Pacific Pasts: An Invitation to Remake History*, ed. Robert Borofsky, 1–30. Honolulu: University of Hawai'i Press, 2000.
Brantlinger, Patrick. *Dark Vanishings: Discourse on the Extinction of Primitive Races, 1800–1930.* Ithaca, NY: Cornell University Press, 2003.
Brody, David. "Building Empire: Architecture and American Imperialism in the Philippines." *Journal of Asian American Studies* 4, no. 2 (2001): 123–45.
Brown, Marie Alohalani. *Facing the Spears of Change: The Life and Legacy of John Papa ʻĪʻī.* Honolulu: University of Hawai'i Press, 2016.
Brown, Michael F. "Cultural Relativism 2.0." *Current Anthropology* 49, no. 3 (2008): 363–83.
Buschmann, Ranier, Edward R. Slack Jr., and James B. Tueller. *Navigating the Spanish Lake: The Pacific in the Iberian World, 1521–1898.* Honolulu: University of Hawai'i Press, 2014.
Campbell, Gavin James. "'To Make the World One in Christ Jesus': Transpacific Protestantism in the Age of Empire." *Pacific Historical Review* 87, no. 4 (2018): 575–92.
Capozzola, Christopher. *Bound by War: How the United States and the Philippines Built America's First Pacific Century.* New York: Basic Books, 2020.
Chakrabarty, Dipesh. "The Time of History and the Times of Gods." In *The Politics of Culture in the Shadow of Capital*, ed. Lisa Lowe and David Lloyd, 35–60. Durham, NC: Duke University Press, 1997.
Chang, David A. *The World and All the Things upon It: Native Hawaiian Geographies of Exploration.* Minneapolis: University of Minnesota Press, 2016.
Charbonneau, Oliver. *Civilizational Imperatives: Americans, Moros, and the Colonial World.* Ithaca, NY: Cornell University Press, 2020.
Choy, Catherine Ceniza, and Judy Tzu-Chun Wu. "Gendering the Trans-Pacific World." In *Gendering the Trans-Pacific World*, ed. Catherine Ceniza Choy and Judy Tzu-Chun Wu, 3–9. Leiden: Brill, 2017.

Christian, Eloise. "Preface." In David Malo, *Hawaiian Antiquities (Moolelo Hawaii)*. Translated by Nathaniel B. Emerson, xix–xx. 1903; repr., Honolulu: Bishop Museum Press, 1951.

Clark, Dan E. "Manifest Destiny and the Pacific." *Pacific Historical Review* 1, no. 1 (1932): 1–17.

Clymer, Kenton. *Protestant Missionaries in the Philippines, 1898–1916: An Inquiry into the American Colonial Mentality*. Urbana: University of Illinois Press, 1986.

Clymer, Kenton. "Southeast Asia: Where We Have Been, Where We Can Go?" *Diplomatic History* 45, no. 2 (2021): 223–39.

Coffman, Tom. *Nation Within: The History of the American Occupation of Hawaiʻi*. Rev. ed. Durham, NC: Duke University Press, 2016.

Comaroff, Jean, and John L. Comaroff. *Ethnography and the Historical Imagination*. Boulder, CO: Westview Press, 1992.

Comaroff, Jean, and John L. Comaroff. *Of Revelation and Revolution*. Vol. 1, *Christianity, Colonialism, and Consciousness in South Africa*. Chicago, IL: Chicago University Press, 1991.

Compoc, Kim. "Considerations from the U.S.-Occupied Pacific." In *Filipinx American Studies: Reckoning, Reclamation, Transformation*, ed. Rick Bonus and Antonio Tiongson, 267–74. New York: Fordham University Press, 2022.

Compoc, Kim. "Weaving Our Sovereignties Together: Maximizing Ea for Filipinx and Hawaiians." *Amerasia* 43, no. 3 (2019): 316–35.

Connery, Christopher L. "Pacific Rim Discourse: The U.S. Global Imaginary and the Late Cold War Years." In *Asia/Pacific as a Space of Cultural Production*, ed. Rob Wilson and Arif Dirlik, 30–56. Durham, NC: Duke University Press, 1995.

Conroy-Krutz, Emily. *Christian Imperialism: Converting the World in the Early Republic*. Ithaca, NY: Cornell University Press, 2015.

Conroy-Krutz, Emily. "Foreign Missions and Strategy, Foreign Missions as Strategy." In *Rethinking American Grand Strategy*, ed. Elizabeth Borgwardt, Christopher McKnight Nichols, and Andrew Preston, 311–28. New York: Oxford University Press, 2021.

Cook, Kealani. *Return to Kahiki: Native Hawaiians in Oceania*. New York: Cambridge University Press, 2018.

Cronon, William. *Nature's Metropolis: Chicago and the Great West*. New York: W. W. Norton, 1991.

Cumings, Bruce. *Dominion from Sea to Sea: Pacific Ascendancy and American Power*. New Haven, CT: Yale University Press, 2009.

Curtis, Heather D. *Holy Humanitarians: American Evangelicals and Global Aid*. Cambridge, MA: Harvard University Press, 2018.

CuUnjieng Aboitiz, Nicole. *Asian Place, Filipino Nation: A Global Intellectual History of the Philippine Revolution, 1887–1912*. New York: Columbia University Press, 2020.

D'Arcy, Paul. "Sea Worlds: Pacific and South-East Asian History Centered on the Philippines." In *Oceans Connect: Reflections on Water Worlds Across Time and Space*, ed. Rila Mukherjee, 23–38. Delhi: Primus Books, 2013.

Daws, Gavan. *Shoal of Time: A History of the Hawaiian Islands*. Honolulu: University of Hawaiʻi Press, 1968.

Deloria, Philip J. *Playing Indian*. New Haven, CT: Yale University Press, 1999.
Dening, Greg. "History 'in' the Pacific." *Contemporary Pacific* 1, no. 1/2 (1989): 134–39.
Dippie, Brian W. *The Vanishing American: White Attitudes and U.S. Indian Policy*. Middletown, CT: Wesleyan University Press, 1982.
Dirlik, Arif. *What Is in a Rim? Critical Perspectives on the Pacific Region Idea*. Boulder, CO: Westview Press, 1993.
Dizon, Salud C., and Maria Elinora P. Imson. "Preface." In Isabelo de los Reyes y Florentino, *El folk-lore filipino*, xi–xii. Translated by Salud C. Dizon and Maria Elinora P. Imson. Quezon City: University of the Philippines Press, 1994.
Doeppers, Daniel F. "Manila's Imperial Makeover: Security, Health, and Symbolism." In *Colonial Crucible: Empire in the Making of the Modern American State*, ed. Alfred W. McCoy and Francisco A. Scarano, 489–98. Madison: University of Wisconsin Press, 2009.
Doty, Helen. "Introduction to the New Edition." In Abraham Fornander, *An Account of the Polynesian Race, Its Origin and Migrations, and the Ancient History of the Hawaiian People to the Times of Kamehameha I*, ix–xii. Rutland, VT: Charles E. Tuttle Company, 1969.
Drinnon, Richard. *Facing West: The Metaphysics of Indian-Hating and Empire-Building*. Minneapolis: University of Minnesota Press, 1980.
Dudden, Arthur Power. *The American Pacific: From the Old China Trade to the Present*. New York: Oxford University Press, 1992.
Dunch, Ryan. "Beyond Cultural Imperialism: Cultural Theory, Christian Missions, and Global Modernity." *History and Theory* 41, no. 3 (2002): 301–25.
Dunch, Ryan. *Fuzhou Protestants and the Making of a Modern China, 1857–1927*. New Haven, CT: Yale University Press, 2001.
Dvorak, Greg. "Oceanizing American Studies." *American Quarterly* 67, no. 3 (2015): 609–17.
Eperjesi, John R. *The Imperialist Imaginary: Visions of Asia and the Pacific in American Culture*. Hanover, NH: Dartmouth College Press, 2005.
Fairbank, John K., ed. *The Missionary Enterprise in China and America*. Cambridge, MA: Harvard University Press, 1974.
Finney, Ben R. *Sailing in the Wake of the Ancestors: Reviving Polynesian Voyaging*. Honolulu: Bishop Museum Press, 2003.
Fish Kashay, Jennifer. "Agents of Imperialism: Missionaries and Merchants in Early-Nineteenth-Century Hawaii." *New England Quarterly* 80, no. 2 (2007): 280–98.
Fish Kashay, Jennifer. "Savages, Sinners, and Saints: The Hawaiian Kingdom and the Imperial Conquest, 1778–1839." PhD diss., University of Arizona, 2002.
Forbes, David W., ed. *Hawaiian National Bibliography, 1789–1900*. Vol. 4, *1881–1900*. Honolulu: University of Hawai'i Press, 1998.
Fuchs, Lawrence H. *Hawaii Pono: A Social History*. New York: Harcourt, Brace & World, 1961.
Fujikane, Candace, and Jonathan Y. Okamura, eds. *Asian Settler Colonialism: From Local Governance to the Habits of Everyday Life in Hawaii*. Honolulu: University of Hawai'i Press, 2008.

Geiger, Jeffrey. *Facing the Pacific: Polynesia and the U.S. Imperial Imagination*. Honolulu: University of Hawai'i Press, 2007.

Geissler, Suzanne. *God and Sea Power: The Influence of Religion on Alfred Thayer Mahan*. Annapolis, MD: Naval Institute Press, 2015.

Gin Lum, Kathryn. *Heathen: Religion and Race in American History*. Cambridge, MA: Harvard University Press, 2022.

Gin Lum, Kathryn. "The Historyless Heathen and the Stagnating Pagan: History as Non-Native Category?" *Religion and American Culture* 28, no. 1 (2018): 52–91.

Go, Julian. "Introduction: Global Perspectives on the U.S. Colonial State in the Philippines." In *The American Colonial State in the Philippines*, ed. Julian Go and Anne L. Foster, 1–42. Durham, NC: Duke University Press, 2003.

Go, Julian. *Patterns of Empire: The British and American Empires, 1688 to the Present*. New York: Cambridge University Press, 2011.

Gonschor, Lorenz. *A Power in the World: The Hawaiian Kingdom in Oceania*. Honolulu: University of Hawai'i Press, 2019.

Gonzalez, Vernadette Vicuña. *Securing Paradise: Tourism and Militarism in Hawai'i and the Philippines*. Durham, NC: Duke University Press, 2013.

Grabill, Joseph L. "The 'Invisible' Missionary: A Study in American Foreign Relations." *Journal of Church and State* 14, no. 1 (1972): 93–105.

Grabill, Joseph L. *Protestant Diplomacy and the Near East, 1820–1960*. Minneapolis: University of Minnesota Press, 1971.

Green, Michael. *By More than Providence: Grand Strategy and American Power in the Asia Pacific since 1783*. New York: Columbia University Press, 2017.

Grimshaw, Patricia. *Paths of Duty: American Missionary Wives in Nineteenth-Century Hawaii*. Honolulu: University of Hawai'i Press, 1989.

Guyatt, Nicholas. *Providence and the Invention of the United States, 1607–1876*. New York: Cambridge University Press, 2007.

Harris, Paul William. "Cultural Imperialism and American Protestant Missionaries: Collaboration and Dependency in Mid-Nineteenth Century China." *Pacific Historical Review* 60, no. 3 (1991): 309–38.

Harris, Paul William. *Nothing but Christ: Rufus Anderson and the Ideology of Protestant Foreign Missions*. New York: Oxford University Press, 1999.

Harris, Susan K. *God's Arbiters: Americans and the Philippines, 1898–1902*. New York: Oxford University Press, 2011.

Hasinoff, Erin. "The Missionary Exhibit." *Museum History Journal* 3, no. 1 (2010): 81–102.

Hau'ofa, Epeli. "Our Sea of Islands." *Contemporary Pacific* 6, no. 1 (1994): 147–61.

Hawkins, Michael C. *Making Moros: Imperial Historicism and American Military Rule in the Philippines' Muslim South*. DeKalb: Northern Illinois University Press, 2013.

Higham, John. *Strangers in the Land: Patterns of American Nativism, 1860–1925*. New Brunswick, NJ: Rutgers University Press, 1955.

Hill, Patricia R. *The World Their Household: The American Women's Foreign Mission Movement and Cultural Transformation, 1870–1920*. Ann Arbor: University of Michigan Press, 1985.

Hixson, Walter L. *American Settler Colonialism: A History*. New York: Palgrave Macmillan, 2013.
Hofstadter, Richard. *The Paranoid Style in American Politics and Other Essays*. London: Cape, 1966.
Hoganson, Kristin L. *Fighting for American Manhood: How Gender Politics Provoked the Spanish-American and Philippine-American Wars*. New Haven, CT: Yale University Press, 1997.
Hollinger, David A. *Protestants Abroad: How Missionaries Tried to Change the World but Changed America*. Princeton, NJ: Princeton University Press, 2017.
Horne, Gerald. *The White Pacific: U.S. Imperialism and Black Slavery in the South Seas after the Civil War*. Honolulu: University of Hawai'i Press, 2007.
Hudson, Winthrop S. "Protestant Clergy Debate the Nation's Vocation, 1898–1899." *Church History* 42, no. 1 (1973): 110–18.
Hunter, Jane. *The Gospel of Gentility: American Women Missionaries in Turn-of-the-Century China*. New Haven, CT: Yale University Press, 1984.
Hutchison, William R. *Errand to the World: American Protestant Thought and Foreign Missions*. Chicago, IL: University of Chicago Press, 1986.
Igler, David. *The Great Ocean: Pacific Worlds from Captain Cook to the Gold Rush*. New York: Oxford University Press, 2013.
Ileto, Reynaldo. "Outlines of a Nonlinear Emplotment of Philippine History." In *The Politics of Culture in the Shadow of Capital*, ed. Lisa Lowe and David Lloyd, 98–131. Durham, NC: Duke University Press, 1997.
Ileto, Reynaldo. *Pasyon and Revolution: Popular Movements in the Philippines*. Quezon City: Ateneo de Manila University Press, 1979.
Ileto, Reynaldo. "Tagalog Poetry and the Image of the Past during the War against Spain." In *Perceptions of the Past in Southeast Asia*, ed. Anthony Reid and David Marr, 379–400. Singapore: Heinemann Educational Books, 1979.
Imada, Adria L. *Aloha America: Hula Circuits through the U.S. Empire*. Durham, NC: Duke University Press, 2012.
Immerwahr, Daniel. *How to Hide an Empire: A History of the Greater United States*. New York: Farrar, Straus & Giroux, 2019.
Inglis, Kerri A. *Ma'i Lepera: Disease and Displacement in Nineteenth-Century Hawai'i*. Honolulu: University of Hawai'i Press, 2013.
Iriye, Akira. *Across the Pacific: An Inner History of American-East Asian Relations*. New York: Harcourt, Brace & World, 1967.
Iriye, Akira. "A Pacific Century?" In *Pacific Histories: Ocean, Land, People*, ed. David Armitage and Alison Bashford, 97–117. Basingstoke: Palgrave Macmillan, 2014.
Jacobs, Margaret D. "Seeing Like a Settler Colonial State." *Modern American History* 1, no. 2 (2018): 257–70.
Johnson, R. Park. "The Legacy of Arthur Judson Brown." *International Bulletin of Missionary Research* 10, no. 2 (1986): 71–75.
Jolly, Margaret. "Imagining Oceania: Indigenous and Foreign Representations of a Sea of Islands." *Contemporary Pacific* 19, no. 2 (2007): 508–45.

Jones, Arun W. *Christian Missions in the American Empire: Episcopalians in Northern Luzon, the Philippines, 1902–1946*. Frankfurt am Main: Peter Lang, 2003.
Kameʻeleihiwa, Lilikalā. *Native Land and Foreign Desires: Pehea Lā E Pono Ai?* Honolulu: Bishop Museum Press, 1992.
Kaplan, Amy. *The Anarchy of Empire in the Making of U.S. Culture*. Cambridge, MA: Harvard University Press, 2002.
Kaplan, Amy. "'Left Alone with America': The Absence of Empire in the Study of American Culture." In *Cultures of United States Imperialism*, ed. Amy Kaplan and Donald E. Pease, 3–21. Durham, NC: Duke University Press, 1993.
Karpiel, Frank. "Notes & Queries: The Hale Naua Society." *Hawaiian Journal of History* 33 (1999): 203–12.
Kauanui, J. Kēhaulani. *Hawaiian Blood: Colonialism and the Politics of Sovereignty and Indigeneity*. Durham, NC: Duke University Press, 2012.
Kauanui, J. Kēhaulani. "Imperial Ocean: The Pacific as a Critical Site for American Studies." *American Quarterly* 67, no. 3 (2015): 625–36.
Kauanui, J. Kēhaulani. *Paradoxes of Hawaiian Sovereignty: Land, Sex, and the Colonial Politics of State Nationalism*. Durham, NC: Duke University Press, 2018.
Kauanui, J. Kēhaulani. "A Sorry State: Apology Politics and Legal Fictions in the Court of the Conqueror." In *Formations of United States Colonialism*, ed. Alyosha Goldstein, 110–34. Durham, NC: Duke University Press, 2014.
Kay, E. Alison. "Missionary Contributions to Hawaiian Natural History: What Darwin Didn't Know." *Hawaiian Journal of History* 31 (1997): 27–52.
Kenny, Gale L. "The World Day of Prayer: Ecumenical Churchwomen and Christian Cosmopolitanism, 1920–1946." *Religion and American Culture* 27, no. 2 (2017): 129–58.
Klein, Kerwin Lee. *Frontiers of the Historical Imagination: Narrating the European Conquest of Native America, 1890–1990*. Berkeley: University of California Press, 1999.
Knight Lozano, Henry. *California and Hawaiʻi Bound: U.S. Settler Colonialism and the Pacific West, 1848–1959*. Lincoln: University of Nebraska Press, 2021.
Koenig, Sarah. *Providence and the Invention of American History*. New Haven, CT: Yale University Press, 2021.
Kramer, Paul A. *The Blood of Government: Race, Empire, the United States, and the Philippines*. Chapel Hill: University of North Carolina Press, 2006.
Kramer, Paul A. "Empires, Exceptions, and Anglo-Saxons: Race and Rule between the British and United States Empires, 1880–1910." *Journal of American History* 88, no. 4 (2002): 1315–53.
Kramer, Paul A. "Power and Connection: Imperial Histories of the United States in the World." *American Historical Review* 116, no. 5 (2011): 1348–91.
Kualapai, Lydia. "The Queen Writes Back: Liliʻuokalani's *Hawaii's Story by Hawaii's Queen*." *Studies in American Indian Literature* 17, no. 2 (2005): 32–62.
Kurashige, Lon, Madeline Y. Hsu, and Yujin Yaguchi. "Introduction: Conversations on Transpacific History." *Pacific Historical Review* 83, no. 2 (2014): 183–88.

Kuykendall, Ralph Simpson. *The Hawaiian Kingdom*. 3 vols. Honolulu: University of Hawai'i Press, 1938–67.

Lears, T. J. Jackson. *No Place of Grace: Antimodernism and the Transformation of American Culture, 1880–1920*. 1981; repr., Chicago: University of Chicago Press, 2021.

Lepore, Jill. *These Truths: A History of the United States*. New York: W. W. Norton & Company, 2019.

Lester, Alan. "British Settler Discourse and the Circuits of Empire." *History Workshop Journal* 54, no. 1 (2002): 24–48.

Lewis, David. *We, the Navigators: The Ancient Art of Landfinding in the Pacific*. Honolulu: University of Hawai'i Press, 1994.

Lico, Gerard. *Arkitekturang Filipino: A History of Architecture and Urbanism in the Philippines*. Quezon City: University of the Philippines Press, 2008.

Linnekin, Jocelyn. "The Politics of Culture in the Pacific." In *Cultural Identity and Ethnicity in the Pacific*, ed. Jocelyn Linnekin and Lin Poyer, 149–74. Honolulu: University of Hawai'i Press, 1990.

Lott, Eric. *Love and Theft: Blackface Minstrelsy and the American Working Class*. Twentieth anniversary ed. New York: Oxford University Press, 2013.

Love, Eric T.L. *Race over Empire: Racism and U.S. Imperialism, 1865–1900*. Chapel Hill: University of North Carolina Press, 2004.

Lyon, Jeffrey (Kapali). "Davida Malo, Nathaniel Emerson, and the 'Sins' of Hawaiians: An Analysis of Emerson's *Hawaiian Antiquities* as a Guide to Malo's *Moʻolelo Hawaiʻi*." *Hūlili: Multidisciplinary Research on Hawaiian Well-Being* 7 (2011): 91–132.

Lyons, Paul. *American Pacificism: Oceania in the U.S. Imagination*. New York: Routledge, 2006.

Lyons, Paul, and Ty P. Kāwika Tengan. "Introduction: Pacific Currents." *American Quarterly* 67, no. 3 (2015): 545–74.

Maffly-Kipp, Laurie. "Eastward Ho!: American Religion from the Perspective of the Pacific Rim." In *Retelling U.S. Religious History*, ed. Thomas A. Tweed, 127–48. Berkeley: University of California Press, 1997.

Mancini, J. M. *Art and War in the Pacific World: Making, Breaking, and Taking from Anson's Voyage to the Philippine-American War*. Berkeley: University of California Press, 2018.

Marsden, George M. *Fundamentalism and American Culture: The Shaping of Twentieth-Century Evangelicalism, 1870–1925*. New York: Oxford University Press, 1980.

Marshall, Anne E. *Creating a Confederate Kentucky: The Lost Cause and Civil War Memory in a Border State*. Chapel Hill: University of North Carolina Press, 2010.

Matsuda, Matt K. "AHR Forum: The Pacific." *American Historical Review* 111, no. 3 (2006): 758–80.

Matsuda, Matt K. *Pacific Worlds: A History of Seas, Peoples, and Cultures*. New York: Cambridge University Press, 2012.

Mawson, Stephanie J. *Incomplete Conquests: The Limits of Spanish Empire in the Seventeenth-Century Philippines*. Ithaca, NY: Cornell University Press, 2023.

McAlister, Melani. *The Kingdom of God Has No Borders: A Global History of American Evangelicals*. New York: Oxford University Press, 2018.

McCoy, Alfred W. *Policing America's Empire: The United States, the Philippines, and the Rise of the Surveillance State.* Madison: University of Wisconsin Press, 2009.

McCoy, Alfred W., Francisco A. Scarano, and Courtney Johnson. "On the Tropic of Cancer: Transitions and Transformations in the U.S. Imperial State." In *Colonial Crucible: Empire in the Making of the Modern American State,* ed. Alfred W. McCoy and Francisco A. Scarano, 3–33. Madison: University of Wisconsin Press, 2009.

McCullough, Matthew. *The Cross of War: Christian Nationalism and U.S. Expansion in the Spanish-American War.* Madison: University of Wisconsin Press, 2014.

McDougall, Brandy Nālani. "Moʻokūʻauhau versus Colonial Entitlement in English Translations of the Kumulipo." *American Quarterly* 67, no. 3 (2015): 749–79.

McDougall, Brandy Nālani. "'We Are Not American': Competing Rhetorical Archipelagoes in Hawaiʻi." In *Archipelagic American Studies,* ed. Brian Russell Roberts and Michelle Ann Stephens, 259–78. Durham, NC: Duke University Press, 2017.

McGregor, Davianna Pōmaikaʻi. *Nā Kuaʻāina: Living Hawaiian Culture.* Honolulu: University of Hawaiʻi Press, 2007.

McKenna, Rebecca Tinio. *American Imperial Pastoral: The Architecture of U.S. Colonialism in the Philippines.* Chicago, IL: University of Chicago Press, 2017.

McWilliams, Tennant S. "James H. Blount, the South, and Hawaiian Annexation." *Pacific Historical Review* 57, no. 1 (1988): 25–46.

Memmi, Albert. *The Colonizer and the Colonized.* Translated by Howard Greenfield. 1965; repr., Boston: Beacon Press, 1991.

Mendoza, Victor Román. *Metroimperial Intimacies: Fantasy, Racial-Sexual Governance, and the Philippines in U.S. Imperialism, 1899–1913.* Durham, NC: Duke University Press, 2015.

Merry, Sally Engle. *Colonizing Hawaiʻi: The Cultural Power of Law.* Princeton, NJ: Princeton University Press, 2000.

Metaxas, Virginia. "'Licentiousness Has Slain Its Hundreds of Thousands': The Missionary Discourse of Sex, Death, and Disease in Nineteenth-Century Hawaiʻi." In *Gender and Globalization in Asia and the Pacific: Method, Practice, Theory,* ed. Kathy E. Ferguson and Monique Mironesco, 37–55. Honolulu: University of Hawaiʻi Press, 2008.

Miller, Stuart Creighton. *"Benevolent Assimilation": The American Conquest of the Philippines, 1899–1903.* New Haven, CT: Yale University Press, 1982.

Miller-Davenport, Sarah. *Gateway State: Hawaiʻi and the Cultural Transformation of American Empire.* Princeton, NJ: Princeton University Press, 2019.

Mislin, David. *Saving Faith: Making Religious Pluralism an American Value at the Dawn of the Secular Age.* Ithaca, NY: Cornell University Press, 2015.

Mojares, Resil B. *Brains of the Nation: Pedro Paterno, T. H. Pardo de Tavera, Isabelo de los Reyes, and the Production of Modern Knowledge.* Honolulu: University of Hawaiʻi Press, 2006.

Moore, Colin D. *American Imperialism and the State, 1893–1921.* New York: Cambridge University Press, 2017.

Moran, Katherine D. "Catholicism and the Making of the U.S. Pacific." *Journal of the Gilded Age and Progressive Era* 12, no. 4 (2013): 434–74.

Moran, Katherine D. *The Imperial Church: Catholic Founding Fathers and United States Empire.* Ithaca, NY: Cornell University Press, 2020.
Morgan, Francesca. *A Nation of Descendants: Politics and the Practice of Genealogy in U.S. History.* Chapel Hill: University of North Carolina Press, 2021.
Morley, Ian. *Cities and Nationhood: American Imperialism and Urban Design in the Philippines, 1898–1916.* Honolulu: University of Hawai'i Press, 2018.
Moser, Patrick. "The Hawaii Promotion Committee and the Appropriation of Surfing." *Pacific Historical Review* 89, no. 4 (2020): 500–527.
Nachman, Steven R. "Lies My Informants Told Me." *Journal of Anthropological Research* 40, no. 4 (1984): 536–55.
Ngai, Mae M. *Impossible Subjects: Illegal Aliens and the Making of Modern America.* Princeton, NJ: Princeton University Press, 2004.
Nishimoto, Warren S. "The Progressive Era and Hawai'i: The Early History of Pālama Settlement, 1896–1929." *Hawaiian Journal of History* 34 (2000): 169–84.
Nogelmeier, Marvin Puakea. *Mai Pa'a I Ka Leo: Historical Voice in Hawaiian Primary Materials, Looking Forward and Listening Back.* Honolulu: University of Hawai'i Press, 2010.
Norbeck, Mark D. "The Legacy of Charles Henry Brent." *International Bulletin of Missionary Research* 20, no. 4 (1996): 163–68.
Novick, Peter. *That Noble Dream: The "Objectivity Question" and the American Historical Profession.* New York: Cambridge University Press, 1988.
O'Brien, Jean M. *Firsting and Lasting: Writing Indians Out of Existence in New England.* Minneapolis: University of Minnesota Press, 2010.
Ocampo, Ambeth R. "Rizal's Morga and Views of Philippine History." *Philippine Studies* 46, no. 2 (1998): 184–214.
Okihiro, Gary Y. *Island World: A History of Hawai'i and the United States.* Berkeley: University of California Press, 2008.
Oliveira, Katrina-Ann R. Kapā'anaokalāokeola Nākoa. *Ancestral Places: Understanding Kanaka Geographies.* Corvallis: Oregon State University Press, 2014.
Oliver, Kendrick, Uta A. Balbier, Hans Krabbendam, and Axel R. Schäfer. "Special Issue: Exploring the Global History of American Evangelicalism: Introduction." *Journal of American Studies* 51, no. 4 (2017): 1019–42.
Osorio, Jonathan Kamakawiwo'ole. *Dismembering Lāhui: A History of the Hawaiian Nation to 1887.* Honolulu: University of Hawai'i Press, 2002.
Pease, Mary Ball Johnson, Caroline Scribner Johnson, Adelaide Johnson Howell, and Mary Johnson Parker, eds. *Mahlon Johnson Family of Littleton, New Jersey: Ancestors and Descendants.* Morristown, NJ: Mahlon Johnson Association, 1931.
Peel, J. D. Y. *Religious Encounter and the Making of the Yoruba.* Bloomington: Indiana University Press, 2000.
Poblete, JoAnna. *Islanders in the Empire: Filipino and Puerto Rican Laborers in Hawai'i.* Urbana: University of Illinois Press, 2014.
Porter, Andrew. *Religion versus Empire? British Protestant Missionaries and Overseas Expansion, 1700–1914.* Manchester: Manchester University Press, 2004.

Preston, Andrew. *Sword of the Spirit, Shield of Faith: Religion in American War and Diplomacy.* New York: Alfred A. Knopf, 2012.

Prieto, Laura R. "'New Women,' American Imperialism and Filipina Nationalism: The Politics of Dress in Philippine Mission Stations, 1898–1940." In *Women in Transnational History: Connecting the Local and the Global,* ed. Clare Midgley, Alison Twells, and Julie Carlier, 77–97. New York: Routledge, 2016.

Prieto, Laura R. "'Stepmother America': The Woman's Board of Missions in the Philippines, 1902–1930." In *Competing Kingdoms: Women, Mission, Nation, and the American Protestant Empire, 1812–1960,* ed. Barbara Reeves-Ellington, Kathryn Kish Sklar, and Connie A. Shemo, 342–66. Durham, NC: Duke University Press, 2010.

Putney, Clifford. "The Legacy of the Gulicks, 1827–1964." *International Bulletin of Missionary Research* 25, no. 1 (2002): 28–35.

Putney, Clifford. *Missionaries in Hawai'i: The Lives of Peter and Fanny Gulick, 1797–1883.* Amherst: University of Massachusetts Press, 2010.

Rafael, Vicente L. *Contracting Colonialism: Translation and Christian Conversion in Tagalog Society under Early Spanish Rule.* Ithaca, NY: Cornell University Press, 1988.

Rafael, Vicente L. *White Love and Other Events in Filipino History.* Durham, NC: Duke University Press, 2000.

Raferty, Judith. "Textbook Wars: Governor-General James Francis Smith and the Protestant-Catholic Conflict in Public Education in the Philippines, 1904–1907." *History of Education Quarterly* 38, no. 2 (1998): 143–64.

Ratnapalan, Laavanyan M. "Science and Politics in the Hawaiian Kingdom: The Progress of the Honolulu Social Science Association, 1882–87." *Journal of Pacific History* 53, no. 2 (2018): 133–47.

Ratnapalan, Laavanyan M. "Sereno Bishop, Robert Louis Stevenson, and 'Americanism' in Hawai'i." *Journal of Imperial and Commonwealth History* 40, no. 3 (2012): 439–57.

Ratnapalan, Laavanyan Michael. "'This Greater Issue of Light against Darkness': Sereno Edwards Bishop, Missionary Religion, and the Hawaiian Islands, 1827–1909." *Journal of Religious History* 43, no. 1 (2019): 3–24.

Reed, James Eldin. "American Foreign Policy, the Politics of Missions and Josiah Strong, 1890–1900." *Church History* 41, no. 2 (1972): 230–45.

Reeves-Ellington, Barbara, Kathryn Kish Sklar, and Connie Shemo. "Introduction." In *Competing Kingdoms: Women, Mission, Nation, and the American Protestant Empire, 1812–1960,* ed. Barbara Reeves-Ellington, Kathryn Kish Sklar, and Connie A. Shemo, 1–16. Durham, NC: Duke University Press, 2010.

Reuter, Frank T. *Catholic Influence on American Colonial Policies, 1898–1904.* Austin: University of Texas Press, 1967.

Robert, Dana L. "Introduction." In *Converting Colonialism: Visions and Realities in Mission History, 1706–1914,* ed. Dana L. Robert, 1–20. Grand Rapids, MI: William B. Eerdmans Publishing Company, 2008.

Robert, Dana L. *Occupy until I Come: A. T. Pierson and the Evangelization of the World.* Grand Rapids, MI: William B. Eerdmans Publishing Company, 2003.

Roberts, Brian Russell. *Borderwaters: Amid the Archipelagic States of America.* Durham, NC: Duke University Press, 2021.

Roberts, Brian Russell, and Michelle Ann Stephens. "Introduction: Archipelagic American Studies: Decontinentalizing the Study of American Culture." In *Archipelagic American Studies*, ed. Brian Russell Roberts and Michelle Ann Stephens, 1–54. Durham, NC: Duke University Press, 2017.

Robin, Ron. *Enclaves of America: The Rhetoric of American Political Architecture Abroad, 1900–1965.* Princeton, NJ: Princeton University Press, 1992.

Rohrer, Judy. *Staking Claim: Settler Colonialism and Racialization in Hawai'i.* Tucson: University of Arizona Press, 2016.

Rosenberg, Emily S. *Spreading the American Dream: American Economic and Cultural Expansion, 1890–1945.* New York: Hill and Wang, 1982.

Rosenthal, Gregory. *Beyond Hawai'i: Native Labor in the Pacific World.* Berkeley: University of California Press, 2018.

Ross, Dorothy. "Historical Consciousness in Nineteenth-Century America." *American Historical Review* 89, no. 4 (1984): 909–28.

Salesa, Damon. "The Pacific in Indigenous Time." In *Pacific Histories: Ocean, Land, People*, ed. David Armitage and Alison Bashford, 31–52. Basingstoke: Palgrave Macmillan, 2014.

Salmond, Anne. *Aphrodite's Island: The European Discovery of Tahiti.* Auckland: Viking, 2009.

Sanneh, Lamin. *Translating the Message: The Missionary Impact on Culture.* Maryknoll, NY: Orbis Books, 1986.

Satia, Priya. *Time's Monster: History, Conscience, and Britain's Empire.* London: Allen Lane, 2020.

Schulz, Joy. "Birthing Empire: Economies of Childrearing and the Formation of American Colonialism in Hawai'i, 1820–1848." *Diplomatic History* 38, no. 5 (2014): 895–925.

Schulz, Joy. "Empire of the Young: Missionary Children in Hawaii and the Birth of U.S. Colonialism in the Pacific." PhD diss., University of Nebraska, 2011.

Schulz, Joy. *Hawaiian by Birth: Missionary Children, Bicultural Identity, and U.S. Colonialism in the Pacific.* Lincoln: University of Nebraska Press, 2017.

Schumacher, John N. "The 'Propagandists' Reconstruction of the Philippine Past." In *Perceptions of the Past in Southeast Asia*, ed. Anthony Reid and David Marr, 264–80. Singapore: Heinemann Educational Books, 1979.

Schumacher, John N. "Rizal and Filipino Nationalism: A New Approach." *Philippine Studies* 48, no. 4 (2000): 193–229.

Scott, William Henry. "An Historian Looks into the Philippine Kaleidoscope." *Philippine Studies* 24, no. 2 (1976): 220–27.

Seat, Karen K. *"Providence Has Freed Our Hands": Women's Missions and the American Encounter with Japan.* Syracuse, NY: Syracuse University Press, 2008.

Shalev, Eran. *Rome Reborn on Western Shores: Historical Imagination and the Creation of the American Republic.* Charlottesville: University of Virginia Press, 2009.

Sharp, Andrew. *Ancient Voyagers in Polynesia.* Berkeley: University of California Press, 1964.

Shoemaker, Nancy. *Pursuing Respect in the Cannibal Isles: Americans in Nineteenth-Century Fiji*. Ithaca, NY: Cornell University Press, 2019.
Silva, Noenoe K. *Aloha Betrayed: Native Hawaiian Resistance to American Colonialism*. Durham, NC: Duke University Press, 2004.
Silva, Noenoe K. *The Power of the Steel-Tipped Pen: Reconstructing Native Hawaiian Intellectual History*. Durham, NC: Duke University Press, 2017.
Sivasundaram, Sujit. "Science." In *Pacific Histories: Ocean, Land, People*, ed. David Armitage and Alison Bashford, 237–60. Basingstoke: Palgrave Macmillan, 2014.
Slotkin, Richard. *Gunfighter Nation: The Myth of the Frontier in Twentieth-Century America*. New York: Atheneum, 1992.
Smith, Bernard. *European Vision and the South Pacific, 1769–1850: A Study in the History of Art and Ideas*. New York: Oxford University Press, 1960.
Smith, Ryan K. *Gothic Arches, Latin Crosses: Anti-Catholicism and American Church Design in the Nineteenth Century*. Chapel Hill: University of North Carolina Press, 2006.
Smith, Tom. "American Missionaries and the Boundaries of Evangelicalism in the Philippines." In *Global Faith, Worldly Power: Evangelical Internationalism and U.S. Empire*, ed. John Corrigan, Melani McAlister, and Axel R. Schäfer, 97–121. Chapel Hill: University of North Carolina Press, 2022.
Smith, Tom. "American Protestant Missionaries, Native Hawaiian Authority, and Religious Freedom in Hawai'i, c. 1826–50." In *The Early Imperial Republic: From the American Revolution to the U.S.-Mexican War*, ed. Michael A. Blaakman, Emily Conroy-Krutz, and Noelani Arista, 139–57. Philadelphia: University of Pennsylvania Press, 2023.
Smith, Tom. "Hawaiian History and American History: Integration or Separation?" *American Nineteenth Century History* 20, no. 2 (2019): 161–82.
Smith, Tom. "History, 'Unwritten Literature,' and U.S. Colonialism in Hawai'i, 1898–1915." *Diplomatic History* 43, no. 5 (2019): 813–39.
Smith, Tom. "Islanders, Protestant Missionaries, and Traditions Regarding the Past in Nineteenth-Century Polynesia." *Historical Journal* 60, no. 1 (2017): 71–94.
Smylie, John Edwin. "Protestant Clergymen and American Destiny: II. Prelude to Imperialism, 1865–1900." *Harvard Theological Review* 56, no. 4 (1963): 297–311.
Sotomayor, Antonio. "The Triangle of Empire: Sport, Religion and Imperialism in Puerto Rico's YMCA, 1898–1926." *The Americas* 74, no. 4 (2017): 481–512.
Stanley, Brian. *The Bible and the Flag: Protestant Missions and British Imperialism in the Nineteenth and Twentieth Centuries*. Leicester: Apollos, 1990.
Stannard, David E. *Before the Horror: The Population of Hawai'i on the Eve of Western Contact*. Honolulu: Social Science Research Institute, 1989.
Steinbock-Pratt, Sarah. *Educating the Empire: American Teachers and Contested Colonization in the Philippines*. New York: Cambridge University Press, 2019.
Stephanson, Anders. *Manifest Destiny: American Expansion and the Empire of Right*. New York: Hill & Wang, 1995.
Stoler, Ann Laura. *Along the Archival Grain: Epistemic Anxieties and Colonial Common Sense*. Princeton, NJ: Princeton University Press, 2009.
Stoler, Ann Laura, ed. *Haunted by Empire: Geographies of Intimacy in North American History*. Durham, NC: Duke University Press, 2006.

Stratford, Elaine. "Imagining the Archipelago." In *Archipelagic American Studies*, ed. Brian Russell Roberts and Michelle Ann Stephens, 74–94. Durham, NC: Duke University Press, 2017.

Sutton, Matthew Avery. *American Apocalypse: A History of Modern Evangelicalism*. Cambridge, MA: Belknap Press, 2014.

Takaki, Ronald. *Pau Hana: Plantation Life and Labor in Hawaii, 1835–1920*. Honolulu: University of Hawai'i Press, 1983.

Tan, Samuel K. *Filipino Muslim Perceptions of Their History and Culture as Seen through Indigenous Sources*. Zamboanga City: SKY Publications Series, 2003.

Teaiwa, Teresia. "Reading Paul Gauguin's *Noa Noa* with Epeli Hau'ofa's *Kisses in the Nederends*: Militourism, Feminism, and the 'Polynesian' Body." In *Inside Out: Literature, Cultural Politics, and Identity in the New Pacific*, ed. Vilsoni Hereniko, 249–63. Lanham, MD: Rowman & Littlefield, 1999.

Thigpen, Jennifer. *Island Queens and Mission Wives: How Gender and Empire Remade Hawai'i's Pacific World*. Chapel Hill: University of North Carolina Press, 2014.

Thomas, Megan C. *Orientalists, Propagandists, and Ilustrados: Filipino Scholarship and the End of Spanish Colonialism*. Minneapolis: University of Minnesota Press, 2012.

Thomas, Nicholas. *Islanders: The Pacific in the Age of Empire*. New Haven, CT: Yale University Press, 2010.

Thompson, Lanny. "Heuristic Geographies: Territories and Areas, Islands and Archipelagoes." In *Archipelagic American Studies*, ed. Brian Russell Roberts and Michelle Ann Stephens, 57–73. Durham, NC: Duke University Press, 2017.

Thompson, Lanny. *Imperial Archipelago: Representation and Rule in the Insular Territories under U.S. Dominion*. Honolulu: University of Hawai'i Press, 2010.

Thompson, Michael G. *For God and Globe: Christian Internationalism in the United States between the Great War and the Cold War*. Ithaca, NY: Cornell University Press, 2015.

Trask, Haunani-Kay. *From a Native Daughter: Colonialism and Sovereignty in Hawai'i*. Rev. ed. Honolulu: University of Hawai'i Press, 1999.

Turnbull, David. *Masons, Tricksters, and Cartographers: Comparative Studies in the Sociology of Scientific and Indigenous Knowledge*. Amsterdam: Harwood Academic, 2000.

Tyrrell, Ian. *Reforming the World: The Creation of America's Moral Empire*. Princeton, NJ: Princeton University Press, 2010.

Vandome, Robin. "American Scientists and Their Fictions: Professional Authorship and Intellectual Identity, 1870–1900." *Journal of American Studies* 53, no. 2 (2019): 478–506.

Wacker, Grant. "The Holy Spirit and the Spirit of the Age in American Protestantism, 1880–1910." *Journal of American History* 72, no. 1 (1985): 45–62.

Walls, Andrew F. *The Missionary Movement in Christian History: Studies in the Transmission of the Faith*. Maryknoll, NY: Orbis Books, 1996.

Walther, Karine V. *Sacred Interests: The United States and the Islamic World, 1821–1921*. Chapel Hill: University of North Carolina Press, 2015.

Walther, Karine V. "'The Same Blood as We in America': Industrial Schooling and American Empire." In *Religion and U.S. Empire: Critical New Histories*, ed. Tisa Wenger and Sylvester A. Johnson, 151–78. New York: New York University Press, 2022.

Weinberg, Albert K. *Manifest Destiny: A Study of Nationalist Expansionism in American History*. Baltimore, MD: Johns Hopkins Press, 1935.
Weir, Christine. "'White Man's Burden,' 'White Man's Privilege': Christian Humanism and Racial Determinism in Oceania, 1890–1930." In *Foreign Bodies: Oceania and the Science of Race, 1750–1940*, ed. Bronwen Douglas and Chris Ballard, 283–303. Canberra: ANU E Press, 2008.
Welch, Richard E., Jr. *Response to Imperialism: The United States and the Philippine-American War, 1899–1902*. Chapel Hill: University of North Carolina Press, 1979.
Wenger, Tisa. *Religious Freedom: The Contested History of an American Ideal*. Chapel Hill: University of North Carolina Press, 2017.
Wenger, Tisa, and Sylvester A. Johnson. "Introduction." In *Religion and U.S. Empire: Critical New Histories*, ed. Tisa Wenger and Sylvester A. Johnson, 1–16. New York: New York University Press, 2022.
Wexler, Laura. *Tender Violence: Domestic Visions in an Age of U.S. Imperialism*. Chapel Hill: University of North Carolina Press, 2000.
Williams, Ronald C., Jr. "'Aole Hoohui ia Hawaii': U.S. Collegiate Teams Debate Annexation of Hawai'i and Independence Prevails, 1893 to 1897." *Hawaiian Journal of History* 43 (2009): 153–80.
Williams, Ronald C., Jr. "Claiming Christianity: The Struggle over God and Nation in Hawai'i, 1880–1900." PhD diss., University of Hawai'i, 2013.
Williams, Ronald C., Jr. "'Ike Mōakaaka, Seeing a Path Forward: Historiography in Hawai'i." *Hūlili: Multidisciplinary Research on Hawaiian Well-Being* 7 (2011): 67–90.
Williams, Ronald C., Jr. "To Raise a Voice in Praise: The Revivalist Mission of John Henry Wise, 1889–1896." *Hawaiian Journal of History* 46 (2012): 1–36.
Williams, William Appleman. "The Frontier Thesis and American Foreign Policy." *Pacific Historical Review* 24, no. 4 (1955): 379–95.
Wilson, Rob. *Reimagining the American Pacific: From South Pacific to Bamboo Ridge and Beyond*. Durham, NC: Duke University Press, 2000.
Wood, Houston. *Displacing Natives: The Rhetorical Production of Hawai'i*. Lanham, MD: Rowman & Littlefield, 1999.
Woods, Colleen. *Freedom Incorporated: Anticommunism and Philippine Independence in the Age of Decolonization*. Ithaca, NY: Cornell University Press, 2020.
Woods, Fred E. "A Most Influential Mormon Islander: Jonathan Hawaii Napela." *Hawaiian Journal of History* 42 (2008): 135–57.
Wulf, Karin. "Bible, King, and Common Law: Genealogical Literacies and Family History Practices in British America." *Early American Studies* 10, no. 3 (2012): 467–502.
Young, Kanalu G. Terry. *Rethinking the Native Hawaiian Past*. New York: Routledge, 1998.
Young, Marilyn Blatt. *The Rhetoric of Empire: American China Policy, 1895–1901*. Cambridge, MA: Harvard University Press, 1968.

Index

Figures are indicated by f.

Abbott, Lyman, 54
ABCFM. *See* American Board of Commissioners for Foreign Missions
An Account of the Polynesian Race (Fornander), 122
Adams, John, 209
Adams-Onís Treaty (1819), 6
African Americans, 19, 49, 80, 88, 175
Agassiz, Louis, 84
Aglipay, Gregorio, 181, 212, 228
Aglipayan church, 181, 188, 196, 220, 228–29
Agoncillo, Felipe, 209
Aguinaldo, Emilio, 147–48, 204–5, 207, 228
'Ahahui 'Euanelio o Hawai'i (Evangelical Association of Hawai'i). *See* Hawaiian Evangelical Association
'ai kapu, 35, 36, 45, 73
Alanakapu Kauapinao (chiefess), 122
Alaska, 6, 153
Alexander, J. M., 152
Alexander, Samuel, 124
Alexander, William DeWitt, 41, 72, 81, 86, 88, 106, 111, 122, 134; HHS and, 83; on *hula* dances, 98; Kalākaua and, 75–76, 77, 105; with knowledge production, 84; legacy, 82; with overthrow and annexation of Hawai'i, 55
Alexander & Baldwin, 38
ali'i. *See* chiefs
Ali'i Nui (high chiefs), 70, 99
Allardyce, John C., 40, 41
Allen, Thomas, 85–86
American Baptist Missionary Union, 141
American Bible Society, 183
American Board of Commissioners for Foreign Missions (ABCFM): criticism of, 34, 50, 72; global reach of, 39, 53; in Hawai'i, 14, 31–32, 34–35, 37, 39–46, 48–53, 55–59, 61, 64, 66–67, 71–72, 75, 103–4, 140, 151; HEA and, 42–43, 52, 58, 103; in Micronesia, 148; in Mindanao, 142, 158, 186, 192; with missionary collections, 85; *Missionary Herald* and, 34, 40–41, 45, 57, 59, 102–3, 192; in Philippines, 141–43, 150, 158, 166, 176, 179, 182, 186, 192, 193, 206, 221–22
American Historical Review (journal), 205
Anderson, Rufus, 34, 37, 39, 41–42, 45, 46, 57
Anglican Church, 60, 72, 104
Anglican Church Chronicle (periodical), 72
animism, 10, 14, 147, 178, 212, 227, 237

annexation, Hawai'i, 25–26, 28, 62, 116, 120, 133–34, 137, 235; with completion of mission history, 26, 101–10; with mission history and overthrow, 26, 32, 37–38, 54–63; opponents, 27, 39, 59–60, 79, 80; supporters, 38, 55, 77, 81–82, 96
annexation, Philippines, 133, 137
architecture, Philippines: history and, 184–96; with infrastructure and modernization, 190–91
Arellano, Cayetano, 208
Arista, Noelani, 35
Armstrong, Clarissa (mother), 49
Armstrong, Richard (father), 49
Armstrong, Samuel Chapman, 49–50, 73, 129
Army, US, 146–47
Artigas y Cueva, Manuel, 224
Asia, 2, 4, 10, 217
Assembly Herald (magazine), 151, 192
assimilation, 7, 109, 113, 146, 147, 213
Associated Press, 80
Atherton, Joseph B., 46
Atkinson, Alatau Tamchiboulac, 77
Atlantic Ocean, 5, 152
Aurora, Manuel, 223
Australia, 153
awit (song or romance), 213

Bagobo people, 179, 227
Bancroft, Hubert Howe, 2
Barrow, Terence, 128, 131
Barton, James L., 109
Bathalà (deity), 211
Bayonet Constitution (1887), 26, 38, 48, 93, 247n31
Beckwith, Martha Warren, 238
Bederman, Gail, 45
Bell Trade Act (1946), 239
Bemis, Samuel Flagg, 12
Benedict, Ruth, 222
Bethlehem Presbyterian Church, Chicago, 1
Beveridge, Albert J., 160; with empire and God, 2, 17, 137, 138, 146, 153, 154, 210; imperial historicism and, 17; Pacific Ocean and, 1–2, 3, 4, 6
Beyer, H. Otley, 231
Bicknell, Ellen Bond (wife), 64
Bicknell, James, 64, 65–67
"bicultural identity," 38

Bigler, Henry W., 71
Bingham, Clara (daughter-in-law), 51
Bingham, Hiram, 43–44, 73, 82, 87–88, 111, 124; ABCFM and, 35; centennial celebration, 93; criticism of, 41, 69; women and, 45
Bingham, Hiram II (son), 41, 43, 103
Bishop, Artemas (father of Sereno), 31
Bishop, Charles Reed, 85
Bishop, Cornelia (wife of Sereno), 31
Bishop, Elizabeth (mother of Sereno), 31
Bishop, Pauahi (wife of Charles), 85
Bishop, Sereno, 45, 49, 75, 77, 79, 107, 109, 134; as annexationist, 32, 55, 96; with completion of mission history, 101; on descendants of missionaries, 46; HEA and, 43; Kalākaua and, 57; with knowledge production, 84; on Lili'uokalani, 45–46, 87; missionaries defended by, 41, 54–55, 80–81; with mission history in Hawai'i, 31–32, 92–93; with overthrow and annexation of Hawai'i, 56, 58, 62; *Reminiscences of Old Hawaii* and, 110–11, 112–13; with *Washington Evening Star* letters, 62, 80–81, 87, 90–92, 94, 95, 116; *Why Are the Hawaiians Dying Out?* and, 112–13
Bishop Museum, 85
Black, Robert F., 142, 166, 192
"blackbirders," labor and, 6
blackface minstrelsy, 91
Blaine, James, 62
"blood compact," 209
Blossom, John, 91
Blount, James H., 39, 55–56, 78–79, 90
Blumentritt, Ferdinand, 210–11, 212
Board of Genealogy, Hawai'i, 64–65, 68, 213
Boas, Franz, 5, 18
Bocobo, Jorge, 224
Boki (Native Hawaiian chief), 72
Bond, Elias (father), 50, 64
Bond, Ellen. *See* Bicknell, Ellen Bond
Bond, Ellen (mother), 64
Bonifacio, Andrés, 147, 212
"boomerang" effect, of Protestant mission, 233
Boston, U.S.S., 38
Boston Journal (newspaper), 114
Brain, Belle M., 62–63, 73

INDEX   313

Brent, Charles Henry, 141, 146, 165, 216; with Catholic Church in Philippines, 167, 170, 180, 194–202; evolutionism and, 175; Filipinization and, 221; on Magellan, 214; with Providence and US empire, 149–50, 153–57, 210; with slow progress of Philippine history, 175–76; with stereotypes of Filipinos, 193; World War I and, 222
A Brief History of the Hawaiian People (Alexander, W. D.), 82, 86, 122
Briggs, Charles W., 142, 151, 157–58, 166, 175, 214; Catholic Church and, 172, 173, 182; on church buildings, 188, 194–95; on Philippines, 180, 184; *The Progressing Philippines*, 142, 143, 228; racism and, 190
Britain, 13, 72, 74–75, 95, 180, 201
British and Foreign Bible Society, 180
Brown, Arthur Judson, 143, 145, 149–50, 156, 162, 163, 214, 225; with architecture of Protestant churches, 191; on Catholic Church in Philippines, 172–74, 178, 181–82, 201; on Protestant worship in Philippines, 189–90
Brown, Marie Alohalani, 238
Brown, Roy H., 176, 192
Bryan, William Jennings, 166
Buchanan, James, 209
Buddhism, 229
Buencamino, Felipe, 208
Bureau of Missions, New York, 18
Burgess, John W., 84

California, 6, 8, 233
Calvinists, 26, 41, 236
Camus, Manuel R., 200
Canada, 141, 153
Cano, Juan Sebastián del (Captain), 214
Castells, Francisco, 179–80
Castle, Alfred (grandson), 105
Castle, Caroline Dickinson (sister), 53
Castle, G. P. (brother), 83
Castle, William R., 77, 83
Castle, William R., Jr. (son), 99–100, 109, 111, 114–15, 124
Castle & Cooke, 37–38
cathedral, in Old Manila, 186f
Catholic Church, 75; conversions, 59, 73–74, 172; missionaries in Hawaiʻi and, 72–74; in Philippines, 10, 14, 19, 160–65, 168, 170–73, 178, 180–202, 219; Protestant mission and, 15, 139, 218; Spain and, 2, 19, 23, 164, 171–73, 205
Cavite insurrection (1872), 214–15
census of 1903, Philippines, 231
Central Union (Fort Street) Church, Honolulu, 31–32, 41–42, 43, 46–47, 83, 91–92
Chafee, Adna (General), 191
chiefs (*aliʻi*), 9, 27, 65, 68–70, 84, 95; Christianized, 31, 32, 73; high, 70, 99; Native Hawaiian women, 35, 44–45, 70, 73, 99, 105, 122
children, 40, 107; education and, 42, 48, 49, 93, 124, 140, 182; infant mortality, 143. *See also* descendants of Protestant missionaries, in Hawaiʻi; Hawaiian Mission Children's Society
China, 2, 5, 10, 41, 150, 152, 156, 158, 168, 217, 239; ABCFM in, 39; Philippines and, 226–27
Chinese migrants, 25, 48, 74, 80, 98
Christian Advocate (journal), 141, 148
Christian and Missionary Alliance, 141, 223
Christian Conference of the Pacific Area, YMCA, 239
"Christian internationalism," 230
Christianity, 8, 54, 99, 101; conversions, 5, 13, 35–37, 53, 59, 66, 73–76, 92, 105, 142, 166, 172, 176, 180, 190–91, 197, 229; God and, 59, 211; missions, 5, 61, 63; *One Hundred Years of Christian Civilization in Hawaii* (pageant), 106–7, 108f. *See also* Catholic Church; Protestant mission; Young Men's Christian Association
Christianization: of Hawaiʻi, 9, 31, 32, 34–35, 47, 61, 100, 102, 104; of Philippines, 8, 180
Christus Redemptor (Montgomery), 144, 151–52
Clark, N. G., 34, 48
Clay, Henry, 209
Cleveland, Grover, 39, 55–56, 59, 78–80, 82, 90
climate change, 5
Coan, Lydia Bingham (wife), 93
Coan, Titus, 48
Coan, Titus Munson (son), 54–55, 118, 124
Cochran, Bourke, 160
Coffman, Tom, 238

"colonial domesticity," 143
colonialism, 8, 14, 20, 63, 235; nationalist, 212, 223, 228–29; settler, 9, 79, 124; violence, 5, 12, 19, 37, 81, 139, 146–49, 161, 208, 237
colonization, 8; of Native Hawaiians, 9; of Philippines, 10–11, 13
Columbian Exposition, Chicago World's Fair (1893), 116, 130
Columbus, Christopher, 82, 214, 226
Committee of Safety, 26, 38, 79
Committee on Hawaiian Evangelization, 51–52, 118
commoners (maka'āinana), 65, 113
Condict, Alice Byram, 20, 140, 144, 174, 184–88, 189, 208
Congregationalists, 15, 36–37, 44, 46, 54, 72, 142, 143, 151
Congress, US, 9, 26, 55, 79–80, 92, 223
Constitution, US, 146, 154–55
Cook, James, 4, 35, 72
Cooke, Charles M., 85
Cooke, Clarence (son), 105
corpulence, status and, 112
cosmology, 13, 65, 67, 71, 85, 129, 213, 260n76
Craig, Austin, 219, 231
creation myths, Tagalog, 229
The Crisis of Missions (Pierson), 36, 179
Cristianos Filipinos, 223
Cristianos Vivos Metodistas, 223
Cuba, 2, 133
Cubans, 12, 133
cultural anthropology, 5
cultural relativism, 121, 124, 222
culture: "bicultural identity," 37–38; "missionary," 46, 47, 75; Native Hawaiian, 22, 28, 41, 65, 84–85, 107, 109, 119, 124
Czech Republic, 210

Daggett, R. M., 69
Damien (priest), 73–74
Damon, Ethel Moseley (granddaughter), 105, 106
Damon, Frank (son), 41
Damon, Samuel C., 41
Damon, Samuel M. (son), 85, 100
Dana, Richard Henry, Jr., 34
Daniel, John W., 79
Darwin, Charles, 4, 84, 85

Daughters of Hawai'i, 102, 106
Declaration of Independence, US, 209
decolonization, 23, 221, 225, 230, 233, 239
Decoration Day, 88–89
De los Reyes, Isabelo, 211–12, 231
Democratic Party, US, 39, 79, 155, 166, 221
depopulation, in Hawai'i, 27, 37, 64, 76, 113
descendants of Protestant missionaries, in Hawai'i, 86, 134; ABCFM and, 32, 51–53; with annexation and completion of mission, 26, 101–10; with annexation and overthrow, 55–63; "bicultural identity" of, 38; childhood of, 41–42, 124, 129–30; with classification of Hawaiian tradition, 117–25; criticism of, 38–40, 46–48, 56, 78–80, 89–90; in defense of first-generation missionaries, 41, 50; on HEA board, 43; with historical narratives, 20, 22–23, 27, 33, 37, 60, 63, 75, 101, 107; with HMCS membership, 42, 46; *hula* dances and, 98–101; with innovation, 53–54; kinship networks and, 94–95; with labor, 37–38; as liminal, 33–34, 67, 78, 101, 125–32, 235; with memory, strenuous life and creation of American Hawai'i, 110–17; on oral tradition of Native Hawaiians, 67
Dewey, George (Admiral), 133, 137, 140, 145, 148, 149, 179–80
Dibble, Sheldon, 35, 43, 66, 73, 106, 118, 122
Disciples of Christ, 141, 190, 223
diseases, 37, 74, 113
Dole, Daniel (father), 38
Dole, Emily (mother), 38
Dole, James (cousin), 38
Dole, Sanford, 38, 40, 42, 77, 81, 106, 238; birthday celebration for, 90–91; HHS and, 83; Social Darwinism and, 84
"domesticating" colonialism, 20
Dyer, Frances J., 152

educated Filipinos. *See ilustrados*
education, 161–62; assimilation with, 109; with Hawaiian language banned, 78, 82, 99, 107; history textbooks, 107, 162; industrial, 49; schools, 42, 48, 49, 93, 124, 140–41, 182
Ellinwood School for Girls, 141
Emerson, John S. (father), 93, 117
Emerson, Joseph (brother), 83, 106

INDEX   315

Emerson, Nathaniel Bright, 52, 75, 92, 171, 213, 235; with classification of Hawaiian tradition, 117–25; with completion of mission history, 101–2; on Hale Nauā, 65; HHS and, 83; *hula* dances and, 100, 101; as liminal, 125–26; *The Long Voyages of the Ancient Hawaiians* and, 121; *Pele and Hiiaka* and, 118, 126–28, 131; "The Prick of Honor," 129; science and, 130, 237, 238; social science and, 22, 131; *Unwritten Literature of Hawaii* and, 118, 120–21, 124, 127, 130
Emerson, Oliver P. (brother), 43, 47, 53, 56–57, 113–14; ABCFM and, 59; with completion of mission history, 101, 103, 109
Emerson, Ursula (mother), 93, 117
empire: British, 95; Japan, 62, 95
empire, US: with crisis of mission in Philippines, 154–59; expansion, 1–4, 6–7; God and, 137–39, 144–45, 149; Philippines and, 23, 135–36, 169, 209–10, 220–21; Philippines and spiritual shortcomings of, 159–67; Protestant mission and, 11–19, 235; Providence and Protestant missionaries in Philippines, 145–54, 173–74, 210
Enlightenment, 17
Episcopal Church, 193, 195–96, 195f, 198–99
Episcopalians, 5, 141–43, 150, 196, 199
erasure, 45, 127
European intellectual traditions, 205, 212
Evangelical Association of Hawai'i ('Ahahui 'Euanelio o Hawai'i). *See* Hawaiian Evangelical Association
Evangelical Union, 142–43, 151, 153, 157, 181–82, 183, 197
evolutionism, 171, 173–75, 201, 212
explorers, 5, 44, 72, 77, 209, 214

fiction writing, 211
Field Museum, 84
"fiesta politics," 208
Fiji, 152
Filipinization, 221, 224, 225
Filipino nationalism, 221–22, 224–25, 229, 239; historical thought and, 23, 205–13, 230–31, 233; *ilustrados* and, 10, 147, 205, 208, 210–13, 215–16, 219; missionaries with elision of historiography and, 206, 214–20, 231

Filipinos, 6, 116, 138, 146, 182; with Hispanicized population, 178, 212, 237; idolatry and, 172, 180, 215; racism and, 147, 172, 175, 190, 193; with Tagalog, 147, 152, 212, 213, 229. *See also ilustrados*
Fisher, Jessie Shaw, 107, 108f
Fleming, Daniel Johnson, 217
Fleming H. Revell press, 62
folklore: Flilipino, 210–11, 215, 224; Hawaiian, 53, 68, 84, 117–18, 120, 130, 134
Forbes, Anderson O., 43
Forbes, W. Cameron, 161, 224, 225
Foreman, John, 216
Fornander, Abraham, 122–23
Fort Street Church, Honolulu, 40, 41. *See also* Central Union Church, Honolulu
Fox, Evelyn (sister), 142
Fox, Florence (sister), 142
Fox, Isabel, 142
Fragments of Hawaiian History ('Ī'ī), 238
France, 75, 141
Frazer, James, 123
Frear, Walter, 104
The Friend (periodical), 25, 41, 73, 101–2, 110, 118

Gage, H. B., 74
genealogies, 18, 87, 213; Board of Genealogy, 64–65, 68, 213; of Hawaiian monarchy, 27, 236; of Native Hawaiians, 9, 19, 22, 33, 35, 63–65, 68–71, 76, 86, 120–22, 127, 236, 238; Protestant missionaries with, 67–68; white supremacy with, 17
Germany, 180, 201
Gibson, Walter Murray, 71
gift giving (*hookupu*), 90–91, 134
Gilsheuser, Henry, 193
Gin Lum, Kathryn, 6, 20–21, 87–88, 125, 255n87
Glotfelter, J. H., 144
God: Christianity and, 59, 211; Filipinos with, 212; in nature, 84; Providence with US empire and missionaries, 145–54, 173–74, 210; US and, 2, 17, 137–39, 144–45
Great Britain. *See* Britain
Great Reform Meeting, 93
Groves, J. M., 223
Guam, 12, 100, 133, 204
Guano Act (1856), 6, 7

guerilla warfare, in Philippines, 146
Gulick, Ann Eliza Clark (daughter-in-law), 107, 109, 113, 114
Gulick, Charles Thomas (nephew), 39–40
Gulick, John T. (son), 39, 84, 85
Gulick, Julia (daughter), 39
Gulick, Luther (son), 39, 42
Gulick, Orramel Hinckley (son), 39, 53, 92, 103, 107, 113, 114; with completion of mission history, 102, 109; on *hula* dances, 98–99
Gulick, Peter, 39
Gulick, Sidney (grandson), 39
Gulick, Thomas (son), 39, 113
Gulick, William (son), 39
Guyatt, Nicholas, 138
Gynberg Ballads (Atkinson), 77

Hale Nauā society, 64–71, 76–77, 85
Hall, G. Stanley, 114
Hall, William W., 43, 55
Hamilton, Charles R., 220
Harper's Bazaar (magazine), 56, 91
Harris Memorial Training School, Manila, 140–41
Harrison, Benjamin, 62
Harrison, Francis Burton, 221, 222
Harty, Jeremiah, 161, 163
Harvard University, 84, 117
Hauʻofa, Epeli, 7
Hawaii (Castle, W. R., Jr.), 111, 114–15
Hawaiʻi: ABCFM in, 14, 31–32, 34–35, 37, 39–46, 48–53, 55–59, 61, 64, 66–67, 71–72, 75, 103–4, 140, 151; California and, 8; Christianization of, 9, 31, 32, 34–35, 47, 61, 100, 102, 104; cosmology, 65, 67, 71, 85, 129, 213, 260n76; Daughters of Hawaiʻi, 102, 106; depopulation in, 27, 37, 64, 76, 113; Filipino workers in, 6, 116; folklore, 53, 68, 84, 117–18, 120, 130, 134; Hale Nauā society, 64–71, 76–77, 85; historical pageant, 75–76, 89, 106–7, 108f; with history as contested terrain, 68–75; identity, 89–96; *Ka Moʻolelo Hawaiʻi*, 66, 118; memory with strenuous life and creation of American, 110–17; with "missionary" defined, 37–48; "missionary" denigration of Indigenous understandings, 75–78; with mission history recalibrated, 48–54; *One Hundred Years of Christian Civilization in Hawaii* (pageant), 106–7, 108f; *Pioneer Days in Hawaii*, 113–14; populations, 42, 81; Protestant mission and, 14–16; Protestant mission history in, 18–19, 31–32, 34–37; *Reminiscences of Old Hawaii*, 110–11, 112–13; Republic of Hawaiʻi, 26, 38, 45, 56, 62, 82, 99, 134; *Scenery in Hawaii*, 116; seizure of, 1–2; sovereignty of, 27, 59–60, 63, 68–69, 83, 86, 89, 95–96, 102, 131; stereotypes of, 129; Supreme Court, 81; tourism and, 6, 8–9, 97, 99–100, 109–17, 131, 240; *Unwritten Literature of Hawaii*, 118, 120–21, 124, 127, 130; US empire and, 4, 6–7, 15; white settlement in, 8, 80–81, 109, 131; YMCA in, 46, 47, 239. *See also* annexation, Hawaiʻi; missionaries, in Hawaiʻi; Native Hawaiians; Protestant missionaries, in Hawaiʻi; tradition, Hawaiian

Hawaiian Antiquities (Emerson, N. B.), 118. *See also Ka Moʻolelo Hawaiʻi*
Hawaiian Booth Committee, 98–99, 107
Hawaiian Evangelical Association (HEA, ʻAhahui ʻEuanelio o Hawaiʻi, Evangelical Association of Hawaiʻi): ABCFM and, 42–43, 52, 58, 103; board members, 43, 47; Committee on Hawaiian Evangelization, 51–52, 118; HMCS and, 32, 103; as Indigenous organization, 43; members, 46, 47, 59, 64, 75; with overthrow and annexation, 55, 58; Pālama Settlement and, 98; role of, 32, 42–43; with weaponized history, 102; women and, 43
Hawaiian Historical Society (HHS), 82–84, 93, 102, 105, 117, 121, 122, 134
Hawaiian League, 26, 32, 38, 46
Hawaiian Mission Children's Society (HMCS), 94, 102; ABCFM and, 50–51; Committee on Hawaiian Evangelization, 51–52, 118; founding and role of, 42; HEA and, 32, 103; members, 42, 43, 46, 47; as memorial society, 103; with overthrow and annexation, 55
Hawaiian Star (newspaper), 77
Hawaiian Yesterdays (Lyman, H.), 113
Hawaii Holomua (newspaper), 38
Hawaii Promotion Committee, 116
Hawaii's Story by Hawaii's Queen (Liliʻuokalani), 60, 69, 86–87, 110

INDEX 317

Hawkins, Michael, 167
Hay, John, 209
HEA. *See* Hawaiian Evangelical Association
heathenism, 48, 55, 58, 60, 64, 76, 102
"heathen" people, 6–7, 14, 34, 36, 54, 57, 124, 172, 236
Hewahewa (*kahuna*), 117
HHS. *See* Hawaiian Historical Society
Hibbard, David S., 140, 149, 152, 158, 178, 193, 206, 214, 221, 230–33, 237; *Making a Nation* and, 143, 226; Muslims and, 228–29; on Rizal, 219–20
high chiefs (*Ali'i Nui*), 70, 99
Hilo Boarding School, 48, 49
Hinduism, 226, 227, 229
Hispanicized Filipino population, 178, 212, 237
historical consciousness, missionaries and, 16–21
"historical hopefulness," 12
historical narratives: annexation of Hawai'i and, 28; colonialism and, 63; descendants of missionaries with, 20, 22–23, 27, 33, 37, 60, 63, 75, 101, 107; Filipino nationalism and, 230; with genealogies and memory, 87; Hawaiian tradition and, 67, 99, 114, 238; *ilustrados* and, 219, 233; malleability of, 28; Muslims in Philippines with, 213; Native Hawaiians and, 19, 22, 67, 77, 85–87, 89, 92, 96; performance and, 19, 75–76, 87, 88, 92–93, 105–7; Philippines, 181, 202, 213, 219, 230, 233, 237; Protestant missionaries producing, 3, 8, 19–21, 35, 135, 207, 214–15, 230, 233–34; science and, 85; as tool of imperialism, 16, 19, 21; Yoruba people, 281n140
historical pageant, Hawai'i, 75–76, 89, 106–7, 108f
historiography: Filipino nationalist language and, 23; *ilustrado*, 212, 213; missionaries with elision of Filipino nationalist, 206, 214–20, 231; Philippine, 212, 220
history: with architecture in Philippines, 184–96; *Brief History*, 82, 86, 122; as contested terrain in Hawai'i, 68–75; Filipino nationalists and, 23, 207–13; *Fragments of Hawaiian History*, 238; genealogies and, 122–23; Hawai'i and Protestant mission, 31–32, 34–37; Hawai'i and recalibrating mission, 48–54; HHS,

82–84, 93, 102, 105, 117, 121, 122, 134; *ilustrados* and, 10, 205, 208, 210–13, 215–16, 222, 231; missionaries and Philippine, 171–77; missionaries in Philippines producing, 143; *Missions and Modern History*, 17; "No Value as History," 87; overthrow, annexation of Hawai'i and mission, 26, 32, 37–38, 54–63; place and, 260n76; textbooks, 107, 162; weaponized, 16, 56, 102
HMCS. *See* Hawaiian Mission Children's Society
Hoar, George Frisbee, 81
Hollinger, David, 233
Honolulu Social Science Association, 81, 82–83, 94, 112
hookupu (gift giving), 90–91, 134
Hoomanamana—Idolatry (Bicknell), 64, 65
House of Representatives, Hawaiian, 38
hula dances, 65, 75–76, 98–101, 107, 118, 120–22, 124, 130–31
Hyatt, Alpheus, 84
Hyde, Charles McEwen, 46–47, 50, 64, 74, 94, 122; ABCFM, 52, 56, 57–58; Bishop Museum and, 85; HMCS and, 47; in opposition to Hawaiian monarchy, 55, 77

identity: "bicultural," 38; claiming Hawaiian, 89–96; settler, 22, 47
idolatry: Catholic Church and, 172, 199; Filipinos and, 160, 172, 180, 215; *Hoomanamana—Idolatry*, 64, 65; Native Hawaiians and, 36, 54, 56, 58, 64, 65, 77, 106, 112, 119
Iglesia Evangélica, 142, 182
Iglesia Evangélica Metodista, 223
Iglesia Filipina Independiente, 196
Igorot people, 227
'Ī'ī, John Papa, 36, 238
ilustrados (educated Filipinos), 147; historical narratives and, 219, 233; with history, 10, 205, 208, 210–13, 215–16, 222, 231
Imada, Adria L., 76
imperial archipelago, 7, 27
imperial historicism, 17–18, 167, 216
imperialism, historical narratives as tool of, 16, 19, 21
India, 140, 151, 179, 217, 227, 239
Indian Ocean, 6, 10, 218
Indigenous churches, 34, 59, 223

Indigenous people: with assimilation, 7, 109, 113; Hawai'i with "missionary" denigration and, 75–78; as "heathens," 6–7, 14, 34, 36, 54, 57, 124, 172, 236; with intellectual traditions, 19, 101; Malays, 10, 193, 212, 218, 228; Melanesians, 4; men, 45; Micronesians, 4; in Philippines, 179, 227; women, 20; Yoruba, 281n140. *See also* Native Hawaiians
industrial education, 49
infant mortality, 143
Institute for Pacific Relations, 239
intellectual traditions, 5, 8, 19, 101, 212
Intramuros, Manila, 184
Ireland, John, 160
Islam, 10, 15, 180, 213, 218, 229, 237
The Islands of the Pacific (Alexander, J. M.), 152

Jackson, Andrew, 79
Jacobs, Margaret, 116
Japan, 6, 152, 180, 217, 239; ABCFM, 39, 53; empire, 62, 95; migrants from, 25, 48
Japanese sugar plantation workers, 62
Jefferson, Thomas, 146
Jim Crow, 45, 175
Johnson, Anna, 142
Johnston, Mercer Green, 141, 151, 156, 163, 165, 171, 195; Catholic Church and, 172, 199–200, 219
John the Baptist (biblical character), 175–76
Jones, Peter C., 46
Jones Law (1916), 221, 224
Jordan, David Starr, 175
Judd, Albert Francis, 43–45, 48, 55
Judd, Albert Francis, Jr. (son), 124
Judd, Laura Fish (mother), 20, 43–44, 48

Ka'ahumanu (queen regent), 35, 45, 73, 105, 107
Ka Hoku o ka Pakipika ("The Star of the Pacific") (newspaper), 86, 127–28
kahu (royal attendants), 36
kahuna (priest), 80, 117, 128
Kalākaua (r. 1874–91), 26, 56–58, 60, 74, 88, 109, 247n31; Anglican Church and, 72; Hale Nauā society and, 64–66; *hula* performances and, 98, 118, 120–22; lineage, 69–70, 86, 91–92; pageantry and, 75–77, 105
Kalakaua's Reign (Alexander), 76

Kalaniana'ole, Jonah Kūhiō (Prince Cupid), 92
Kalanimoku (Native Hawaiian chief), 72
Kalaw, Maximo, 223, 231
Kamakau, Samuel M., 73, 83
Kame'eleihiwa, Lilikalā, 70
Kamehameha I (r. 1795–1819), 35, 45, 70, 91, 93–94, 107, 115
Kamehameha II (Liholiho) (r. 1819–24), 35
Kamehameha III (Kauikeaouli) (r. 1825–54), 35, 36
Kamehameha IV (Alexander Liholiho) (r. 1855–63), 35, 70, 72
Kamehameha School for Boys, 48
Kamehameha V (Lot Kapuāiwa) (r. 1863–72), 57, 93
Ka Mo'olelo Hawai'i (*Hawaiian Antiquities*) (Malo), 66, 118
Kapihenui, M. J., 127–28
Kapi'olani (queen regent), 45, 105, 107
Kapuāiwa, Lot. *See* Kamehameha V
Katipunan secret society, 147, 212
Kauanui, J. Kēhaulani, 69
Kauikeaouli. *See* Kamehameha III
Kawaiaha'o Church, Honolulu, 93
Keli'iahonui (chief), 112
Keohokālole (chiefess), 91
Keōpūolani (queen regent), 35, 45
Kershner, Bruce, 190
Kidd, Benjamin, 174
Kīlauea, 45, 126
kinship, 9–10, 22, 89, 94–96, 212–13
Kirchmayer, Johannes, 193
knowledge production, 3, 84, 122, 125–26, 130, 170, 206, 232, 234–40
Korea, 152
Korean laborers, 116
Kramer, Paul, 212, 235
Kuakini (governor of Hawai'i island), 112
Kualapai, Lydia, 86, 110
The Kumulipo, 69, 70, 238

labor: Chinese migrants, 25, 48, 74, 80, 98; descendants of Protestant missionaries with, 37–38; Filipino workers in Hawai'i, 6, 116; Japanese, 25, 48, 62; Korean, 116; violence, racism and, 233
Lagarda, Benito, 208
Lake Mohonk Conference on the Indians and Other Dependent Peoples (1912), 222–23, 228

Lallave, Nicolas, 179–80
land, 19, 22, 54, 68, 164
language, Filipino. *See* Tagalog
language, Hawaiian, 52–53, 123, 126, 129; English in schools instead of, 78, 82, 99, 107; HEA and, 43; newspapers, 9, 59, 127–28; oral traditions, 68, 107, 120; preservation of, 102
languages, in Philippines, 182, 215
Laubach, Frank, 142, 158, 173, 186, 188, 218, 222, 230–32, 237; *The People of the Philippines* and, 143, 206, 217, 226–28; Rizal and, 220
Leadingham, John, 53
Lears, T. J. Jackson, 125–26, 196
Legazpi, Miguel López de, 162, 209, 214
leprosy, 37, 74
LeRoy, James A., 205, 216
"Lessons from the Hawaiian Islands" (Armstrong, S. C.), 49
Life and Light for Woman (magazine), 151
Liholiho. *See* Kamehameha II
Liholiho, Alexander. *See* Kamehameha IV
Liholiho, Emma (wife), 70, 72, 76
Liliha (high chiefess), 99
Lili'uokalani (r. 1891–93), 57, 79, 109; abdication, 26; criticism of, 87; *Hawaii's Story by Hawaii's Queen* and, 60, 69, 86–87, 110; *The Kumulipo* and, 69, 238; lineage, 70, 86, 91–92, 253n31; overthrow of, 9, 14, 38–40, 54–61; racism and denigration of, 45–46; supporters, 39, 53, 56, 59–60, 90, 210; US and, 27, 39, 40, 56, 59–60
Lincoln, Abraham, 146
Lingle, W. H., 168–69, 191
Linnekin, Jocelyn, 95
literacy, Muslims in the Philippines, 142, 233
literature: Hawaiian tradition as, 126; *Unwritten Literature of Hawaii*, 118, 120–21, 124, 127, 130
Livingston, Edward, 209
The Long Voyages of the Ancient Hawaiians (Emerson, N. B.), 121
Lorenzana, Avelina, 229, 231
Lott, Eric, 91
lū'au (traditional feast), 105, 115, 116, 134
Luna, Antonio, 205
Lunalilo (r. 1873–74), 70
Lund, Eric, 142, 218
Luther, Martin, 173

Lyman, David (father), 49
Lyman, Henry, 109, 113
Lyman, Rufus (brother), 93
Lyman, Sarah (mother), 49
Lyons, Lorenzo, 50

Mabini, Apolinario, 204–5, 209–10, 231
Madagascar, 10
Maffly-Kipp, Laurie, 14–15
Magellan, Ferdinand, 214, 226–27
Mahan, Alfred Thayer, 5, 62
Maine, U.S.S., 12, 133
"majority-ocean nation," US as, 7
maka'āinana (commoners), 65, 113
Making a Nation (Hibbard), 143, 226
Malay peoples, 10, 193, 212, 218, 228
Malaysia, 152, 217
Malinowski, Bronisław, 5
Malo, David, 66, 118, 128–29
manifest destiny, 2, 5, 81
manifestos: by Aguinaldo, 207; by Mabini, 204–5, 209–10
Manikan, Braulio, 142
Marcos, Ferdinand, 239
Marquez Benitez, Paz, 224
Mary Johnston Hospital, Manila, 143
Mayo, Katherine, 224
McDougall, Brandy Nālani, 238
McKinley, William, 2, 155, 166, 221, 226; Hawai'i and, 26; Philippines and, 138, 146–47, 151, 153, 160
McKinley Tariff Act (1890), 43
McKinnon, William, 188
Mead, Margaret, 5, 222
Mediterranean Sea, 5, 152
Melanesian people, 4
Melville, Herman, 5
Memmi, Albert, 16, 130, 165
memoirs, 20–22, 43–45, 48, 86, 110–11, 237–38
memory: historical narratives with genealogies and, 87; with strenuous life and creation of American Hawai'i, 110–17
Methodist Episcopal Church, 20, 104, 140–41, 148
Methodists: Cristianos Vivos Metodistas, 223; with Mary Johnston Hospital, 143; missionaries in Philippines, 142, 151, 163, 166, 182, 183, 192, 193, 217, 223, 225; WFMS, 140–41

Metropolitan Presbyterian Church, Washington DC, 56
Micronesia, 42, 62, 148, 152
Micronesian island groups, 39
Micronesian people, 4
Middle Ages, 172
Mid-Pacific Institute, Honolulu, 105
Mid-Pacific Kirmess, Hawai'i, 98, 107
migrants: Chinese, 25, 48, 74, 80, 98; Japanese, 25, 48
migration, Asian, 9, 80
military, US, 41, 134, 142–43, 204; Army, 146–47; church buildings damaged by, 186; naval bases, 5, 239–40; Union Army, 88, 117
Military Bases Agreement (1947), 239
Mindanao, Philippines, 227; ABCFM in, 142, 158, 186, 192; Muslims of, 142–43, 178, 180, 218, 233
missionaries, in Hawai'i: Catholic Church, 72–74; culture, 46, 47, 75; defense of, 40–41, 50, 81–82; defined, 37–48; with denigration of Indigenous understandings, 75–78; with foreign policy, 13; historical consciousness and, 16–21; memoir, 22, 43–45, 110–11, 238; as pejorative, 32, 38–41, 47; writing, 21–22, 35, 80, 120, 126, 129. *See also* Protestant missionaries, in Hawai'i
missionaries, in Philippines: architecture and history, 184–96; with Brent and Catholic Church, 167, 170, 180, 194–202; with Filipino nationalist historiography, 206, 214–20, 231; with history production for US audiences, 143; with national imperial project, 13–14, 135; with Philippine history, 171–77; US empire and, 23, 135–36, 145–66, 169; writing, 135, 148, 174, 190, 213, 217, 219, 237. *See also* Protestant missionaries, in Philippines
Missionary Herald (periodical), 34, 40–41, 45, 57, 59, 102–3, 192
Mission Hospital School of Nursing, 141
missions: Christian, 5, 61, 63; Hawai'i and recalibrating history of, 48–54. *See also* Hawaiian Mission Children's Society; Protestant mission
Missions and Modern History (Speer), 17
mobility, 5, 6, 9–10, 116, 121

monarchy, Hawaiian, 44, 92; criticism of, 47, 59, 75–77, 87, 120; genealogies of, 27, 236; idolatry and, 36; mission history, annexation and overthrow of, 26, 32, 37–38, 54–63; opponents, 55; overthrow of *'ai kapu*, 35, 36, 45, 73; queen regents, 35, 45, 73, 105, 107; with royal attendants, 36; sovereignty and, 69; supporters, 38–39, 53–56, 59–60. *See also* annexation, Hawai'i; Kalākaua; Kamehameha; Lili'uokalani
Monroe Doctrine, 81
Montgomery, Helen Barrett, 144, 151–52
Moody, Dwight L., 36
Moots, Cornelia Chillson, 140, 142, 143, 158, 162
Morga, Antonio de, 211
Morgan, Lewis Henry, 171
Mormonism, 59, 71, 74, 75
Morrow, W. C., 119, 126
Morse, Elijah Adams, 55
Mott, John R., 154
museums, missionaries with, 18, 85, 103
Muslims, in Philippines, 171, 178, 180, 212, 223, 229; with historical narratives, 213; literacy and, 142, 233; Propagandists and, 147; Protestant missionaries and, 14, 142–43, 218

Nakuina, Emma, 84
Nāpela, Jonathan, 71
nationalism. *See* Filipino nationalism
nationalist colonialism, 212, 223, 228–29
nationalist drama, Tagalog, 213
Native Americans, 17, 49, 87, 112, 216
Native Hawaiians, 11, 40; culture, 22, 28, 41, 65, 84–85, 107, 109, 119, 124; genealogies of, 9, 19, 22, 33, 35, 63–65, 68–71, 76, 86, 120–22, 127, 236, 238; historical narratives and, 19, 22, 67, 77, 85–87, 89, 92, 96; idolatry and, 36, 54, 56, 58, 64, 65, 77, 106, 112, 119; land and, 19, 22, 54, 68; oral traditions of, 67–69, 82, 86–88, 107, 114, 120; pastors, 34, 46–47, 50, 58, 61, 101, 109; population, 37; racism and, 45–46, 54, 91–92, 172; *Why Are the Hawaiians Dying Out?*, 112–13; women chiefs, 35, 44–45, 70, 73, 99, 105, 122. *See also* monarchy, Hawaiian
nature, God in, 84

naval bases, US, 5, 239–40
"Negritos," 212, 227
The New Era in the Philippines (Brown, A. J.), 143
New York Daily Tribune (newspaper), 130
New York Evening Post (newspaper), 54, 56
New York Herald (newspaper), 41
New York Public Library, 84
New York World (newspaper), 56
New Zealand, 84, 122–23, 128, 152
North Pacific Missionary Institute, 46, 53
"No Value as History" (Bishop, S.), 87

Ocampo, Pablo, 228
oceanic colonialism, 8, 235
Okihiro, Gary, 9
Old Glory and the Gospel (Condict), 144, 184
Oldham, Marie (wife), 217
Oldham, William F., 217, 223
Old Manila, 184, 185f, 186f, 274n109
Oleson, W. B., 48, 51
Olympia, U.S.S., 133
One Hundred Years of Christian Civilization in Hawaii (pageant), 106–7, 108f
'Ōpūkaha'ia, 35–36, 105
orally transmitted genealogies, 9, 69, 86
oral traditions, of Native Hawaiians, 67–69, 82, 86–88, 107, 114, 120
Oregon Treaty (1846), 6
Organic Act (1900), 26
Osías, Camilo, 229, 231
Otis, E. S., 163
Our Country (Strong), 37
overthrow. *See* annexation, Hawai'i

Pacific Air Forces, US, 240
Pacific Commercial Advertiser (newspaper), 41, 98–99, 121
Pacific Fleet, US, 240
Pacific Ocean: expansion into, 1–3; with "heathen" people, 6–7; heterogeneous, 4–11; with intellectual traditions, 5; as sacralized space, 14–15
Pacific peoples, 8–11, 94
paganism, 50, 64, 88, 102, 109, 119–20, 171–72, 180
Pālama Settlement, Honolulu, 98
Palekaluhi, Abraham K., 99
Palmer, Julius A., 79, 90
Pardo de Tavera, Trinidad, 208, 231

Paris, treaty of (1898), 133, 137, 148
Paris Basis, for YMCA membership, 200, 276n166
Paris Exposition (1889), 211
Parker, Alton B., 166
Partido Federalista, 208, 222
pastors, Native Hawaiians, 34, 46–47, 50, 58, 61, 101, 109
Paterno, Pedro, 211, 231
patriarchy, 20, 45–46
Peel, J. D. Y., 281n140
Pele (goddess), 45, 85, 105, 126–27
Pele and Hiiaka (Emerson, N. B.), 118, 126–27
Pentecost, George, 151, 219
The People of the Philippines (Laubach), 143, 206, 217, 226–28
performance, historical narratives and, 19, 87, 88, 105
Perry, Matthew C. (Commodore), 6
Pettigrew, Richard F., 79
Phelps, Austin, 36–37
Philippine-American War (1899–1902), 11, 138, 143, 146–49, 161, 186
Philippine Assembly, 165, 222
Philippine Commission, 147, 160–61, 221
Philippine Historical Association, 224
Philippine Presbyterian, 157
Philippine Revolution, 147–48, 204–5
Philippines: ABCFM in, 141–43, 150, 158, 166, 176, 179, 182, 186, 192, 193, 206, 221–22; annexation of, 133, 137; Catholic Church in, 10, 14, 19, 160–65, 168, 170–73, 178, 180–202, 219; census of 1903, 231; Christianization of, 8, 180; colonization of, 10–11, 13; folklore, 210–11, 215, 224; guerilla warfare in, 146; historical narrative, 181, 202, 213, 219, 230, 233, 237; historiography, 212, 220; Indigenous people in, 179, 227; industrial education in, 49; languages in, 182, 215; Methodist missionaries in, 140–43, 151, 163, 166, 182, 183, 192, 193, 217, 223, 225; Mindanao, 142–43, 158, 178, 180, 186, 192, 218, 227, 233; missionary turn to long past of, 220–33; *The New Era in the Philippines*, 143; Old Manila, 184, 185f, 186f, 274n109; *The People of the Philippines*, 143, 206, 217, 226–28; *The Progressing Philippines*, 142, 143, 228; Presbyterians

Philippines (continued)
 missionaries in, 140–43, 178, 182, 190–94, 223, 225; Protestant mission and, 13–16, 18–19; seizure of, 1–2; with social sciences and taxonomy, 215–17; Spanish past and, 169–73, 177–83, 184; with spiritual shortcomings of US empire, 159–67; Supreme Court, 188; tourism and, 240; as unincorporated territory, 132, 137–38; US empire and, 4, 6, 7, 15, 23, 135–36, 169, 209–10, 220–21; YMCA in, 140, 142, 165, 180, 192, 200, 217, 218. See also Filipinos; missionaries, in Philippines; Muslims, in Philippines; Protestant missionaries, in Philippines
The Philippines and the Far East (Stuntz), 141, 143
The Philippine Islands (Foreman), 216
Pierson, Arthur T., 36, 51, 154, 155, 179
Pioneer Days in Hawaii (Emerson, O.), 113–14
Plymouth Church, Brooklyn, 54
police violence, 239
politics: "fiesta," 208; Filipino nationalism and, 221, 222; Partido Federalista, 208, 222. See also Democratic Party, US; Republican Party, US
Polynesian Society, 84, 123
polytheism, 180, 211
populations: deaths in Spanish-American War, 146; depopulation in Hawai'i, 27, 37, 64, 76, 113; Hawai'i, 42, 81; Philippine census of 1903, 231
Portland Basis, for YMCA membership, 200, 276n166
Prautch, Arthur W., 140, 163
Prautch, Eliza (wife), 140
Presbyterian missionaries, in Philippines, 140–43, 178, 182, 190–94, 223, 225
Price, Francis M., 148
"The Prick of Honor" (Emerson, N. B.), 129
priest (*kahuna*), 80, 117, 128
The Progressing Philippines (Briggs), 142, 143, 228
Propagandists, 147
Protestant mission, 124, 149; "boomerang" effect of, 233; Catholic Church and, 15, 139, 218; conversions, 5, 13, 35–37, 53, 75, 76, 92, 105, 142, 166, 176, 180, 190–91, 197, 229; imperial historicism and, 17–18; new age of, 36; US empire and, 11–19,

235. See also American Board of Commissioners for Foreign Missions
Protestant missionaries, in Hawai'i, 8; annexation and completion of mission, 26, 101–10; history, 18–19, 31–32, 34–37; overthrow and annexation and history of, 26, 32, 37–38, 54–63; women, 19–20, 43–46. See also descendants of Protestant missionaries, in Hawai'i
Protestant missionaries, in Philippines, 1–3, 8; Americans, 139–45; historical narrative and, 135, 207, 214–15, 230, 233–34; Muslims and, 14, 142–43, 218; outdoor service in Philippines, 189–90, 189f; with Providence and US empire, 145–54, 173–74, 210; Spanish past and, 169–73, 177–83, 184; with turn to long past, 220–33; with US empire and crisis of mission, 154–59; women, 19–20, 140–44, 148, 151–52, 182
Providence: providential language, 207, 228; with US empire and missionaries, 145–54, 173–74, 210. See also God
Pua, Samuel K., 38
Puerto Ricans, 116
Puerto Rico, 2, 12, 132, 133, 137–38
Puhi, Daniel, 92
Pukui, Mary Kawena, 238
Punahou School, for missionary families, 42, 93, 117, 124
Puritans, 17, 59, 87–88, 156

Quezon, Manuel, 221–24

race, social science and, 84, 86, 135, 173–77; blackface minstrelsy, 91; Filipinos and, 147, 172, 175, 190, 193; Native Hawaiians and, 45–46, 54, 91–92, 172; racism, 11, 39, 79; violence, 11, 146, 210; violence, labor and, 233
Rafael, Vicente L., 213
Rapanui, 10
Ratnapalan, Laavanyan M., 246n5
Reformation, 72, 173–74
Reminiscences of Old Hawaii (Bishop, S.), 110–11, 112–13
Republican Party, US, 1, 55, 79, 133, 137, 155, 166, 221, 224
Republic of Biak-na-Bato, 147
Republic of Hawai'i, 26, 38, 45, 56, 62, 82, 99, 134

Restarick, Henry B., 104–5
"rhetorical archipelagoes," 7–8
Rice, Mary, 54–55
Ripley, C. B., 192
Rizal, José, 210–12, 219–20, 231
Rizal Day, 219
Robertson, James A., 205, 231
Rodgers, James B., 140, 151, 174–75, 176–77, 180, 182, 199; *ilustrados* and, 219; at Lake Mohonk Conference, 223, 228; with Presbyterian church in Philippines, 191–94; Protestant mission and, 218
Rohrer, Judy, 71
Romanes, George John, 84
Rome, 198
Rooker, Frederick, 163
Roosevelt, Theodore, 62, 112, 156–57, 161–62, 165–66, 221
Rossiter, Stealy, 153
royal attendants (*kahu*), 36
Royal Geographical Society, 216
Russia, 152–53, 180

St. Louis, World's Fair (1904), 223
St. Luke's Episcopal Church, Manila, 193, 198
Samoa, 12, 90
Sandwich Islands, 34
San Francisco Call (newspaper), 56
San Francisco Chronicle (newspaper), 56
Satterlee, Henry, 150
Scenery in Hawaii (pamphlet), 116
Schulz, Joy, 110
Schurman, Jacob, 160
science, 130, 237, 238; deep time and, 86; Hale Naua society and, 68; historical narratives and, 85. *See also* social science
Scott, William Henry, 238–39
settler colonialism, 9, 79, 124
settler identity, white, 22, 47
settler mission, 15, 43
Seventh-day Adventists, 141, 223
Seven Years' War, 214
Seward, William, 6
Shearman, Thomas G., 54–55, 60, 74
Sikatuna, Datu, 209
Silliman Institute, Philippines, 140, 182
Silliman Truth, 152
Silva, Noenoe K., 65, 68, 95
Sivasundaram, Sujit, 237

slavery, 34
Smith, James Francis, 161, 165
Smith, James William, 93
Smith, Jared, 50, 57
Smith, Juliette (sister), 50, 57
Smith, Lowell, 93
Smith, Ryan K., 191, 196
Smith, S. Percy, 84, 123
Smith, William O., 42, 55, 85
Smithsonian, 84, 130
Social Darwinism, 84, 175
social science, 23, 28, 84, 97, 100, 167, 169; emergence of, 16, 171; Emerson, Nathaniel Bright, and, 22, 130–31; evolutionism and, 201; Honolulu Social Science Association, 81, 82–83, 94, 112; *ilustrados* and, 212, 216; missionaries and, 18; with Philippines and taxonomy, 215–17; race and, 86, 135, 173–77
Society Islands, 151–52
song or romance (*awit*), 213
Sons of the American Revolution, 88
sources, structure and, 21–23
South America, 10, 218
Southeast Asia, 10, 227
Southeast Asian people, 213
sovereignty, of Hawai'i, 27, 59–60, 63, 68–69, 83, 86, 89, 95–96, 102, 131
Spain: ABCFM in, 39; Catholic Church and, 2, 19, 23, 164, 171–73, 205; with colonization, 10; Philippines and, 169–73, 177–83, 184
Spanish-American War (1898), 1–2, 12–14, 25, 62, 133, 137–38, 145–46, 148, 161
Spanish Inquisition, 172
Spaulding, Winifred, 140–41, 183
Speer, Robert E., 17
Spofford, Harriet Prescott, 91
Staley, Thomas N., 72
Stallings, J. F., 79
"The Star of the Pacific" (*Ka Hoku o ka Pakipika*) (newspaper), 86, 127–28
status, corpulence and, 112
stereotypes, 129, 182, 193, 223
Stevens, John L., 38–39, 62
Stevenson, Robert Louis, 74
Stoddard, Charles Warren, 74
Stoler, Ann Laura, 22
"A Stranger Asks Bliff about the Historical Procession," 77

Strong, Josiah, 37, 154
structure, sources and, 21–23
Student Volunteer Movement, 11–12, 14, 36, 50–51, 154, 176, 236
Stuntz, Homer C., 141, 143, 145, 146, 150–51, 163, 166, 175, 181, 223; on Catholic Church in Philippines, 164, 171–72, 192, 193, 201; on colonial violence, 148–49; on idolatry in Philippines, 215; Magellan and, 214; Philippines and, 228; on Protestant missionaries in Philippines, 179–80; with social sciences and Philippines, 215–17
Sucesos de las Islas Filipinas (Morga), 211
sugar plantations, labor, 62
sugar planters, 37–38, 43, 74
supreme courts, 80–82, 188
surfing, 115, 116

Taft, William Howard, 160–64, 166, 177–78, 188, 205, 221
Tagalog, 147, 152, 212, 213, 229
Tahiti, 64, 75
Thoburn, James, 151, 179–80, 217
Thompson, Carmi, 224
Thompson, Lanny, 7–8
Thompson, Michael G., 230
A Thousand Years Ago (play), 105
Thrum, Thomas G., 104
Thurston, Asa (grandfather), 38, 106
Thurston, Lorrin, 38, 39, 77, 82, 90, 91, 105, 238; Bishop, Sereno, and, 110–12; volcano tourism and, 116
Thurston, Lucy (grandmother), 38, 106
Tinguian people, 227
Tirona Benitez, Francisca, 224
Tobera, Fermin, 233
torture, 146, 148
tourism, 9, 99, 109–17; militarism and, 240; settlement and, 8, 97, 100, 109, 114, 131; volcano, 116
trade, 5, 10, 26, 211, 229, 236, 239
tradition, Hawaiian: classification of, 117–25; denigration of, 75–78, 100; fetishization of, 69; historical narration and, 67, 99, 114, 238; as literature, 126; motifs in, 70
traditional feast (*lūʻau*), 105, 115, 116, 134
Trask, Haunani-Kay, 9, 112
Treaty of Wanghia (1844), 6
Turner, Frederick Jackson, 5, 156

Twain, Mark, 34–35
Tydings-McDuffie Act (1934), 224–25
Tylor, E. B., 123, 171

unincorporated territories, 132, 137–38
Union Army, 88, 117
United Brethren of Christ, 141, 223, 229
United States (US), 4, 7, 75, 78, 143, 181, 209; California, 6, 8, 233; Congress, 9, 26, 55, 79–80, 92, 223; Constitution, 146, 154–55; Democratic Party, 39, 79, 155, 166, 221; God and, 2, 17, 137–39, 144–45; *ilustrados* and, 208; Liliʻuokalani and, 27, 39, 40, 56, 59–60; with memory, strenuous life and creation of American Hawaiʻi, 110–17; Pacific Ocean and expansion of, 1–3; Republican Party, 1, 55, 79, 133, 137, 155, 166, 221, 224. *See also* empire, US; military, US
United Study of Missions, 144
University of Santo Tomas, 180, 204
Unwritten Literature of Hawaii (Emerson, N. B.), 118, 120–21, 124, 127, 130
US. *See* United States

Vancouver, George, 72
Vatican, 163, 164, 198
venereal disease, 37, 113
Venn, Henry, 34
Vicuña Gonzalez, Vernadette, 6, 22, 100
violence, 112, 178, 219; colonial, 5, 12, 19, 37, 81, 139, 146–49, 161, 208, 237; oppression and, 224; police, 239; racial, 11, 146, 210, 233; of Spanish Inquisition, 172
volcano tourism, 116
voting rights, for women, 45

Wacker, Grant, 12
Wake Island, 12
Wallace, Alfred R., 84, 217
Warne, Frank W., 144
Washington, Booker T., 49
Washington, George, 145, 146, 208
Washington Evening Star (newspaper), 56, 62, 80–81, 87, 90–92, 94, 116
Waterhouse, Henry, 46
Webster, Daniel, 209
Weir, Christine, 123
West Africa, 281n140
Westervelt, William D., 51–53

WFMS (Woman's Foreign Missionary Society), 20, 140–41
white settlement, 8, 80–81, 109, 131
white supremacy, 11, 17, 38, 39, 84, 91, 155, 175
Why Are the Hawaiians Dying Out? (Bishop, S.), 112–13
Wilcox, Albert (brother of George), 124
Wilcox, George, 124, 128
Wilcox, Robert, 41
Wilkes, Charles, 5
Williams, Ronald, 61
Willis, Alfred, 60, 72
Wilson, Woodrow, 17, 166, 206, 220–21
Winne, Jane Lathrop, 106
Winter, Carrie Prudence, 44
Wise, John Henry, 53
Wisner, Julia, 140, 145
Woman's American Baptist Foreign Mission Society, 142
Woman's Board of Missions, 142, 144, 182
Woman's Foreign Missionary Society (WFMS), 20, 140–41
Woman's Missionary Friend (magazine), 152
women, 40, 43–44, 84; Daughters of Hawai'i, 102, 106; missionaries, 19–20, 43–45, 140–44, 148, 151–52, 182; Native Hawaiian chiefs, 35, 44–45, 70, 73, 99, 105, 122; patriarchy and, 20, 45–46
Wood, Leonard, 161, 224, 225
Worcester, Dean Conant, 222, 279n59
Wordsworth, William, 119
World War I, 12, 141, 194, 203, 206, 222, 224, 225, 230
World War II, 239
Wright, George William, 1, 2–3
writing, 211; of historical narratives by Native Hawaiians, 19, 67, 86–87, 128; missionary, 21–22, 35, 80, 120, 126, 129, 135, 148, 174, 190, 213, 217, 219, 237

Yale University, 84
YMCA. *See* Young Men's Christian Association
Yoruba people, 281n140
Young Men's Christian Association (YMCA): in Hawai'i, 46, 47, 239; Paris Basis for membership, 200, 276n166; in Philippines, 140, 142, 165, 180, 192, 200, 217, 218; Portland Basis for membership, 200, 276n166
Yzendoorn, Reginald, 105

Zamora, Nicolas, 223

www.ingramcontent.com/pod-product-compliance
Lightning Source LLC
Chambersburg PA
CBHW030521230426
43665CB00010B/718